NEHRU

By the same author

A Book of India

The Rise of Modern India

The Introduction of English Law into India

Shahar Ke Kutte (a collection of short stories in Hindi)

The Break-up of British India

The Evolution of India and Pakistan Select. Documents 1858–1947 (edited jointly with C. H. Philips and H. L. Singh)

B. N. Pandey

NEHRU

STEIN AND DAY/*Publishers*/New York

First published in the United States of America, 1976

Printed in the United States of America
Stein and Day/*Publishers*/Scarborough House,
Briarcliff Manor, N. Y. 10510

Library of Congress Cataloging in Publication Data

Pandey, Bishwa Nath, 1929–
Nehru.

Bibliography: p. 464
1. Nehru, Jawaharlal, 1889-1964.
DS481.N35P29 954.04′092′4 [B] 75-37858
ISBN 0-8128-1931-4

To
VALERIE

Contents

List of Illustrations

MAPS

Acknowledgements for permission to reproduce illustrations are due to the following: Nehru Memorial Museum and Library, New Delhi, 1–5, 8; the Trustees of the Low Estate, and the London Evening Standard, 6–7.

The map on page 292 is reprinted from Michael Brecher, *Nehru: a political biography* (Oxford University Press, 1959).

NEHRU

Preface

NEHRU is a formidable and fascinating subject for a full-size biography. Formidable for the vast expanse of his career as a nationalist and as a prime minister, and for the wide range of his interests and involvements. For over thirty years, from 1916 to 1947, he was one of India's foremost nationalists; for seventeen years, from 1947 to 1964, he nourished, as its first prime minister, the world's largest democracy. During the half-century of his active political life he was ardently interested in everything of national and international importance. He was the world's most committed and yet its most refined enemy of absolutism, exploitation and discrimination, and he strove to give reality to his vision of a new world order based on peace and co-existence. He was the first statesman in the Afro-Asian world to lead his country of millions along an untrodden path of non-alignment and a mixed economy. The multifarious roles he played in his life and the mighty problems he faced at each stage and level in themselves would have made the task of his biographer most difficult, but added to these are millions of words he wrote and spoke during his lifetime. He was indeed a most prolific writer. Books and articles apart, even his letters often tended to turn into booklets. And then he was a very willing speaker, prone to giving half a dozen performances in a single day, unprepared and unrehearsed. And yet he was not a person who released his own tensions fully in his writings, speeches, or even in his outbursts of temper. He sustained throughout his life an inner conflict and tension, and while living simultaneously in the worlds of ideas and realities he strove continuously to level the barrier which separated them.

Among the various fascinations of Nehru the one which weighed most heavily with me was the spectacle of him as unique in the twentieth century in that he succeeded in politics with qualities which are commonly considered to be major handicaps in that profession. Nehru was a man of intellect, of vision and of essential goodness. He was honest and sincere, kind and considerate, dispassionate and indecisive; he was untouched by ruthlessness, malice and pettiness; he had no aptitude for manœuvres and for dreary details of organisation, and his personality had a sprinkling of vanity, conceit and romance which, in his case, bejewelled rather than blemished it. How could he have succeeded so elegantly and wielded such enormous power in a profession in which men of his stamp so often miserably fail? How and why did Nehru become a leader of men? To what extent were the peculiarities of Hindu tradition and the Indian environment responsible for his rise to power?

Another compelling aspect of the subject is Nehru's relationship with Gandhi. How could such an unbreakable bond have existed between these two who were poles apart from each other in their demeanour, outlook and ideologies? Gandhi, for example, was quite indifferent to the democracy to which Nehru was devoutly committed. Gandhi would have been happier were society ruled by a single man who was spiritually emancipated. Again, the Mahatma was strongly opposed to industrialisation, a process which for Nehru was both desirable and inevitable. A closer study of their relationship may give the impression that Nehru, while deriving his power from the Mahatma and the people, used it continuously to protect India not only from communism and fascism but also from Gandhism itself.

The questions aroused by a consideration of the career of Nehru are innumerable. To mention only a few of the broader aspects of the subject which appear to require an answer: What did Nehru achieve in his lifetime at the national and international levels? How consistent was he in pursuing his avowed policies? How did his life as a nationalist shape his style as a prime minister?

These, together with a number of other aspects of the subject – some relating to Nehru's family background, his upbringing, his domestic and social life, his relationships with his father, wife and daughter, his own understanding of the problems of human relationships, and the impact of all of these on his public life – have been treated in this book. The research for it was begun in the spring of 1969 and carried almost continuously for over six years. It is based almost entirely on primary sources, largely on private papers.

Many people, in England and India, have helped in the making of this book. To each I express my deep gratitude, but some names ought to be mentioned here. The Right Honourable Harold Macmillan blessed the launching of the project, tried to obtain for it the support of Mrs Indira Gandhi and expressed to me freely his views on the problems which Nehru faced during his prime ministership. Lord Mountbatten showed his enthusiasm and good will for the project by sitting for a long recorded interview and securing for me a fruitful meeting with the late Sri V. K. Krishna Menon. Sir Cyril Philips may not remember the occasion when one afternoon over a cup of tea he gave me the kind of encouragement which, being on the first lap, I badly needed at that time. He assured me that it was not inordinately presumptuous in a historian to study as vast a theme as the career of Nehru from 1889 to 1964. Professor Kenneth Ballhatchet (head of the South Asia section of the History Department and for three years Chairman of the South Asia Centre of the School of Oriental and African Studies) gave his full support to this study and offered valuable advice on ways and means of sustaining it.

It was my privilege to have received from the beginning the full support and co-operation of Mrs Vijayalakshmi Pandit. Her importance to a biographer of Nehru lies less in the fact that she was Nehru's most beloved sister as in the circumstance that she was possibly the only one in whom her brother could confide throughout a major part of his life. Mrs Pandit put at my disposal her private papers which consist of her brother's correspondence with her both before and after independence. But for these letters I would not have acquired the necessary insight into Nehru's inner conflicts, and his thinking on a wide range of subjects, personal, national and international. While discoursing on Nehru and his contemporaries to me Mrs Pandit demonstrated that objectivity, precision and forthrightness which, together with humanity and elegance, characterise her own life-style. I am sure she would feel offended if I were to seek her forgiveness for probing into the lives and conflicts of the Nehrus – particularly those of her father Motilal Nehru, her brother, and her niece Mrs Indira Gandhi – whom she has so dearly loved.

Among a number of active and retired Indian politicians whom I met, my association with Sri Morarji Desai turned out to be most fruitful. I first met him in the spring of 1969 when he was India's Deputy Prime Minister and Minister of Finance. Our meetings grew frequent over the years, and he gave me an inside view of the working of the state and union cabinets during the Nehru era. He also allowed me access to his private papers, which contain correspondence between Nehru and himself during the post-independence period. The late Dr Syed Mahmud, whom I met when he was in failing health, gave me access to what he rightly considered his most precious possession – the letters of Kamala Nehru. He also put at my disposal his post-1947 correspondence with Nehru.

The Director (Miss Joan Lancaster) and the staff (particularly Dr Richard Bingle) of the India Office Library have throughout been very helpful, and on several occasions they have provided me with special facilities. The Director and Miss D. Keshwani of the National Archives of India were equally kind and hospitable to me and my staff. Most of my research, however, was carried out in the Nehru Memorial Museum and Library which, for its most amiable working conditions and its high standard of efficiency, is one of the best archives in India. Its Director, Dr B. R. Nanda, and Deputy Director, Dr V. C. Joshi, could not have been more considerate to me and my research assistants. They obtained the Prime Minister's prior approval of my application for access to the Nehru papers, and they have over the last six years offered me valuable advice and guidance on a number of problems.

This work, which soon after its inception turned into an expensive enterprise involving over half a dozen visits to India and the maintenance there of a staff consisting of research assistants and typists, would not have been possible without the funds advanced to me by my publishers and a grant from the Social Science Research Council, London. The Central Research Fund of the University of London also contributed from its resources. The School of Oriental and African Studies helped me in many ways. Apart from giving me leave of absence for research in India, it enabled me, with the aid of a grant, to pursue a study, through seminars and a conference, of 'Leadership in South Asia' – a theme which emerged out of my project on Nehru and required to be examined separately.

Five adults and one child have been deeply involved in this work. James Wright of Macmillan has watched the growth of this work with infinite patience. At every stage he has offered me his seasoned editorial experience and friendly care. Together with his wife Gilli, he has gone over the entire text and tidied it up in various places. My old friend and colleague Malcolm Yapp has borne a heavy burden. Throughout he has inspired me by taking a lively and keen interest in this work. He has read the entire manuscript, chapter by chapter, and saved me from many errors. I have greatly benefited from his sound knowledge of the history of European expansion in Asia and from his insight into the defence mechanisms of the British Empire. Eleanor Curzon, a friend of the family, displayed her goodwill by volunteering to work as my research assistant. She spent six months in India collecting and typing documents for me and succeeded in putting out in these months work which would normally have taken a year to accomplish. But for my wife Valerie I would not have been able to pursue the sustained and concentrated research required for this work. Apart from being a full-time housewife and mother, she willingly undertook to function as my research assistant and secretary in India and, at a later stage, as my typist – being the only one who could conveniently decipher my handwriting, she typed the entire manuscript for the publishers – and protector. In the latter capacity she protected me from our four-year-old daughter Tara, who at her age had to learn ' not to disturb Daddy while he is writing chapters '. As a token of my appreciation and understanding for Valerie's endurance over the last six years and the sacrifice she has made for the sake of this work, I dedicate this book to her.

School of Oriental and African Studies,
University of London,
London.
15 September 1975

B. N. PANDEY

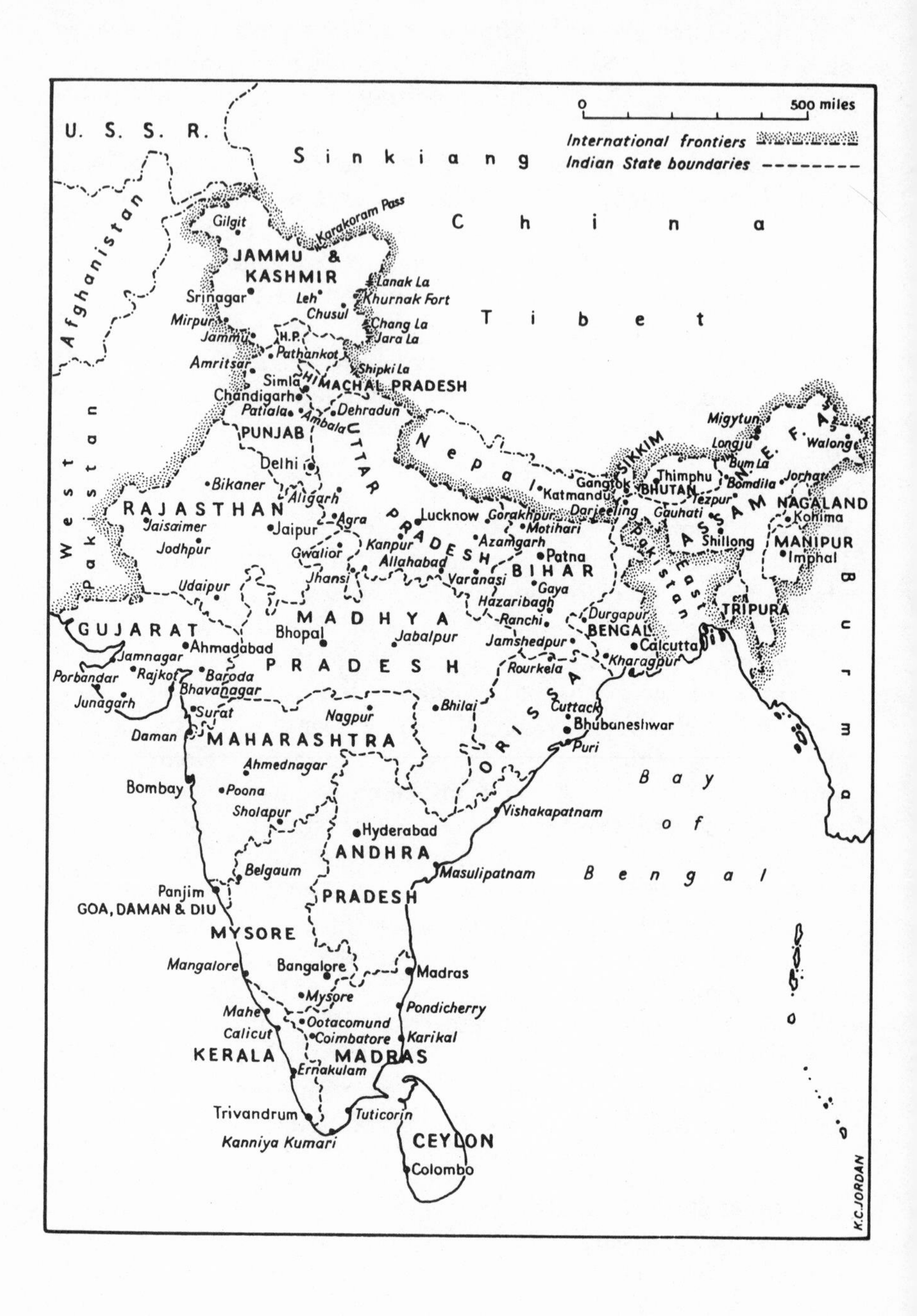

0
500 miles
International frontiers
Indian State boundaries
U. S. S. R.
Sinkiang
China
Tibet
Afghanistan
West Pakistan
Gilgit
Karakoram Pass
JAMMU & KASHMIR
Srinagar
Leh
Chusul
Lanak La
Khurnak Fort
Chang La
Jara La
Mirpur
Jammu
H.P.
Pathankot
Amritsar
Shipki La
Simla
HIMACHAL PRADESH
Chandigarh
Patiala
Ambala
Dehradun
PUNJAB
UTTAR PRADESH
Nepal
Delhi
Bikaner
Aligarh
RAJASTHAN
Jaisalmer
Jodhpur
Jaipur
Agra
Lucknow
Gorakhpur
Motihari
Katmandu
Gangtok
Darjeeling
SIKKIM
Thimphu
BHUTAN
Migytun
Longju
Bum La
Bomdila
Walong
N.E.F.A.
Jorhat
Tezpur
Gauhati
ASSAM
NAGALAND
Kohima
Shillong
MANIPUR
Imphal
East Pakistan
TRIPURA
Burma
Kanpur
Azamgarh
Gwalior
Allahabad
Patna
BIHAR
Jhansi
Varanasi
Gaya
Udaipur
Hazaribagh
Ranchi
MADHYA PRADESH
Bhopal
Jabalpur
Jamshedpur
Durgapur
BENGAL
Calcutta
Kharagpur
GUJARAT
Ahmadabad
Jamnagar
Rajkot
Porbandar
Baroda
Bhavanagar
Junagarh
Rourkela
ORISSA
Cuttack
Bhubaneshwar
Puri
Surat
Nagpur
Bhilai
Daman
MAHARASHTRA
Ahmednagar
Bombay
Poona
Sholapur
Bay of Bengal
Vishakapatnam
Hyderabad
ANDHRA PRADESH
Masulipatnam
Belgaum
Panjim
GOA, DAMAN & DIU
MYSORE
Mangalore
Bangalore
Madras
Mysore
Pondicherry
Mahe
Ootacomund
Calicut
Coimbatore
Karikal
KERALA
MADRAS
Ernakulam
Trivandrum
Tuticorin
Kanniya Kumari
CEYLON
Colombo
K.C.JORDAN

CHAPTER ONE

Sowing of the Seed

I am going back to India with the firm conviction that I have sown the seed of your future greatness and I have not a shadow of a doubt that you have a great career before you.

Motilal Nehru to Jawaharlal Nehru, 16 October 1905, London

MOTILAL NEHRU wrote these lines to his son Jawaharlal on the day of his return to India with his wife and five-year-old daughter, after placing Jawaharlal at Harrow and, as he hoped, laying the foundations of his future career; the boy was then fifteen. But what career did Motilal Nehru envisage for his son? In building up his hopes for his future, Motilal was perhaps over-influenced by his own aspirations and, indeed, by the existing conditions in colonial India.

Motilal Nehru was forty-four in 1905. Of light-brown skin, he was a stern-looking man. He had a ferocious temper, inherited from his mother; his bark was worse than his bite, but he used his tongue to beat opponents into submission. There were some conflicting traits in his character. He was ostentatious, but efficient and meticulous; demonstrative, but passionately sincere. He was proud, vain and aggressive, but self-confident and enterprising. Rational and independent in his thinking, agnostic in his beliefs, he was at the same time deeply committed to his family, caste and community. With him the family was all that counted. He occasionally bowed to the Hindu gods, gave way to some superstitions and bathed in the holy rivers. He was tolerant towards his enemies but contemptuous of weakness in his friends. He was too much of an authoritarian ever to turn into a loyal follower; yet he could not make friends of his followers, among whom he aroused fear more than admiration. He had the ability to carve out a principality for himself in a feudal state, but would have found it difficult to lead in a democratic society. He was a shrewd businessman but spent money like a prince. He was cool and practical in his dealings with the people, but emotional and willing to make sacrifices in the interests of his family. He would have changed his entire way of life if he had thought it necessary in order to keep his son's respect. It was the end that mattered most with him, hence he could at times be less than scrupulous about the means; but he always stayed within the bounds of legality, for as a lawyer he dreaded revolution and despised terrorism.

Some of the conflicting traits in his personality can be traced to the various environments and cultures to which he had been exposed. He was born in Agra, United Provinces, in an upper-caste – Kashmiri Brahmin – Hindu family of fairly modest means, his mother dying in childbirth. The family culture was a Hindu–Muslim blend. Hindu beliefs, customs and social values were mixed with Persian speech, dress, diet and manners.

As a child Motilal was under the care of his two elder brothers – Bansidhar and Nandlal. He spent the first ten years of his childhood with Nandlal, who had become tutor to the raja in the small Hindu princely state of Khetri. Nandlal's career in the state lasted for less than ten years, but during that time he rose from the humble position of tutor to that of a chief minister. Motilal thus grew up among the traditional aristocracy. He must have had some aspirations towards the princely way of life. He was not, and would never become, an aristocrat, but he had ambitions to live like a prince.

His English education started in Kanpur, United Provinces, under the guardianship of the eldest brother Bansidhar, who was posted there as a government servant, and continued at Muir College, Allahabad, where his other brother Nandlal had set up in legal practice and was thus able to support him. Allahabad had become the capital of United Provinces (then called North-West Provinces) after the Mutiny of 1857 when the Muslim cities of Agra, Lucknow and Delhi fell into disrepute. Within fifteen years a European township had grown up there with a High Court, a secretariat, a cantonment, and the Muir College which was founded in 1872 and was to grow into the first university of the province (and the fourth in India, after Calcutta, Madras and Bombay) in 1887. Motilal failed to take the examinations in full and consequently was not awarded a degree. This was perhaps the only failure which was to remain with him in later life; the remorse he felt made him attach a little too much importance to academic distinction. He held his incomplete liberal education accountable for not being made a High Court judge, a part-time professor at the local law college or the Honorary Vice-Chancellor of Allahabad University. But as a restless youth he did not have the patience to spend another year or so in completing his formal education. Instead he moved on to vocational training, passed the lawyer's examination with distinction, completed his three-year apprenticeship at the Kanpur district court, and moved back to Allahabad in 1886 to practise in the High Court as a junior counsel under the aegis of his brother Nandlal. But Nandlal died the following year, leaving behind a widow and seven children. Motilal, then twenty-six, assumed responsibility for his brother's family; his own first wife had died, and he had married again. As a beginner in the profession with few briefs, very little income, and a large family to maintain, Motilal would have found it difficult to make both ends meet; but Nandlal had left a capital sum, his life savings, which came under Motilal's control.[1] It was not much but just enough to support the family during his early years at the Bar. Later Motilal was to discharge his obligations most handsomely towards his brother's family. Not only was he to spend enormous sums on the education and maintenance of his nephews (some of whom were educated in Britain) but also to refund to them with interest their father's legacy.[2]

Though Motilal inherited his brother's practice, his success at the Bar was really the product of his own hard work and force of personality. In less than ten years he moved to the very top of the ladder. In 1896, at the age of thirty-five, he was one of the four leading advocates in the High Court, earning Rs. 2000 (approximately £170) a month. By 1905 his income had multiplied five times, and he was recognised as one of the two most successful advocates in the province, the other being Sundarlal Dave.[3]

Motilal attributed his success solely to his industry, and he attributed other people's failures to their lack of it: 'To my mind it is simple enough. I want money, I work for it and I get it. There are many people who want it perhaps more than

I do but they do not work and naturally enough don't get it.'[4]

He claimed, with justice, that he was the 'founder of the fortunes of the Nehru family'.[5] He was also the first to adopt Nehru as a surname.

With the change in his life-style he had begun, in the middle nineties, to accept Anglo-Indian culture. In his adaptation and emulation of English culture he was more courageous and less restrained than his colleagues at the Allahabad Bar. In fact he was the only one among the leading men of the province who took wholeheartedly to anglicisation. The others had adopted the English language and, in some cases, European dress merely as professional equipment, while living a strictly traditional life in their homes. Among upper-caste Hindus the traditional life meant, among other things, the strict observance of culinary taboos and caste rules which in effect neutralised mobility and social integration. Sundarlal Dave, who was to become a vice-chancellor and then a High Court judge, would not eat while travelling.[6] If a Congress session was to be held in Madras, three days away by rail, he would stay away rather than break this rule. Madan Mohan Malaviya of the Allahabad Bar, who was to become a leader of all-India status, would not allow Vedic hymns to be recited by girls in the presence of non-Hindus.[7] Malaviya overflowed with love for all mankind but he made a distinction, solely on grounds of physical purity, between upper-caste Hindus on the one hand and the rest of the human race on the other.

Motilal had accepted the symbols and to some extent the essence of anglicisation. He had moved to the civil lines, an exclusive residential area for Europeans, and then in 1900 bought a palatial home which he named Anand Bhawan. His was the first Indian house to have all the modern amenities, including electricity, a swimming-pool, well-laid-out gardens and tennis courts. He was to be the first civilian in Allahabad to own motor-cars, directly imported from France. He broke all Hindu taboos on food, drink and social intercourse. His house contained a European kitchen and wine cellar. He employed on his domestic staff Muslims, Untouchables and English governesses, who would not be acceptable in an orthodox home. He imposed English upon his family as the language of conversation, which often resulted in long spells of silence. He had defied the Hindu taboos after two visits to Britain, first in 1899 and again in 1900. On each occasion he had refused to submit to any purification ceremony; instead he had willingly turned into a social rebel and an outcaste, and gathered some local followers. With rationality as his yardstick he had defied many customs and superstitions, and marched firmly on the road to modernisation.

In Motilal's case anglicisation had manifold implications. It implied acceptance of the British connection with India as providential. This in turn meant accepting for India an inferior status. India had to progress – politically, socially and economically – under the British aegis. Moderate, constitutional politics therefore seemed to him appropriate. Anglicisation further implied being equated with the English, which in the Indo-British context depended on the explicit recognition of an Indian by the English as his equal. Motilal could not bear the thought of being inferior to any Briton on any grounds. He was convinced of the irrationality of racial discrimination and was inclined to believe that only uncultured Britons indulged in it. He wanted to believe that racialism was not a common British disease. When, as late as 1927, his son and daughter-in-law were to complain about discrimination as practised by some London hotels, Motilal had to advise them always to lodge in a first-class hotel.[8] British racialism was taboo as a topic of family conversation, especially in Motilal's presence. It was best to avoid it, otherwise it might cause an emotive reaction against anglicisation, and virtually against modernisation – for these were then indistinguishable. A colonial power was virtually the exclusive agency of modernisation in its colony. A reaction, psychological or political, against the colonial power often involved rejection of certain modern norms and forms, otherwise useful, which that power had introduced – intentionally or otherwise – into the life of its colony.

For Motilal, however, Europeanisation did not mean a complete divorce from the Hindu tradition. Consequently his household exhibited several cultures in separate layers; it was a house of contrasts where the old and the new co-existed in peace. The inner sanctum was exclusively Hindu, presided over by his orthodox wife. An English governess functioned side by side with the traditional Hindu (Pandit) and Muslim (Maulvi) teachers. European, Hindu and Muslim kitchens catered for three different tastes in three different styles. The swimming-pool and the lawns contrasted with the place of family worship. Horse-riding and tennis had their place but wrestling, Motilal's favourite sport, was still patronised. The norms of western individualism and privacy were accepted but not allowed to violate the caste rules or erode the joint-family structure.

Anand Bhawan, however, was not a house of conflict, at least until Gandhi appeared on the Indian scene. Diverse cultural patterns ran parallel with each other, causing no friction. Motilal, the grand patriarch, harboured no self-doubt. This was so partly because he was not an intellectual; he was not so sensitive and imaginative as his son was to become. He was decisive; once his mind was made up he nourished no lingering doubts. He released his tensions in rocking bursts of laughter or temper. The year 1905 was perhaps the happiest of his life. Later he was to become famous, doubting and disconsolate.

This portrait of the father provides some insight into his aspirations for his son; but it is important to understand that Motilal did not envisage a political career for him. To understand this fully we must consider the state of Indian politics in 1905.

There were no corridors of power. The provincial and central legislative councils, comprising an official majority and non-official Indian minority, functioned as mere consultative and advisory bodies. These legislative bodies absorbed, in 1905, not more than fifty nominated Indians who were supposed to represent 'types and classes rather than areas and numbers'.[9] The rulers believed that India was unsuited to any system of representation which closely imitated the parliamentary systems of western Europe.[10] Membership of a council carried for an Indian no prospect of executive or ministerial responsibility. An Indian with ambitions in public life, like G. K. Gokhale, could at the most aspire to become a member first of the provincial legislative council, then of the central council, and ultimately of the British Parliament.[11] The membership yielded no other rewards than a superficial contact with the guardians of the Raj, a forum for rhetoric and the status of an honourable gentleman among a handful of constituents. Nonetheless, the legislative councils of British India symbolised the constitutionalism of the British imperial system, distinguishing it from the French and Dutch systems in Indo-China and Indonesia respectively. They were the nurseries for the growth of liberal nationalism. The British never attempted to dissolve them. On the contrary, the powers of the legislative councils, as well as the proportion of Indian representation in them, were to be successively increased in 1909, 1919 and 1935. Nor were these councils to be entirely abandoned by the Indians even during the dominance of the Gandhian non-constitutional, non-violent style of nationalism. It was in the council chamber that the final transfer of power in 1947 was to take place.

Outside legislative councils the political life of India was nourished by a number of provincial parties, and by a single all-India organisation – the Indian National Congress. Twenty-five years old in 1905, Congress was still a floating organisation that acquired visible form once a year, at its session which occupied the last week of December. It was an élitist organisation controlled by a caucus of about a dozen leaders,[12] including three retired Englishmen from the Indian Civil Service – Allan Octavian Hume, Sir William Wedderburn and Sir Henry Cotton. These guardians of the Congress constituted the first generation of Indian leadership. They belonged to the politically conscious provinces of Bengal, Bombay and Madras. Except for Dadabhai Naoroji and Gokhale, respectively the oldest and the youngest members of the inner circle, all the others were born during the 1840s and had reached adulthood in the 1860s when the British Raj, having suppressed the Mutiny of 1857, appeared as the single unassailable power in India. They had accepted the British connection as providential and had led the Congress movement since its foundation in 1885, on strictly constitutional lines. They represented the interests of the Indian middle class and asked for increased Indian participation in the administrative, legislative and military organs of the State. They did not ask for self-government; to them this would have been like a precocious child asking for freedom from parental control.

In fact, they were the mature offspring of the Raj, but lacked the confidence to break the apron-strings. Some believed that chaos and anarchy would follow if the British withdrew from India. Theirs was thus the politics of petition and participation, not of revolution and replacement. They were nationalists and their movement was national, but their concept of an Indian nation was wide enough to contain the British as senior partners.

The British response to the overtures of Congress, however, was harsh and sarcastic. The harshness stemmed from a general fear of any Indian party, however loyal in the beginning, turning into a potential contender for power. The sarcasm was the result of over-stressing the narrow base of Congress, and the unrepresentative status of its leaders. Lord Dufferin (Governor-General of India from 1884 to 1888), who was the godfather of Congress, had soon become disillusioned and attacked it as the product of an infinitesimal section of the Indian community, unrepresentative, misguided and disloyal.[13] Lord Curzon (Governor-General of India from 1899 to 1905) believed that Congress was tottering to its fall. He wanted to assist it to a peaceful demise.[14] British hostility towards Congress and disregard for its leaders had made Gokhale, the youngest member of the Congress caucus, realise with sadness that public men like himself were in a helpless position, for they belonged neither to the Government nor to the masses.[15] Yet the Congress leaders persisted in their constitutional politics, hoping that the policy-makers in London might concede what the British administrators in India had withheld from them.

A section of the Indian élite had grown militant mainly in reaction to British indifference and Congress passivity. The members of this group challenged the propriety of British rule in India, and rejected the supremacy of western civilisation. Their demand was for self-government. They were unscrupulous about methods, which could include anything from boycotting British goods and terrorising individual Britons to armed revolt and conspiracy with anti-British foreign powers.

The militant nationalism which appeared in the late 1890s never gathered any great strength in India. It never turned into an all-India underground movement. Even in the provinces of Bengal and the Punjab, where it was strongest in the first decade of this century, it lacked organisation. The reasons for the feebleness of militant nationalism are many. But perhaps the most important is the unshackled growth of constitutional nationalism represented by Congress up to 1920. If the British Government had ever banned Congress during this period (which it did not, in spite of its growing hostility towards it) the ranks of the militant nationalists might have been swollen by a number of desolate patriots. Even though it was never banned, when constitutional nationalism seemed too feeble to attain any results – as it did in the first decade of the present century – the militant nationalists gained ground and strength. The Government suppressed them with various measures, but most effectively by introducing the constitutional reforms of 1909 which, as intended, strengthened the liberal stream in national politics.

The relative affluence of the upper middle class and the preponderance within it of the lawyer element are other factors that discouraged the growth of militant nationalism in India. Militancy involved danger to life, confiscation of property and the ending of careers. It thus implied risks which self-made men of the middle class were most reluctant to take. The lawyers, who provided leadership at all levels in the national movement, were by their professional training and social background conditioned against participating in terrorist and conspiratorial activities. The lawyer was committed to constitutionalism. He was at home while arguing in a law court, debating in the council chamber, negotiating at a conference table, even heading a lawful procession or addressing a lawful public meeting; but he would be opposed to a revolutionary movement which justified murders and conspiracies, and tended to undermine the very system in which the lawyer had flourished and which he was trained to protect. It is, therefore, not merely a coincidence that the high-ranking militant leadership included hardly any lawyers.[16]

Militant nationalism thus tended to thrive in regional pockets on local grievances. It had its first great opportunity in October 1905, when Curzon implemented his plan for the partition of Bengal with a display of complete disregard for the opinion of the Hindu Bengali middle class. The militant nationalists gained strength in the anti-partition agitation and strove to turn a provincial grievance into a national tragedy with a view to capturing the leadership of Congress. The concern of the Congress barons was aroused as much for their own leadership as for the survival of Congress. They feared that the Government would destroy the young Congress rather than let it fall under militant control. The struggle for supremacy began in 1905. It was to last for two years, and end in the defeat of the militant nationalists and the subsequent imprisonment of their leader Bal Gangadhar Tilak.

Although the militant nationalists were to be outmanœuvred, they were to show an advantage over their rivals in having followers among the lower middle class. They achieved this by their use of Indian languages and cultural symbols, and through their support for local grievances. But a lower-middle-class following had its own disadvantage. The members of this class, with low incomes and little leisure, could not be easily mobilised and assembled at places distant from their home town or province. It is for this reason that the venue of the Congress session was to become a vital issue in the struggle for power between the constitutionalists and militants. If the session of 1907 had been held in Nagpur instead of in Surat the militants might have captured the leadership.

This was the political scene in India in 1905. The constitutional reforms of 1909 were still in the future, and the struggle between the constitutionalists and the militants was in its infancy, when Motilal was laying the foundations of his son's career. Although Motilal had attended, between 1888 and 1892, a few sessions of Congress, two of which were held in his home town, he was in 1905 on the whole non-political. In fact he considered politics a refuge for those who had been failures in life. All this prevented his thinking of a public life for his son. Neither did he consider his own profession necessarily the best for him. He knew from his own experience that success in the legal profession depended as much on chance as on hard work. Although with his large practice he could guarantee a good start for his son, a successful career at the Bar nonetheless seemed to lack the opportunity to wield the kind of power he wanted for him. Though a successful Indian advocate could be appointed to a judgeship of the High Court, it was nonetheless an uncertain prospect. Besides, the judicial office in colonial India did not have the same aura of power and prestige as a high executive post.

What Motilal wanted for his son was firstly the best English education money could buy, and then an entry into the Indian Civil Service, the core of the Establishment, the steel frame of the Empire in India. Having failed to get a degree for himself, Motilal encouraged his son to collect as many academic distinctions and degrees as possible before sitting the competitive examination for the Indian Civil Service.

Jawaharlal was to spend three years each at Harrow and Cambridge, and to study science in order to become a Senior Wrangler. With such academic achievements to his credit, the father assured the son, the Indian Civil Service would be 'child's play'.[17]

The Civil Service was the most sought after profession among young Indians of the upper middle class. This was more for the prestige and power which membership carried than for the financial rewards it offered. In 1905 a district magistrate earned just over £2000 a year,[18] but he exercised enormous power and responsibility in his district. He was the collector of revenue, dispenser of justice (in minor cases), and preserver of peace and order. A member of the Indian Civil Service, whether British or Indian, was sure at some point in his career to get the charge of a district. Although in theory membership of the Indian Civil Service was open to all through the competitive examination, in practice it was made difficult for Indians to compete with the British on equal terms. The Indians were handicapped in many ways, one of them being the fact that the competitive examinations were held exclusively in London. Thus, of a total of about a thousand members of the Indian Civil Service in 1903, only forty-two were Indians.[19] The proportion of Indians in the Service remained well under seven per cent until the First World War, after which it steadily increased.[20] Of this small percentage, most were Hindu Bengalis. Until 1905 not a single Kashmiri had entered the Service. Motilal was thus hoping that his son might be the first member of the Kashmiri community to attain this distinction. In the event it was not his son but his nephew Brijlal Nehru who was to become the first Kashmiri member of the 'superior governing class'. Jawaharlal was to be spared for a more challenging profession. Harrow and Cambridge were intended to turn the young Nehru into a faithful associate of the British Raj. They turned him into a loyal nationalist.

CHAPTER TWO

The Growth of an Intellectual, 1905–12

It would be something for any man to speak about his connection with these great institutions, but in your case I am perfectly certain that it will be the institutions who will own you with pride as one of their brightest jewels.

Motilal Nehru to Jawaharlal Nehru, 26 July 1907

Even Balliol could not have made me a greater friend of the English than Harrow and Trinity made me, but that friendship, I am afraid, does not extend to the British Government in England and India.

Jawaharlal Nehru, 1933

THE fifteen-year-old Jawaharlal was not 'vastly surprised at anything' when he first arrived in England.[1] He had been brought up in the best of both Indian and English cultures, had learnt to be at home in but not committed to either. His father and mother represented two diverse strands in his family background. In contrast to his father – domineering, rational, modern – his mother Swarup Rani was delicate, sensitive, uneducated and traditional. She was beautiful, short of stature, and belonged to the fresher stock of emigrants from Kashmir.[2] Jawaharlal respected and feared his father but he loved his mother, confided in her, even dominated her.[3]

His communication with Swarup Rani began to weaken when he entered Harrow, but not his concern for her. He could not share with her his experiences at Harrow. She would not have understood. Besides, his slight knowledge of Hindi, in which alone he could communicate with her, began to fade. Accordingly, his weekly letters to her became shorter. Yet he carefully respected her wishes. He did not ask her openly to stop sending him parcels of Indian sweets and savouries which were invariably stale by the time they reached London from Allahabad. He assured her that he would observe all the Hindu rituals on his birthday, including wearing the sacred thread (Brahminical cord) but excluding the distribution of alms among the poor, of whom there were few in the town.[4]

Swarup Rani became more possessive with Jawaharlal, especially after November 1905 when she lost another baby son within days of his birth.[5] She had already lost a son before the birth of Jawaharlal. She began to feel inadequate, insecure, and apprehensive of a widening gulf between herself and Jawaharlal. All the same, she did not change her way of life to keep pace with her son. She was aware that she would never succeed, therefore she did not attempt it. Her one visit to Europe in the summer of 1905 ran counter to her traditional way of life, and rather than change her life-style she never made another attempt. She did not even yield to Motilal's advice that she should learn English. Her helplessness often made her a little jealous of Motilal, resentful towards and isolated from other members of the joint family, and more solicitous of Jawaharlal's assurances of his love for her. Her constant anxieties pushed her frequently into a state of morbid depression. She poured out her grievances and fears in her letters to Jawaharlal. She told her son that his father rebuked her for her ignorance of English, that she did not like his father's speech delivered at a conference, and that everybody at Anand Bhawan was against her. She expressed to Jawaharlal her fear that he might not respect her after his return. Throughout his stay in England, he responded to his mother with kindness and tact, while carefully avoiding taking her side. He asked her not to take his father's remarks seriously as he must have made them when very tired.[6] He expressed his surprise at her disapproval of his father's speech, adding that there was nothing wrong with the speech and that he himself liked it (in fact Jawaharlal did not like that particular speech and his mother knew it before she wrote to him).[7] He asked her not to be resentful towards other members of the family, explaining that 'Papa is doing to his brother's children what I would do towards my brother's children'.[8] Assuring his mother of his never-diminishing respect for her, he remarked: 'It is bad if an illiterate man does not respect his mother. But it is considered very bad if an educated man does not respect his mother. What is the use of education if it does not teach one how to behave with one's parents?'[9] Assuring her further that his great ambition in life was to make both his parents happy,[10] he begged her not to worry, grumble and grieve. He advised her to keep herself occupied in useful pursuits like reading Hindi newspapers and books.[11] Her anxieties never subsided nor did Jawaharlal's concern for her. She often caused additional strain on his nerves, but he bore it with a sense of pride and duty. She constituted for him an unbreakable link with the Indian culture and tradition which he could never entirely abandon.

From this heterogeneous cultural background Jawaharlal entered Harrow with an incipient desire to play a dominant role in life. To some extent his parents were responsible for generating in their only son the desire for the limelight. The excessive love they bestowed upon him and the overpowering personality of his father aroused in the solitary child an urge for freedom and power. He could satisfy this in his childhood only by setting his mind free from the bondage of love. He often dreamed of 'flying high up in the air' without any assistance.[12] This remained a constant urge in his life and even at the height of his power his mind would fly to yet higher spheres.

Theosophy was another factor. He was introduced to it by his Irish tutor Ferdinand T. Brooks, who took charge of him when he was eleven. Two years later, at the age of thirteen, Jawaharlal was formally initiated as a member of the Theosophical Society.[13] The feeling of being 'one of the elect' gave him, temporarily, a sense of identity. Brooks also cultivated in young Jawaharlal an aptitude for reading widely and retentively. He read the novels of Scott, Dickens, Thackeray, Wells, Lewis Carroll, Kipling, Mark Twain, Cervantes, Jerome K. Jerome, Du Maurier, Conan Doyle and Anthony Hope, also poetry and travel books (such as Nansen's *Farthest North*), which gave wide scope for flights of imagination.[14] From his mother and aunt he learnt the stories of the Indian epics – Ramayana and Mahabharata. Like any other sensitive Indian child, he developed an adoration for their heroes – Rama, Krishna, Arjuna – and a longing to acquire their strength and power to destroy evil, or just to overcome fear.

A cause was not hard to find. There was the fear of the English to be overcome. It was his duty, the duty of every

Indian, to stand up against 'the overbearing character and insulting manners of the English people, as well as Eurasians, towards Indians'.[15] 'Instances of conflicts between the ruler and the ruled' were discussed by young members of the Nehru family, and Jawaharlal was glad when an Indian was reported to have hit back at an arrogant Englishman.[16] His resentment was not against English people as such (in his heart he rather admired them) but against the English as alien rulers of India, in which role they often asserted their racial superiority, appeared arrogant and smug. Nationalistic ideas filled his mind and he ' mused of Indian freedom and Asiatic freedom from the thraldom of Europe'.[17] He dreamt of brave deeds, of how, sword in hand, 'he would fight for India and help in freeing her'.[18] The young Jawaharlal was, thus, deeply interested in any event which might render the European less impregnable. The Boer War (1899–1902) interested him. At that early age of ten or eleven he began to read newspapers 'to get the news of the fighting'.[19] His sympathies were all with the Boers; while his future mentor M. K. Gandhi, then in South Africa, was raising an ambulance corps to help the British against the Dutch. The Russo-Japanese War (1904–5), however, vindicated Jawaharlal's hopes more satisfactorily. For the first time in modern history an Asian nation was defeating a western power. In May 1905, Jawaharlal arrived in London by train from Dover, reading joyously the news of the decisive naval victory of Japan over Russia in the strait of Tsushima.[20] And, when Jawaharlal first entered the gates of Harrow, England too had moved from Victorian complacency into the uncertainty of the Edwardian era. The Boer War had raised doubts in the minds of the British about the civilising mission of the Empire. The Irish national movement, the Suffragettes, the growing class consciousness among the working people who seemed less inclined to accept their poverty as the judgement of God, all threatened to erode Victorian ideals and values. The rich of Britain, however, were not unduly concerned and lived a life of ostentation, luxury and waste in the midst of working-class poverty.

It was in the affluent sectors of English society that Jawaharlal spent the seven years of his studentship in England. He lived luxuriously, even by British standards. In this he was encouraged by his father, but it also suited his own inclinations. In keeping with the Edwardian style of life, Jawaharlal spent his holidays travelling to Paris quite frequently, to Ireland twice, to Norway once, and to almost all the fashionable holiday resorts in England and Wales. He spent two long vacations in India, first in 1906 and again in 1908. In his first year at Cambridge he asked his father in vain to buy him a motor-car – a most luxurious and unusual mode of transport for a student in those days. The Edwardian spirit of adventure suited his temperament, particularly in the last two years of his stay in England, from October 1910 to August 1912, when he was studying for the Bar, had too much time on his hands and was restless. In those years Jawaharlal developed expensive tastes (including gambling at cards) in trying to live the life of a 'man about town', whose typical evening would consist of a visit to the theatre and then a late supper with champagne at the Savoy.[21] His annual expenses rose above £800, a sum which in those days was enough to support a comfortable life in London for three years.[22] This aroused his father's anxieties, but he did not blame Jawaharlal, for at least in this respect he was proving himself his 'father's son'.[23] Jawaharlal's style of life in London contrasted greatly with that of Gandhi and Vallabhbhai Patel. When Gandhi was a student in London he spent only sixpence on three meals a day.[24] When Patel was in London for his Bar studies, from 1910 to 1913, he walked from his lodgings to the Middle Temple and back.[25]

Jawaharlal also indulged his love of sport – from paper chase, ' two hares ' and cricket at Harrow to tennis and rowing at Cambridge. He did not, however, distinguish himself at any particular game except perhaps in flying kites, an occupation that suited his temperament, and which he popularised in Cambridge by getting good-quality kites sent to him from India by his parents.[26] He never made the Harrow cricket team against Eton at Lord's. He was not tubbed at the Trinity boat club; on joining the club he was weighed and found 'the lightest person of the lot', hence immediately made a cox.[27] Neither did he fully benefit from the principles of the team games. He regarded himself as an 'outsider', reluctant to let his individuality merge into a group, share its enthusiasm and be bound by its loyalty.

The growth of Jawaharlal as an intellectual and a nationalist, however, was not stifled either by the anti-intellectual, anti-scientific, games-dominated conservative environment of his public school, by the imperialist atmosphere of Cambridge or by the carefree, opulent life he led throughout his stay in England. Cambridge intensified his nationalist aspirations. The comforts of life, which he took for granted, neither aroused in him any fondness for the capitalist order nor prevented him from being academically interested in socialism. At the end of his educational career he emerged as non-aligned as he was before, but with a longing to submerge himself in an all-absorbing cause.

In spite of himself, Jawaharlal's scholastic achievements were second-rate. This was mainly because the subjects in which he was examined were not those in which he had any keen interest. Considerations other than his interests determined the choice of subjects, while at Harrow he did not have much choice anyway. He was not good at learning languages and he had no patience with Latin, in which he made very little progress, in spite of private tutoring. He found the atmosphere at Harrow uncongenial and the physical discomforts almost unbearable. The school houses seemed too primitive, and the rooms looked to him like 'miserable caged hovels' from which there was no easy exit in case of fire.[28] They were terribly cold, there was no fire in the mornings, and he detested washing in freezing water.[29] The best room in the Headmaster's house was occupied by the Indian Prince of Gaikwar. Jawaharlal had more right to the room than anybody else when the Prince left Harrow. Instead another Indian prince (the son of the Maharaja of Kapurthala) was allotted the room, although he was junior to Jawaharlal.[30] Jawaharlal felt he had been wronged, and the incident did not make him feel kindly towards the princely order. Furthermore, he had no great regard for the Headmaster Dr Joseph Wood, whom he considered a 'stuffy old fellow' whose main concern was to make money for the school.[31]

Despite these inconveniences Jawaharlal managed to do well in his first term and came top of his form. But his visit to India in the summer of 1906 unsettled him. On his return to Harrow he suffered from homesickness, his life grew more 'solitary and lonely', and the school became more uncongenial, almost like a prison.[32] Soon after his return he wrote to his father:

> You can hardly imagine how much the hope of seeing you keeps me up.
>
> I have no doubt whatever that my coming to Harrow was the right thing, nor do I think that it has done me no good. But sometimes I feel rather lonely and wish I was in more congenial surroundings. This is quite natural and I am sure you will appreciate it.[33]

Jawaharlal decided to leave Harrow sooner than expected. Against the Headmaster's advice, he took the Cambridge entrance examination in the summer of 1907 and passed it with distinction. At the close of his Harrow career he evidently felt no nostalgia – 'I would have liked to have stayed on for another year if I had been younger but under the circumstances it is undoubtedly the best thing for me to leave.'[34]

In his choice of studies at Cambridge, Jawaharlal was to some extent influenced by considerations of competing successfully in the Indian Civil Service examination. The natural sciences figured prominently in the Civil Service syllabus. He opted for a natural science tripos in physics, chemistry and geology, although his interests were not confined to these. In the course of a year he realised that he was very poor in physics because he had no background in mathematics.[35] He gave up physics and took botany. The Cambridge atmosphere was more congenial. He felt 'elated at being an undergraduate with a great deal of freedom, compared to school, to do what I choose'.[36] He pursued a number of non-academic interests and lived an altogether fuller life. His return to Cambridge from his second visit to India in the summer of 1908 was almost like a homecoming. But the more he felt at home the more he was reminded that he was 'a foreigner', an 'intruder', in England.[37]

At this time nothing could hold Jawaharlal's interest for long. He was reluctant to become deeply involved in any situation, and was consequently always restless. By the time he took the second part of the tripos he was tired of Cambridge. Though he obtained a second – he had expected a third – he had no wish to stay longer to study law for the LL.B. and LL.D. degrees, which his father wanted him to get.[38] Nevertheless the occasion was duly celebrated at Anand Bhawan in a princely style. Motilal gave a gala dinner, champagne flowed freely for several days, the domestic servants received cash and increases in their salaries, and Jawaharlal in London received an extra hundred pounds from his proud father to spend on a holiday in France.[39]

It was at this point that a firm decision about Jawaharlal's professional career was taken. The Indian Civil Service was ruled out in favour of the Bar. The main reasons for abandoning the Civil Service were Jawaharlal's lack of interest in it and his fear that he might not pass the examination or might pass it in a lower grade, in which case he might be offered a posting in Ceylon like his cousin Brijlal Nehru, who had passed in a lower grade in 1907.[40] Jawaharlal did not make his own decisions – he would have taken the examination if his father had insisted – but Motilal's initial enthusiasm for the Civil Service had subsided in course of time. For Motilal it was no longer a grand novelty – a member of the Nehru family, and for that reason the first Kashmiri, had already entered the service. Besides, he saw no prospects in it because 'the deserving and un-deserving' were all herded together, and every opportunity was taken 'to humiliate the Indian members of the I.C.S.'.[41] The Bar, on the other hand, seemed to offer the highest position and rank to the deserving. Motilal's mind was finally made up when a judge of the Allahabad High Court remarked that with such a good practice at the Bar it would be very silly of him to send his son into the Civil Service.[42] Motilal, therefore, advised Jawaharlal to take law degrees: 'With a school training at Harrow and an M.A. LL.D. (Cantab) you will be worth half a dozen civilians any day. As for success at the Bar, leave that to me.'[43] Motilal felt confident that his son would rise 'in his father's profession'.[44]

Jawaharlal was not interested in legal studies either, but he accepted his father's advice without protest. His ardent desire after leaving Cambridge was to spend a year or so at any of the 'decent' Oxford colleges, even if it was to pursue legal studies. As Oxford's intake of Indians was minimal, it was an achievement for an Indian to be offered a place. To outmanœuvre any possible bar against Indians, Jawaharlal applied to some Oxford colleges without disclosing his Indian nationality, for once the head of the college offered him a place 'it will be hard for him to get out of his promise when he found out that I was an Indian'.[45] He was keen on Balliol and Oriel, but both declined. He was offered a place by St John's which he did not accept.

Jawaharlal was interested in the study of the social sciences – economics, history, political science, even philosophy – and, although he finally moved to London in October 1910 for his Bar studies at the Inner Temple, he toyed with the idea of studying economics at the London School of Economics.[46] At this point Jawaharlal became acutely conscious of the lack of opportunities to pursue his real scholastic interests. In a moment of frustration he blamed his father, indirectly, for turning him into a mere lawyer:

> Law and science are all very well in their own way but no man, however great a lawyer he may be, will or should be excused for his want of knowledge in certain other subjects. I would much rather risk my success at the Bar than go through life as a mere lawyer with no interest in anything save the technicalities and trivialities of law.[47]

A 'mere lawyer', Motilal retorted, 'has not yet been known to succeed in his profession and the lawyers who have succeeded and will succeed have generally something more than mere law to draw upon'.[48] Jawaharlal apologised to his father for having so forcefully expressed his views. He settled down 'to do law and law alone', abandoning the idea of joining the London School of Economics.[49] He did not, however, forsake his interest in the social sciences. He pursued his studies informally and often haphazardly for the rest of his life.

Legal studies seemed to Jawaharlal far less interesting than the natural sciences. As they did not absorb him he spent most of his time in pursuit of pleasures and high living, and became increasingly restless. But he had to pass the examinations and he did. He passed the examinations in constitutional law, Roman law, and even in real property, which, he thought, was a 'godless subject'.[50] He employed a coach to prepare him for the Bar final examination, which he thought he had no hope of getting through. Nonetheless he passed it in June 1912 and was called to the Bar.

It was a year when Motilal could proudly count the achievements made by the scions of the Nehru family. Three of his nephews had been educated in Britain; of these two had entered the Indian Civil Service and the third had become a highly qualified medical man. His son was now a graduate of Cambridge and a barrister. His fondest hopes of seeing the Nehru name become famous were being realised. These young Nehrus and their descendants, he felt sure, would 'go on adding fresh lustre to the family name as years go by'.[51]

Jawaharlal's development as a nationalist was more consistent, though he did not attain in this period any measure of dedication to the cause; this was to some extent due to his intellectual and generally uncommitted state of mind. His initial resentment against British power was kept aflame by instances of British discrimination against Indians. He suspected even the English law courts of discriminating against Indians.[52] He saw iniquitous discrimination in the attempt made by John Morley (Secretary of State for India, 1905–10) in March 1909 to devise means of limiting the number of Indian students at Cambridge.[53] He was incensed at the disregard shown to distinguished Indian visitors (the Maharaja of Bikaner and the Aga Khan) on Convocation Day in Cambridge in June 1911. The Indians were the only recipients of honorary degrees who were not cheered, and the Chancellor did not get up when giving them the degree, 'although he got up for everyone else, even for such a villain as Lee-Warner'.[54]

Jawaharlal's pride and sensitivity intensified his awareness of the inferior and humiliating position generally occupied by Indians in the British imperial order. In this order, he realised, there was no prospect for Indians ever to attain a status equal to that of their British so-called mentors. He therefore became more appreciative of political methods which openly defied, slighted or challenged British power. He also felt attracted towards any political system which did not discriminate between people on grounds of race, colour or religion. He was thus drawn towards the strategy of the Indian extremists and the socialism of the British Fabians. Yet as an intellectual and an individualist he was unable to commit himself fully either to the ideology of the extremists or to the collectivism of the Fabians. All the same, his political views clashed with those of his father. But instead of modifying or suppressing them, which was his usual practice, he kept on trying to convert his father to them, knowing full well that his father was too proud and aggressive a person to pursue for long the self-effacing politics of the Indian moderates.[55]

Jawaharlal was politically conscious when he entered Harrow. He kept in touch with Indian political developments through Indian nationalist periodicals, some of which like the *Indian People* were regularly sent to him from India. He was also briefed continually by his father, who on his return to India in November 1905 was drawn, first as an observer and then as a partisan, into the country's politics, which had suddenly grown defiant and aggressive. In protest against the partition of their province, the English-educated Bengali-Hindus had forged a new style of agitation based on the boycott of everything British, and the adoption of everything Indian. The anti-partition movement seemed to Indianise, for the first time, the national movement, which had until then progressed on western lines. It also constituted a challenge to the moderate politicians who controlled Congress. Motilal informed Jawaharlal of the advent of this new era in British Indian history, symbolised by the ritualistic discarding of European for Indian costumes – dhoti and chaddar – and highlighted by the departure of Curzon from India 'unwept, unhonoured and unsung'. 'If this movement only continues,' he warned his son, 'you will on your return find an India quite different to the India you left.'[56] Jawaharlal was most gratified by the news of the boycott and swadeshi.[57]* His nationalist views, however, seemed out of place in the conservative atmosphere of Harrow. He realised that in his background, interests and inclinations he was different from his fellow Harrovians. At times he suspected he was too precocious. Motilal

*For a definition of swadeshi, see below, page 67.

had to assure him that there was nothing unusual: 'An Indian boy is generally more thoughtful than an English boy of the same age. In fact there is very early development in India which Englishmen call precocity.'[58] This might be so, but Jawaharlal could not share the true spirit of the Harrovians who were, as a contemporary novelist put it, 'repeating the creed of their fathers, knowing that creed will be so repeated by their sons and sons' sons'.[59] He wished he had gone straight to a university instead of to Harrow.[60] The Liberal victory at the general election of January 1906 gratified him, but before long he realised that the Liberals, whether imperialists or Little Englanders, were in no way different from the Conservatives in their policy towards India. Ireland could divide them, but India received the same blanket treatment from all political parties and from all factions within each party.

The Liberal victory aroused new hopes among the Indian moderates and strengthened their position against the extremists. In this crisis Motilal was drawn to take sides. His original enthusiasm for the new Bengali style of politics soon subsided. At the 1905 annual session of Congress, held in December in Banaras, Motilal was disillusioned by the irresponsibility, dishonesty and stupidity of the anti-partition agitators of Bengal.[61] This was the first occasion on which he had come into close contact with Gokhale, the Congress president for the Banaras session. Gokhale's integrity and his style of leadership impressed Motilal. At the Banaras Congress Motilal also realised that there was a prospect of his assuming the leadership of his province, which was then outside the vortex of Indian politics. He also saw in the extremist politics of boycott, which included not only the boycott of British goods but also of English courts and schools, a threat to his own profession and life-style. Moderate politics suited his temperament, and he rallied to its support at the annual session of Congress held in Calcutta during the last week of December 1906. He attended the Congress session virtually as the leader of moderate opinion in his province.

It was at this session that the battle between the extremists and the moderates was to be fought over the aims and methods of the Congress movement. Calcutta was the stronghold of the extremists, and they far outnumbered the moderates at the Congress session. Motilal saw in this struggle no noble cause but a dishonest bid for power on the part of the Bengali politicians. He prepared the delegates from his own province to oppose publicly the extremist resolution in favour of self-government – a resolution which to him meant nothing less ridiculous than giving a 'formal notice to the British Government to quit and hand over the reins of government to the oily Babus'.[62] The battle, however, was not fought; it was postponed to the next session of Congress. In 1907 both moderates and extremists canvassed for support in the provinces. The politically backward United Provinces was the target for both parties. Tilak visited Allahabad in January 1907, and won the students to his cause by what Motilal called 'his wild and revolutionary propaganda'.[63] At this point Motilal finally made up his mind, accepted the presidency of the first United Provinces provincial conference, and entered the political arena. With this also began the politicisation of United Provinces. Politics was 'entirely a new line' for him, but he entered it fearlessly and with an independent mind. When Gokhale visited Allahabad in February, Motilal sat beside him as the leader of his province.

The political dialogue between father and son now began. Jawaharlal was glad of his father's decision but unhappy at his dislike of the Bengali extremists. 'Their erratic methods', he wrote to Motilal, 'have made me respect them far more than I ever did.'[64] It was owing to the activities of the extremists, Jawaharlal pointed out, that Congress had begun to feature prominently for the first time in British newspapers. Motilal, however, followed the moderate line in his presidential speech at the provincial conference on 29 March 1907. He was true to his beliefs in endorsing the various blessings that India had enjoyed under British rule, and in hoping that many more would be bestowed upon her if only John Bull were sufficiently aroused, for he meant well: 'it was not in his nature to mean ill'.[65]

Jawaharlal found his father's speech too moderate. 'As regards John Bull's good faith,' he wrote to his father, 'I have not as much confidence in him as you have.'[66] While not questioning his son's lack of faith in the British, Motilal nonetheless tried to dispel Jawaharlal's impression that the Indian extremists were all courageous and self-sacrificing. He blamed the 'extremist fools' for the deportation of Lajpat Rai in May 1907. Lacking in moral and physical courage, he explained to his son, the extremists kicked up a row with another set of cowards – the British administrators in the provinces – to impress the latter with their power and importance. The British administrators 'got frightened and not knowing exactly what to do and how to account for the existing state of things' laid their hands on the most prominent man in the Punjab – Lajpat Rai.[67] The deportation of Lajpat Rai, Motilal maintained, frightened the extremists into submission, and on hearing the news their 'great hero', the Bengali Bipin Chandra Pal, cancelled the 'fiery speech' with which he had been going to earn cheap martyrdom in Madras and hastily retired into meditation.[68] Not a single Bengali patriot, Motilal assured Jawaharlal, had yet gone to jail if he had anything to lose by doing so.

Jawaharlal's respect for individual extremists diminished somewhat. But his fondness for extremism increased during the summer of 1907 when he visited Ireland for the first time. He at once felt an affinity with the Sinn Fein movement, the aggressive, self-reliant new kind of Irish nationalism. He learnt more about the ideology and strategy of Sinn Fein from *The New Ireland*, a booklet by an English journalist Sydney Brooks, which was published in the summer of 1907.[69] Sinn Fein believed 'that the salvation of Ireland must be sought and achieved by Irishmen on Irish soil'.[70] The old nationalist attitude of seeking concessions from England was to be abandoned, and a vigorous boycott of English language and institutions (a method of passive resistance first used by Francis Deak, the Hungarian nationalist, against Austrian imperialism) was to be initiated. Irishmen were urged not to take up arms against England, but to stay at home in Ireland and boycott English law courts, the English parliament, English educational institutions and English manufactured goods. Ireland and India presented identical pictures to Jawaharlal. In both countries people were listless, numbed by rhetoric into inaction. Irish parliamentarians and Indian liberals seemed alike to him. Gokhale and his own father appeared to be the Indian counterparts of Redmond and Dillon. Thus there arose in Jawaharlal's mind the image of extremists as the Sinn Fein of India. He conveyed this impression to his father, asking him to read Brooks's *New Ireland* and see for himself the striking resemblance between the two groups.[71]

Motilal was not converted. He continued to fight faithfully for the moderates, and he was fully gratified by their victory over the extremists at the Surat session of Congress in December 1907. Jawaharlal, on the other hand, refused to be browbeaten. Instead of suppressing his views and becoming a little sarcastic in his communications with his father, which he usually did when confronted by him on any issue, he became more ardent and explicit in his criticisms of moderate politics in India. He told his father openly that the moderates were not the 'natural leaders' of the country as they arrogantly claimed to be, and that he was convinced that in a few years' time 'there will hardly be any so called "moderates" left' in India.[72] He resented the contention of the Indian moderates that chaos and anarchy would follow if the British left India.[73] It seemed to him pathetic that the moderates relied so naïvely on British goodwill when the British, while conceding the possibility of India's achieving self-government one day, saw this as not happening (as the *Saturday Review* put it in one of its June 1908 issues) for 'some million generations', the time required to educate Indians up to the colonial standard.[74] His individual defiance of the British was manifested on such occasions as the funeral of King Edward VII and the coronation of George V, when he complained of the disturbance to his studies, while his father respectively mourned and celebrated as a loyal subject of the Crown.

Their political differences, however, did not create bad blood between father and son. Politics had not yet become a dominant theme in the life of either. For Motilal it was a game which he played during High Court recesses. He had discovered to his own surprise that he could be as successful in politics (so long as it did not involve the masses) as he was in his own profession. Starting as a mere delegate in 1905, he had become a provincial leader in 1907, was elected to the provincial legislature in February 1910 when the new legislative bodies under the Act of 1909 were inaugurated, organised the annual session of Congress in Allahabad in December

1910 and was invited to attend the King's Delhi durbar in December 1911 – which he attended dressed in clothes bought for him in London, ironically enough by Jawaharlal. He had mastered the political game as well as launched in 1909 in Allahabad a nationalist daily newspaper – *The Leader*. He had thus, by 1912, created for himself a sound base in liberal politics.

Jawaharlal had during the same period fallen in with the extremists, but with some reservations. He was attracted to boycott as a political weapon but not to its correlative, the revival and glorification of Hindu tradition – on which, with a view to Indianising the national movement, the extremists, who were all Hindus, had fallen back. This new nationalism, substantially Hindu, did not appeal to Jawaharlal. For example, he disliked the speech which B. C. Pal gave in Cambridge, because it did not take the Muslims into consideration and contained repeated references to the 'spiritual mission of India', to India as 'God's chosen country' and to Indians as a 'chosen race'.[75] He was unreceptive to religious and spiritual images. Besides, he had not yet discovered the rich heritage of India.

His interest in nationalist politics, however, did not reach the point of dedication, although it was already greater than his interest in anything else. In this, as in other fields, he was reluctant to commit himself completely; it was as if he were afraid of being misjudged. His intellect rebelled against the notion that there were any absolutes of right and wrong. How, then, could he commit himself fully to one thing and be labelled? Non-alignment was more congenial to him, for it gave room not only for his doubts and conflicts, but also for his reluctance to make final and ruthless decisions.

He displayed an even more noncommittal attitude, verging on total indifference, towards the question of marriage. In principle he was opposed to an arranged caste-marriage; but he never let his views clash with his father's. In fact he put himself entirely in his father's hands. Occasionally he lodged mild protests with his mother – in order, it seemed, to keep his conscience clear, rather than to seek any remedy. Motilal assumed the customary parental responsibility for selecting a suitable bride for his son. Young Jawaharlal told his father his abstract views – that he had such a very high opinion of marriage that the practice of it was sure to disappoint him: 'This sounds like the saying of the Irishman who declared that he had such a great regard for truth that he refused to drag it into his own petty affairs, but really there is some sense in it.'[76] Motilal began the search for a bride, but the choice was restricted. The girl, of course, had to be an Indian. Haunted by the fear that his son might fall in love with an English girl, he wrote to him as follows:

> I will therefore give you a bit of advice though I think in your case it is unnecessary. You must not confuse real love with a passing passion or a feeling of pleasure in the society of a girl. I do not believe in love at first sight and no right thinking man will ever believe in it. Real love takes time to develop and is mutual. You know of the arguments against Indians marrying English women. The moment you suspect that any girl has inspired a feeling of some sort in you break off at once and do not let it grow and you will be all the happier for it.[77]

To drive his point home further, Motilal made it clear that he could not bear the idea of having Eurasian grandchildren; such a marriage might cut Jawaharlal off from his 'devoted parents'.[78] Jawaharlal had to dispel his father's fear by assuring him that there was 'no danger of that happening'.[79]

The search was further restricted to Kashmiri girls of the Brahmin caste.[80] Here Motilal was acting contrary to the progressive social views he often expressed on the platform, where he publicly denounced caste as an evil 'which has dragged us down the social scale and made us the laughing-stock of modern civilization'.[81] But Motilal was by no means the only social reformer who did not practise in private life all he preached in public. Jawaharlal, too, had strong views about caste. He believed that India could allow the individualism of the West only when the caste system disappeared.[82] Thus he was opposed in principle to the strict confinement of the search to a particular caste and community. He told his mother that one should do what one considered right, and not conform to caste restrictions just because a handful of people would be annoyed if one disregarded them.[83] Motilal, on the other hand, was determined, however evil the caste system might be, not to be the first one in his community to defy it. Jawaharlal became indifferent and told his father that, on the whole, it would perhaps be better if he married a Kashmiri girl.[84]

The other qualities that Motilal wanted in the girl (apart from her being a Kashmiri Brahmin) were that she should be good-looking, moderately educated but docile (he disapproved of highly educated, obstinate, self-willed girls, certainly of any girl who was a medical doctor) and belong to a cultured and respectable family.[85] The search, already so limited, appeared more difficult in view of the practice of early marriage among Indian girls, particularly among high-caste Kashmiris. This difficulty could be overcome only by 'reserving' a girl when young, and then letting her be educated and groomed till Jawaharlal finally returned to India, by which time she too would have reached marriageable age; but this would mean an age gap of ten years between the couple.

Starting in 1906, Motilal's search for a 'faultless' bride for his only son did not reach fruition during the seven years of Jawaharlal's stay in England. Girls were found and rejected; some for their poor looks and some for their lack of culture. At least one girl, who scored good marks on all points, was rejected because Motilal found her father ugly and uncultured.[86] When the combination of what Motilal called 'looks' and 'books' began to seem unattainable, he asked Jawaharlal which of the two he would prefer. His reply was indecisive. While agreeing with his father that the 'outer features generally take after the inner person', he pointed out that 'beauty is after all skin deep and without certain other qualities would be more harmful than beneficial'.[87] This did not make Motilal's task any easier. Nonetheless, he assured his son that 'unless I am absolutely certain that I have found the most suitable match for you I will not tie you down to anyone'.[88]

Beneath Jawaharlal's placidity and acquiescence in the matter lay resentment and disapproval. In the last two years of his stay in England – from 1910, when he reached the age of twenty-one, to August 1912, when he left for India – Jawaharlal became increasingly conscious of the deprivation and degradation involved in an arranged marriage. Temperamentally romantic and adventurous, he saw no prospect of fulfilling himself in such a situation. Handsome, with sensuous lips and dreamy eyes, he was a little inhibited by his shyness and constant awareness of a small bald patch.[89] His personality did not radiate instant warmth, but he was by no means a cold-blooded prig, as – he thought in his moments of self-chastisement – his friends must think him. In the last two years of his London life he came into contact with a few girls and was drawn romantically towards at least one.[90] But as soon as he felt he was getting emotionally involved he began to extricate himself. He would rather repress his feelings than upset his devoted parents.

All the same, he protested to his mother: 'There should be no marriage without mutual love. I consider it a crime and a ruination of one's life if one has to marry merely for the sake of creating children.'[91] This protest, though embodying his genuine grievances, was couched in an impersonal style and contained no threat of direct resistance. In April 1912, when Motilal sent him the photograph of a girl hoping that he might fall in love with her,[92] Jawaharlal retorted:

> There is not an atom of romance in the way you are searching girls for me and keeping them waiting till my arrival. The very idea is extremely unromantic. And you constantly expect me to fall in love with a photograph. The days for that are gone by. The girl whose photograph you sent me is very probably a very nice person but I can hardly say I am enamoured of her from the photo.[93]

In the same letter Motilal had suggested an alternative choice – 'a Delhi girl' – who satisfied all requirements except that of age; she was only twelve. But he told Jawaharlal that a doctor had given it as his considered opinion 'that there should be a difference of seven or eight years between the age of the girl you are to marry and your own age'.[94] The 'Delhi girl', the last to be unearthed in the six-year search, elicited the following comments from Jawaharlal:

> As regards the Delhi girl surely she is too young for me. I am nearly ten years her senior and that is a rather big difference. I could not possibly marry her until she was eighteen or nineteen and that is six or seven years hence. I would not mind waiting as I am not in a matrimonial state of mind at present.[95]

This brought to an end the long correspondence on marriage, for Jawaharlal returned to India in August 1912. It also brought to an end the search for a bride, for in all probability it was the 'Delhi girl' whom Jawaharlal was to marry in February 1916. He was then twenty-six, and Kamala (born on 1 August 1899) was sixteen.

In almost every aspect of his life in England Jawaharlal encountered conflict between his personal aspirations and family obligations. What he complied with outwardly he often resented inwardly. Basically scrupulous and compassionate, he was also, as an intellectual, free from blind faith and strong prejudices, and was inclined to look at a question from several angles. He could not always summon the ruthlessness to put his opinions into practice. Thus when conflicts created emotional crises he tended to escape into abstract thought. During his last two years in England he became slightly cynical and hedonistic under the mounting pressure. He disliked the imperial face of Britain but was most friendly towards individual Britons. His sympathies lay with India but he was ill at ease with individual Indians. He was shy and reserved but cherished a desire for the limelight. He was drawn towards ideas but had no great aptitude for the dreary details of organisation and implementation. He was capable of great vision but not necessarily insight. He could give an inspired performance on stage but would dread the job of stage-manager. Conscious of the meticulous care and loving protection continuously bestowed upon him by his father, he generally longed to be independent, adventurous and aggressive. In his last years in London he was unable even to manage his finances, which were steadily worsening. It was thus almost with relief that he left England for India. 'It is a jolly good thing', he wrote to his father, 'that I am returning home soon, otherwise I might conceivably get into trouble.'[96]

However, beneath his desire to escape confrontation and involvement lay his longing to commit himself fully to a noble cause and thereby release himself from the bondage of doubts and conflicts. He did not reach this state of commitment as an outsider in England. A stranger now in the India to which he was returning, he was to achieve it.

CHAPTER THREE

Waiting for a Leader, 1913–19

IN September 1912, when Jawaharlal returned to India, the political life of the country in so far as it was represented by Congress seemed complacent and placid. Congress had crushed its extremist wing immediately after the Surat crisis, and since then it had proceeded on a strict constitutional path under the vigilant control of its moderate masters. Sir Pherozeshah Mehta and Gokhale between them formed the body and soul of Congress.

To young Jawaharlal, Congress politics seemed dull. Within three months of his arrival in India he attended, for the first time, the annual session of Congress. It appeared to him like a theatre where well-to-do English-educated Indians were playing the role of gentlemen politicians in their 'morning coats and well-pressed trousers'.[1] His father was one of them. The extremist fire in Congress, which had brightened his nationalist vision while he was in London, seemed to have gone out for ever. Tilak was in Burma serving his six-year term of imprisonment (the longest single term of imprisonment ever served by any of the most prominent nationalists, including Gandhi and Jawaharlal). Among the extremist leaders Tilak was perhaps the only big figure. The Bengali extremists, though rich in new ideas, lacked Tilak's courage, perseverance and capacity to endure suffering. Aurobindo Ghose had abandoned politics in 1910 and retired to Pondicherry in search of spiritual enlightenment. B. C. Pal was in 1911 languishing in London, heartbroken and penniless.[2] His ambition to become a leader by sheer power of oratory had not been achieved. He returned to India but never again played a leading role.

Jawaharlal did not look for political stimulation outside Congress. This was partly because he was young (only twenty-three in November 1912) and uncommitted; partly because politics was then, even for elders like his father, a vacational pastime in which only those who earned enough money in their profession could participate and excel; partly because there was no political life outside Congress which was suitable for Jawaharlal.

There were the individual terrorists, unorganised and leaderless, having a precarious existence in the shadow of government's repressive measures. There were the Indian revolutionaries, in Europe and America, surviving on slender promises of help occasionally given to them by powers hostile to Britain. These terrorists and revolutionaries were to gather some strength for a short while after the outbreak of the First World War. But terrorism was utterly uncongenial to the tender disposition of Jawaharlal, who then, as in later life, could not even bear the sight of death and deliberately avoided visiting a dying friend or colleague.[3] Equally antipathetic to Jawaharlal were the communal political parties – the incipient All-India Hindhu Sabha (which later, in April 1921, changed its name to Mahasabha) and the six-year-old Muslim League; they espoused the Hindu and Muslim interests respectively. However, a handful of young English-educated Muslim leaders, inside and outside the League, having come under the influence of pan-Islamism, were becoming restive and hostile to British power. Pan-Islamic feelings were then generated by the entanglement of European powers in the Near and Middle East. The sensitive Muslim mind in India interpreted every conflict between a Christian and a Muslim power as a further onslaught of Christianity against Islam. The Ottoman Empire, the greatest surviving independent Muslim state, was what Islamic India turned to as an example. The precarious existence of the Turkish Empire accordingly aroused great concern among the Indian Muslims. The division of Persia in 1907 into British and Russian spheres of influence; the Italian attack on Libya, then a province of the Ottoman Empire in 1911; the imposition of a French protectorate over Morocco in 1911; and finally the Balkan War of 1912 in which Bulgaria, Serbia, Greece and Montenegro jointly and successfully attacked the Turks – in these events Muslim India saw the gradual destruction of the Islamic world by a conspiracy of the Christian powers, headed by Britain. The status of the Sultan of Turkey as Caliph took on a new meaning. The Muslim fears were shared by some Britons. Wilfrid Scawen

Blunt accused Britain of hostility towards Islam and urged the Indian Muslims to join hands with the Hindu Congress and resist the Christian onslaught on the independent Muslim states.[4] The suspicion among the Indian Muslims that Britain was steadily becoming anti-Muslim in her policies was increased by the revocation of the partition of Bengal in 1911 and by the rejection in July 1912 by Lord Crewe, the Secretary of State for India, of a scheme for the foundation of a Muslim university. This growing suspicion was to be whipped up to a frenzy in August 1913 over the Kanpur mosque case (when, as a part of a road-widening scheme, the Kanpur municipality proposed to remove a washing-place attached to the mosque), resulting in riots and the loss of twenty-three lives.

Anti-British feeling was, in 1912, growing among a small group of young middle-class Muslims (some of whom had received their education in Britain) and among the orthodox ulama – the Muslim scholars in the Islamic religious sciences.[5] The 'radical Muslims' stood in the same relation to the loyal Muslim League as the extremists had occupied in relation to the moderate Congress. They were opposed to the upper-class leadership of the League and its dependence upon the British. Like the Hindu extremists the radical Muslims based their politics on religion, rejected the secular concept of a nation based on the unity of language or country, and acknowledged a common historical tradition as the sole determining factor of a nation.[6] A common historical tradition, however, meant different things to the Hindus and Muslims of India. In the case of the Hindus, as their historical tradition had been confined to the territorial boundaries of India (where they were in the majority), their nationalism, even of the communal kind, was essentially territorial. Thus Hindu nationalists, of all denominations, could conveniently affirm their loyalty first to the country and then to their community or caste. Among them the emphasis on the territorial aspect of nationalism was strong enough to enable them to widen the scope of their historical tradition and to include within its fold the non-Hindu traditions and heroes of India. In the case of the Muslims, on the other hand, their historical tradition had communal, rather than territorial, roots. Forming a minority community in a country which once they had ruled, and lagging far behind the Hindus in terms of economic, educational and political advancement, the Indian Muslims took comfort in asserting their membership of a large Islamic community. In consequence they felt obliged to profess their foremost loyalty not to India where they lived, but to Turkey and other independent Muslim states of the Middle East.

This was the state of Indian politics in the autumn of 1912. Jawaharlal entered Congress politics as a matter of course. Congress represented the bourgeois, mendicant politics of his own upper middle class, of which he was a vehement critic from inside.[7] He thus began his part-time political apprenticeship with little enthusiasm. He was, however, no ordinary apprentice. The eminence of his father and the high position Motilal had acquired in the political hierarchy of the country enabled Jawaharlal to come into close contact with the leaders of the land. From this privileged position Jawaharlal could observe the strength and weakness of the leaders as well as the formulation or abandonment of a policy, a strategy or an alliance. He could look at the actors in the dressing-room, so to speak, before watching their performance on stage. None of the leaders, whether militant or moderate, not even his father, made an overpowering impression on him. He noticed the lack of purpose in the moderate leadership and the lack of scruples among the militants, both Muslims and Hindus.

More than four years were to pass before Jawaharlal became politically excited and had his enthusiasm aroused by the Home Rule leagues of Tilak and Mrs Annie Besant. In the intervening period his political activities included attending some of the annual sessions of Congress and playing occasionally the role of an uncertain moderate agitator in his home town of Allahabad. By coincidence his first public work consisted of raising funds (through the United Provinces South Africa Relief Fund of which he became secretary in 1913) for the passive-resistance campaign in South Africa organised and led by his future mentor Gandhi, whom he was to meet for the first time in 1916. Still diffident about public speaking, he was obliged to deliver his first speech, on 20 June 1916, to a small audience, consisting of the prominent citizens of Allahabad, assembled to protest against the Indian Press Act of 1910. It was an outburst of emotion on the part of a young nationalist rather than a coherent speech. Calling the Act 'mischievous' and 'poisonous' Jawaharlal warned that there was no hope 'in this world for those Indians who thought otherwise'.[8] The speech was duly reported in the nationalist daily, the *Leader*, and Jawaharlal won his first publicity. Motilal, who was then holidaying in Kashmir, wrote to Jawaharlal to say that he liked his speech, 'though not very informative it has the rare merit of being free from commonplaces'.[9]

For the first four years after his return to India, Jawaharlal led an aimless life. He began his professional career in 1912 as a junior barrister under his father's supervision. But his heart was not in it. His sensitive nature dreaded being engulfed in what seemed to him the dullness and futility of the legal profession. For him the atmosphere of the High Court and Bar Library lacked intellectual stimulus. A sense of the 'utter insipidity of life' began to grow upon him.[10] Motilal was aware of his son's want of interest in the Law. Frequently he asked Jawaharlal to concentrate and work hard, hoping that through sheer hard work his son might become more involved.[11] Jawaharlal worked on his father's briefs, sometimes hard enough to please his father, but without ever acquiring a vocational interest.

His capacity for hard work in these years might have been slightly affected by his constant concern for his health and appearance. Apart from his steadily growing baldness, which he tried in vain to stop by applying various ointments, he developed acute stomach trouble in 1913 and took a course of homeopathic treatment during which he had to regulate his diet and abstain from eating meat. He was not completely cured. In 1915 his stomach ailment grew into chronic dyspepsia, and sugar was found in his urine.[12] This disorder persisted; in later years he had an operation for piles. Persistent stomach disorders added a new element to his temperament – irritability.

Involved neither in his profession nor in the politics of India, Jawaharlal found comfort in his private life. He often started the day by riding, sometimes with his young sister Nan. From ten in the morning till four in the afternoon, he was in the High Court with his father. He spent the evenings playing tennis, dining and playing bridge with his Indian and

British friends.[13] And then there was Kamala, to whom he was married in Delhi on 8 February 1916.

Nearly a year before her marriage Kamala had moved from Delhi to Allahabad, where she lived in the home of a relative. This arrangement had been made to assist her adjustment to the life-style of the Nehru family. Kamala's background was utterly different from that of the Nehrus. Her parents were orthodox in their outlook and traditional in their way of life. Her father, Jawaharmal Kaul, a Kashmiri Brahmin, and a prosperous businessman of Delhi, was not as well placed socially as the Nehrus. Kamala had had almost no education when Motilal chose her as his future daughter-in-law. Her grooming by Nan's English governess Miss Hooper made very little difference. She was shy, desperately unsure of herself, and faced the problem of being a suitable companion not only for her future husband but also for his two sisters, especially Nan, with little confidence. Born on 18 August 1900, Nan (the future Mrs Vijayalakshmi Pandit) was only one year younger than Kamala. Europeanised, vivacious and highly intelligent, Nan was also exceedingly beautiful. She was the darling of the family, and Jawaharlal's favourite sister. She was to become his closest confidante. He communicated with her more freely than he did with any other member of his family, including his wife and daughter. Since she had never been put into a school and given a formal education and discipline, Nan had developed an open personality with few restraints on her feelings and mode of expression. Nan's personality was to clash with that of Kamala. Kamala, with her undistinguished appearance and simple demeanour, felt still more conscious of her inadequacies in Nan's presence. As they were very much of an age, their relationship began with a tinge of competitiveness. In this unacknowledged confrontation Nan was dominant. Kamala's pride, together with her lack of confidence, continually held her back from attempting to learn or change. For fear of losing face in case of failure, she nervously resisted making the effort. When once, soon after her marriage, Motilal, who had offered to tutor her privately, asked her to write an essay, she developed a headache which Motilal rightly diagnosed as 'a result of pure nervousness at her inability to produce anything likely to be approved'.[14] 'The first thing to strengthen her', Motilal counselled Jawaharlal, 'and make her feel so entirely at home with us is to get rid of all nervousness.'[15] Kamala did not get rid of her nervousness. She chose to withdraw within her secret self and languish in the aura of helplessness and jealousy. Later she was to grow yet more conscious of her inadequacies, and of her inability to keep pace with her husband.

Easy-going on the surface but restless underneath, Jawaharlal was waiting for something exciting to happen, something which could absorb him fully and tap all his latent energies. He did not possess Gandhi's faith, or his energy to create by himself a situation suited to his genius. He had to be led before he could lead. It was a chance combination of factors that produced a political situation which stirred Jawaharlal into action. The outbreak of world war in 1914; the release of Tilak and the conclusion of Gandhi's South African satyagraha* in the same year; the Easter uprising of the Irish nationalists and the foundation of the Home Rule leagues in 1916: these were the factors which created in India an aggressive new political impulse and made available to the country a man who eventually gave to this impulse an identity, a purpose and a strategy.

The Muslim militants who had been riding high on the wave of anti-British feeling readily gave their loyalty to Turkey when she joined the war against Britain in November 1914. The problem they faced was how to save the Islamic world and to destroy or damage the British Raj. They had no strong organisation – the Muslim League was still under the control of the loyalists. But even with an organisation what could they do to achieve their vague objective, but pass resolutions and make angry speeches? They opted for terrorism and conspiracy, which turned out to be even less effective. The king of the neighbouring Muslim state of Afghanistan was urged by letter either to attack India directly or to persuade Germany to attack her. Afghanistan did not attack until too late, in the first week of May 1919, and then mainly to strengthen the position of her new king by rallying round him the disaffected nobles and army. Equally unsuccessful were the

*For a description of satyagraha, see below, pp. 68–9.

isolated attempts made to raise a rebellion in India. In February 1915 the Government suppressed a rebellion (ill-organised by the Ghadr Party which had been founded in 1913 in San Francisco largely by the Sikh emigrants to North America) in the Punjab even before it began. Some militant Muslim leaders – Muhammad Ali, Shaukat Ali and A. K. Azad – were interned in May 1915. Muslim militancy was stranded.

The Muslim League came to the rescue. At this point the Muslim League, under the leadership of Muhammad Ali Jinnah – a constitutional nationalist with no affection for pan-Islamism – modified its former loyalist code of conduct, opened its doors to the militants and linked with Congress in the preparation of a joint constitutional scheme for India. The liberals in both the Muslim League and Congress were uniting to reap jointly the fruits of the constitutional reforms which they expected Britain's Liberal Government to introduce during the course of the war or immediately after it ended. Constitutional reforms had been in the air since Lord Hardinge (Viceroy 1910–16) set the tone through his despatch of 25 August 1911, which urged the London government to introduce some measure of reform in the provinces. The Irish Home Rule Act of 1914 (suspended during the course of the war), which conceded self-government to Ireland, excluding most of Ulster, further increased the Indian expectation. The outbreak of the war made the prospect of reforms seem certain to the Indian liberals. If only India could present to the British a united front and a scheme embodying its constitutional demands, the British would be obliged to concede more than they otherwise would. Jinnah, who in the future was to play the role of an Indian Sir Edward Carson, was at this point all for Indian unity. It was at his insistence and owing to his endeavour that the League–Congress *rapport* began in the last week of December 1915, when both the parties held their annual sessions in Bombay at the same time. The union yielded a constitutional scheme, which was informally thrashed out in Anand Bhawan most probably in October 1916,[16] and formally adopted by both parties, as the Congress–League scheme, at their annual sessions held in Lucknow in December of the same year. The Congress–League scheme was modelled on Gokhale's constitutional proposals, which he had submitted a few days before his death in February 1915 to the Governor of Bombay. The scheme asked the British to declare their intention of conferring self-government on India at an early date, and in the meantime to grant a greater share to Indians in the provincial and central governments.

The British thinking on the Indian problem, as represented by the administration of Lord Chelmsford (Viceroy 1916–21), was proceeding on identical lines, almost uninfluenced by the Indian demand, for it was at his first executive-council meeting in April that Chelmsford had asked: what is the ultimate goal of British rule in India? By June 1916 an answer was found: to endow India in successive stages with the largest measure of self-government compatible with the maintenance of the supreme authority of British rule. The Chelmsford scheme substantially embodied current British thinking on India. It implied that India was not fit then for full self-government, and that her rate of progress must depend upon the improvement and wide diffusion of education, the softening of racial and religious differences, and the acquisition of political experience. The British planners did not visualise India becoming a self-governing dominion during their lifetime or that of their successors. The Indian expectation was not much different. Nobody in India, not even Tilak, then believed that the next instalment of reforms would give India full self-government. The difference between the two, the Indian liberals and the British, lay in the questions when and why. It was these questions which were to cause duplicity, procrastination, insincerity and confusion among the British, and disillusion, anger, restlessness, division and belligerency among the Indians. The Indian leaders were to be disappointed by the Government of India Act of 1919 – the result of a series of events set in motion by Chelmsford's scheme of 1916 – but not so much with what it offered as with how and why it was offered.

It was not, however, this sudden animation of liberal politics in India which aroused Jawaharlal's enthusiasm. In fact he was repelled by liberal talk and sycophancy, based on a tacit acceptance of India's inability to stand on her own. He noticed with distaste the caution and fear of the liberals as manifested at the annual session of Congress held in Bombay in the last week of December 1915. He did not take much notice of the

Congress–League scheme even though it was conceived in his own house. The principles and style of liberal politics did not suit his temperament. He felt that both 'individual and national honour demanded a more aggressive and fighting attitude to foreign rule'.[17] He had looked in vain to liberal leaders, to S. N. Sastri, M. M. Malaviya, T. B. Sapru, and to his own father, to give a 'brave lead to the country'.[18] But he was not sure of the components of a brave leadership. He was not clear as to what action it should take. He only knew that it had to be aggressive and fearless. Paradoxically it was Mrs Annie Besant of Anglo-Irish parentage who first fitted his description of a brave leader, though only for a short while. Jawaharlal, together with a host of young Indian nationalists, was drawn towards Mrs Besant and her Home Rule movement for negative reasons.[19] These young men regarded the liberals with derision; the liberal leaders distrusted Mrs Besant. Thus, there existed between the young nationalists and Mrs Besant a bond of sympathy, though not of understanding. Mrs Besant was by no means an extremist. Her politics was essentially liberal. She had no vision of an independent India outside the British Empire. She manifested more caution and moderation towards the governors of the Raj than even Malaviya when she stopped Gandhi in the middle of the speech he was delivering on 4 February 1916, at the opening of the Banaras Hindu University.[20] She feared that Gandhi – who was then an unknown quantity, often considered an anarchist – might offend the high dignitaries who had assembled on that occasion. In subsequent years her clashes with Gandhi were to grow in number, and she turned into a great opponent of the non-co-operation movement. The fame and glory that were bestowed upon her in June 1917 as a national heroine faded in less than three years.

Mrs Besant had been mainly occupied with her theosophical activities since her arrival in India in the late 1890s. At the outbreak of war in 1914 she suddenly decided to break into politics as a mediator between the liberals and the extremists. The occasion arose when Tilak, after his release from imprisonment, wanted to be taken back into Congress. Mrs Besant offered to negotiate with the liberals on behalf of the extremists. 'In view of the political changes which will follow the war,' she argued with Gokhale, it was advisable 'to close the breach between the extreme wing and the moderates', and to present to the British the face of a united India.[21] Mrs Besant assured her liberal friend that the extremists had abandoned their previous stand and were ready to accept the Congress creed, which was to attain self-government within the Empire through constitutional means. Gokhale was not convinced that Tilak's ideology and methods had changed. Tilak's own statement of his position made in December 1914 showed that he did not believe in the present methods of Congress, which rested on association with government where possible and opposition to it where necessary. In place of these, Tilak wanted to substitute the method of pure and simple opposition to government, using constitutional means – 'in other words a policy of Irish obstruction'.[22] Tilak's entry into Congress, Gokhale feared, might endanger not only Congress but his own leadership. He closed the Congress door against Tilak.

Stimulated by her own ambition to make an impact on Indian politics and inspired by the Irish Home Rule example, Mrs Besant proposed at a conference, held in Bombay soon after the 1915 annual session of Congress, that a Home Rule League be started in India. Her proposal was rejected by the liberal leaders, including Motilal Nehru.[23] The young nationalists, including Jawaharlal Nehru, were very disappointed at this. They were attracted towards the idea of a Home Rule League as an alternative organisation to Congress. To Jawaharlal the term 'home rule' brought back memories of the enthusiasm he had felt in 1907 for the Irish Home Rule movement. For Mrs Besant and Tilak the Home Rule League was mainly a means to capture Congress. Tilak stole a march on Mrs Besant and started his Home Rule League in April 1916. Mrs Besant founded her League in September of the same year. Thus, three months before the Lucknow session of Congress, two Home Rule leagues had come into existence – that of Tilak, confined to Maharashtra, and that of Mrs Besant operating over the rest of India.

Tilak's entry into Congress in 1916 was facilitated partly by the absence of a strong opposition to him (Gokhale and Mehta had died in 1915) but mainly by his Home Rule League, which had provided him with a base in organisational politics. Lucknow thus witnessed not only unity between the two wings of Congress but also between Congress and the Muslim League as symbolised by their joint scheme. It was indeed only a surface unity, for Indian politics was still provincially based and even in the provinces it was divorced from the masses. Then there were the young nationalists, Hindus and Muslims, the future leaders of the country. Their pride, aggression and aspirations did not find satisfaction in the lame proceedings of the political parties or in their joint manifesto – the Congress–League scheme. The extremism of Tilak, who was now sixty, seemed to have waned during the six years of his imprisonment. He was now a staunch supporter of the Congress–League scheme, which did not ask for complete independence.

It was partly to capture the imagination and support of the young nationalists and partly to strengthen her own political position, which was still tenuous, that Mrs Besant plunged into the politics of propaganda. She adopted a dual role. As a British woman she attacked the Raj for its misdeeds, false promises and lack of vision; as an adopted Indian she played the role of a 'tom-tom', waking up the sleepers to the service of their motherland. Her emotion-laden speeches and articles caused stirrings among educated Indians and anxiety among the guardians of the Raj. The Governor of Madras, Lord Pentland, decided to silence her, and she was accordingly interned in June 1917.

Pentland's action turned Mrs Besant into a martyr and India's heroine. Her image changed overnight. For Jawaharlal and the young nationalists she became the symbol of courage, defiance and suffering. Her example – a British-born lady of seventy suffering in the service of Mother India – was at once used by young nationalists to put India's political 'cowards' to shame. Some liberals, including Motilal Nehru and Jinnah, who had opposed Mrs Besant's Home Rule proposal in 1915 were converted to the policies of the Home Rule League.

Perhaps the largest sympathy and support for Mrs Besant was in United Provinces. Jawaharlal put his heart and soul into the movement and became its leading organiser. The Allahabad Home Rule League was founded in June with Motilal as its president and Jawaharlal as its joint secretary.

Branches of the League were started at other places in the province and a plan was thrashed out to turn the Allahabad Home Rule League into a provincial league. At the same time Jawaharlal, together with other prominent citizens of Allahabad, withdrew in protest from the Indian Defence Force, which they had originally decided to join, more with a view to acquiring military training than to defending the Raj. Jawaharlal showed more zest for agitation and attack than for organisation. He took advantage of the occasion to release his pent-up resentment and lambasted both the moderate politicians and the Indian bureaucracy:

> Ours have been the politics of cowards and opium-eaters long enough and it is time we thought and acted like live men and women who place the honour and interests of their country above the frowns and smiles of every Tom, Dick and Harry who has I.C.S. attached to his name.[24]

Politics of 'protests and representations', he exhorted, must be abandoned for the politics of non-co-operation: 'Every one of us who holds an honorary position under the Government should resign it and refuse to have anything to do with the bureaucracy.'[25] This will be the test, Jawaharlal argued, to find out the 'faint hearts or wobblers' for whom there was no need in the Home Rule League; 'the wheat will be all the purer when the chaff is removed'.

In June 1917 boycott and passive resistance had begun to capture the imagination of young Indians. Gandhi's first experiment in India with his satyagraha (or passive resistance) had begun in April 1917 in Champaran, a few hundred miles away from Allahabad. It was successfully concluded in less than three months, on 10 June. In spite of Gandhi's wishes to the contrary, it had been publicised by the nationalist newspapers. Thus, when the United Provinces provincial congress met in Lucknow on 10 August under the presidency of Motilal Nehru, there was talk among the young nationalists who had assembled there of resort to passive resistance. Motilal was not willing to dabble in any wild, unconstitutional methods. He still believed in pressure politics. He exerted his dominance over the conference just enough to keep it moderate and confined to its main purpose of protesting against the internment of Mrs Besant. Motilal's eyes were set on the impending reforms, which were announced on 20 August 1917, by Edwin Montagu, the Secretary of State for India. Tension and excitement subsided, hopes and expectations emerged. To relax the political atmosphere further, Chelmsford released Mrs Besant on 17 September, hoping that the Indian politicians, who disliked her, would be glad to see her disappear into oblivion.

Mrs Besant, however, was to reap the rewards of her martyrdom before being edged out of the political scene. Tilak had proposed that she should be installed as the President of Congress, which was to meet in Calcutta for its 1917 annual session. The old extremists and the young nationalists organised their support for Mrs Besant. Her candidature was opposed by the Bengali moderates headed by S. N. Banerjea, B. N. Basu and A. C. Majumdar. To put labels on the political groupings which existed at that time, however, would be misleading. In terms of objects and methods, there was hardly any difference between S. N. Banerjea, M. A. Jinnah, Mrs Besant, Tilak and Motilal Nehru. The difference perhaps lay in their aptitudes for being defiant and aggressive within the limits of constitutional politics. In this political framework the alliances and alienations between leaders were based more on grounds of personal prejudices, personal advancement, and at times on political expediency than on political conviction. The young Indians, whether theosophists, socialists or pure nationalists, was not yet committed to any theory of revolution. Young India had not yet felt the impact of the world's two revolutionary experiences of 1917 – the Russian Revolution and Gandhi's satyagraha. Thus, all they seemed to have in common was their defiant mood towards the British Raj and their resentment at the mendicant style of Indian politics. An occasional spark on the political horizon brightened their hearts, and they rallied round it hopefully only to be disappointed soon afterwards. They were in search of a new political style which the existing Indian leadership was unable to offer. In the latter part of 1917 they gathered round Mrs Besant and enrolled themselves in her Home Rule League.

Mrs Besant arrived in Allahabad, her power base, on 17 September to receive a grand welcome; her carriage was unhorsed and dragged by young men from the railway station to Anand Bhawan. The struggle for the control of Congress began. The supporters of Mrs Besant wanted to bring Congress under the leadership of herself, Tilak and Motilal. The method used was to flood the ensuing Congress session with the Home Rule Leaguers and like-minded aggressive nationalists. A firm grip over the Congress by the 'extremists', it was hoped, would turn Congress into an effective pressure-organ which would be very useful at a time when negotiations were in progress between the Indian leaders and Montagu for constitutional changes.

Jawaharlal enthusiastically accepted the task of raising in United Provinces a large contingent of delegates, consisting of Home Rule Leaguers and 'other advanced politicians', for the Calcutta session of Congress.[26] At the same time he organised local agitations for the release of Muhammad Ali and Shaukat Ali, who had been interned since 1915. He aligned himself with what he then thought were the progressive forces in the national movement. Nearly 5000 delegates assembled in Calcutta for the Congress session; most of them were 'extremists'. The opposition of old liberals to Mrs Besant was locally weakened by C. R. Das, an ally of Tilak and Motilal. Mrs Besant was elected to the Congress presidency. The old liberal guard, being overpowered by the new force in Calcutta, parted company with Congress. In August 1918 they boycotted the special session of Congress which met in that month to consider critically the Montagu–Chelmsford Report. The liberals held a separate conference of their own in November 1918 gratefully to appreciate and wholeheartedly to support the reform scheme of the Government. In December 1919 they gave their breakaway faction a name – the National Liberal Federation of India.

The liberals' breakaway somewhat impaired the unity of Congress and its image as a national assembly. It also provided the Government with an option. The Chelmsford administration could now lean on the liberals in case the 'extremist' Congress rejected the reforms which were in the pipeline. The new Congress that emerged at the beginning of 1918 tried, through various means, to overcome this handicap. It tried to play down the strength of the liberal faction, focus on the significance of the Congress–League scheme as representing the unity and solidarity of the two communities, and widen its base by including in its ranks the constituents of the lower middle class and masses. The campaign for the support of the masses was in part caused by the Montagu–Chelmsford Report published in July 1918. In evaluating the position of the educated and politically conscious Indians the authors of the Report maintained that their number did not exceed five per cent of the population, and that they did not and could not represent the remaining ninety-five per cent of the non-politically minded population, whose interests and advancement thus remained a primary responsibility of the Government.[27] Through this analysis of the Indian conditions, the authors of the Report created at once a justification not only for a gradual and guided constitutional progress but also for the indefinite continuance of the British Raj in India. The Congress leaders took it as a challenge, and the latter part of the year witnessed a Congress movement for peasant support. The only way Congress could prove to the Government that it had mass support was to enrol peasant delegates for the annual session. Motilal, aided by Jawaharlal, launched the campaign for raising at least 500 peasant delegates from United Provinces for the ensuing Congress session to be held in December in Delhi.[28]

Having given Congress the semblance, if not the substance, of a national assembly, the Congress leaders expressed their disappointment at the Montagu–Chelmsford Report and raised their demands high in asking for almost full autonomy in the provinces and diarchy at the centre – more than the Congress–League scheme of 1916 had asked for. All the same, they did not, at either of the two sessions of Congress held in 1918, reject outright what the Montagu–Chelmsford Report offered. They knew that their liberal rivals would step in if they withdrew from the political arena. Besides, they had no alternative plan of action in case of a stalemate caused by their total rejection. They were essentially constitutionalists; like their liberal rivals they felt at home in a council chamber while negotiating and bargaining but lost in the wilderness of a battlefield. Yet in the autumn of 1918 they were more on the verge of a battlefield than the threshold of a council chamber. Their pride had been hurt by the Montagu–Chelmsford Report, their faith in the constitutionalism of the Raj had been shaken by the Rowlatt Committee Report (published in April

1918), and their young followers, who had looked up to them hopefully so far, were beginning to feel disillusioned and restive. They faced, further crisis of leadership. There was no leader of all-India status to command the loyalties of the provincial barons. Tilak had nearly acquired the image of a national leader but he had left for London in August to fight a private defamation suit against Sir Valentine Chirol. Tilak's popularity rested on his mass-style politics. But he was an exception. Since Indian nationalism had been the affair of a narrow intelligentsia, insulated from the masses, the leadership had been accordingly oligarchic. Thus, at the end of 1918, Indian nationalism in its confrontation with the British Raj faced crises of unity, action and leadership. It was on the crest of these crises that Gandhi emerged as a leader.

Jawaharlal's capitulation to Gandhi was as inevitable as the latter's rise to power in 1919. Gandhi's power and leadership showed qualities which Jawaharlal had seen to be utterly lacking among the Indian leaders, including his father. In fact he himself was wanting in some of the qualities which he admired in Gandhi. Both Jawaharlal and Motilal were fascinated by Gandhi's strength and faith, his courage, his utter sincerity and lack of vindictiveness, his sheer energy, and the apparent harmony between his thought and conduct.[29] Yet it was not his qualities but their effect, not the ingredients but the total radiant image of his personality, which dazzled the beholders and compelled admiration. The messianic image of his personality instantly assured his followers that he had tremendous inner reserves of power and would not be daunted by the mighty British Raj. Gandhi's image fitted well into the Indian tradition. It was in harmony with the popular Indian belief in supermen and saints, in the paramount virtue of spiritual power, and in the emergence of a saviour from time to time 'whenever' (according to the Gita) 'there is decline of righteousness, and unrighteousness is in the ascendant'. It was not, however, Gandhi's mahatmaship but his theory of action which drew Jawaharlal towards him. When Gandhi launched his satyagraha for the first time on a national level in March–April 1919, against the Rowlatt Act, Jawaharlal was on fire with enthusiasm and wanted to join the movement immediately. It seemed to Jawaharlal that Gandhi offered at last 'a way out of the tangle, a method of action which was straight and open and possibly effective'.[30] It was the open, defiant face of the satyagraha, not its spiritual body, that gripped Jawaharlal's fancy. In fact he did not then understand its spiritual and moral implications; in later years, when he did, he remained uncommitted to them. Though Jawaharlal was inwardly converted to Gandhi's satyagraha, he was dissuaded from plunging into it by his father. Motilal was sceptical then about the effectiveness of satyagraha, critical of its unconstitutional character, and apprehensive of the sufferings it might inflict on his only son and, in effect, upon the whole of the Nehru family. Motilal's ruling passion was his love for Jawaharlal; he did not then anticipate that his opposition to Jawaharlal's participation in the movement would in any way diminish his son's respect for him. Later when he suspected that this might happen he himself plunged, in his own way, into Gandhi's movement, leading the way for his son. This is not to say that Motilal was not influenced by other factors in changing his political style; the Amritsar tragedy of April 1919, for example, shook his whole legal and constitutional assumptions. But his main incentive came from his son. When he joined Gandhi it was not as a convert, but as the father of a convert.

The emergence of Gandhi as a leader in 1919 was unavoidable. Had there been no Rowlatt Act and no Khilafat cause, Gandhi would, in all probability, have found another cause suitable for the implementation of his satyagraha, and thereby made a dominant impact on the political horizon of India. He had already, between 1917 and 1918, successfully launched satyagraha in different situations and at three different places – at Champaran (April–June 1917), at Ahmedabad (February–March 1918) and in Kaira (March–June 1918). The satyagraha had been launched in Champaran (Bihar) in support of cultivators' grievances against the indigo-planters, at Ahmedabad (Gujarat) in support of a labour strike against the mill-owners and in Kaira district of Gujarat for the remission of land revenue. In those years Gandhi had also toyed with the idea of starting satyagraha to stop indentured labour emigration from India and to secure the release of Mrs Besant from internment. Since satyagraha implied the dictatorship of one man, each satyagraha had given Gandhi fame and confidence.

At the beginning of 1919 his credit was very high, and his determination for further experiments equally strong. He believed that the political, economic, social and moral life of India was at its lowest ebb and that an over-all regeneration of India could be achieved only through satyagrahas and not through constitutional reforms. In fact he was indifferent towards the emphasis given to the impending reforms by the Indian leaders. Gandhi believed that the real reform which India needed was not so much in the running of the government as in people's orientation towards swadeshi.[31] Swadeshi, meaning 'of one's own country', implied that people gave preference to everything Indian – to goods produced in India (particularly the hand-spun cloth, called khadi), to the Indian languages and to other cultural, educational and social institutions indigenous to India. He believed that the use of swadeshi would not only restore to India its dignity and self-sufficiency but would also keep India's millions of artisans and peasants self-employed, fed and clothed.

Launching of further satyagrahas in 1919 was also necessary for the advancement of Gandhi's leadership. In the previous two years Gandhi had launched his satyagrahas on his own, outside Congress and institutional politics. This was so mainly because he had no hold on Congress. He was not then thought of as a candidate for leadership.[32] But Gandhi had to be the leader, partly because he disapproved of the existing standard of Indian leadership, which seemed to him divorced from truth and morality, but mainly because his satyagraha technique could not be worked unless he was at the helm. If India accepted the weapon of satyagraha she had to accept Gandhi as its chief. Hence, proving the effectiveness of satyagraha had to be the first phase in Gandhi's strategy; capturing political organisations came only after that. Three successive local satyagrahas had by December 1918 proved the effectiveness of the technique. India accepted satyagraha in 1919, and Gandhi emerged as the leader at the Amritsar Congress held in December of the same year. By December 1920, Gandhi was in full control of India's political organisations, both of Hindus and Muslims.

In this initial phase of his political career in India, Gandhi did not occupy a subordinate position in the leadership hierarchy. This was so because of the unique ideology with which he had returned to India in January 1915, after having lived in South Africa for nearly twenty-two years (1893–1914). It was so also because there was no established hierarchy in India after the death of Gokhale in 1915 until the emergence of Gandhi himself as the leader in 1919. But it may also have been because of Gandhi's unique political background. Gandhi had begun his political career in South Africa as an apprentice leader. He had no leader to contend with when he decided, in 1894, to arouse political consciousness among the Indians in South Africa and lead them. The Indian community, consisting of merchants and indentured labour, contained no political rivals. Twenty-two years of unrivalled leadership might have conditioned him against occupying a subordinate position. He began his life in India as a leader and remained one until his assassination in January 1948. This gave him enormous self-confidence, which in turn supported his humility and magnanimity. Though he did not in fact owe his career to anyone, he expressed his gratitude to Gokhale and acknowledged him as his political mentor. It was not so much Gokhale's political wisdom or patronage as his integrity, humility, non-violent attitude, and belief in the virtues of endurance and suffering that inspired Gandhi to acknowledge him as his master. And indeed Gokhale was the only one among the Indian leaders who took an active interest in Gandhi's South African satyagrahas. Gokhale served as a link between Gandhi and India; his visit to South Africa in 1912 gave Gandhi's struggle great moral support, and also good publicity in India. But this is not to say that Gokhale had a hand in the making of Gandhi. Gandhi was the sole creator of satyagraha – its ideology and method. He was also the sole builder of the organisational base for his satyagraha. He combined in himself the role of theorist, strategist and organiser. He had, during his South African phase, grown into a uniquely self-contained operator.

Gandhi's personal style of leadership emerged from his intuitively conceived spiritual philosophy of satyagraha. The uniqueness of his satyagraha lay in the emphasis it put on inner thought and motivation. The satyagrahi, while vindicating truth (through non-co-operation and civil disobedience) by the infliction of suffering not on the opponent but on himself, must also have love and sympathy for the opponent and must not suffer from hatred, anger and remorse. The satyagrahi's persistent love for the opponent while suffering at his hands, according to Gandhi, could alone fulfil the main object of his satyagraha, which was not only to attain recognition of the justice of its cause but also morally to uplift the opponent. Thus, it was not only self-suffering but also self-control which were required of a true satyagrahi. The failure of a satyagraha, consequently, implied that insufficient self-control was exercised by the satyagrahis. It was this aspect of the satyagraha which distinguished it from both western passive resistance and the Indian dharna.[33] Further, it separated Gandhi from his co-workers and followers and turned him into a mahatma, for only Gandhi could profess to exercise the degree of self-control required from a true satyagrahi. The dictatorship of the Mahatma thus virtually emerged from a ready acceptance by his followers of their relative inadequacies and failings.

Gandhi, however, did not forge his satyagraha with political ends in view. His entry into politics was accidental. He began his quest for truth first in the spiritual world with the sole purpose of overcoming his personal fears and failings. Through his experiments in self-suffering and self-control, and through his faith in God (or Truth), he acquired spiritual power and overcame his fears. With this reserve of power he began his work in the political field, believing that what was good for him was good for all and that the technique which he had used for his personal redemption could also be effectively applied to serve political ends.[34] The success of satyagraha in redressing specific local grievances had strengthened Gandhi's faith in its efficacy, and at the beginning of 1919 he was eager to launch it at a national level. An all-India satyagraha, Gandhi might have reckoned, would bring him out of the political isolation into which he had deliberately retreated in the latter part of 1918. His campaign to recruit Indians for the Army to defend the Empire 'in its life and death struggle' had made him unpopular. The Congress leaders and pan-Islamists did not support his recruiting campaign. No leader was convinced by his argument that India's unconditional support for Britain during the war would win British gratitude and that Britain at the end of the war would willingly concede Indian demands, as embodied in the Congress–League scheme of 1916.[35] The war ended in November. The Congress leaders set their sights on the impending reforms, while the pan-Islamists, already distressed at the virtual disappearance of the Ottoman Empire, looked with grave apprehension to the peace conferences where the fate of Turkey was to be decided. Gandhi was left in isolation.

The Rowlatt Act of March 1919 was both the occasion and the cause of Gandhi's satyagraha. Indeed, Muslim sensitivity, high food-prices, and epidemics had made Indian conditions a little more explosive. But the politically conscious and constitutionally minded Indians, liberals and extremists alike, were hopefully looking forward to the reforms promised by the Montagu–Chelmsford Report. To these men the Rowlatt Act seemed like an explosion, damaging their self-respect and shaking their faith in the fairness of the Indian bureaucracy. The Act gave to political India a psychological shock; the physical terror it held forth could affect only very few. It was the principle underlying the Act and the bureaucratic thinking that had gone into its making that aggrieved political India. Its timing aroused suspicions regarding the genuineness of British intentions. For the Chelmsford administration, however, it was a necessary measure and quite in keeping with the bureaucratic tradition. The Act invested the Government of India with discretionary power to short-circuit the processes of law in dealing with terrorists. The Government believed that the danger of terrorism existed in India and that the ordinary law had failed to cope with it. It further believed that the Defence of India Act, being a war-time measure, could not be prolonged. Likewise the Regulation of 1818, being too repressive a measure, could not be revived. It was also thought undesirable to resort to an ordinance. Thus, in the absence of any special provision to deal with the situation the Government went to the Legislature openly and honestly for a new Act.[36]

Leaders of almost all political groups in India attacked the Rowlatt legislation;[37] and Gandhi, having condemned it as the 'symptoms of the deep-seated disease', took this opportunity to prove the potency of his satyagraha and, in effect, India's 'capacity for resistance to arbitrary or tyrannical rule'.[38] Gandhi's call to satyagraha on 6 April 1919, however, had to be suspended on 18 April. It grew violent soon after it was launched. Violence aroused in Gandhi fear and repentance. While admitting his mistake in having 'called upon the people to launch upon civil disobedience before they had thus qualified themselves for it', he asserted that the satyagraha was not the direct cause of violence in Ahmedabad and that the Punjab violence was unconnected with his movement.[39] If Gandhi's own explanations are accepted it would seem that he showed insufficient insight in starting it and a good deal of courage in stopping it. But, then, he showed the same lack of insight and abundance of courage in starting and suspending his next national satyagraha – the non-co-operation movement. Was Gandhi so naïve as to think that the people would purge themselves of their latent violence in less than a year and be prepared for his next satyagraha? Or did he think that non-co-operation as compared with civil disobedience would be less likely to arouse violence? Answers to such questions have to be no. Perhaps a plausible explanation may be found in the implicit achievements rather than the seeming failures of his satyagrahas. The Rowlatt satyagraha advanced Gandhi's leadership. It was also the first attempt to initiate mass mobilisation. In these terms it provided an incentive for a further satyagraha. In less than six months, after the suspension of the Rowlatt satyagraha, Gandhi fixed his eyes on a bigger issue – the Khilafat question – and appealed to the Hindus to unite with Muslims in fasting and hartal (a strike), and to observe 17 October 1919 as a Khilafat Day. On 24 November, while presiding over the All-India Khilafat Conference held in Delhi, Gandhi envisaged the idea of starting a non-co-operation movement in support of the Khilafat demands.[40] But in the second half of 1919 the Muslim leaders were divided among themselves on the Khilafat cause. The Hindus were largely uninterested in the fate of Turkey. Gandhi had to wait till the beginning of 1920 when the Khilafat issue, being joined with the Punjab wrongs, turned into a big enough issue to merit his next national satyagraha.

While Jawaharlal watched Gandhi's rise to power with enthusiasm and a growing feeling of commitment, Motilal viewed it with some alarm. At the beginning of 1919 Motilal occupied a middle position, between his old liberal friends on the one hand and Gandhi on the other. He had moved away from the liberals, relinquished his interests in the liberal newspaper, the *Leader*, and launched his own English daily, the *Independent.* His main difference with the liberal group lay in his emphasis on a rapid constitutional advance leading to full responsible government for India within fifteen years. He no longer believed in the politics of mendicancy, and its utter dependence on British goodwill. For example, in February 1919 he was against sending an Indian deputation to Britain. Self-reliance had become the hallmark of his political thinking. In his concept of Indian nationalism there was no place for pan-Islamism or pan-Hinduism. He was not concerned with the question of the Khilafat but he was agitated over the Rowlatt Act.[41] Yet Motilal was not in favour of the satyagraha.[42] He regarded the Rowlatt satyagraha as a misadventure. He looked on Gandhi's rising popularity, in spite of the failure of his Rowlatt satyagraha, with a degree of helplessness and distrust. He regarded Gandhi as a challenge not only to his own leadership but also to institutional politics – to Congress and the Muslim League – which was being steadily overshadowed by the Mahatma. Possessed of a rational mind of his own and being eight years older than Gandhi, he resisted coming under the spell of the Mahatma. The only way, he thought, in which he could oppose Gandhi was to strengthen the institutional politics and his own position in it. He was, for example, against Gandhi independently calling the people to support the Khilafat agitation by boycotting the peace celebrations which were being organised by the Government. 'In my opinion,' Motilal counselled his son, 'this is not a matter for independent idiosyncrasies and whatever action is taken it must be on behalf of the Indian National Congress and the Muslim League jointly.'[43] He was at the same time cautious – aware that he might find himself swimming against the tide. If Gandhi at any stage appeared to have the whole of public opinion behind him, Motilal might capitulate, but until this happened he was determined to preserve his own identity and those of Congress and the Muslim League. But more important to him was Jawaharlal's opinion of his father; however, since the short-lived Rowlatt satyagraha of April, no occasion had arisen for open conflict between father and son. In the latter half of

1919 Motilal and Jawaharlal were together occupied with their public work for the Punjab.

The Jallianwala Bagh tragedy of 13 April 1919 shook Motilal and aroused his utter distrust of the Indian bureaucracy.* But he did not abandon his constitutional approach to the Indian problem. In fact the Punjab tragedy made him realise the need for having more powers given to the Indians in the impending constitutional reforms as safeguards against a recurrence of such an event.[44] From June till November 1919, Motilal, aided by Jawaharlal, was fully occupied in defending the victims of the Punjab martial law, and also in working on the Congress sub-committee which was appointed in June to enquire into the tragedy.[45] The fact that Motilal charged no fees for defending the various accused gladdened Jawaharlal. Motilal's legal and political work for the Punjab raised his political stature from a provincial to a national leader. In November 1919 he was elected to the presidency of Congress. By the beginning of December, Motilal had formed his own definite views on the proposed constitutional reforms. Though he was not fully satisfied with them, he was all for accepting them: 'we should utilise the new Act as much as possible and try to get it improved at the earliest possible opportunity'.[46]

Acceptance of the reforms by Congress, Motilal hoped, would bring the liberal faction back into the organisation. Accordingly he invited the liberals to attend the Congress session in Amritsar. Congress, however, had become too unpredictable and aggressive for the liberals. They did not come back to it; instead they held their own separate conference in Calcutta at the same time that Congress met in Amritsar under Motilal's presidency. The breach between Motilal and the liberals was now sealed. This gratified Jawaharlal immensely. Jawaharlal calculated that his father, now cut off from his liberal moorings, would be able to pursue a more aggressive kind of nationalism.

In view of what followed soon afterwards, the Amritsar Congress session (held in the last week of December 1919)

*The killing of about 500 of the 20,000 unarmed Indians who had unlawfully assembled for a protest meeting on a piece of wasteland in Amritsar (Punjab) called the Jallianwala Bagh. At the command of General Dyer, ninety soldiers fired 1650 rounds of ammunition continually for ten minutes.

was a non-event. The decisions made in Amritsar were abandoned soon afterwards in the wake of Gandhi's non-co-operation movement of 1920. And yet Gandhi's movement was apparently unrelated to the Amritsar Congress. The real question facing the leaders at the Amritsar Congress (attended by 7031 delegates, 1095 peasant delegates and thousands of spectators) was not whether to accept the new reforms as embodied in the Government of India Act of 23 December 1919, but how to accept them. Opinion was divided on the manner of acceptance. The Act seemed inadequate in relation to the Indian demands which, over the last two years, had been raised high, more in a bargaining than a fighting spirit. Gandhi had disapproved of this style of politics as immoral and often counselled the politicians in private first to lay out their minimum demands and then if necessary fight for them with their lives. He was there in Amritsar watching the constitutionally minded politicians grappling with the dilemma into which they had led themselves. The general consensus among the leaders was to accept the Act but only after condemning, in the strongest possible terms, its inadequacies, so as to ensure that it was improved in the near future. Behind this issue lay a general resentment (assuaged to some extent by the well-timed royal proclamation) against the Indian bureaucracy for its woodenness and arrogance as manifested in the manner in which it had forced through the Rowlatt Act and brought about the Amritsar tragedy. Hence, in expressing their resentments and frustrations some, like C. R. Das, were emotionally driven to the point of rejecting the Act. Gandhi, aloof and reluctant to intervene, was manœuvred by Motilal and Malaviya into the arena. With his support the resolution, accepting the Act, was passed.[47] Of the twenty-one leaders (including the President and excluding the Punjabi leaders) who sat on the elevated platform on the opening day of the Congress session, Gandhi was the only one who was uninterested in the Act and the reforms. He then thought that the Indian problems were not going to be solved by constitutional reforms. The Act as such, he thought, contained enough for politicians to chew on. Mass uplift and mass mobilisation through satyagraha were on his mind. He believed that India's future lay in the politics of suffering, not in that of the council chamber. His own role as a leader lay outside institutional politics. Seen in this light Gandhi's satyagraha of 1920 was not really a contravention of the stand he took at Amritsar. Equally unenthusiastic about the Act were Gandhi's young converts; Rajagopalachariar, Rajendra Prasad and Jawaharlal Nehru attended the session as members of the All-India Congress Committee. Their elders had agreed to work out the Act. What future, then, lay ahead for the satyagrahis?

At the beginning of 1919 Jawaharlal inwardly bowed to Gandhi's truth and satyagraha, and basked in their rays throughout the year. But like the other followers of Gandhi he too had no clear understanding of his mentor's thought. He was in fact the youngest (thirty in 1919) and the only one among the four notable disciples whom Gandhi had acquired since 1917 who had not yet worked with the master as a satyagrahi. Rajendra Prasad had gone through his initiation in Champaran at the age of thirty-three, Vallabhbhai Patel in Kaira and Ahmedabad when he was forty-three, and C. Rajagopalachariar at forty in the course of the Rowlatt satyagraha. These three disciples of Gandhi were in future to become Jawaharlal's colleagues. They were also to constitute the core of the right-wing opposition to Jawaharlal's leadership. Their early initiation, however, did not give them any better insight into Gandhi's thought or any advantage over Jawaharlal. Thus, Jawaharlal's political reflections at this time were inconsistent with Gandhian thought.[48] They exhibited the rudiments of the basic differences that later developed between him and Gandhi. His political thinking seemed to revolve round his two strong sentiments – his aversion for the British Empire, and his attachment to individualism and democracy. Democracy in imperial Britain was choked by the combined forces of capital, militarism, an overgrown bureaucracy and a capitalist press. Hence the problem 'before us is to free democracy from their malign influences'. His appreciation of the Russian Revolution was generated more by his intense dislike for capitalist imperialism than by his positive understanding of the merits of bolshevism. But his love for individual liberty counselled him against orthodox socialism: 'Life under socialism would be a joyless and soulless thing, regulated to the minutest detail by rules and orders framed by the all powerful official.'[49] Yet his individualism did not pull him towards the farthest extreme – pure anarchism: 'Pure Anarchism postulates a community of saints and few of us, if any, with the exception of Mr Gandhi, have any claims to sainthood.'[50]

India, however, was not presently concerned with these problems. She had first to pass through the nationalist phase and then, when the time came, 'perhaps some form of communism will be found to suit the genius of the people better than majority rule'.[51] Thus, in his political ponderings there was no emphasis given to non-violence or to the non-industrial, self-sufficient village economy. Yet Jawaharlal was not then aware of how different his thinking was from that of his master. At the beginning of 1920, while giving some good advice to a friend on the eve of his marriage, Jawaharlal wrote:

> I shall only express the fervent hope that you and your partner in life will ever follow the path of truth whatever may be the consequences. Be a Satyagrahi in body, in mind, and in soul and your people and your country will glory in you.[52]

By the autumn of 1919 Jawaharlal had committed himself to Gandhi's truth and satyagraha, but he was unaware of their spiritual and moral connotations.

CHAPTER FOUR

The Plunge into the Politics of Suffering, 1920-1

> No country has ever risen without being purified through the fire of suffering. The mother suffers so that her child may live. The condition of wheat-growing is that the seed grain should perish. Life comes out of death. Will India rise out of her slavery without fulfilling this eternal law of purification through suffering?
>
> *Gandhi, June 1920*

> Bolshevism and Fascism are the ways of the West today. They are really alike and represent different phases of insensate violence and intolerance. The choice for us is between Lenin and Mussolini on the one side and Gandhi on the other. Can there be any doubt as to who represents the soul of India today?
>
> *Jawaharlal Nehru, October 1923*

THE years 1920 and 1921 were perhaps the happiest of Jawaharlal's life. He was, in those years, fully committed, for the first and the last time. Action on his part during this period was a wholehearted expression of his self; in later years it was often an attempt to run away from himself.[1] Action, with or without attachment, and aggression without vengefulness were the hallmarks of his character. Later in his life, while consoling his sister on the death of her husband, he wrote: 'I have myself found that work, hard continuous work, is the best occupation and antidote for a disturbed mind. It brings a certain calmness of spirit and makes one forget oneself in impersonal activity.'[2]

After 1920 his life became substantially public and his activities more impersonal. He began to become more attached to ideas than to persons. Neither his profession nor his domestic affairs could fill his life. He had utterly lost his interest in legal work. There was joy, tenderness and loyalty in his family life but these were often overshadowed by conflicts and tensions from which he longed to escape. His wife Kamala had been ailing since the birth of her first child Indira Nehru in November 1917. Her feelings of inadequacy were further aggravated by self-reproach that she had failed to give birth to a son. Her failing health gave her no strong hope for the future. In 1920 she was suffering from that chronic illness which in 1925 was diagnosed as tuberculosis. In 1924 she gave birth, prematurely, to a son who died two days later. Kamala's silent suffering and her growing sense of insecurity caused tension and loneliness in Jawaharlal's family life. He sought solace and compensation in the world of ideas and action:

> We are attached to people, to some more than others. We are also attached to ideas and all that they represent and it is ultimately these ideas that make us function and largely fill our lives. If our attachment is to persons alone, there is nothing or very little left when they leave us.[3]

While in prison in 1922, he derived comfort and consolation in quoting from Byron's *Marino Faliero*:

> Such ties are not
> For those who are call'd to the high destinies
> Which purify corrupted commonwealths. . . .[4]

Jawaharlal's activity often stemmed from his passionate attachment to grand ideas. While inspired with such ideas he acted with tremendous enthusiasm and vigour. But when his faith in ideas waned and his mind was filled with doubts and conflicts he lost heart in his actions. Persistence in activity then became for him a matter of discipline, an escape from himself. Action was not an end in itself; an activity far removed from its goal seemed to him dull and futile. Though drawling and soft-spoken he was not a relaxed, slow-walking, dominant man like Gandhi or Vallabhbhai Patel. Jawaharlal's dominance emanated from his intellect and his energy. In committing himself to Gandhi's satyagraha in 1920 he was more full of zest and hope than Vallabhbhai Patel, Rajendra Prasad, C. Rajagopalachariar, or perhaps even Gandhi himself.

At the beginning of 1920, while the Congress leaders were preparing to work the reforms of 1919, Gandhi was making ready for the inauguration of his non-co-operation movement. Gandhi's main objective for his satyagraha was the creation of a mass force. He believed that mass mobilisation in India depended on Hindu–Muslim unity. Thus he saw the Khilafat cause as offering a great opportunity for uniting the two communities into a single mass movement. Gandhi could not hope either to resolve the Khilafat question or to redress the Punjab wrongs. He aimed only at channelling the aggrieved and agitated Indian opinion into the satyagraha movement. His sole concern was for the regeneration of India not for the revival of the Turkish Empire. The success of his strategy depended on the persistence among the Muslims of an acute grievance on the Khilafat question, on the winning of Muslim hearts by the Hindus through their unconditional support for the Khilafat cause, and on the acceptance by both communities of the strategy of non-violent non-co-operation. On each of these counts Gandhi had to face and overcome difficulties. The Khilafat movement was not wide and persistent among the Muslims. The Khilafat group itself was divided between the moderates, who were reluctant to resort to any revolutionary action, and the extremists, who considered a non-violent satyagraha incompatible with their religion and militancy. In January 1920 (less than one month after the conclusion of the Amritsar Congress and five months before the peace treaty regarding Turkey was announced) Gandhi re-entered the Khilafat camp. He pledged unconditional Hindu support on the Khilafat question and offered to start the non-co-operation movement if the question were not amicably resolved. Since terrorism and conspiracy had failed to yield any result and the Khilafatists were lost for a strategy, they accepted Gandhi's non-violent satyagraha, but as a policy not as a creed. By the time the peace treaty was announced in May 1920, Gandhi had turned Khilafat into 'a question of questions'. The peace treaty, with its aura of finality, and with its terms not so severe as anticipated by the Indian Muslims, seemed to dampen the Khilafat spirit. At this point Gandhi stoked the embers by pronouncing the treaty 'a staggering blow' to the Indian Muslims, and advocating non-co-operation as the only alternative.

Securing Hindu support for an ultra-national cause was a more difficult task. The Hindu leaders of Congress were not touched by the plight of Turkey. Gandhi turned Hindu reluctance into willing co-operation by joining the 'Punjab wrongs' with the Khilafat grievances. The publication in May 1920 of the report by the Government-appointed Hunter Committee revived the memory of the Punjab tragedy. The Hindu leaders were angry to find that the majority of the committee members, all British, justified the imposition of martial law in the Punjab and did not fully condemn the perpetrators of the tragedy. Gandhi seized this opportunity and launched himself as the champion of Indian self-respect. He condemned the Hunter Report as illustrative of the fact that Indian feelings counted for little in the British Empire. On 30 June he linked the Punjab with Khilafat as twin reasons for resorting to the non-co-operation movement.

Gandhi had surged so far on the full support of the Muslim extremists and on his steadily growing popularity among the masses. Congress had not yet accepted his non-co-operation programme, and most of the Congress leaders were either opposed to or sceptical about it. Yet no Congress leader had mustered enough courage to oppose Gandhi openly. Though reluctant to offer individual resistance to him, the Congress leaders hoped to organise an institutional opposition to his programme at the special session of Congress which had been fixed to meet in September in Calcutta to consider the non-co-operation plan. Gandhi, anticipating opposition from Congress leaders, planned to overpower Congress by presenting to it his non-co-operation movement as a *fait accompli*. With this in view he inaugurated his movement a month before the Congress session. He offered his explanation: 'But when one has an unshakable faith in a particular policy or action, it would be folly to wait for the Congress pronouncements. On the contrary one must act and demonstrate its efficacy so as to command acceptance by the nation.'[5]

Gandhi indeed had faith in his programme but he also relied on the support of his loyal lieutenants and the masses. The month of August witnessed the capitulation of the provincial congresses, one after the other, to Gandhi's non-co-operation programme which had been formally launched on the first day of the month, the day that also coincided with the death of Tilak. The capitulation was absolute in some cases (Bihar, Gujarat, Sind, Delhi and United Provinces) and qualified in others (Bengal, Bombay, Central Provinces, Madras, Andhra and the Punjab). Though all provincial congresses accepted non-co-operation in principle, some were opposed to it and some deferred their decision upon the most controversial aspect of the programme – the boycott of the legislative councils. Gandhi's programme of gradual non-co-operation (which, though starting with the resignation of titles and honorary posts, boycott of courts, councils and government educational institutions, could at any point be extended to the withdrawal of Indians from the Army and Civil Service, and the non-payment of taxes, rents and land revenue) posed an ultimate threat to the survival of the Raj but an immediate menace to the constitution-minded lawyer-politicians of India. The law courts were the source of their livelihood and the councils were the objects of their political ambitions. Non-co-operation for them meant abandoning their life-style, earning their livelihood by spinning and weaving, and fulfilling their political ambitions in the politics of suffering, most assuredly behind prison bars. They were thus determined to resist, but their resistance was steadily weakened by the mobilisation of national enthusiasm behind Gandhi. They felt defeated even before the confrontation. Some capitulated in Calcutta, some at the Nagpur session of Congress in December 1920; some left Congress and some retired from politics altogether. But the bulk of the body that surrendered to Gandhi did so helplessly, hence half-heartedly, hoping that the period of suffering would be short. Congress accepted Gandhi's non-co-operation programme in Calcutta by a small majority, and in Nagpur by a vast majority. Gandhi emerged as the father of the nation and became 'a symbolic expression of the confused desires of the people'.[6]

It was not, however, easy for Jawaharlal to plunge into Gandhi's politics of suffering. Unlike the other important lieutenants of Gandhi, Jawaharlal had to reckon with a distinguished father. It was not enough for him that his father consented to his joining the Gandhian satyagraha; he wanted his father to take the plunge himself, as if to atone for the life of ease and comfort the Nehrus had led so far. But there was also an element of romance and melodrama in Jawaharlal's aspirations. His fondness for the spectacular was excited by the vision of his father and himself handcuffed together and marching along the streets towards the prison. This would also have pleased Gandhi.[7]

Motilal, however, was not yet willing to take the plunge. In the first half of 1920 he was precariously holding his ground on the constitutional side of the fence, his heart set on the implementation of the reforms and his eyes on the movements of Gandhi. He resented Gandhi's plan of satyagraha which, he thought, was in utter disregard of the Congress policy devised in Amritsar. He believed that Gandhi's defiance stemmed from his mounting popularity: 'There is such a thing as trusting too much to one's popularity. Mrs Besant is paying for it, and others have done the same. It will be a great grief to me if Gandhi follows suit.'[8]

Perhaps Motilal would have felt more relieved than grieved if Gandhi had fallen in February 1920, when he wrote the above lines to his son. But, realising that an open break with Gandhi would be injudicious, Motilal tried to tame him by bringing him into institutional politics. With this end in view Motilal persuaded Gandhi to accept the presidency of Mrs Besant's Home Rule League. Gandhi eventually accepted the presidency but used the organisation to strengthen his satyagraha movement.[9]

Motilal further hoped that the Government might lessen the national tension, and accordingly disarm Gandhi, by pursuing a liberal policy both in the implementation of the Act of 1919 and in the treatment of the Punjab victims. In this too he was disappointed. The Government excluded Congress from representation on the advisory committee which was constituted to frame rules for the implementation of the reforms. Against this Motilal protested, in February, to the Prime Minister, Lloyd George, but in vain.[10] At the same time the Privy Council dismissed the appeal which Motilal had arranged to be filed against the judgement of the Punjab martial-law courts. This meant that at least two of the convicted Indians, whom Motilal considered 'as innocent as the baby born', were to be hanged.[11] Later, in June and July, the House of Lords and the British public demonstrated their open support for General Dyer, who had in the previous year made a show of imperial strength at the cost of Indian lives.[12] This further intensified national tension.

These events, which took place between February and July,

weakened Motilal's resistance to the politics of satyagraha. During the same period he gradually lost his interest in his profession and in the 'occupation of making money'.[13] Politics acquired a stronger grip on him, and he began to long to be a full-time public worker.[14] And yet he felt helpless. His entire family, including his thirty-year-old son, was dependent on him. He had earned a good deal, but spent lavishly and had no considerable savings on which he could draw. However, his financial anxieties were to some extent mitigated by his being occupied, from February to September 1920, in earning what turned out to be his last great fee. He was in those months away from Allahabad in Arrah, a district town of Bihar, engaged in defending a big civil suit, for which he received a total fee or over £10,000. Thus, by August 1920, Motilal had come to stand on marginal ground, on the edge of constitutional politics and on the verge of the Gandhian satyagraha. Sometimes his problems seemed to him real, sometimes academic. It was at this stage that he was pulled into the Gandhian camp by his son.

Jawaharlal had become Joint-Secretary of the United Provinces congress and also made his first mark as a satyagrahi. In May 1920 in Mussoorie, a popular hill-station of United Provinces, he refused to obey a government order undertaking not to communicate with some Afghan delegates who were staying in the same hotel as himself, his ailing wife and mother. He was consequently forbidden to stay there.[15] The order, though meaningless, betrayed the Government's suspicion of the young Nehru as a militant nationalist. Jawaharlal was excited by this recognition. 'Greatness is being thrust on me,' he reported to his father.[16] He wanted to defy the order to leave Mussoorie and to court imprisonment. But Motilal opposed this idea, for he was not yet prepared to see the family separated. 'If you go to jail,' he warned his son, 'I have to follow.'[17] The order to leave Mussoorie turned out to be a blessing in disguise. His act of defiance acquired for him some publicity in the province; it also gave him the opportunity by chance to be drawn into a peasant movement and discover the rural India for himself.

From Mussoorie he returned to the oven-hot June temperature of Allahabad and there he met a crowd of peasants who had marched fifty miles from the rural interior of Pratapgarh district to Allahabad city 'with the intention of drawing the attention of the prominent politicians there to their woebegone condition'.[18] Having listened to them, Jawaharlal came to realise that millions of Indians were being exploited by a handful – not more than 5000 – of big land-owners (called taluqdars and zamindars). June 1920 thus marked the beginning of Jawaharlal's visits to rural India and his increasing involvement in the plight of the peasants. Here in the villages of his own province he discovered, among other things, a potential base for the national movement which had until then drawn its support entirely from the cities and towns of India. He realised how easy it was to win the affection and trust of the peasants through a show of genuine concern for their cause. His own image among them – the son of a wealthy man educated abroad, who feared neither the British officers nor the mighty Indian zamindars, who had forsaken the comforts of the palatial home to travel hundreds of miles of dusty roads in the scorching heat and come to their squalid villages to listen to their grievances – drew them in thousands around him. They showered affection on him and looked on him as their saviour. Their faith in him filled Jawaharlal with self-confidence and a new sense of responsibility which often frightened him.[19] To unload or to share with them his growing sense of personal responsibility he tried to communicate with them and point out to them that their miseries originated from a political and social system which it might take a hard and long struggle to change. His conversational and rather personal style of speaking was useful. But it was almost impossible fully to convey in Hindi to illiterate peasants the thoughts and arguments he usually conceived in English. He was not adept at dressing his ideas in the language of the masses, in using the idioms, phrases, parables and cultural images to which they could respond. Yet they listened to him reverently, not understanding a great deal of what he said. To see a town-dweller of Jawaharlal's princely background was for them an achievement in itself, and they felt as refreshed and hopeful as they might feel after bathing in a holy river. Returning home after the meeting they might ask the wise man of their village about what Jawaharlal had said; and the village leader, though he himself might not have understood the essence of the speech, nonetheless would give them his own version of the meeting. Thus, sometimes, the masses were given to understand the opposite of Jawaharlal's meaning. He was aware of the vast distance between himself and the masses, and the more they gathered round him and the more they showered on him their affection and confidence the more he wondered why. Was he gaining their goodwill under false pretences? Or was it the result of some fanciful image of him that they had formed?[20] He did not find the answer in 1920 but in subsequent years he realised that it was his image as an honest, self-sacrificing princely leader which drew the masses towards him; and it was not hard for him to live up to that image.

His first involvement in mass politics aroused in him a sense of power which in turn strengthened his urge for further sacrifice. With this new self-confidence Jawaharlal first established his dominance over the Congress organisation of his province. In the absence of his father and other older provincial leaders, Jawaharlal, with the support of other young nationalists, manipulated the United Provinces congress committee to vote, at its meeting of 22 August 1920, for Gandhi's non-co-operation movement.[21] The capitulation of the United Provinces congress, engineered by his son, left Motilal no option but to plunge into the politics of non-co-operation. He formally entered the Gandhian camp in the first week of September when the non-co-operation plan was debated and approved at the special session of Congress held in Calcutta.

From September 1920 until December 1921, when both courted their first imprisonment, Motilal occupied himself in settling the financial and domestic affairs of his family while Jawaharlal busied himself in preaching to the people of his province the politics of satyagraha. Commitment to the non-co-operation movement, in Motilal's case, involved him in giving up his legal practice. Though he was willing to sacrifice for the nation, he was utterly opposed to letting himself and his family depend for maintenance on other people or 'being a charge on the nation'.[22] He was thus obliged to take stock of his liabilities and assets, to pay off his debts and then so to invest the balance of his assets as to enable his family to live on the proceeds. He had not thought of a rainy day and had saved only a small percentage of the vast amount of money he had earned in his life. Therefore, no matter how wisely he rearranged his financial affairs at that stage, a change in the lavish style of living to which the Nehrus had been accustomed was certainly required. But even a change in their living standard was in itself not enough. It was further necessary, according to Motilal's calculations, to preserve the remaining assets for the family, and accordingly to stop making large donations to the national fund and spending vast sums of money on public works. On this point he needed the co-operation of his son, for Jawaharlal, as it seemed to Motilal, was anxious to give away to the national cause all that was left of the Nehru fortune. Misunderstandings often arose between them, and Motilal continued to impress upon Jawaharlal the ethics of looking after one's own family while serving the nation, for 'a man who is capable of starving his own children' cannot be of much good to the nation.[23] Motilal managed to retain the family assets, often by threatening to resume his legal practice if Jawaharlal did not restrain his generous impulses. He also continued to discharge another of his parental responsibilities. His daughter, twenty-year-old Vijayalakshmi, was married to Ranjit Pandit on 19 May 1921. Gandhi attended the wedding and blessed the young couple in his own strange fashion – asking them to lead a life of continence and to serve the nation.[24] The advice, though incongruous, was not inconsistent with the national mood, which was then bent on building up its strength and vitality through sacrifice, abstinence and suffering. Vijayalakshmi and Ranjit, however, avoided committing themselves. Motilal was now ready to suffer, if he must, for the nation but he was reluctant to indulge in what seemed to him meaningless self-deprivations. He had given up his legal practice, taken to home-made (hand-spun and hand-woven) khadi garments and contributed four cartloads of foreign clothes and goods to the local bonfire,[25] but he was unwilling to take to a simple vegetarian diet, and give up smoking and drinking. For forty years he had seldom missed his evening drink for eleven months in a year; he had abstained from taking alcoholic drink for one month in every year 'simply to avoid getting enslaved to the habit'.[26] He could not, however, continue his drinking when he was drawn into the temperance movement which was started at Gandhi's bidding. Unlike many of Gandhi's disciples, Motilal was averse to keeping up false appearances. He was thus obliged even to give up drinking for nearly three years during the non-co-operation movement. When he resumed his old habit in December 1923 he made no secret of it, to which Gandhi objected in vain.[27]

Jawaharlal's commitment to Gandhi in 1920–1 was almost absolute. He was so fascinated and overpowered by the superstructure of satyagraha that he readily accepted its religious and spiritual foundations. He came nearer to a religious frame of mind in 1921 than at any other time since his early boyhood.[28] This was, in a way, inevitable. The positive side of the non-co-operation movement called for a total rejection of everything western and for seeking one's identity in swadeshi – everything Indian – language, culture, tradition and religion. The English language, culture and tradition had so far been the only ties to hold together the middle classes of India. Their abandonment, and the search for a national identity, in a country abounding with varieties and contrasts, was beset with formidable problems. Where to find, or how to evolve, an Indian culture acceptable to everyone in a land of many religions, innumerable regional languages and customs, and different historical traditions? Thus, the cultural revolution, as released by Gandhi's non-co-operation movement, impelled many to fall back on their own respective cultures and religions. This, as it turned out, intensified rather than assuaged the divisive forces in Indian society. When Gandhi realised the problem he tried to evolve a common culture which was essentially a collection rather than a merger of cultures into a single whole. Tolerance and co-existence were the keynotes of this cultural style. On the more positive side his disciples were to read the Koran, the Bible and the Gita in turn, to respect all regional languages, and to learn Hindustani, an amalgam of Hindi and Urdu, which he acclaimed as the *lingua franca* of India.

Jawaharlal took to the new cultural awakening and used its symbols and slogans in preaching to the people of his province the strategy of non-co-operation. He tried to overcome his handicaps in communicating to the masses by talking to them in their own language, by using symbols and slogans they understood, and by arousing their fear and concern for the safety of what they valued most – their religion. On 9 November 1920 he told an audience: 'Now the question before you is whether you would or would not co-operate with a government – the British Government – which perpetrated a general massacre of your brethren in the Jallianwala Bagh, dishonoured your sisters, oppressed and beat young boys, made your brethren to crawl on their bellies in Amritsar and which is now attacking your religion.'[29] In June 1921, while explaining to a predominantly Hindu audience why they must support the Muslims in their Khilafat struggle, he said: 'Because if the English succeeded in destroying the Muslim religion, they will try to destroy your religion, our religion, the Hindu religion.'[30]

There was an element of exaggeration, amateurishness, even insincerity (for, though he was closer to religion in those years, he was never devout) in his first public speeches. But it was the inevitable result of an attempt to win quick popular support for a national cause which was incomprehensible to the masses. India's millions had first to be told why before they were told how to fight for political freedom. The easiest and perhaps the only way of securing mass involvement was to convince the people that all their local grievances, whether of a caste, communal or economic description, were caused by an alien rule over India. It was the British Raj which was responsible for the general poverty and degradation of Indian society, for the killing of innocent Indians, for the exploitation of peasants by landlords, for fostering communal rivalry and tension between the communities, and even for cow-killing; most of the cows, Jawaharlal pointed out to an audience, were killed to feed European soldiers, who 'cannot live without beef'. It was difficult enough to explain to the people the imperative need for swaraj or independence, and its meaning, but a much more arduous task to indoctrinate them in the cult of non-violence. Jawaharlal himself was far from being non-violent either in thought or deed. He had accepted non-violence as a policy, not as a creed. He thus asked the people to observe non-violence on grounds of expediency. He reminded them that they, with their swords, spears, even guns, stood no chance against the physical might of the British.[31] The gospel of non-violence, however, did not filter down to the masses. Being released by the national movement from their fear of the Government they – when aroused – grasped every opportunity to use physical violence gainfully. In late 1921 Jawaharlal had his first experience of how ignorant peasants could be misled. The peasants of the Fyzabad district of his province were told by an unscrupulous local man that it was the wish of Mahatma Gandhi that they loot the property of a particular landlord. They carried this out shouting, 'Mahatma Gandhi Ki Jai' ('Hail, Mahatma Gandhi').[32]

In the years 1920–1 Jawaharlal used two media to gain support for the non-co-operation movement. He communicated to the peasants of his province through his speeches delivered in Hindi. He appealed to the middle classes through his articles, and 'letters to the editor', written in English and published in the national newspapers. In his writings he used a different style. Here he was more at ease. He valued clarity and simplicity more than brevity. He meticulously painted the situation and the character before setting them together. Many years later Gandhi once remarked on Jawaharlal's capacity to write: 'Inside jail he writes books and when out of jail he writes letters the size of books.'[33] On his prose style, Frances Gunther once remarked to him: 'You write like an angel... the angel with the flaming sword...your words shine, burn, sear, illuminate, and heal.'[34]

When on the offensive, his style was soaked with sarcasm but without the slightest touch of crudity. Attacking the government of his province in January 1921 for the firing by the police on the kisans (peasants) in the Rae Bareli district (in which thirteen kisans were killed), he wrote:

> And what of the kisans? Poor, miserable, down-trodden men and women, ever in want, ever suffering, seldom complaining. What of them? Their blood lies on the banks of the Sai river, their bodies rot under a thin layer of sand, or in the open, a prey to the beasts who feast on the dead. . . . Yet not a word of sympathy came from the Governor. He sat in his palace well looked after, well-fed. What did he reck of the hungry millions? What did he care for the sorrowing widows and orphans? They were but the victims of law and order. The Pax Britannica must be preserved even though the peace it gives is the peace of the grave.[35]

Since English remained the language of the Indian national movement, Jawaharlal's mastery of it was to give him a distinct advantage over his other colleagues in the Congress High Command. He was to become the master draftsman of his party and the chief interpreter of the government documents sent to Congress.

In these years Jawaharlal also showed his own distinctive style as a fighter. Unlike Gandhi, and very much in the fashion of the Nehrus, Jawaharlal believed first in identifying and isolating the enemies. He considered not only the British Raj but the Indian liberals and the landed aristocracy as the enemies of the freedom movement. He was almost alone in labelling the 'Indian lackeys' of the Raj as the enemies of the nation. In fact he was more contemptuous of the individual liberals than of the British. He considered them inane, weak and hypocritical, of no use to any great cause. He hated the British system and occasionally, though momentarily, some individual Englishmen, but he never lost his respect for them: 'In spite of everything I am a great admirer of the English, and in many things I feel even now that an Englishman can understand me better than the average Indian.'[36]

In attacking his enemies he showed more ruthlessness now than ever after in his political career. In subsequent years, when he recovered his intellectualism, gathered more power and came more under Gandhi's liberal influence, his ruthlessness disappeared. Yet underneath his relentlessness of these years lay no malice or desire for vengeance.

His style of attack, as is evident from his speeches and writings, was also his own. He did not attack directly. His technique was not first to hit the enemy and then to explain why. It was the other way round. He paced round his prey leisurely, almost benevolently, drawing the audience to his side. By the time he had finished, the public passion for the thrust had been aroused. Jawaharlal would then administer the final blow, which satisfied all and shocked none. Jawaharlal's condemnation of the British system was tinged with a certain amount of contempt for a class of Britons whom he held guilty of economic imperialism. He read and was greatly moved by Edmund Morel's *The Black Man's Burden* (first published in 1920), which described the cruel manner of the exploitation of the Africans by the Europeans. He made this the subject of a speech delivered on 30 November 1920 in Allahabad, describing how the Englishmen exported ten million Africans to

America in terrible conditions.[37] This speech annoyed the Government, and in June 1921 an unsuccessful attempt was made to prosecute Jawaharlal. He was ready, in fact eager, to court imprisonment. His opportunity came in December 1921. The Congress boycott of the visit of the Prince of Wales to India in November had obliged the Government to undertake various repressive measures, one of them being the banning of Congress volunteer organisations. The Nehrus (father and son) took this opportunity to demonstrate their defiance of the Government. A list of seventy-five volunteers was prepared (Motilal's signature appearing at the top) and was published by the *Independent* on 5 December. On 3 December Jawaharlal had visited Lucknow and openly distributed hartal (strike) notices, creating quite a sensation in the town. In the evening of Tuesday, 6 December, both Motilal and Jawaharlal were arrested at Anand Bhawan. The atmosphere in the city was suddenly charged with emotion. A large crowd gathered in front of Anand Bhawan. Both Motilal and Jawaharlal addressed the crowd and dictated messages. In one of his messages Jawaharlal said: 'I go to jail with the greatest pleasure, and with the fullest conviction that therein lies the achievement of our goal.'[38]

Motilal's address had its usual personal touch: 'Having served you to the best of my ability, it is now my high privilege to serve the motherland by going to gaol with my only son.'[39]

Then they left in a car for the district jail, leaving behind a lonely Kamala, an excited baby Indira and a sad Swarup Rani Nehru. The following day Gandhi was to write a consoling letter to Jawaharlal's mother asking her to consider it a privilege that both her husband and son were going to jail together.[40] The nation witnessed with admiration the Nehrus taking the plunge.

CHAPTER FIVE

Beginnings of Compromise, 1922–5

Surely emotion should not be cheapened; it is too valuable a commodity. The teaching of the West has made me value restraint a great deal and I feel that we as a race are continually indulging in emotionalism and lessening our activity thereby. We pitch everything in too high a key.

Jawaharlal Nehru, March 1924

THE mental and physical discipline which Jawaharlal had acquired at Harrow may have been useful to him when he began his life in prison. Prison life was a challenge, and then there was the additional compensation of being in the company of fellow patriots and of his father. He easily filled his day with a crowded schedule – sweeping and dusting the prison barrack, washing his father's and his own clothes, cooking, spinning, reading, conducting evening classes for the illiterate political prisoners, playing volley-ball, and sometimes lying in the open and indulging in his special hobby of watching the skies, the clouds, and studying their beautiful, changing hues.[1]

While the Nehrus were settling down in Lucknow district jail, each to his six months' term of imprisonment, Gandhi suddenly suspended the non-co-operation movement on 12 February 1922. The Nehrus were shocked at the news. Motilal, who had reluctantly accepted the politics of suffering, now hit back in frustration and anger at what seemed to him a whim of Gandhi. He couldn't understand why a national movement should be suspended and the sufferings and aspirations of thousands of patriots ignored merely because a few villagers had gone wild in Chauri Chaura and set fire to a police station, burning to death twenty-two of its inmates. Jawaharlal was disillusioned, suspecting that there was something wrong with Gandhi's non-violent technique if it could be made inoperative by a single outburst of violence.

It was, however, not simply the Chauri Chaura tragedy which had obliged Gandhi to suspend the movement. The

Indian masses, being for the first time released from the fear of law and being aroused in the name of 'satyagraha for swaraj', a concept which they could not understand, had begun to express their individual grievances. All manner of rivalries came to the surface and filled the air with violence. There was an eruption of communal riots between Hindus and Muslims in almost every part of the sub-continent. The Moplah Muslims of the Malabar coast were initially aroused in the name of Khilafat but then fell back on their long-cherished grievances against the Hindu money-lenders and consequently, in August 1921, 'converted' or killed many Hindus before the Army intervened to restore order. This event set off a chain reaction among the Hindu leaders, some of whom blamed Gandhi's campaign for the raising of Untouchables which, they argued, had aroused among the Muslims the desire to swell their ranks by converting Hindus to Islam.[2] Accordingly the Hindus began a reconversion campaign.[3] The Hindu leaders also stressed, some with genuine concern, the danger of a further Afghan invasion and the re-establishment of Muslim rule in India. Thus, the Hindu–Muslim unity which had been imposed from above began to be shaken from below.

There was also conflict among the Hindus themselves. Inter-caste hostility mounted in almost all parts of India but most noticeably in Bihar, where it led to a scramble for power between the four dominant castes – Kayasthas, Bhumihars, Rajputs and Brahmins – and in Madras between non-Brahmins and Brahmins. In the Punjab (where Sikhs had accepted Gandhi's satyagraha as a means of winning control of the management of their temples from the Hindu priests) tension grew between the Hindus and Sikhs. The non-co-operation movement, particularly the no-rent aspect of it, had also aroused class conflicts between peasants and landlords, particularly in United Provinces and Bengal, and between workers and industrialists, particularly in Bengal and Bombay. These inner hostilities shook the Congress movement, which Gandhi had intended should include within its fold all religions, castes and classes, and exclude none. The movement had thus already gone out of control even before the Chauri Chaura event. Chauri Chaura provided Gandhi with the excuse for suspending the movement but it was not the cause. He confessed to Jawaharlal that the 'Chauri Chaura incident was the last straw', that the people had become aggressive, defiant and threatening, and that not even a hundred out of 36,000 volunteers who had enlisted in just one district conformed to the Congress pledge.[4] He consoled Jawaharlal that 'the cause will prosper by this retreat', and asked him to do some serious study and manual work while in jail, and above all to concentrate on the spinning-wheel.[5]

Gandhi's non-co-operation movement was both a failure and a success. It failed to achieve its ostensible objects – including swaraj, which it was to have bestowed upon India by the autumn of 1921. This was partly because it failed to acquire the full support of the middle classes on whose co-operation above all its success depended.[6] A full upsurge of Indian non-co-operation with the Government might have shaken the British Raj into some kind of submission, for fewer than 200,000 British, soldiers and civilians, then ruled a country of 320 million people, including the population of the Indian states.[7]* The movement also failed to consolidate the unity of the Indian masses. The hostilities between communities, castes and classes and the consequent outbreaks of violence had pushed the movement to a point of chaos.

The success of the movement, however, lay in its bringing about mass mobilisation. Raising the Indian masses, through self-sacrifice, to a state of fearlessness was Gandhi's main objective. He succeeded in creating, for the first time in Indian history, a mass force to which, he hoped, the British would respond:

> My faith, however, in the British nation is such that when we have shown sufficient strength of purpose and undergone

*The British empire in India consisted of what was called British India and the Indian (or princely) states. British India comprised 61·5 per cent of the Indian sub-continent; it was divided into provinces and ruled directly by the British. Over the rest of the Indian territory there were scattered nearly 600 Indian states varying enormously in size, from states the size of France to petty estates unworthy to be ranked as political entities. Over these states the British exercised, through the Political Department of the Government of India, an indirect control and supervision. Though the Indian rulers of these states were subordinate to the British Crown and were deprived of any independent international status, they did enjoy, nonetheless, some measure of internal autonomy.

> enough measure of self-sacrifice, the British people will respond fully. My reading of history is that they do not yield to justice, pure and simple. It is too abstract for their 'common sense'. But they are far-seeing enough to respond to justice when it is allied with force. Whether it is brute-force or soul-force they do not mind.[8]

Hence Gandhi had not conceived non-co-operation 'in hatred and illwill towards a single Englishman'.[9] He had launched the movement to uplift the Indian masses and to prove to the British that India's was a deserving case. The British, however, were reluctant to recognise the strength of Gandhi's mass movement. They over-stressed, almost in desperation, India's inherent disunity, which had been brought to the surface by Gandhi's movement. With all his respect for Gandhi's saintliness and sincerity, the then Viceroy, Lord Reading, tried to convince himself and the British Prime Minister that the main reason for the mass support of Gandhi was economic distress – the poverty and misery of huge sections of the population – and was not the product of any upsurge of political consciousness among them. He hoped that another good monsoon and a fine harvest like that of 1921 would make the masses contented, and that there would be peace and tranquillity in India.[10] The British, thus, discounted Gandhi's movement. Instead British opinion pressed for his arrest as a mark of retribution for his having called for the boycott of the visit of the Prince of Wales to India. Lord Reading sanctioned Gandhi's arrest at a time which he thought was safest for the Raj. Gandhi was arrested in March 1922, tried, and sentenced to six years' imprisonment.

Jawaharlal was one of those who recognised the Mahatma's achievement. Jawaharlal was prematurely released in early March 1922 as a result of an official discovery that he had been wrongly convicted. Leaving his father and comrades behind in prison, he rushed up to Ahmedabad, arriving there in time to attend Gandhi's trial. If the sudden suspension of the movement had created any doubt in Jawaharlal's mind about Gandhi's strength and wisdom, it was at once dispelled by the historic statement which the Mahatma made at his trial on 18 March.[11] Gandhi turned it into a confrontation between the British Raj and Indian nationalism, and his statement had the effect of shifting all moral force and justice from the former to the latter.

Jawaharlal was greatly moved, and his faith in Gandhi's leadership was reinforced. Recharged with enthusiasm he returned to Allahabad resolved to sponsor constructive programmes – spinning and weaving, the boycott of foreign clothes, picketing of liquor shops, the raising of the Untouchables, enrolment in Congress – which Gandhi had imposed upon the nation as an alternative to the mass civil disobedience which had been suspended.[12] It was also necessary to convince the disillusioned Congress workers that non-co-operation had not failed:

> We demonstrated to India and to the world that we had shaken off the sloth and inertia of centuries; that we understood the value of freedom; that we could fight for it and above all that we could sacrifice for it. Is this a little achievement? What country has offered 23,000 or more of its loved ones for the jail as India did in the ever memorable months of December and January? Today India is honoured and India is respected where yesterday we were treated as coolies and despised as slaves.[13]

Yet these constructive programmes were not fully suited to Jawaharlal's temperament. They required patience and perseverance, and enough faith and humility to work unnoticed and unregarded. They could not absorb Jawaharlal's flair and energy and had no room for his defiance, aggression and world outlook. He also felt sad and lonely with his father and Gandhi in prison. Little Indira and ailing Kamala failed to absorb his interest. Furthermore, he sensed a steadily growing opposition to Gandhi's programme and a division within the Congress ranks. Where would he stand if the opposition to Gandhi was led by his own father? Such a prospect tormented him, and he longed to escape from the dull and demoralising realities to the heroic style of politics. Courting imprisonment was the obvious choice. For Jawaharlal it symbolised both action and reward. It would keep the national mood of defiance alive; he would personally get the confidence of the masses, for nothing assures a simple people of the integrity of their leaders more than the leaders' physical sufferings for them. Prison would also save him from taking sides on issues which seemed to him narrow and petty.

Thus, with prison in view, Jawaharlal put more defiance

into the campaign for the boycott of foreign clothes which he organised in Allahabad. Shops dealing in foreign clothes were picketed and recalcitrant merchants fined. Jawaharlal was arrested, tried on charges of criminal intimidation and extortion, and on 19 May 1922 sentenced to twenty-one months. At his trial he emulated the Mahatma and made a long statement in the same style as Gandhi.

Free from the doldrums and diverse, lower-level pulls of political life, and also from domestic tension, Jawaharlal was nearer to Gandhi and to religion during the second term of his imprisonment than ever after. He disciplined himself into becoming a Gandhian satyagrahi and cultivated a taste for self-deprivation. Spinning yarn became his main occupation and fasting his self-purifying hobby. He fasted on every conceivable occasion – a Muslim or Hindu religious day, Gandhi Day, on the anniversary of the death of Tilak and the second anniversary of the non-co-operation movement. Even the occasion of a formal complaint to the prison superintendent was observed by a fast for thirty-five hours.[14] Regular reading of the Gita and Ramayana was as much a religious act as a search for Indian tradition. A conscious attempt to discover and adopt an Indian identity was further manifested in his reading of books on the glories and splendours of ancient and medieval India, by his learning Urdu, and writing letters in Hindi – an arduous task, which he abandoned after exchanging a couple of letters in Hindi with his father. He did not, however, submerge his world outlook and romantic humanism in the narrow and torrential stream of Gandhian nationalism. He read history and made comprehensive notes on subjects ranging from the 'Decline and Fall of the Roman Empire' to 'The Rise of German Social Democracy'. He continued to read the *Nation* and the *New Statesman* as much for the quality of their prose as for their content. The poems of Tennyson, Keats, Shelley, Wordsworth and Byron remained his bedside companions. Among all the Indian nationalist leaders he was by far the greatest reader. He had done little reading since his return from England but he now made good the deficiency. He did not, however, specialise in any particular subject. His interests were varied; he even struggled, though unsuccessfully, to understand the essence of Einstein's Theory of Relativity.

He wrote on one occasion: 'It is better to live far from the madding crowd absorbed in books and in one's immediate surroundings.'[15]

At this point in his life Jawaharlal became convinced that a great event had taken place in India which had changed not only the life of the country but also of the Nehrus. The life which the Nehrus had lived prior to the non-co-operation movement now seemed to him utterly false and useless.[16] Not only had there been no organised intellectual life, Jawaharlal reflected, but very little had been said or done 'that beautifies existence for us or for others, or that will be remembered by anyone after we are dead and gone'.[17] He thought the non-co-operation movement 'took us in hand and removed us from the ruts and placed us on the mountain side':

> We may not reach the top yet awhile but the glory of wider vision is ours. We can see the stars better and sometimes the rays of the morning sun reach us sooner than those in the valleys.[18]

Jawaharlal was conscious of the role he, together with his father, had played in that event, and of the even greater part he might have to play in the future. Motilal was inspired to look more closely at the Nehru family-tree and he proudly informed his son that his maternal grandfather had been tutor to the sons of the last emperor of Delhi (Bahadur Shah) – a very exalted office in the Mogul court.[19] Jawaharlal was preparing himself for this greater role through self-imposed sufferings and hardships. For a short while he even refused interviews in the prison with his father, mother and wife: 'It is, of course, my opinion that the greater the hardship imposed upon us, the greater the benefit, for it will make us stronger. For this reason I liked the hardship of having no interviews.'[20]

He had taken to the prison as a monk takes to a monastery. He was, therefore, embarrassed when dainty food and other comforts were sent to him. He was even more embarrassed when subjected to domestic love and concern. In prison he felt free and in harmony with himself. But this was not to last. When on 29 January 1923 he was told of his premature release he sadly noted in his diary: 'The jailer, however, insists that we are going to be discharged. If so, I suppose we shall have to put up with it, although the last volume of Gibbon has still to be read.'[21]

Jawaharlal had reasons to be reluctant to face the political India that waited outside the Lucknow district prison. Having exhausted its enthusiasm and energy during the storm of the non-co-operation movement, the nation was languishing in a mood of despondency and doubt. Those who had reluctantly surrendered to Gandhi in 1920 had now lost their belief in his infallibility. As a result, at its 1922 annual session, held in December in Gaya, Congress had split into two groups, one consisting of ardent followers of Gandhi who wanted to remain non-co-operators and carry on with the constructive programme which Gandhi had prescribed for the nation, the other comprising the disaffected who wanted to revert to the constitutional mode of opposition to the Raj. Jawaharlal was aware that his father had played a major role in dividing Congress into these two factions, an event which had taken place a month before he came out of prison.

Motilal's faith in the Gandhian strategy of non-co-operation was much reduced when he was released from prison in June 1922. Like his friend C. R. Das, Motilal believed that Gandhi, at the height of his power, had made mistakes, perhaps the greatest being his rejection of Lord Reading's peace offer of December 1921 to hold a round-table conference. Perhaps nothing would have come out of this conference, for Reading had received no authority from the London government to introduce any major constitutional change in India. But the constitutionally minded nationalists then, and in later years, believed that a great opportunity was missed, for the conference would have immediately led to the establishment of full autonomy in the provinces and India would have acquired, according to some speculators,[22] full dominion status by 1939, without having gone through the agony of partition.

Das and Motilal, however, were concerned with the immediate future and they believed that a truce in 1921, when the nation had exhausted its energy, would have saved the non-co-operation movement from ending in total defeat. During his tours as a member of the Congress Civil Disobedience Enquiry Committee, in the latter part of 1922, Motilal convinced himself that the masses were unwilling to become involved in another civil disobedience movement. The constructive programme, Gandhi's alternative to direct action, was utterly unsuited to Motilal's temperament. Thus, for him, the right course was to abandon Gandhi's battlefield and move into the council chamber. Accordingly, Das and Motilal put before the Indian nationalists their strategy of non-co-operation from within the legislative councils of India. The elected Indian members of provincial and central councils were to offer continuous obstruction to the functioning of the Government by voting down every legislative measure sponsored by the Government until the Government was forced to suspend or scrap the constitution of 1919. This plan meant that the Congressmen, who had boycotted the election in 1920, should contest the next election, which was due in November 1923. The plan thus implied a reversal of Congress policy; accordingly it had to be approved by Congress at its annual session. Being fully aware that the proposal for council entry would be strongly opposed by the more ardent followers of Gandhi, Motilal began alerting his supporters, asking them 'to work hard to see that persons in favour of running elections are returned as delegates' to the impending Gaya session of Congress.[23] Of the 3248 delegates who assembled in Gaya, only 2630 voted on the question of council entry; of these 890 were in favour and 1740 against. The resolution for council entry was most effectively opposed by three of Gandhi's foremost disciples, Rajaji (short for C. Rajagopalachariar), Vallabhbhai Patel and Rajendra Prasad. It was a crushing defeat – especially for Das, who was also the president of the Congress session. Das and Motilal, however, were in no mood to abide by the Congress decision. Then and there, on 31 December 1922, they formed their own party – the Congress–Khilafat Swaraj Party – with Das as its president and Motilal its secretary. Congress was divided.

The question which faced Jawaharlal on his release from prison was to which of the two groups he would adhere. Virtually it involved choosing between his father and Gandhi. As an ardent disciple of Gandhi in 1920 Jawaharlal had ruthlessly branded the breakaway liberals as enemies of the nation. Would he do the same again and attack his father and his group for their divergence from the Gandhian path? Would he be a mere Gandhian soldier like Vallabhbhai Patel, whose unshaken faith in Gandhi had impelled him to oppose his own elder brother Vithalbhai Patel for joining the Das–Motilal group? Jawaharlal did not align himself with either group; nor did he approve of one to the derogation of the other.

Nine months of prison life had refreshed him intellectually. He renewed his former style of looking at a problem from different angles. To him the division in Congress did not represent an irreconcilable conflict between the two factions. His family pride and loyalty towards his father strengthened him in his belief that his father was still a staunch nationalist and his council-entry plan merely constituted a change of tactics rather than a total abandonment of the spirit of non-co-operation and defiance. Jawaharlal himself was, in principle, opposed to council entry but he was at the same time disinclined to join the Patel–Rajaji–Prasad camp, for that would be tantamount to submerging himself in a group and accepting a subordinate role in the implementation of the constructive programme, work in which he knew that he could not excel. He had accepted Gandhi as his leader but he was reluctant to accept the orthodox Gandhi-ites even as his equal colleagues, for not only was he poles apart from them, culturally and intellectually, but he also found himself resenting their political style, which seemed to him rigorously ascetic, self-righteous, almost fanatical. His reading of the situation urged him to rise above party factions and adopt the role of a mediator. He could in that capacity join, and most certainly lead, a group of nationalists who wanted reconciliation, at any cost, between the two factions of Congress.[24] A plunge into the politics of compromise gave Jawaharlal a temporary escape from his inner conflict of ideas, desires and loyalties. It was also rewarding; his non-aligned position gave a touch of charisma to his personality and enabled him to win election by midsummer 1923 to several offices – presidency of the Allahabad town congress committee in March, chairmanship of the Allahabad municipal board and secretaryship of the United Provinces provincial congress in April, and finally the secretaryship of the All-India Congress in May.

The point of conflict between the two caucuses of Congress was such that a compromise settlement between them necessarily involved a greater measure of surrender on the part of the Patel–Rajaji–Prasad group. This group was urged not only to accept the Swaraj Party as an integral part of Congress but also to allow the Party to contest the impending election without let or hindrance. Patel, Rajaji and Prasad were, therefore, determined to resist conciliation to the best of their ability. Vallabhbhai Patel implored Jawaharhal: 'You will have our wholehearted support in all other matters, but you must without resentment or anger allow us in this matter which affects the movement vitally to follow our own conviction.'[25]

Jawaharlal was unconvinced. The compromise would not kill the national movement. 'If the Congress really represented the people,' he argued, 'it is natural that it should attempt to go back a little to some kind of constitutional action, whenever large numbers of people are tired of direct action.'[26] He believed, regretfully, that the root of the present problem lay in the acceptance of the non-co-operation policy and programme by the Calcutta Congress in 1920. This acceptance 'overwhelmed us from the very beginning and the weight of numbers paralysed us'. If this had not happened 'we could then have marched on as a compact body, strong in our faith and in our discipline, and, at the right moment, have converted the masses and the Congress to our viewpoint'.[27]

Patel lost the battle, first at the All-India Congress Committee meeting held in Bombay in May and finally at the special session of Congress held in Delhi in September 1923. The compromise was reached under additional pressure exerted by the Muslim Khilafatists, particularly by Muhammad Ali and A. K. Azad who had but little liking for Patel's political style. Thus the comradeship between Jawaharlal and Patel – the two future rulers of India – began on a note of rivalry and mutual distrust for the other's style of leadership. Only their common loyalty to Congress and the country was to keep them together. Patel had much more in common with Rajaji and Prasad. All three had a rural background which had conditioned them to see harmony rather than inherent discord between classes. They were deeply rooted in the Indian tradition and remained so throughout their lives. They had faith in Indian values and Hindu gods. Hence each was self-contained, spiritually and socially. None of them experienced deep inner conflict, and none searched for new attachments or for a synthesis between conflicting values. Though they were ardent followers of Gandhi, they had accepted the Mahatma only as their political leader and not as their spiritual mentor. Their need for Gandhi was limited. For them the Mahatma had far less charisma than he had for Jawaharlal. Being uprooted at an early age from the Indian tradition and unassimilated in the western tradition, Jawaharlal had been continually searching for substitutes and syntheses. His desire for commitment found a new attachment in Gandhi. The Mahatma appeared to him not simply as the political leader and the spiritual master, but as a complete system. He took to Gandhi as a convert takes to his new religion. His surrender, however, was absolute only for the first two years, for Jawaharlal was essentially a man of reason rather than of faith. When his reason clashed with Gandhi's intuition and mysticism, he became puzzled and tormented. In future he was to disagree with Gandhi on a number of occasions, and on each his reason was to take him on a short, but unsuccessful, journey in search of another substitute. His bond with Gandhi, therefore, was never broken.

Jawaharlal's attachment to Gandhi was almost absolute in September 1923 but his interests in comparatively minor politics had worn out. He was by then beginning to feel restless. The municipal work, which had captured his imagination for a little while, was now beginning to weigh heavily upon him. It was minor employment; his real passion lay in a different direction, and 'God willing', he informed his colleagues, 'I shall go that way till our purpose is attained.'[28] On the municipal work, which was his first administrative task, he stamped more of his intellectual outlook than his organisational skill. He examined almost every subject which came up for his consideration in a world context. He dressed a problem in a wide historical perspective and in so doing neutralised its uniqueness as well as its acuteness. For example, on a proposal for electoral reform in the Allahabad municipality, he began by quoting from the eighteenth-century French philosopher Montesquieu to show how important is the matter of regulating suffrage upon which depends the destruction or salvation of states; he then pointed out how this problem was tackled differently in various countries at different times; stressed how difficult it was to deal with such a question; and finally endorsed the general principle of the proposal with a reference to the system then prevailing in New York which attached greater importance to having small electoral districts.[29] Here in his municipal office, bearing some power and responsibility, he revealed his predilection for evolution rather than revolution. On the treatment of prostitutes he reflected: 'The world would be a very different place if we could abolish prostitution and lying and cruelty and oppression and the thousand and one ills that flesh is heir to by resolution. Unhappily we can proceed but slowly with the task of regeneration.'[30]

Municipal work, however, could not satisfy him. He was also afraid that his longer continuance in the office might make his muscle turn to fat, and his spirit yield to a love of security.[31] He needed to involve himself in a heroic deed of self-sacrifice, suffering or defiance. This urge became stronger when he observed Patel's success in Nagpur (July–August 1923) in organising civil disobedience in honour of the national flag.[32] It was at this point, when Jawaharlal was looking for an outlet, that the opportunity was provided by the state of Nabha in the Punjab.

The Government of India had deposed the Maharaja of Nabha and appointed an official administrator in his place. In protest against this the Sikh community had taken to civil disobedience, which in the circumstances meant sending batches of men into the state in defiance of the government order banning such entry. This Sikh agitation attracted Jawaharlal. On 19 September 1923, soon after the conclusion of the special Congress session in Delhi, with two colleagues he joined a Sikh contingent and entered the state of Nabha, almost in the same style as Gandhi had entered Champaran in 1917. He was promptly arrested, and kept in a most unpleasant and insanitary cell while on trial. Jawaharlal's arrest attracted public sympathy and admiration. But it aroused in Motilal an acute parental concern for the safety of his son, and he arrived in Nabha with the special permission of the Viceroy. His father's concern for him embarrassed Jawaharlal.

He wanted to be left alone like his fellow prisoners. The grandeur of suffering would be diminished if his father exerted all his influence to secure his release. He entreated his father to return to Allahabad. Motilal's feelings were hurt: 'I was pained to find that instead of affording you any relief my visit of yesterday only had the effect of disturbing the even tenor of your happy jail life.'[33] But he obeyed and returned to Allahabad, proudly assuring Jawaharlal: 'I am as happy outside the jail as you are in it.'[34]

The trial of Jawaharlal was farcical, a mockery of justice. He was sentenced to thirty months' rigorous imprisonment, but the sentence was suspended and he was ordered to leave the state. He returned to Allahabad as a hero: 'I have returned to Allahabad before after serving much longer periods in jail but nobody took much notice of my return. Yesterday, however, there was quite a seething mass of humanity at the station to welcome and embarrass me.'[35]

His own province immediately honoured him with the presidency of the provincial congress. A feeling of success, partly stemming from the awareness of his growing popularity, released in Jawaharlal a new source of energy. He was undaunted even though suffering from remittent fever, and wrote his lengthy presidential address while running a temperature of 104°.[36] Although in this written address Jawaharlal emphasised the success of the non-co-operation movement in mobilising the masses, he was at the same time aware that, but for the lack of discipline and organisation, the movement would have yielded more than it actually did. India's greatest weakness, as he saw it, was her lack of discipline. Courage and willingness to suffer were not enough. Congress must have a body of regular disciplined volunteers. With this in view Jawaharlal founded in December 1923 an all-India volunteer organisation (the Hindustan Seva Dal) which was to recruit and train volunteers, and to function under the supervision and control of Congress. Though this body was not to find favour with Gandhi, who suspected that violence was latent in such an organisation, nonetheless it made a good start under Jawaharlal's presidency.[37]

It was also at the same annual session of Congress held in December 1923 in Kakinada that Jawaharlal, who since May

1923 had functioned as acting General Secretary of Congress, was formally elected to the post; he held it until December 1925, and accordingly served under two Congress presidents – Muhammad Ali 1923–4 and Gandhi 1924–5. His term of office, however, coincided with a gradual decline in the political morale of the country caused by division in Congress, and the rise of communal politics at sub-national levels. The national movement stood at the crossroads swept by winds which blew in different directions. Gandhi, who was prematurely released from prison in February 1924 on grounds of ill-health, was for a while opposed to the council-entry programme of the Swaraj Party. He smelt violence in the strategy of 'obstruction from within'.[38] Underneath this strategy, he sensed, lay ambition for power rather than earnest self-sacrifice. Against this he put forward the constructive programme, which required of the nationalists self-abnegation and self-control. The cult of the spinning-wheel, which required much greater sacrifice from its votaries, seemed to Gandhi the most effective means of acquiring national strength and unity.[39]

C. R. Das and Motilal Nehru were equally against withdrawing their party from the councils. They believed in neither the creed of non-violence nor the economics of the spinning-wheel. Motilal dug in his heels: 'Gandhiji will either convert the Congress into a spinners' association or else stick to his five boycotts. Neither will suit us or the country.'[40] There seemed no prospect for a compromise while both parties held their ground. In their meeting with Gandhi in Juhu (a seaside resort near Bombay) in May 1924, C. R. Das and Motilal Nehru made it clear that they would on no account withdraw their party from the legislative councils. They believed they had good reasons to pursue their programme and that they possessed high credentials, as the self-sacrificing colleagues and friends of Gandhi, to challenge him if he stood in their way.

In this confrontation the Mahatma took a back seat. Though he had complete faith in his constructive programme, he was at the same time aware that it seemed uninspiring even to those who were on his side. There were possibly three ways in which he could revive his leadership. The first option was to call immediately for a direct satyagraha. This would have disarmed the swarajists and created instant unity in Congress. But he was not prepared to take this course, for he feared it would result in violence and consequently strengthen the Government in its disbelief in 'our professions of truth and non-violence'.[41] Secondly he could get his programme endorsed by a substantial majority in Congress and thereby force the swarajists either to surrender to the will of the majority or withdraw from Congress. The third option was to allow Congress to accept the swarajists and to carry on with both the constructive and the obstructive council-entry programmes. This course would have obliged him to compromise his cherished principles and co-operate with those who disagreed with him fundamentally.

Gandhi thus opted for the second course, which meant a declaration of war against the swarajists. The first battle was fought in June 1924 at the meeting of the All-India Congress Committee held in Ahmedabad. Gandhi asked Congress to endorse his programme. He further sought to drive out of Congress those who did not believe in the constructive aspect of his programme, especially in the cult of the spinning-wheel. This he attempted to achieve by amending the membership clause in the constitution of Congress. His resolution was intended to limit membership to those who gave to Congress regularly a certain amount of self-spun yarn instead of the four annas subscription. Only the whole body of Congress at its annual session, and not its All-India Committee, was competent to consider such a fundamental change in its constitution, but Gandhi seldom cared for the letter of the law when it stood in his way.[42] The illegality as well as the severity of his measure shocked not only the swarajists but also Jawaharlal, who offered to resign from the general secretaryship of Congress. The swarajists led by Motilal Nehru and C. R. Das walked out of the meeting in protest. Gandhi won, but only by a slender majority; if the swarajists had not walked out, he conceded, his resolution might have been defeated.[43] Gandhi had not expected such strong opposition from the swarajists. He had hoped to convert them rather than turn them into his enemies. The proceedings of the Committee further convinced him that not only his opponents but even most of his supporters did not share his absolute faith in non-violence and the spinning-wheel. He thus publicly acknowledged his marginal victory as a great defeat. However, Gandhi did not change his course instantly. His humble utterances only betrayed his anguish at being confronted by a force which he persisted in calling evil. Would he now join hands with the swarajists? Or would he try once again to suppress them? Motilal anticipated a decisive trial of strength at the annual session of Congress, which was to be held that year in Belgaum.[44] He kept his forces alert for this final battle.

In this confrontation during the latter part of 1924 between the Mahatma and Motilal, Jawaharlal occupied a difficult position. His loyalties were divided and confused. Though his faith in Gandhism had been shaken, he still believed that the Mahatma, with his vast mass following, was the undisputed and indispensable leader of the nation. Gandhi seemed to be the great reservoir of power from which alone the Indian leaders could draw their support and legitimacy. At the same time Jawaharlal was not prepared to see his father's leadership being suppressed or destroyed by Gandhi. Since he was not greatly attracted either by Gandhi's or Motilal's programmes his conflicts were personal rather than ideological. No demand on his loyalty was made either by Gandhi or Motilal; nonetheless he felt pulled in different directions. The only course he saw open to him was to stand aside, hoping that the confrontation would resolve itself into a compromise; in doing so he was troubled by doubts. His relationship with his father had grown tense, and he wondered whether his father had expected him to be on his side. The fact of his being financially dependent upon his father tormented him. His daughter was now seven. His wife was expecting another baby. He was himself now in his mid-thirties, having never, for even a short while, fully earned his living. He feared that his father's feelings would be hurt if he discussed the matter with him. He expressed his feelings to Gandhi, who occasionally advised him to take up some remunerative job in a newspaper concern or in a college, or even in a business firm.[45] But for one reason or other Jawaharlal never came round to facing his father on this issue. However, to his great satisfaction, the confrontation between his father and Gandhi gradually subsided into a compromise. A number of factors induced Gandhi to make a *volte-face*.

In spite of his initial condemnation of it, the Swaraj Party stood firm and strong, threatening to divide Congress rather than surrender to it. The Party contained the foremost intellectuals in the country and represented a very strong body of public opinion in favour of council entry. Gandhi further saw that the division in Congress had encouraged communal politicians to come to the front and intensify Hindu–Muslim tension. There was a daily increase in the frequency of communal riots. The Congress weakness also emboldened the Government to stiffen its attitude towards the nationalists, and made it more willing to resort to repressive measures when the opportunity arose. National interest thus demanded unity at all costs. The personal factor, too, played some part. His regard for Motilal Nehru and his concern at Jawaharlal's predicament arising out of the confrontation made Gandhi willing to compromise. Consoling one of his most loyal followers, Rajaji, he wrote: 'I do not know if your mind keeps pace with the swift changes that have come over me. I see as clearly as daylight that we must not resist the evil that has crept into our ranks. We must abdicate power altogether.'[46] Gandhi told his followers that the total surrender on their part now would bring them victory afterwards: 'We must stoop to conquer. Retaining every bit of non-co-operation in our own persons, we must make the path of those who do not believe in it smooth for helping us and helping the country in the constructive effort.'[47]

The occasion for actually signing the treaty of unity and solidarity arose in October–November when the Government retaliated against the Bengal swarajists. Under the agreement concluded between Gandhi and the swarajist leaders in Calcutta on 6 November, the Swaraj Party was permitted to carry on its council programme in the name of Congress. In return the swarajists undertook to support Gandhi's constructive programme. Congress was now virtually united; only one of its erstwhile components – the liberals – still remained outside the fold. Gandhi, now placed at the head of the unity movement, held out his hands for them.[48] The liberals, however, nourished strong objections to the Congress creed and methods, the latter now including the swarajists' programme of obstruction from within the councils. Gandhi therefore offered to moderate still further the aims and activities of Congress. Consequently his presidential speech delivered at the Belgaum Congress on 26 December 1924 turned out to be a supreme exercise in moderation and caution.[49] He interpreted the Congress creed of swaraj to mean the attainment not of complete independence from Britain, but of dominion status within the British Empire. Removing the focus from all controversial aspects of the Congress movement, he declared that the only 'national programme jointly to be worked by all the parties is Khaddar [hand-woven cloth], Hindu–Muslim unity and, for the Hindus, removal of untouchability'. Gandhi's programme aimed at social regeneration. It contained no immediate prospect of a war with the Raj, and it envisaged the retention of the British connection for ever. Gandhi's speech therefore struck Jawaharlal 'as being very uninspiring'.[50] He saw the spirit of aggression and fight being suppressed in the name of national unity. Was this unity viable? Was it necessary? Did the country have to wait for its freedom until it was socially regenerated? Did this not imply that India had first to qualify herself before she asked for political freedom? – an argument which Jawaharlal had resented continuously since his student days in London. Why settle for dominion status? Why not aspire to complete independence and a republican constitution for India?[51] Again, would not the recently aroused mass political consciousness subside if it were not harnessed to a continuing fight against the Raj? The reformist methods of Gandhi, he feared, would not resolve the country's problems. He felt that the situation demanded a revolutionary outlook, planning and solution. But then 'there was no-one among the leaders to offer these'.[52] He himself then had no clear vision of revolutionary methods. Nonetheless, his disenchantment with the Gandhian path paved the way for the search which he began in 1926 for the alternative system.

Thus the years 1924 and 1925 saw Jawaharlal haunted by a number of questions, and by doubts and conflicts which often caused him frustration. A part of his frustration, however, arose from the domestic situation. Throughout 1924 tension had persisted between father and son. Kamala's baby boy, born prematurely in November 1924, had died two days later, leaving her more sick and unhappy than ever before. Her illness was finally diagnosed as tuberculosis in November 1925. Jawaharlal himself was not in the best of health. He was going bald and suffered from piles for which he underwent an operation in February 1925. In these years, therefore, he gradually resigned himself to a state of detachment. He functioned laboriously but aloofly as the General Secretary of Congress.

As Congress Secretary he had to deal with three main problems, each one of which baffled him. He had to organise the finances of Congress, a work for which he had no special aptitude. He had to deal with the problem of a nationwide tension between Hindus and Muslims and the resulting increase in communal riots. He analysed the causes and nature of the riots that had occurred in his own province and came to the conclusion that all such outbreaks were instigated by communal leaders who for their own political advancement played on the religious sentiments and fears of their respective communities. He resented these leaders, but found it impossible to deal with them: 'Whom would I represent? The Hindus are not going to accept me, and why should the Muslims do so?'[53] He wanted to destroy rather than reconcile the communal leadership. But how? He also began to look scornfully at the Indian religions which, he thought, were basically responsible for such a hopeless situation. But how could these religions be brought under control? He realised that the communal leaders represented the upper classes of all groups. If there was a class war, would they not hasten 'to patch up their differences in order to face jointly the common class foe'?[54] His entanglement with the communal problem thus prepared him to accept most willingly any solution which promised to destroy religious and communal leaders. More than a year was still to pass before he came to see that solution in socialism based on a rational system of education. The third problem he faced was the rising tension in the Punjab between the Sikhs and Hindus. He looked at the Punjab situation through the Congress Akali Sahayak Bureau which had been established in Amritsar to help the Sikh Akali movement in its struggle against the Government for the control of the Sikh temples. An analysis of the situation convinced Jawaharlal that religion again lay at the root of the tension. He looked with disfavour at the Akali movement, which was 'largely a separatist movement so far as religion is concerned'.[55] The narrow-mindedness of the Punjabi Hindus and the arrogance of the Sikhs, he concluded, arose out of their religious sentiments and fears.

Jawaharlal was also depressed to observe political discord and divisions re-emerging soon after the Belgaum Congress. The Swaraj Party, which had succeeded in securing a strong foothold in Congress by December 1924, began to disintegrate in 1925. Its dog-in-the-manger policy – to be in the arena of power and not to accept power – had come to be criticised by some of its members who were now in favour of accepting power. Some Hindu swarajists began to argue that the most effective way of strengthening their community against the Muslims was through the acceptance and exercise of ministerial power in the provincial governments. A number of swarajists, led by Maratha Hindus – M. R. Jayakar, M. C. Kelkar and S. B. Tombe – thus opted for what they called the policy of responsible co-operation with the Government. Motilal Nehru, who became the sole leader of the Party after the death of C. R. Das in June 1925, struggled hard to enforce the official policy and maintain unity among the swarajists. His domineering personality and anti-communal outlook, however, prevented him from establishing any *rapport* with the proud Maratha faction, which suspected him of harbouring anti-Maharashtra feeling. Jayakar even suspected him of duplicity: 'Pandit Motilalji takes all liberties with the programme, even to the extent of joining in social festivities with Government officers, but will not extend liberty to others even to suggest a variation.'[56]

The unity could not be maintained against the rising tide of communalism. During the course of 1926 the Party was to split between the Hindu communalists and the secularists. Even though Jawaharlal was not involved in the politics of the council chamber, the disintegration of the Swaraj Party further intensified his concern for national unity. He believed that a unity based on bargains and compromises between various groups could not last for long during peace-time. This kind of unity could only be sustained in an open war with the British, which then seemed too remote a possibility. What, then, should be the basis, the style and the goal of the national movement?

With a mind open and restless, baffled and tired, Jawaharlal stood at the crossroads.

It was at this point that he had to leave for Europe on 1 March 1926 with his wife and daughter. It was a journey undertaken primarily for Kamala's treatment, but he was to discover a possible solution to the Indian problem. He looked forward to his visit to Europe, though with a certain feeling of apprehension.

'It is quite likely that when I get there I shall be looking backward to India! . . . India is so like a woman – she attracts and repels.'[57]

CHAPTER SIX

Emergence of a Leader, 1926–9

Religion as practised in India has become the old man of the sea for us and it has not only broken our backs but stunted and almost killed all originality of thought and mind. Like Sinbad the Sailor we must get rid of this terrible burden before we can aspire to breathe freely or do anything useful.

Jawaharlal Nehru, September 1926

But we need not be communists, nor need we agree with their gospel of communism, in order to appreciate much that they have done.

Jawaharlal Nehru, September 1927

THE Europe to which Jawaharlal was returning after more than thirteen years had changed in the aftermath of the world war. Now it presented the options of communism and fascism, of class warfare and class collaboration. Jawaharlal first settled in Geneva for Kamala's treatment, eager to study these new European phenomena. Geneva, the seat of the League of Nations and the International Labour Office, had become an international city. To a student of international affairs the city offered exciting possibilities. Jawaharlal earnestly organised both his domestic life and intellectual pursuits. The domestic front offered him a new experience. For the first time he was put in a position of direct responsibility for his wife and daughter who, because they knew no French, were entirely dependent on him. He took on these responsibilities with enthusiasm. He rented a modest two-bedroom flat; Kamala was put under Henry Spahlinger's serum treatment for pulmonary tuberculosis; nine-year-old Indira was admitted to a local school. His principal domestic occupations lay in supervising Kamala's treatment and escorting Indira to and from school. He also tried to reduce the family budget. In this he was prompted more by sensitivity to his dependence on his father than by any real need, for though Motilal's resources were reduced there was still sufficient to support a comfortable standard of living for the Nehrus in Europe. The experiment did not last long, for when his father came to know that Jawaharlal had not bought an overcoat for himself until after he was exposed to a severe chill, and that only 'inferior stuff' was bought for Kamala, Motilal warned him against practising such false economy, particularly with regard to Kamala:

> It seems as if you have undertaken the trip merely to demonstrate how cheaply it is possible for a man, wife and child to live in a European town. It was hardly necessary to go so far afield for such a practical demonstration of domestic economy.[1]

In spite of changes of sanatoria and of courses of treatment, Kamala did not improve much during her prolonged stay in Europe. At times her temperature would become normal and she would gain some weight but she was never fully released from the clutches of the mortal disease. Motilal was disappointed to find that, whereas Kamala did not respond to the most expensive treatment Europe could offer, other patients had been cured with little or no treatment.[2] No explanation can be offered for this, except perhaps that Kamala did not succeed in overcoming her feelings of self-pity, loneliness and failure. The first few months of family closeness were disrupted by the arrival of the eighteen-year-old Krishna, Jawaharlal's youngest sister, who had been sent away from India to sort herself out after an unhappy love affair.[3] Later Vijayalakshmi Pandit arrived with her husband Ranjit. They were on holiday and their stay was a short one, but while it lasted Kamala receded into the background. Vijayalakshmi's fondness for her brother and the easy communication between them made Kamala feel inadequate. Even Indira, who in the beginning spoke to her mother in Hindi, after a few months of schooling in Geneva spoke only in English and French.[4] Jawaharlal himself had grown restless after being housebound for the first few months and needed an outlet for his suppressed energy.[5] He became increasingly absorbed in political activities which often took him away from Kamala.

It is difficult to conjecture how much self-confidence Kamala might have gained if Jawaharlal had given her his undivided attention. Perhaps not much, for she had come to believe in her utter incompatibility with her husband. Conscious of her upbringing in a purdah culture she considered herself incapable of standing on her own.[6] She believed in her husband's mission to fight for the independence of India, and more passionately so after her brief visit to London when her sensitive mind rebelled against the racial arrogance of the English.[7] She wanted to be her husband's comrade-in-arms in this fight, but it was too late, and in moments of acute depression she longed to die:

> Death is better than such a life, but even death is frightened of me. Death comes to those who are needed in this world, and does not claim those who are a burden on this earth. I was happy that this tuberculosis would relieve me of this world but I never knew that death itself would fight shy of me.[8]

Indira alone gave her a sense of fulfilment. Kamala believed that women were superior to men, morally as well as intellectually, and she nourished the ambition of fighting for the liberation of Indian women from the purdah culture, which had done so much damage to her own life. Conscious of her own impotence in this, she hung on to her daughter. Unlike her husband she had no aptitude for looking at a problem from different angles, and for shifting the blame on to the system rather than on to individuals. She openly conveyed to her daughter her ideas and impressions, her likes and dislikes of people, friends and relatives. Indira, having reached a receptive age, may well have drawn her mother's opinions into the foundation of her own understanding.

Though his marital life languished in the sanatoria, Jawaharlal's intellectual life prospered steadily. During these years in Europe he formed the bases of the policies which he was to pursue, not always consistently, for the rest of his life. His eagerness to grasp the realities of the European situation with a view to finding a solution to the Indian problem prompted him to undertake a series of visits to European capitals, and to meet a number of individuals, mostly past or present revolutionaries. He visited Italy in the summer of 1926, and though he did not like the rising tide of fascism he admired the fascist method of arousing the youth of the country through the song – 'Giovinezza' – which asked them to 'live dangerously'. The

General Strike in Britain (4–12 May 1926) excited him, and he felt its sudden collapse as a personal blow.[9] He visited England in September and saw the hungry and fear-stricken faces of the workers, punished and terrorised by magistrates who 'were themselves directors or managers of the coal mines'. All his sympathies were for the workers and for the Trade Union Congress on which, he believed, rested the emancipation of the down-trodden class.[10] During his visit to Berlin in the autumn of 1926 he was vastly impressed by the factories, and fully convinced that in industrialisation alone lay the path of progress and the diminution of poverty. He visited Brussels in February 1927 to attend the International Congress of Oppressed Nationalities Against Imperialism as an Indian National Congress representative. There he met nationalists and revolutionaries gathered from many parts of the world – from Asia, Latin America and Europe. The Brussels Congress represented conflicting ideas and interests between socialism and nationalism, and though Jawaharlal plunged into the stream of international socialism he emerged with a certain amount of doubt and uncertainty on the question of how to reconcile the one with the other. Being strongly committed to nationalism he expected the socialist movement to provide space for the nationalistic aspirations of peoples in the colonies. He thus found at the Brussels gathering more in common with the Asian nationalists, particularly from China, than with the revolutionary socialists of Europe for whom nationalism was a term of abuse.[11] His last important visit was to Moscow in November 1927 during the tenth-anniversary celebrations of the Revolution; he was accompanied by Kamala, his sister Krishna, and his father who had arrived in Europe in the summer of that year. The visit lasted only three days, but it was fruitful; it enabled Jawaharlal to endorse, as well as to modify, some of the impressions he had acquired about the Soviet socialist system, and also to write for the Indian newspapers a number of articles on Russia which were collected into a volume called *Soviet Russia*, published in 1928.

On these visits he met a large number of people. Some encounters were interesting for intellectual and historical reasons, though not politically significant. Meeting Romain Rolland in May 1926 was an exciting intellectual experience. He was fascinated by Madame Sun Yat Sen whom he met in Moscow; he found her delightful, young, full of life and energy.[12] Some political contacts, however, were disappointing. His meeting with the members of the Independent Labour Party in England convinced him that, no matter how politically advanced Britons might be, they were imperialist in matters relating to India.[13] Further experiences were to harden him in this view with far-reaching effects in the future: notably in 1945–6 when, if he had been able to place full trust in the Labour Government, it might have been useful. He met some Indian exiles and old revolutionaries whose names were familiar to him. He found them haunted by fear and suspicion and living in the past. There was no trace of the courage which he expected to find in these veterans of the war. He was drawn only towards two Indians – Virendranath Chattopadhyaya, brother of Mrs Sarojini Naidu, and M. N. Roy – and to these more for their intellectual outlook than for their communist politics. Of the two, Chattopadhyaya to some extent influenced Jawaharlal's political thinking, and in later years Jawaharlal felt obliged to explain to him his drift away from the exclusively socialistic into the all-inclusive nationalistic politics. It was not just intellectual flair or leftist politics which attracted Jawaharlal. There was in his fondness for people a definite bias towards the persecuted who were deprived of all worldly blessings, including family love, and who led a hand-to-mouth existence while suffering for a noble cause. He felt drawn towards such people and even envied them, for his own deprivations had not been as great as he would have liked. Chattopadhyaya represented this ideal in the 1920s; V. K. Menon, who had similar personality traits, was to come into Jawaharlal's orbit in the 1930s.

At this time, then, Jawaharlal was formulating, in a world context, goals and concepts for India. The sense of resignation with which he had arrived in Europe was short-lived; but while it lasted he spent some time ski-ing and skating, reading, improving his French and acquiring knowledge of international affairs. Even these pursuits had the definite object of keeping his body fit and his mind fertile. Among the Indian nationalists he was perhaps the only one who took physical fitness seriously. He was all too aware that politicians lost a great deal of time through illness, the cause of which he put down largely to over-indulgence and lack of exercise. In the Indian context a nationalist could perhaps win half the battle for leadership solely by the force of good health and perpetual energy. Jawaharlal, however, drew his overpowering energy not only from his good health but also from his teeming interest and his zeal in his political work.

He came more and more to feel the urgency of a solution to India's problems. His father's regular letters from India presented a distressing picture. Political morale was rapidly deteriorating. With the resurgence of Hindu communalism, national politics was steadily degenerating into communal factions. The communal Responsivists had seceded from the Swaraj Party and together with the Independents formed a National Party. What was left of Motilal's secular Swaraj Party was being torn into pieces by the Hindu Mahasabha and the Muslim League. Motilal's endeavours to keep his party firm against the communal *blitzkrieg* had failed. The communalists – headed by M. M. Malaviya and financed by the Hindu industrialist Birla – had inflicted a crushing defeat on the Swaraj Party at the triennial election held in November 1926. The year ended with the assassination by a Muslim of the Hindu nationalist Swami Shraddhananda, who had in the days of the Rowlatt satyagraha in 1919 risked his life fostering Hindu–Muslim unity. All Congressmen in the Legislative Assembly, Motilal reported to his son in March 1927, were, instead of pursuing their duty in opposing the Government, now 'tumbling over each other to shake hands with officials' and 'stealthily attending official functions' – though taking care that their names were not reported in the press.[14] Even the integrity of some respected nationalists – Lajpat Rai, Vithalbhai Patel, Srinivasa Iyengar – was no longer beyond reproach.[15] The very men who only six years ago had risked their lives, liberty and property as Gandhi's satyagrahis were now afflicted by fear, prejudice and lust for power and wealth.

Gandhi himself had withdrawn from the hurly-burly of active politics; he had at the beginning of 1926 imposed upon himself a year of silence on political matters, and instead became absorbed in promoting the constructive programme and writing his autobiography in instalments for *Young India*.

His advice to agitated politicians like Motilal was to let the evil forces of communalism play themselves out, and in the meantime to 'wait, watch and pray'.[16]

Muslim politics had also become more communalistic. Even the nationalist Muslims were fast losing their confidence in Congress, which seemed to be sinking under the weight of Hindu communalism. Hindu militancy influenced Muslim thinking, and thirty Muslim leaders met in Delhi in March 1927 and decided to renounce the eighteen-year-old Muslim right to a communal electorate, provided that Congress agreed to allow Muslims one-third of the seats in the central legislature, and also to the separation of Sind from the predominantly Hindu presidency of Bombay – a measure which would bring into existence another Muslim province (in addition to Bengal, Punjab, North-West Frontier Province and Baluchistan). The genuineness of the Muslim offer is doubtful. Though some, like M. A. Jinnah, might have felt seriously about this deal, the others backed out of the offer soon after it was made. The Muslim leadership, chronically divided and weak, was very susceptible to government pressure, and Lord Irwin's administration did not feel happy about the Muslim peace offer. The prospect of Hindu–Muslim unity was considered by the administration to be a threat to the Empire in India, and Lord Irwin (an inferior man with mediocre qualities, according to Motilal[17]) hastened to assure the Secretary of State that there was no immediate danger of a Hindu–Muslim agreement, and that most of the Muslims, excluding Jinnah, had made the proposal in order to create dissensions in Congress, for the nationalists led by Lajpat Rai and Malaviya were least likely 'to accept the essential conditions about Sind, Baluchistan and the North-West Frontier Province'.[18]

Irwin's view was proved right. Though the Congress Working Committee finally accepted the offer, during the course of its deliberations the Hindu nationalists had raised the alarm, which provided the Muslim leaders with a good excuse for abandoning it. Even Motilal himself was not agreeable to the extension of constitutional reforms in Baluchistan and North-West Frontier Province, for he anticipated that as soon as legislatures were established in these regions they would drift away from the national politics of Congress and turn into strongholds of Muslim communal politics. Mutual fear and suspicion prevented any agreement being concluded between the leaders of the two communities.

It seemed ridiculous to Motilal that at such a time Jawaharlal should be writing to the Congress Working Committee about the League Against Imperialism, the splendours of the Chinese national movement, the efficacy of Indo-Chinese solidarity, the danger of American imperialism in Latin America, and a host of other topics with which most Congressmen were not even familiar. By April 1927, Motilal had become thoroughly disillusioned and frustrated and, believing that there was 'no room for decent people in the public life of the country', he had almost made up his mind to retire. Summing up the Indian situation, he wrote to Jawaharlal:

> I do not think there is one man among the old or new set of Congressmen who will not go into a fainting fit on hearing the words complete independence for India. . . . Religion is the home of this country and unless a strong personality arises who will knock the prevailing Shibboleths on the head there is no hope for the God forsaken land. Malaviya and Co. are busy promoting what they consider to be the Hindu rights. Gandhi is killing himself over the Charka – M. Ali is thinking of retiring into a mosque and devoting the rest of his life to the reading of the Koran etc. We are fast settling down to the conditions of 20 years ago. I think there can be no greater misfortune for the country than the appointment of a Royal Commission of Reforms at this juncture. Any crumb which will be thrown at us will be gratefully accepted by all the 'sane' people.[19]

Motilal temporarily gave up his leadership in the summer of 1927 and joined his son in Europe for a holiday. He was tired. At the end of the year the European doctors were to tell him he was ill, which at the age of sixty-six he took to be ' the beginning of the end'.[20] But the end was still four years away, and in between lay for the Nehrus years of power and glory, of hopes and sufferings.

Jawaharlal had already formulated his policies for India when Motilal arrived in Europe.[21] His policies incorporated more of nationalistic urges and needs than socialistic imperatives; this was in no small measure due to his unwillingness ever to accept any system in its entirety. He believed that world peace was a noble objective which could be achieved through a world organisation consisting of large federal units and functioning more independently than the League of Nations, which he saw as being steadily choked to death by the war-loving states of Europe. If such an international body came into existence, it would be quite legitimate for the countries of the world to yield up to it a measure of their freedom of action. Just as the emergence of an international organisation seemed a logical progression, so did the coming into being of large blocs of nations; the age of small states living in isolation was over. He thus conceived the idea of an Asian bloc (including the Soviet Union) with India possibly as its nerve-centre. But first India must be free. India's independence was vital for Asia because western imperialism would find no ground to stand on once it had lost its hold on India. The national movement in India, and in all imperialist colonies, was therefore a necessary step towards international socialism. He felt it would be hypocritical to call a national movement reactionary, though he admitted that in independent countries like Greece, Poland, Italy, Spain, Hungary or Germany such movements were tending to become dictatorial, anti-international and unprogressive, and were falling into the imperialistic and capitalistic fold. Nationalism in colonial countries, however, must have 'a broader base and derive its strength from and work specially for the masses, the peasants and the other workers'.[22] The Indian national movement must align itself exclusively with the peasants and labourers. Such an alignment would have two distinct advantages. First, it would give the national movement the substance of real unity, which though not all-inclusive would generate class war, which in turn, Jawaharlal believed, would annihilate communalism. The communal leaders, Hindu and Muslim, belonging as they did to the higher strata of society, would unite to fight their common class foe. An open class war would most assuredly destroy the hold on the nation of caste and communal alliances.

The Indian national movement had to be at once uncompromisingly anti-capitalist, anti-feudal, anti-bourgeois and, of course, anti-imperialist. The movement must aim at establishing a democratic socialist republic in a fully independent India, and must thus reject outright dominion status for India within the British Commonwealth. Such a goal would not only intensify the conflict between the national and imperial forces but it would also revive the nation to manhood, for the Indians' fear of claiming independence as their due was for Jawaharlal 'a vivid illustration of our own mental degradation and of the injury that England had done to us'.[23] He put forward other reasons too. He suspected that a dominion link with Britain might mean retention by Britain of some control over India's defence and foreign policy. Independence, then, would mean very little if it was, for example, of the type which then prevailed in Egypt, 'with a foreign army of occupation to overawe the National Parliament and British cruisers to enforce the decisions of the British Cabinet'.[24] Jawaharlal paid no heed to Balfour's declaration, made in 1926, which defined Great Britain and the Dominions as autonomous communities, equal in status, and in no way subordinate one to another. In this he saw only Britain's desperate attempt to prevent the Dominions from drifting apart. Even if Balfour's definition were accurate, it applied to Dominions (such as Canada, Australia, South Africa) with which Britain had sentimental ties; India, he believed, had no such tie nor even a common economic interest. India would not only be an outsider within the British Commonwealth but she would also tip the balance against Britain; by virtue of her vast population and latent resources, India would inevitably become the predominant partner in the group, and consequently the centre of gravity would shift from London to Delhi, a possibility which no one could imagine Britain permitting.[25]

The 'bully of all eastern nations striving to be free', the friend of every dictator 'whether it be in Italy or Spain or Hungary or Greece', the conservative influence even in the League of Nations – Britain appeared to Jawaharlal 'the most reactionary force in the world'. This was, he reckoned, partly due to 'the comic opera government' she had possessed for some years, but mainly because she 'has had too long a spell of Empire not to be corrupted by it and it will take time to live this down'.[26] He saw no possibility that the two countries might associate in some form of commonwealth until India had attained complete independence and Britain had fully forsaken her imperial attitude. India could associate with Britain on an equal basis only after she was divorced from the imperial wedlock. This was like saying, a British friend of Jawaharlal remarked in later years, that a man and wife cannot possibly live together in harmony and affection until the divorce court has severed the nuptial knot.[27] But it was not a question of a husband and wife separating, Jawaharlal replied, 'but one of, if I may use a similar analogy, the perpetrator of a rape being made to part company with his victim'.[28]

Friendship with all countries formed the core of the foreign policy Jawaharlal then conceived for a free India. A closer contact, however, was to be cultivated with the countries of the East. He ruled out the possibility of a pan-Islamic bloc threatening India. This was pure fancy, for each of the Islamic countries, he confidently asserted, was 'developing on intensely national lines' and there was 'absolutely no room in them for an external policy based on religion'.[29] But there was in his thinking a definite bias towards the Soviet Union and China. There were many reasons for his attraction to Soviet Russia, but the most important one, as he saw it, was her non-imperialist and non-racial outlook: 'The principles, and what is more important the practice, of Soviet Russia have always, with one exception, been in favour of the fullest self-determination of various peoples. She has always been for the oppressed and the exploited'.[30] (The one exception was Russia's suppression of the independence movement in Georgia.) Furthermore, friendship with Russia was a defence necessity for India: 'Russia is our neighbour, a giant sprawling half over Asia and Europe, and between such neighbours there can be either amity or enmity. Indifference is out of the question'.[31] A close relationship between the two countries was possible because they had so much in common, both being vast agricultural countries with only the beginnings of industrialisation and both faced with massive poverty and illiteracy: 'The two countries are today too similar to be exploited by each other and there can be no economic motive for Russia to covet India'.[32] He was not enamoured of the Soviet communist government, though he had adopted the principles of socialism; but he thought it was possible to be friends with Russia without being communist. The example of Turkey was encouraging, for though she was by no means communist she was apparently on the Russian side in her external policy. Then there was much to be learned from Russia, for if she succeeded, as appeared to be the case, in finding a satisfactory solution for all her economic problems India might then adopt some of the Soviet methods in solving her own problems.

India's affinity with China seemed to Jawaharlal to be even more emphatic. Whereas India had problems similar to Russia's, she had in common with China the heritage of a great ancient civilisation. Tradition retained its significance even in his socialistic thinking. Tradition, he believed, was the major constituent of a country's genius, and that genius must find its place in any political system the country might adopt. Hence communism when it came to China would be modified by Chinese genius and would accordingly cease to be pure Marxism: 'Even Soviet Russia, owing to the pressure of the peasantry, has had to give up part of its communism, and in China where the small peasant is the deciding factor, the departure from pure communism will be all the greater.'[33] This belief was, perhaps, partly one of convenience, since his admiration for the Chinese national movement might otherwise have been watered down by the fact that in China the movement was carried by the United Front consisting of the nationalists and communists. The final break between the two had not yet come and when it did, in 1927, Jawaharlal's sympathy gradually shifted from Chiang Kai-shek towards Mao Tse-tung and Chou En-lai.[34] But at present Jawaharlal was fascinated by the Chinese nationalists and their finely developed boycott of foreign goods. He had met the Chinese delegates at the Brussels Congress and had been deeply impressed by their energy, enthusiasm and driving force, and was led to wish regretfully that 'we in India might also develop some of this energy and driving force, at the expense if need be of some of our intellectuality'.[35]

Jawaharlal visualised the emergence of a strong Chinese Socialist Republic in alliance with the Soviet Union – a phenomenon which would dominate the whole of Asia and

Europe and threaten the very existence of the British Empire. Being aware of this possibility, the British, he reckoned, were preparing for a war against China and the Soviet Union; a war they must fight within five years lest China become too strong ever to be beaten down. Thus, in 1927, he was convinced that in a few years' time a world war would break out, in which Britain would align herself against the Soviet Union with other European powers. He felt that India must declare unequivocally now, and keep repeating, that she would not be dragged into such a war without her express consent, and that if she were bullied or hustled into it she would not help in any way. A free India, Jawaharlal visualised, would have no fear of invasion from Russia or China, and if she were ever invaded her vast defence would lie in the support of her peasantry and workers, for they would fight for their country and for their own freedom with the valour and doggedness that come from a new hope. India's main strength, however, was to lie in her peaceful and friendly policy towards all countries.

Jawaharlal displayed more positiveness in his thoughts on India's social and economic problems. Religion, to which he had been drawn in 1920–2, now seemed to him India's deadliest enemy. It was at the root of the stagnation and inertia from which the country was suffering. The very factors which made for India's strength in the past were now a heavy load on her back, preventing her from going forward or adapting herself to present-day conditions. The basis of Indian society was authority – the authority of sacred books, of old customs, of immemorial habits: 'No country or people who are slaves to dogma and the dogmatic mentality can progress, and unhappily our country and people have become extraordinarily dogmatic, and little-minded.'[36] Thus, religion and all that went with it must be scotched before it swamped the country and its peoples. Mass education alone would release Indian society from the clutches of religion, of the joint-family system, and of a host of other social evils: 'I think what is required in India most is a course of study of Bertrand Russell's books, or at any rate some of them.'[37] But large-scale education must go hand in hand with industrialisation. Jawaharlal was fully committed to industrial civilisation. There was for him no other alternative. Gandhi's ideal of a Rama Rajya* meant regressing to a primitive agricultural civilisation which was just not possible: 'I think that western or rather industrial civilisation is bound to conquer India, maybe with many changes and adaptations, but none the less in the main based on industrialism.'[38] Admitting that industrialism had produced some evils in the western world, he argued that this was due to the system under which it had flourished. That system was capitalism, under whose evil influence the progress of science had been prostituted and the beauty of life had been sacrificed to a mad race for profit and wealth. To avoid conflict and competition, industrialism in India must be based on socialist principles; it should be planned and controlled and yet at the same time must leave some room for private enterprise and initiative. He was aware that state ownership of all means of production was not possible even in Soviet Russia.

Nearly two years of free thinking and policy-making for India had revived Jawaharlal's zeal. He had conceived a solution for the Indian problem which he believed was more comprehensive than the Gandhian theory, which seemed to have collapsed in recent years into a dogma of inaction. Gandhi had occasionally tried to restrain Jawaharlal from cultivating too wide a world consciousness: 'On our side there is danger of people again looking to external forces and external aid for salvation instead of seeking to achieve it by evolving internal strength.'[39] Gandhi's views and outlook appeared too narrow to Jawaharlal. He reminded the Mahatma: 'Our salvation can of course come only from the internal strength that we may evolve but one of the methods of evolving such strength should be studying other people and their ideas.'[40] A confrontation between them seemed inevitable, but Jawaharlal felt too confident to be over-awed by such a prospect. He was determined to organise and lead a movement which would challenge both British imperialism and Indian conservatism. The occa-

*This was Gandhi's vision of an ideal state which, he believed, existed in ancient India. It was to be a fully decentralised non-industrial society with the village as its main unit. Each man in this society was to produce with his hands what he needed for his simple existence. This society, Gandhi visualised, would have no room for modern machines, competition, exploitation and profiteering.

sion for him to throw down the challenge arose with the appointment of the Simon Commission in November 1927. He took it as an affront that not a single Indian was included in the Commission, which was supposed to propose further constitutional reforms for India. He revolted against the conception which he believed lay behind the Simon Commission – that the British Parliament was there to give to Indians and withhold from them what it liked, and that Indians were for ever appurtenances of the British Empire. Earlier in the year Indian dignity had been humiliated by Katherine Mayo's book, *Mother India*, which had focused entirely on the evils and immoralities of Indian society. Jawaharlal had commented that it would have been easy enough for anyone so minded to write a similar book about France or Britain or America, and by picking out the most disgusting facts from the police records and Sunday papers to conclude that it was a loathsome country, past all redemption. Many Indian nationalists feared that *Mother India* might come in handy to those members of the Simon Commission and other Britons who sought justification for the continuance of the Raj in the argument that India was not ripe for self-government. Jawaharlal had no such fear; he was opposed to the very idea of Britain sitting in judgement on India. It was in this mood of total defiance that he sailed for India, in the first week of December 1927, accompanied by his wife, daughter and youngest sister; Motilal stayed behind in Europe for a few more months. Jawaharlal reached Madras in good time to blow the wind of change into the annual session of Congress held there in the last week of December.

From December 1927 to December 1929, Jawaharlal played the leadership role in various ways: in setting a new basis and goal for the national movement, in acquiring a new following, in increasing his popularity among the masses, in intensifying the conflict between nationalist India and the British Raj, and in strengthening and mobilising the Congress organisation for the civil disobedience movement of 1930. By the end of this period, at the age of forty, he had come to be recognised by most of his immediate colleagues as a man of superior qualities; he was adored by the masses as their glorious prince, identified by the Government as a leader to be reckoned with and, above all, crowned by the nation as the Congress President.

The controversy over independence or dominion status for India that gripped the nation throughout 1928 was inaugurated by Jawaharlal when, in order to set a clearer goal for the national movement than swaraj – which was vaguely defined and differently interpreted – he moved, on 27 December 1927, at the Madras Congress, the resolution that this 'Congress declares the goal of the Indian people to be complete National Independence'.[41]

This resolution, which Gandhi thought was 'hastily conceived and thoughtlessly passed',[42] was at first not taken seriously by the right-wing Congressmen: Rajendra Prasad pointed out that the resolution would turn Congress into the laughing-stock of the world; some condemned it as downright 'stupid'. For Jawaharlal and his leftist followers in Congress, however, the new creed of independence symbolised defiance and revolt. Indeed it required, in the late 1920s, great courage and initiative to propound this creed, for not only was it then the government view that it was seditious to talk of complete independence,[43] but the majority of Congressmen too could not, at that time, foresee an India fully set free from British influence.

Jawaharlal intended to win support for his independence movement from the educated youth and the masses – labourers and peasants. With this support forthcoming, he calculated, it might be possible to dispense with the upper-class element in the national movement. But he intended these changes to take place within the Congress organisation itself, for he never thought of starting a rival party. His strategy thus lay in exercising pressure and persuasion over Congress to broaden its base and march firmly towards its new goal. He founded pressure groups – the Republican Party of Congress (December 1927) and the Independence for India League (August 1928) – to secure the support of the masses for a socialist republican ideal, to launch a crusade against communalism (no member of the Independence for India League was to belong to any communal party) and to carry out propaganda for the Independence of India.

He forged a direct link with Indian youth through his

speeches and articles published mostly in the nationalist dailies, the *Hindu* and *Tribune*.[44] Each of his articles brought a flood of letters from young men pledging their full support and loyalty. Youth organisations emerged in almost every province of India, each offering its presidency to Jawaharlal. His young socialist colleagues started a number of youth journals and magazines. By the autumn of 1928, Jawaharlal was elected to the presidency of the All-India Youth Congress. He thus gained a new following among the youth of India. They understood his language and to some extent his ideas. Yet it was his image, more than his goals and concepts, which drew young India towards Jawaharlal: the image of a youthful personality, of courage and defiance, of a self-denying patriot and hero, of an intellectual with a world outlook. They could not aspire to emulate Gandhi, who was austere and incomprehensible; but they longed to copy Jawaharlal, whose attributes seemed attainable. There was an enthusiastic response among them to Jawaharlal's call to live dangerously, 'to stand for progress, rebellion and action and not passive inactivity'.[45] But their energy and enthusiasm once aroused needed to be contained in an organised and disciplined movement. Jawaharlal was an inspired performer but a poor stage-manager, for he had no great aptitude for the dull details of organisation and for the persistence and perseverance it required. In addition, the vastness of the country obliged him to rely upon his provincial lieutenants for the implementation of his ideas, and a certain aloofness and loftiness in his character inhibited him from being sufficiently intimate with his colleagues and lieutenants. This handicapped him in forming and running a party or a group within a party. He admitted to Gandhi, rather penitently, in 1929:

> It is my good fortune that I have more the good will of a number of people but with this good will there is also a lack of confidence. I represent nobody but myself. I have not the politician's flair for forming groups and parties. My only attempt in this direction – the formation of the Independence for India League last year – was a hopeless failure so far as I was concerned.[46]

But this failing – based as it was partly on his reluctance to align himself with any sub-group – had certain advantages.

Among other things, it gave his leadership a continental status. In times of crisis caused by divisions in the national movement he could, with enormous ease, soar above political factions. He thus derived his strength more from his ever-growing popularity among the young and the peasantry than from his steady hold on any organisation. The Republican Party died soon after its birth, the Independence for India League staggered on for some time and then collapsed, but Jawaharlal's popularity steadily grew.

Throughout 1928 the political atmosphere in urban India was alight with defiance. All political parties except a faction of the Muslim League had decided to boycott the Simon Commission, whose members were now in India. The Madras session of Congress had not only instructed the nation to boycott Sir John Simon and his team, but also asked all parties in India to unite and meet the British challenge (as thrown at Indians by Lord Birkenhead, the Conservative Secretary of State for India) that Indians could not produce a constitution of their own. In pursuance of a Congress directive the representatives of all parties (including Liberal, Labour, Muslim League, Sikh League, Hindu Mahasabha) had met, and in May 1928 they appointed a sub-committee under Motilal Nehru, who had by then returned from Europe, to draft the outlines of a constitution for India. Jawaharlal, who had again been nominated in December 1927 as one of the general secretaries of Congress, also acted as secretary of this sub-committee which came to be popularly called the Nehru Committee after his father. The leaders of the two opposing factions, Motilal and Simon, were, as it happens, good professional friends. The Nehru Committee's report, however, was prepared (most of the drafting was done by Motilal with the help of Jawaharlal and Tej Bahadur Sapru) in less than three months, and nearly two years ahead of the Simon Commission's report.

Motilal applied all his professional skill to the drafting of the Report, but it was not entirely to Jawaharlal's liking. While admitting, rather over-optimistically, that the Nehru Report had given 'the finishing kick to communalism', Jawaharlal was aggrieved to find that under the pressure of right-wing thinking and in order to maintain the façade of all-party unity the Report restricted the national goal only to dominion status, which contradicted the independence resolution passed at the Madras Congress, and, of course, utterly disregarded his own principles which he had passionately preached for over six months to his supporters and had clearly avowed to his leftist colleagues, including S. C. Bose.[47] As a result, Jawaharlal's relations with his father became severely strained during the latter part of 1928. Earlier in the year he had confronted Gandhi, who had warned him against overstepping the mark with his socialist ideas and encouraging mischief-makers and hooligans.[48] Gandhi had also reminded him that the time was not yet ripe to dispense with the rich and educated upper middle classes and to turn Congress into a peasant–worker movement.[49] Jawaharlal had at first rebelled, accusing the Mahatma of indecisiveness: 'During the non-co-operation period you were supreme; you were in your element and automatically you took the right step. But since you came out of prison something seems to have gone wrong and you have been very obviously ill at ease'.[50] Gandhi challenged him to come into the open: 'Write to me a letter for publication showing your differences. I will print it in "Young India" and write a brief reply'.[51] But his respect for Gandhi's wisdom and his regard for the power he exercised on the mind and heart of the people, and some doubts concerning the efficacy of his own strategy, made Jawaharlal retract to some extent, though he was not reconciled to Gandhi on the points of difference between them:

> No one has moved me and inspired me more than you and I can never forget your exceeding kindness to me. There can be no question of our personal relations suffering. But even in the wider sphere am I not your child in politics, though perhaps a truant and errant child?[52]

The personal bond between the two had been restored and this bond was to keep them together in politics in spite of the enormous differences between their respective approaches.

Jawaharlal's opposition to the Nehru Report was, like his confrontation with Gandhi, based on a point of strategy. A national demand for independence would demonstrate an utter rejection of the Raj, would intensify the conflict with the imperial system and mobilise the masses behind the national movement. He knew very well that even a demand for dominion status was not going to be accepted by the British Government unless it had a sanction and force behind it. The call for independence would create that mass sanction and embolden Congress to declare war against the Raj. The demand for dominion status represented a middle-class council-chamber politics and consequently would fail to arouse the revolutionary spirit among the masses. The Nehru Report thus seemed to prevent Jawaharlal's strategy of resistance finding its way into national policy. But he was not disheartened, nor did he abandon his hope of setting the national movement on the war-path. He was convinced that the Nehru Report would be unacceptable to the Government, and thought it would be wise to let the rightists abandon their optimism in their own time. He must, however, ensure that when their moment of great disappointment came, instead of stooping further down, they would rise up and join the war party.

Jawaharlal thus continued building up a belligerent force amongst the young, the labourers and the peasants. There was labour unrest in the industrial cities of Bombay, Bengal and Bihar. This was to erupt into a number of major strikes early in 1929, and to attract on the one hand the sympathy and support of the Communist Party of Britain[53] and on the other the fear and wrath of the Government of India which, suspecting that there lay behind these industrial troubles a communist conspiracy to undermine the British Raj, rounded up thirty-one labour leaders in March 1929 and put them on trial in Meerut. Jawaharlal reached the urban labour force through the trade unions, and, while steering a middle course between the rightists and leftists, managed to establish a *rapport* with both wings. By late 1928 he was elected President of the All-India Trades Union Congress. His name was put forward by the moderate group because he stood the best chance of defeating the other candidate, who was a radical.[54] Jawaharlal increased his popularity among the rural masses as well. Not only did he draw large rural gatherings in his own province but he was also now next to Gandhi in attaining popularity in provinces other than his own. Province after province invited him to preside over its conferences, and his national stature grew day by day. Wherever he went he drew large crowds, even in the south where, in his own words, he was 'carried about from place to place like a performing animal' and made to hold forth in face of the strong language-barrier.[55]

While Jawaharlal was building up a fighting spirit among the masses, Motilal was involved in the politics of bargaining and gaining agreement among all parties on his report, which was to be considered at the national convention of all parties in Calcutta in December 1928. Even though his report had been ostensibly accepted at the All-Parties Conference in Lucknow in August, the Hindu and Muslim communalists persisted in opposing it for different reasons. Some Hindu leaders opposed the Report mainly because it conceded the creation of Sind as a separate province – an act which, they feared, would weaken the Hindu hold on the economy of that province.[56] The Muslim leaders (excluding the Congress Muslims like Dr Ansari) found that the Report took away all the Muslim rights and privileges (including their rights to a separate electorate and to representation in legislatures in a proportion greater than the percentage of their population) and gave hardly anything in return. They even suspected that the creation of another Muslim province would mean nothing if real power was to be vested in a Hindu-dominated centre under the unitary form of government which the Report prescribed for India. Determined to see his report through the national convention, Motilal began to manœuvre. He had already forestalled the Hindu attack on his report at the Lucknow conference by suppressing the Sind Committee Report which augured financial doom for a separated Sind.[57] Now he concentrated on minimising the leftist and Muslim opposition. He asked Gandhi to strengthen his position against the leftists, including his own son, by recommending 'the adoption of Dominion Status by the Congress without prejudice to the ultimate goal of Complete Independence'.[58] Gandhi complied by explaining to the people that swaraj was like a rose which smells just as sweet whether it is called dominion status or independence. Motilal planned to weaken Muslim opposition through propaganda and stratagem. Vast sums of money, most of which was contributed by G. D. Birla, the Hindu capitalist, were spent in producing and circulating copies of the Nehru

Report among the Muslims. He made a deal with Lajpat Rai, the Hindu leader; the latter was to mount a stiff Hindu opposition to the Muslim demands.[59] It was calculated that in the face of firm Hindu opposition the Muslim leaders would reduce their demands to a minimum. When that happened Lajpat Rai was to come forward at the Calcutta convention and, on behalf of the Hindu communalists, accept the minimum Muslim demand. The artifice was a success in the beginning but ultimately rebounded on Motilal. Lajpat Rai delivered his tirade from a Hindu Mahasabha platform, and the Muslim demands began to shrink. Then the unfortunate happened; Lajpat Rai died on 17 November about a month before the Calcutta convention. His militant speech was widely circulated at the Calcutta convention as his last will and testament, and it stiffened Hindu resistance even against the most modest Muslim demands.

Calcutta presented a great political spectacle in the latter part of December 1928. Representatives of eighty-seven parties of various denominations met on the twenty-second in the Congress-dominated national convention.[60] Never before had so many parties assembled together and achieved so little. The year had been one of bargainings and compromises for Congress. Its presidency was therefore, at Gandhi's suggestion, offered to Motilal Nehru, 'the man for honourable compromise'. Besides, Bengal and other major provinces wanted him to wear the crown. Calcutta received Motilal – the President-elect – in grand style. Then the business began. Each major party was holding its annual session simultaneously with the national convention. Motilal first faced opponents from within the Congress ranks. S. C. Bose and Jawaharlal attacked the dominion clause of the Nehru Report. Gandhi put all his political weight behind a compromise formula. He asked Congress to accept the Report in its entirety and to give the Government an ultimatum that if dominion status was not conceded to India by December 1929, then Congress would revive non-violent non-co-operation. His original suggestion to give a two-year time-limit to the Government was thus, under leftist pressure, reduced to one. The idea of an ultimatum with a time-limit soothed Jawaharlal. It also served his purpose. He knew that the Government would not comply and that Congress would be obliged to take the militants' road. The time-limit was thus for him a year in which to prepare Congress and the country for war. But his young radical colleagues did not share his optimism and foresight. He thus sang their chorus half-heartedly, until S. C. Bose's amendment to Gandhi's compromise resolution was defeated by 1356 votes to 973.

Muslim opposition to the Nehru Report came from Jinnah, who implored the convention to alleviate the Muslim fear of the Hindus by accepting their minimum demands. As Muslim opinion was then divided into at least three major sections, and a section of the Muslim League was already supporting the Nehru Report, Jinnah's representation did not carry much weight and he was hooted down and silenced by the Hindu communalists on the Congress side.

The Nehru Report appeared to have emerged unscathed, but it had only the semblance of unity behind it. Many knew that its life would be short, though some politicians may have taken it seriously and, knowing that a further instalment of constitutional reform was in the offing, believed that dominion status might be conceded by the British within the time-limit set by Congress. But the Government of India was certain from the very day the Congress ultimatum was issued that 'this condition cannot be fulfilled'.[61] It also believed that the ultimatum was a bid for time during which Congress intended to prepare itself for the civil disobedience movement. At the same time the Government recognised Jawaharlal as the leader of the new party and wondered whether it was possible to forestall the impending movement by immediately convicting him on some charge or other.[62] Congress recognition of Jawaharlal's leadership soon followed.

The task of organising and strengthening Congress for direct action fell on Jawaharlal, who had been reappointed its General Secretary at the Calcutta Congress. Throughout 1929 he performed this function with considerable zeal and efficiency. Inspections of Congress provincial headquarters were started; Jawaharlal himself inspected nearly half a dozen provinces.[63] Soon after the stock-taking, he launched a vigorous campaign for extending and strengthening the organisation in provinces where it was weak, and for consolidating and regularising it where it was strong. Recruitment was speeded up; by mid-1929 the total Congress membership (in twenty-one linguistically constituted Congress provinces) was brought up to 477,440.[64] He reached the masses not only through the rural congress committees, but also through a number of peasant and labour organisations which had been (at his suggestion made in the previous year) affiliated to Congress.[65] His presidency of the Trades Union Congress and of several youth organisations gave him a leverage over the most active section of the urban populace. He missed no opportunity to gain new constituents. He even approached the Anglo-Indians, who had hitherto remained aloof from any movement which bore the epithet 'Indian'.[66] The Anglo-Indians responded to him hopefully, partly owing to their disillusionment at being told repeatedly by the Simon Commission and the Government of India that they must regard themselves as 'Natives of India'.[67] If they were to behave as Indians, how could they ignore Jawaharlal – the voice of India, the bridge between Indian and English cultures?

By mid-1929, Jawaharlal was in the running for the Congress presidency. This was not always a mark of leadership; at times it was offered for other reasons. Indeed Gandhi played an important role in the selection, and it was mainly owing to his overpowering influence that the candidate of his choice was often elevated to this office uncontested. Gandhi acted almost like a judge, but his choice was often confined to the recognised competitors for the post. Jawaharlal had been considered for it in 1927 while he was in Europe: in the estimation of Gandhi and Motilal he was then probably the best choice, the next best being Vallabhbhai Patel.[68] When sounded on the matter, Jawaharlal had emphasised his differences with Gandhi on the question of Congress goals, and pointed out that he did not believe in the policy of wait and see and trusting providence to right the matter.[69] The negotiation was carried no further, however, mainly because Gandhi was seized by another consideration. Hindu–Muslim tension had reached its nadir, and Gandhi calculated that a Muslim president might regain for Congress the confidence of the Muslims; hence the 1927 presidency was offered to Dr Ansari.[70] In 1928 two names captured the limelight – Motilal for his Nehru Report, and Vallabhbhai Patel for his success in organising the peasants of Bardoli district, Gujarat, in a no-rent satyagraha against the large increase in the land tax which had been imposed, somewhat arbitrarily, by the Bombay Government. Jawaharlal was perhaps more popular than his father and Patel but he was also a radical, suspect in the eyes of the Congress right-wingers who controlled the party machine.[71] The Congress presidency thus lay between Motilal and Patel, and Gandhi recommended the former.

The election of the Congress President for 1929 was significant; it was like selecting a general to conduct an impending war. The obvious choice was Gandhi, but the competition lay between Vallabhbhai Patel and Jawaharlal. Between these two future rulers of India there was little trust or understanding. Patel saw Jawaharlal as a dreamer and an idealist. Jawaharlal saw in Patel a mere soldier of limited imagination. The right wing closed its ranks behind Patel, who had a firm hold over the party organisation and was loyally supported by Rajendra Prasad and Rajaji. Jawaharlal had captured the imagination of young India, and was more popular among the masses. He had decidedly more appeal for the Muslims. In a way the contest between the two symbolised the contest between the Party and the people. It was, however, the party organisation which had to choose the President. The Congress constitution empowered the provincial Congress committees to nominate candidates and vote for the presidency.[72]

Of the eighteen provincial Congress committees, ten recommended Gandhi, five Patel and three Jawaharlal.[73] Pressure was put on Gandhi to accept the presidency, but he was reluctant. It was not his style to accept an office in institutional politics; he preferred to operate as a super-president. He was also aware that not all Indians were with him; the young socialists and the new generation, for example, were decidedly critical of his policies and methods. He decided to decline. The contest was now between his two principal lieutenants. It was not a hard decision for Gandhi. At the meeting of the All-India Congress Committee in September 1929, Gandhi withdrew his name for the presidency in favour of Jawaharlal. Patel accepted Gandhi's decision and dropped out of the running. Jawaharlal was thus unanimously elected as the Congress President.

A number of factors influenced Gandhi's decision. The foremost was his own belief in Jawaharlal's qualities of leadership. In recommending him to the nation Gandhi said:

> In bravery he is not to be surpassed. Who can excel him in the love of the Country? . . . And if he has the dash and the rashness of a warrior, he has also the prudence of a statesman. A lover of discipline, he has shown himself to be capable of rigidly submitting to it even where it has seemed irksome. . . . He is pure as crystal, he is truthful beyond suspicion. He is a knight *sans peur, sans reproche.* The nation is safe in his hands.[74]

His recommendation was also in fact an endorsement of the people's choice. The young, restless India (socialists, students, peasant and labour leaders) looked up to Jawaharlal for leadership. Jawaharlal's presidency promised unity on a wider Congress base.

Then there were personal considerations. Gandhi's fondness for Jawaharlal had been often ruffled by their intellectual differences. He calculated that Jawaharlal's radicalism might become tempered if he were saddled with the responsibility of the Congress presidency. And the risk of Jawaharlal running wild with Congress was minimal, for an organisation having a well-defined constitution and well-known traditions, Gandhi assured the rightists, was the least likely to be ruled by an individual. Besides, Congress was then substantially dominated by the right-wingers.

What, then, of Patel, the hero of Bardoli? He certainly excelled Jawaharlal in organisational ability, practical wisdom, ruthlessness and tenacity of purpose. But these qualities were partly due to his being set in his style and way of thinking. He lacked intellectual flair, dynamism, world outlook. His qualities fitted him for running a government in a stable society, but in the Indian context he was destined to be the runner-up if the competition lay between him and Jawaharlal. He could not lead Jawaharlal but he could function as a brake on him. The role into which he was first cast by Gandhi he was to play for the rest of his life, and often to the annoyance of Jawaharlal. Gandhi thus felt no remorse when he backed the winning horse. He had no fear of losing Patel's loyalty, for Patel was committed to the Mahatma as a soldier to his commander. Besides, he had been promised the Congress presidency of the following year.

Jawaharlal's reactions were mixed. He was happy to be elevated to the highest office the nation then offered, but he would have felt happier if the office had come to him in a normal way, via an election, rather than as a gift from Gandhi. It hurt his pride that he should be led into the office, as it seemed to him, through a trap-door rather than through the main entrance.[75] He swallowed his pride, but he could not ignore the fact that the Congress he was to lead was the stronghold of the right-wingers. His socialist friends and colleagues, especially those abroad – for example, Chattopadhyaya from Berlin – warned him that he was being trapped by the 'cunning Mahatmaji' and that if it was too late for him to escape he must at least endeavour to bring about a split in Congress 'in order to destroy a patched-up unity and clear the way for a solid anti-imperialist movement'.[76]

Jawaharlal himself did not suspect the Mahatma of dubious motives, and recognised, moreover, that Gandhi was indispensable to the national movement. He also doubted the efficacy of pushing the right–left conflict in Congress to breaking-point. Such a split might become inevitable if the rightists backed out of the ultimatum which Congress had given to the Government or were bullied by the Government into accepting something which was far less than they had asked for, but should not be manœuvred just as a matter of principle.

Such a situation arose when Irwin, the Viceroy, made his first move to placate Congress. In his statement of 31 October he assured the Indian leaders that it was the intention of His Majesty's Government to concede dominion status to India, but he did not specify when this was to be. This vague promise satisfied the rightists, however, and on the following day they issued on behalf of Congress a manifesto (signed, among others, by Gandhi and Motilal) expressing their willingness to negotiate with the British Government at the proposed Round Table Conference. Their only proviso was that a scheme of dominion constitution for India should be drawn up at the Conference. Jawaharlal opposed the Manifesto, but Gandhi pointed out that its terms were consistent with the Congress ultimatum. He thus reluctantly added his signature to the

Manifesto, only to discover that some liberal-minded leaders were prepared to step down further if the Delhi Manifesto was not accepted by the British as a basis for negotiation. If such a passive line were not scotched outright, then the prospect of a straight fight with the British would be completely blighted.

He therefore applied personal pressure to stop Congress treading a conciliatory path. He resigned from the Congress Working Committee and even threatened to renounce his presidency.[77] He then lodged his complaint with Gandhi:

> I accepted the presidentship of the Congress with great misgivings but in the hope that we shall fight on a clear issue next year. That issue is already clouded and the only reason for my acceptance has gone. . . . I cannot be president if the policy of the Congress is what might be described as that of Malaviyaji.[78]

He had some difficulty in explaining to his somewhat surprised radical colleagues why he had put his signature to the Delhi Manifesto. He assured them that it was done 'to give some rope to those' who wanted to adopt a compromising policy.[79] He had reasons to hope that the Delhi Manifesto would not be accepted by the Government and that Congress would declare war at its next annual session. As it turned out, he was right. The Delhi Manifesto failed to break any new ground with the British Government. The pacifists in Congress were persuaded to bury their differences and march on to the battlefield together.

Lahore, the capital of the Punjab, was heavy with excitement and anxiety when Congress assembled there for its annual session in the last week of December 1929. The citizens crowded into every available space, even clambering on to roofs and trees, to hail their President-elect, who, as if to symbolise the uniqueness of the occasion, rode up on a white charger, leading a detachment of Congress cavalry, like a general marching towards the battle front. The occasion had a personal significance for Motilal: this was the first time in the history of Congress that a son had succeeded his father as President. Motilal proudly made over charge to Jawaharlal, saying that what the father was unable to accomplish the son would achieve.

In his presidential address Jawaharlal restated his goals and policies for Congress. While confessing that he was a socialist and a republican, he admitted that in the present circumstances it might not be possible to adopt a full socialist programme. Taking his stand on the main issue of independence he said:

> Independence for us means complete freedom from British dominion and British imperialism. Having attained our freedom I have no doubt that India will welcome all attempts at world co-operation and federation, and will even agree to give up part of her own independence to a larger group of which she is an equal member.[80]

Gandhi himself moved the main resolution – that Congress now stood for complete independence (swaraj); that Indians should immediately boycott all legislatures and committees constituted by the Government; and that the All-India Congress Committee was authorised to launch a programme of civil disobedience. This resolution was passed at the stroke of midnight on 31 December, exactly on the hour when the Congress ultimatum expired. The flag of independence was unfurled and, with a roar of 'Long live revolution', Congress went to war.

CHAPTER SEVEN

The Introspective Warrior, 1930–6

If we can succeed in prison in learning forbearance and the art of getting on with others, who happen to be different from us, then we have learnt the secret of success in public activity, and indeed life itself. And after all what is truth? Who can say with absolute definiteness which is the correct way? The modern scientific spirit therefore is very far from being dogmatic in anything. It gropes for truth and dare not be too positive.

Jawaharlal Nehru, October 1932

In the dawn of 1930 urban India was filled with excitement, hope and anxiety. As usual, prominent Indian astrologers supplied the expectant populace with their prophecies: Congress was to have a disastrous time between April and July 1930.[1] April was to be especially bad for persons born under the influence of Libra (Gandhi) and Scorpio (Jawaharlal). As the Round Table Conference was to be held (in autumn 1930) under the influence of Mars and Jupiter, a large measure of agreement was bound to be reached between different parties on important issues. March 1931 would bring victory to Congress. The future contained three significant years – 1933, 1937 and 1949 – of which one was to witness the outbreak of a world war and in another India was to attain full independence.

The news of the confrontation between Congress and the English Raj trickled down to the rural populace. But the curious peasant, when the matter was explained to him by the village wise man, still could not comprehend the concepts of swaraj or of the Congress Raj. He nourished neither love nor hatred for the alien rulers whom he had hardly ever seen. He lived far outside the arena in which the racial arrogance of the British Raj slashed at the sensitive pride of more ambitious Indians and bred in them a strong anti-British feeling. Fear and helplessness were his constant companions: fear of his own people – the revenue officer, the landlord, the money-lender, the village priest – who ruled his destiny; helplessness arising out of the perpetual meagreness of his resources. His plight was in some measure redeemed by his ignorance and religiosity: the former prevented him from aspiring to better things, the latter enabled him dutifully to endure. He was in fact more in harmony with his environment than were the factory workers in the city. For him the British Raj was remote and irrelevant.

How was he, then, to be drawn into a movement for independence? Jawaharlal was engrossed by this question. Swaraj must represent more than the substitution of one Raj for another; it must promise the peasant immediate relief from his specific grievances and quick improvement in his way of life. Alternatively, he could be galvanised in the name of religion, a method which now appeared to Jawaharlal not only distasteful but also full of disastrous consequences. Rejection of the use of religious slogans and symbols made his task of communication with the peasantry more difficult. He had first to arouse among them an awareness of their hardships and grievances, then to convince them that the party solely responsible for their distress was the British Raj, and finally to present to them the remedy of swaraj, which aimed not only at freeing the country from an alien rule but at establishing in India a socialist republic, a people's Raj, in which every citizen would have equal rights and be entitled to enjoy the fruits of his labour.[2] It was difficult for a caste-ridden Hindu peasantry to understand such egalitarian principles; besides, did they really approve of the levelling down of social barriers, which they believed were God-ordained?

Jawaharlal approached the young people in a simpler and more direct way. His emotive slogan – 'Who lives if India dies? Who dies if India lives?'[3] – was aimed at arousing the passions of the young, who clearly were not going to remain content with a non-violent boycott of their schools and colleges. They were bound to step over the mark at some point. Jawaharlal's main objective was to keep this defiant spirit high; he was not worried about a few violent outbursts, though he certainly did not welcome the young men offering him their loyalty, as they occasionally did, in letters written in their own blood.

In the Indian context Jawaharlal's secular style was less effective than that of a leader who appealed to the masses in the name of religion. A Muslim nationalist, Abdul Ghaffar Khan, for example, received a ready response from his Muslim followers when he urged them to fight against the slavery of the British rule, on the impeccable grounds that no slave could be a true Muslim.[4]

The fact was, however, that the peasants had a very limited capacity to endure additional deprivations and sufferings for any length of time – a point which Jawaharlal never fully realised. He attributed to the peasantry a measure of his own personality and often interpreted their adoration of him as implying the determination and capacity for a prolonged fight.

In terms of endurance the city workers were no better. The trade union movement, weak at the best of times, was incapacitated still further by internal factions, and there was, of course, no union fund to feed workers while on strike. Even the industrialists and businessmen, who gave generous donations to the Congress fund and were prepared to endure the boycott programme, were willing to sustain their losses only for a limited period of six months.[5] A leading industrialist, P. Thakurdas, warned Motilal Nehru that if the Congress war was prolonged beyond that period, then the endurance of the commercial community would most certainly collapse.[6]

In facing the problem of how to call the nation to war Jawaharlal wavered between idealism and reality. For him it should be a people's war based on the active support of the peasantry, labour and lower middle class, otherwise it would become yet another upper-class liberal movement such as Congress had abandoned for good in 1920. For its sustenance and vigour, however, a mass movement ought to be directed also against the Indian capitalists and landlords who were, in Jawaharlal's estimation, not only the exploiters of the people but also collaborators with the British Raj. But this strategy was not only beset with a host of uncertainties and problems but was also opposed by the bulk of the Congress right wing, including Gandhi.

The support of the upper classes, with their influence and wealth, seemed vital for the survival of the national movement. An open class war would push this section of society on to the side of the British and, together, they might starve the people's movement into submission. Besides this, there were doubts about the feasibility of organising the peasantry into a non-violent revolution. With its theme of non-violence, the Indian movement had no precedent. Jawaharlal had accepted non-violence as a policy, and though he occasionally condoned mob violence and even praised the bravery of a young terrorist martyr he never believed in the efficacy of the violent method. Being so persuaded, he was even against secret societies:

> In our country the whole basis of our struggle having been open defiance in order to inculcate character and backbone in our people – and in this it has succeeded to a remarkable extent – it is very difficult to switch on to an entirely different method.[7]

Acceptance of violence and secret societies spelled for Jawaharlal the end of the present struggle and the beginning of a different type of struggle such as he was never willing to undertake, even when, as in 1933, the movement reached rock bottom and the Gandhian way stood discredited.

Jawaharlal's dilemma, therefore, arose from his acceptance on the one hand of the non-violent method and, on the other, of the principles of socialist revolution; in moments of acute conflict, however, he found his attachment to the former was the stronger. He was temperamentally sympathetic to the morality and humanism of satyagraha. Basically he always preferred persuasion to force and compassion to ruthlessness. His attachment to socialism was rational and, because of its alienness, qualified. Initially he had looked to socialism and its communist manifestation in Soviet Russia as the panacea for the ills of poverty, racialism, communalism, exploitation and colonialism. Now, at the beginning of 1930, he was somewhat perplexed by the narrowness and rigidity of the socialists, particularly those of the radical brand based in Europe, at their interpretation of Indian nationalism and, above all, at their description of Gandhi as a bourgeois reactionary set on betraying his country to the British imperialists.[8] Jawaharlal severed his connection with the League Against Imperialism which he had joined in 1927 while in Europe.[9]

His dissociation from the League marked not the rejection of his socialist sentiments but an assertion of his firm faith in the Gandhian-style national movement. Nationalism at all costs was his motto, and he was even prepared to abandon the class war if it threatened to weaken the nationalist attack on the British Raj. Jawaharlal was thus unable to go all the way either with the Indian socialists, who had no scruples against the use of violence and conspiracy, or with the Gandhi-ite right-wingers who were wholly opposed to an attack on propertied interests. This attitude also determined his future role in criticising both the leftists and rightists, and at the same time protecting them against each other. Neither wing considered him an enemy and to neither was he a committed friend. A movement based on the best of the two systems would have appealed to him most, but in January 1930 he was unable to evolve such a system. Thus, on the eve of the war for which he above all was responsible, he wavered uncertainly between one standpoint and another and, lacking his youthful conviction, fixed his hopes on the Mahatma, praying that the master of the non-violent revolution would once again arouse the nation and this time lead the masses to victory.

It was a heavy responsibility for Gandhi, the more so because he was not prepared to involve the masses in direct action. He had learnt from his non-co-operation movement that a mass moment could not remain non-violent for long and that the moment violence occurred governmental repression would begin and the movement would soon collapse into complete submission. He would have preferred to leave the masses with his constructive programme, and to let his trained satyagrahis (the inmates of his ashram – a spiritual retreat) take direct action through what he called the individual as opposed to the mass civil disobedience movement. But the left wing gave him no choice: young and militant India would revolt against Congress itself rather than participate in anything less spectacular than a mass revolution. Gandhi's eagerness to avoid total war was evident from his readiness to strike some agreement with the Government just before the Lahore Congress. His reluctance to lead the entire nation to battle persisted even after the Lahore Congress. On 31 January 1930 he made his last bid for a truce by offering to call off the impending civil disobedience movement if the Viceroy conceded his eleven points. These included demands for total prohibition of alcohol, reduction of land revenue and military expenditure by fifty per cent, abolition of the salt tax, and paradoxically, the right of Indians to carry arms. If these demands were accepted by the Government, Gandhi assured the nation, then India would have achieved the substance, if not the entirety, of independence.

Gandhi's offer seemed to Jawaharlal like a move to surrender before the battle had begun. He anxiously reminded Gandhi that his offer was inconsistent with the Congress resolution and argued that the eleven points did not even constitute the semblance of independence. Even to Motilal, who was by no means anxious for a long-drawn-out confrontation with the Raj, Gandhi's offer seemed like an anticlimax coming as it did so soon after 26 January when India celebrated the declaration of independence.[10] Gandhi assured Jawaharlal privately that 'our case has been strengthened not weakened by the 11 points'.[11] He also assured the people that there was a consistent line running through his seeming inconsistencies: 'Independence means at least those eleven points, if it means anything at all to the masses. Mere withdrawal of the English is not independence. By mentioning the eleven points I have given a body in part to the illusive word independence.'[12]

The Government, however, did not concede a single point, and Gandhi was now left with no choice but to start the movement. All eyes were fixed on the supreme commander of the Indian National Army. The politicians and world press paused – some with apprehension and admiration, others with amusement – to see how this little man of India was going to shake the mighty British Empire. India's pledge for independence, which contained some shades of the American Declaration of Independence, received a certain degree of appreciation in the United States, and an enthusiastic Senator had moved a resolution for American recognition of Indian independence. At the same time a Labour under-secretary for India had stated that none knew better than the Indians themselves how foolish it was to talk of complete independence. In India the Irwin administration put on a supremely confident face, though underneath this lay an apprehension that the movement might assume a larger dimension on account of the deep resentment all thinking Indians felt against the inferior racial status which the British accorded them.

On 2 March, Gandhi announced to the world the nature

and timing of his satyagraha. As civil disobedience meant breaking one or more unjust laws, Gandhi, after careful consideration, chose to break what seemed to be the most unjust of all laws, the Salt Act of 1890. This gave the Government a monopoly over salt manufacture and made it an offence, punishable by six months' imprisonment and a fine, for any private person to manufacture a commodity which formed such a vital part of the diet of every man. What made the monopoly particularly unjust was the profit government derived from salt taxation, which fell most heavily on the poor man, taking from him every year nearly three days' income. However, it was not so much the economics of the matter that determined Gandhi's choice but the comparative ease with which the masses could break this law (it was simple to manufacture salt either from sea-water or salt-earth), and the popular appeal which this kind of disobedience would have. Gandhi, with a select batch of trained volunteers from his ashram, was to defy the law first; the people were then to follow his example. The provincial congress committees were authorised to select other laws for breaking. Non-co-operation was to run side by side with civil disobedience; lawyers and students were to boycott courts, schools and colleges.[13] The nationalist councillors had already walked out of the legislative councils.

Gandhi's theatrical ability was manifested in the manner in which he chose to break the Salt Law. On 12 March, with seventy-eight of his followers, he marched on foot from his Sabarmati ashram (Ahmedabad) through the hinterland of Gujarat to Dandi, situated on the salty shore of the Gulf of Cambay (Arabian Sea) – a journey of 241 miles. The sixty-one-year-old Mahatma walked ten miles or more every day for nearly twenty-four days, and on each day publicity increased and the national spirit rose higher. Jawaharlal felt overwhelmed. His doubts disappeared, and he inwardly saluted the Mahatma for his remarkable feat. Both he and Motilal met Gandhi on his march and, to mark the occasion, they made a gift to the nation of their old palatial house in Allahabad. The house was renamed Swaraj Bhawan and became national property from 6 April – the day Gandhi (having reached Dandi the previous day) ceremoniously broke the law by picking up a lump of natural salt from the sea.

Commencing on 6 April, the civil disobedience movement lasted for nearly eleven months, until the Gandhi–Irwin Pact brought an interlude of truce on 5 March 1931. The second movement broke out with the arrest of Gandhi on 4 January 1932, and lingered on until 8 May 1933, when Gandhi officially suspended it, first for six weeks, then in July for another six weeks, in September for a year, and finally in May 1934 for an indefinite period. Jawaharlal did not conform to the official schedule and maintained his individual defiance of the Raj even when Congress was not at war. As a result he was in prison for about four years (precisely for 1460 days) in the period from 1930 to 1935.[14] During his short spells of freedom in these years, he found the realities of politics too inflexible to be moulded to his ideals. It was a frustrating experience for him as he sincerely believed that the fullness of life comes from attempting to fit ideas to action. Sometimes jail seemed preferable to a freedom where his ideals could be polluted and his conscience strained by the grey choices of politics.

Prison became his refuge, a place where he could read, write and think. He was not a poet and he could not, as he might have wished, 'compose poetry and inscribe it on the prison wall with the help of an improvised utensil'.[15] Instead he took to writing prose with a view to turning his captivity into the sweetest days of his life. There were before him the examples of Hugo Grotius, Cervantes and John Bunyan. Here, in words if not in action, he felt free, positive, decisive, and close to his vision. But between the author and politician, between the rational and emotional Jawaharlal, there always lay an unmapped area of fallibility, a no-man's-land where compromises could be made.

He wrote prolifically: two large books, and a number of articles which were published in two collections. *Glimpses of World History* (1934) emerged from his attempts to educate Indira in letters written between October 1930 and August 1933. It was the continuation of an exercise which had earlier given birth to the *Letters from a Father to His Daughter* (1929). The *Glimpses* – covering the entire span of human progress from the beginnings of ancient civilisations in Asia to the crisis in capitalist civilisation as marked by the Depression and Roosevelt's New Deal – was written, as he explained to his literary agent, in a sort of jumpy way with a connecting link, and it contained many personal and intimate touches.[16] The inspiration for this venture came from H. G. Wells's *Outline of History*, and the justification from his own belief in the unity of the world, 'each part influencing, and being influenced by, the other' to an extent that it was 'quite impossible now to have a separate history of nations'.[17] In his world outlook, however, Asia figured dominantly, and it is this Asian-centred approach of the *Glimpses* which distinguishes it from other universal histories.

His *Autobiography*, written entirely in prison from June 1934 to February 1935, bears signs of the stresses he was undergoing on account of the suspension of the civil disobedience movement and the re-emergence of the 'opportunist' and liberal politicians who were, for him, not only out of date but cowards and traitors to the national cause. Jawaharlal gave the manuscript to Gandhi, who read it in his bathroom (the only other work which had the privilege of being put in the Mahatma's watery 'library' was Hitler's *Mein Kampf*[18]). Gandhi did not like Jawaharlal's scathing criticism of the liberals who had, as he reminded Jawaharlal, served the nation according to 'their own light'; none could serve the country better just by attacking them.[19] Jawaharlal, however, had neither time nor inclination to revise his manuscript.

In a later defence of his *Autobiography*, he maintained that it contained a frank account of his inner feelings and that he believed that the liberals, having co-operated with the Government when it was at war with Congress, were thus responsible for the repressive legislation the Government introduced to suppress the national movement.[20] The liberals rose up in arms against Jawaharlal when his *Autobiography* was published in 1936. As they saw it, the book revealed Jawaharlal's contempt for all men who differed from himself. One of them remarked that the book contained 'the conceited vapourings of a fretful child spoilt in early life by a doting father'.[21] A German Nazi, then resident in India, took offence at Jawaharlal's 'sneering' at the Nazi use of the term Aryan.[22] On the whole, however, the book was favourably received among educated Indians, and the left-wingers particularly relished his tirades against the liberals.[23] Some critics were a little disappointed at the dearth of personal details regarding his ambitions, his attitude to sex and his friends.[24] They wondered whether he had any friends. Jawaharlal retorted that worthwhile people were hard to come by, hence he had been mainly interested in ideas and principles.[25]

Apart from *Glimpses* and his *Autobiography*, Jawaharlal wrote during this period a number of articles, essays and speeches which found their way into two collections, *Recent Essays and Writings* (1934) and *India and the World* (1936). Various problems of Indian and international significance attracted his attention and he wrote, as he reflected on them, in a rambling style. One of the articles, 'Whither India', written in 1933, came near to being his political manifesto. This summed up his aspirations for India and the world. He stood for India's freedom within the framework of an international co-operative socialist world federation, for social and economic equality, and for ending all exploitation of nation by nation and class by class.[26]

For such a prolific writer as Jawaharlal, who had evolved a distinguished style in English, the task of choosing a national language for India could have been exacting as well as embarrassing. Yet, in early 1935 when he gave his thoughts to this problem, he at once reached the conclusion that Hindustani (or Hindi), written in both Nagari and Urdu script, must become the national language of India (because it was spoken by more people than any other language of India), even though it was poor not only in comparison with English but also in relation to other major Indian languages.[27] He even tried his hand at writing a few essays in Hindi.

Prison itself formed the topic for an article or two:

> Prison is the best of universities if only one knows how to take its courses. Physically of course one has the chance of regular and simple living. Mentally, its effect is still more noteworthy. Our Age is the Age of Indifference. People have no real beliefs left – nothing sacred – nothing worthwhile almost. And so we suffer from ennui and life itself becomes a burden. We have lost entirely our sense of perspective – well, jail gives it back to us to some extent and we begin to appreciate the little things, which we hardly noticed before.[28]

Jawaharlal's prison life was not physically distressing. As a Class A political prisoner, with additional privileges, he had time and opportunity to pursue his interests. Between 1921 and 1945 he spent almost nine years in nine different jails: seven of these were in his own province of United Provinces, one in Calcutta and the last was the Ahmednagar Fort in the Bombay presidency. His prison accommodation varied in small points, though he always had a cell to himself, often placed in a barrack or quarter of the prison shared with other political prisoners, who usually irritated him. He resented the loss of privacy: 'This close association in a barrack had most of the disadvantages of married life with none of its advantages.'[29] Mosquitoes and bedbugs were an inevitable accompaniment to prison, and being a light sleeper they caused him many a sleepless night. But there were compensations. The jail authorities provided him with a servant – a common convict, who cooked for him the simple vegetarian food which he usually preferred whilst in prison. And he had a private bathroom. His normal exercise was taken in the yard of his quarters, but because he took pleasure in running he was often given special permission to exercise in the mornings outside his quarters although within the prison walls. When an ungenerous prison officer allowed him to indulge in this hobby only on alternate days, he protested: 'The direction that I should have the fresh air and exercise "every other day" must have been based on an assumption that I differ on alternate days, perhaps after the fashion of Dr Jekyll and Mr Hyde and that only one part of me should be favoured.'[30]

On a typical prison day he would wake at six, take his exercise in the morning and spend the rest of the day reading, writing, spinning, and sometimes lecturing to his fellow political prisoners on general science and international affairs. About 9 p.m. prisoners were locked in their cells, and he went to bed soon after. Books and foreign periodicals arrived for him almost every week. He was restricted to one visit from outside every two weeks and was allowed to write and to receive only one letter in the same period. Both the incoming and outgoing letters were censored by the prison authorities. He kept a prison diary but the entries were not made regularly. He often wondered why he did this:

> For others to read later or to read it myself in after years? Ridiculous habit – to keep a journal for the purpose of recording futilities. After all there can be little worthwhile to record in prison. And yet it is a bit of a relief at times.[31]

Yet it was not always easy, even for him, to put up with jail life. In moments of strain and agitation the deprivations and loneliness of the prison environment could become unbearable: 'The object of jail appears to be first to remove such traces of humanity as a man might possess and then to subdue even the animal element in him so that ultimately he might become the perfect vegetable.'[32] In such moments he hungered for life's little delights, and his family, friends and relatives all became the dearer for the deprivation. Then he could suddenly feel grateful to the prison for arousing in him such a longing. He derived from his agonies a kind of self-assurance that he had not become insensitive and impervious towards the 'little delights' of human life.

As for Jawaharlal's activities outside prison, the first interlude (11–19 October 1930) was for him the least frustrating. During that brief respite he succeeded in putting new life into the civil disobedience movement, at least in his own province of United Provinces. The movement was beginning to lose momentum. Fewer people were now going to jail, and urban India seemed exhausted. Over 30,000 people had courted imprisonment, but the non-violent face of the movement had been tarnished by sporadic outbreaks of violence in Chittagong (Bengal), Sholapur (Bombay) and Peshawar (North-West Frontier Province). Government reprisals, especially in Peshawar (where the Muslim 'Redshirts' organisation of Abdul Ghaffar Khan had been in full control of the city for five days in April), had been severe enough to weaken the urban defiance. The Government, its initial complacency shattered by the unexpectedly large support the movement gained at the start, resorted to the stratagem of winning away from Congress the Muslims and the commercial community. Government propaganda reminded the Muslims in the Punjab and North-West Frontier Province that their interests were not safe with Congress, which was essentially a Hindu organisation. At the same time Irwin urged the leaders of the commercial community to dissociate themselves from Congress tyranny and assured them of government protection against any harassment.[33] The movement had thus run out of steam everywhere except in Bombay, where it was continuing, though slowly.

Jawaharlal at once sensed the staleness in the movement.

The only way, he decided, that the movement could be revitalised was by involving the rural masses in a no-rent campaign. The Depression of 1929 had brought about a phenomenal fall in the price of agricultural products and consequently put the cultivators of India under the severe distress of money scarcity and starvation – conditions conducive to the building up of a peasant movement. The strain was badly felt by the peasants in United Provinces, the most populous and economically the most backward of the Indian provinces. The average holding of a tenant in this province was three to four acres. Being a sugar-cane- and wheat- growing area it was hit hard because the price a peasant got for sugar-cane and wheat was estimated to be respectively thirty-five and fifty per cent less than the cost of production.[34] The tenant was thus in no position to pay his rent. Peasant proprietors and smaller landlords, being equally handicapped, were unable to pay land revenue to the Government. In the case of a tenant, the penalty for failure to pay rent was eviction, and the landlord was entitled to use physical coercion.

Jawaharlal took the initiative and sanctioned a no-tax campaign in the district of Allahabad; the other districts were permitted to follow suit. He did, however, conform, though half-heartedly, to the official Congress policy of not sponsoring class war, and accordingly he called upon both parties, landlords (zamindars) and peasants (kisans), not to pay. He addressed a number of meetings and a large peasant conference, and was duly arrested, tried for sedition and sentenced to two years' rigorous imprisonment. He returned to Nani prison (Allahabad) after eight days' absence. His re-arrest and conviction raised the tempo of the civil disobedience movement, not only in United Provinces but throughout India, though only temporarily.

His arrest also galvanised his ailing father into a final spurt of activity. Motilal had been ill since the beginning of the year, though hardly inactive. On the arrest of Jawaharlal in April he had taken charge of the Congress presidency and vigorously worked for the movement until June, when he himself was arrested and put in the same prison as his son. The prison conditions were unsuited to his failing health, and he suffered from occasional attacks of fever. His son's presence was a great compensation; it was in fact his last chance to spend any length of time in the company of Jawaharlal. He was, however, subjected to additional strain as a result of the peace negotiations between Congress and the Government through the mediation of Sapru and Jayakar, the liberal leaders, since he himself was responsible for this move.

Prior to his arrest he had expressed to Jayakar his wish for a truce on certain conditions.[35] Again on 20 June 1930, ten days before his arrest, Motilal had made a statement to a correspondent of the London *Daily Herald* putting forward the possibility of Congress entering into a negotiation with the Government provided the latter gave certain assurances. Motilal's overtures came as a relief to the Government, which felt threatened by the growing support for the Congress movement given by the young, women, business and commercial interests, and, above all, by the Muslims in North-West Frontier Province.[36] Sapru and Jayakar were encouraged by the Viceroy to begin negotiations. They first visited Gandhi in Yeravda prison and then, on 27 July, the Nehrus in Nani prison. As there was no chance of progress until Gandhi and the Nehrus could consult with one another directly, the Government arranged on 10 August for the transportation of the Nehrus by special train from Nani (Allahabad) to Yeravda prison in Poona. Jawaharlal was against any such negotiation from the first and feared 'a false or weak move' on the part of Congress.[37] The conditions that the leaders finally laid down for the truce were the result of his influence. Congress would suspend the civil disobedience movement and participate in the forthcoming Round Table Conference in London only on condition that India was given a complete national government, with complete control of the defence forces and the economic machinery, and the right to secede from the British Empire. As the situation of the Government had by then improved, the Viceroy refused to accept these conditions; the negotiations thus ended with no result other than to aggravate Motilal's illness.

While at Yeravda he began to bring up blood in his sputum, and his condition continued to deteriorate after his return to Nani prison on 19 August. As a result, he was prematurely discharged on 8 September 1930, and was bedridden when Jawaharlal was re-arrested. Although he was by now used to his son's imprisonments, the pang of separation was especially severe, since he felt his life's journey was drawing to a close. He was denied the satisfaction of his son's company, but could yet reach Jawaharlal's heart. Would it not make his son happy and proud if he kept the fight going in his absence? Characteristically, he resolved to 'get well at once', and his old body immediately responded to his will.[38] His sputum cleared, and he was active once more. He conferred with workers and issued detailed instructions for a course of action, arranged for an all-India celebration on his son's birthday (Jawaharday), at which the offending passages from Jawaharlal's speech, for which he had been convicted, were read out at public meetings.[39] He invigorated the civil disobedience movement and himself, but neither could live for long on nervous energy. His mortal disease reasserted itself after a few weeks, and he was persuaded to take a health cruise in the Bay of Bengal.

With this object in view he came to Calcutta in November, but his condition worsened and he had to remain in Calcutta for treatment. As a result of chronic asthma his lungs had become fibrous, and his heart and liver were both affected. On his own initiative the Governor of Bengal unofficially released Dr B. C. Roy – the eminent physician who was then a political prisoner – to examine Motilal.[40] It was not so much the treatment, however, as the prophecy of an astrologer which, at this point, revived Motilal's hopes of survival. The astrologer predicted that the influence of the stars responsible for his bad health would last till May 1931 and that there would be occasions for serious anxiety during this time.[41] His confidence returned and he even began treating his own doctors! To one, who was suffering from a minor ailment, Motilal prescribed an ointment which he himself had made from the leaves of a local plant. The Calcutta doctors, however, had nothing to offer; his condition had passed beyond cure.

Jawaharlal, Gandhi and other members of the Congress Working Committee were prematurely released on 26 January 1931 to reconsider, in view of what had been achieved at the Round Table Conference (12 November 1930–19 January 1931), the advantages of calling off the civil disobedience movement and co-operating with the British Government in evolving further the constitutional reforms for India. The leaders rushed to Allahabad where Motilal, having returned from Calcutta, now lay at death's door: 'like an old lion mortally wounded and with his physical strength almost gone, but still very leonine and kingly'.[42] His eyes shone with joy at the sight of Jawaharlal, but for his son it was an agonising experience. When Gandhi arrived, Motilal announced: 'I am going soon, Mahatmaji, and I shall not be here to see Swaraj. But I know you have won it and will soon have it.'[43] He firmly believed that, when swaraj came, his son – the foundation of whose greatness he had the satisfaction of having laid with his own hands – would become its first executive. He serenely resigned himself to the inevitable end, which came peacefully at dawn on 6 February 1931. In the evening, when Gandhi dedicated Motilal's pyre at the altar of the nation, Jawaharlal felt desolate and old. He had lost not only a father, but an intimate companion, the principal witness of his past. From now on Gandhi would fill the parental vacuum.

Jawaharlal resumed in earnest the responsibility for his household, which now consisted of his mother, wife, daughter and his youngest unmarried sister Krishna; Vijayalakshmi, being married, needed no support. He declared to both his sisters that, though in law he was the heir to his father's property, he had no wish to inherit property and that they must consider themselves as joint sharers with him and his mother in what was left of their father's fortune.[44] Though his political career prevented him from being able to earn his living, he assured his sisters that, if it ever became necessary, he was perfectly capable of earning money in a variety of ways. He cared little for money, but this was partly because he was never (even after the death of his father) destitute for lack of it, and partly because, as happened in later years, he could make a living through his writings.[45] Money, of course, was always essential to the Nehrus. It enabled them to meet the cost of travel, communications, secretarial and other assistance, and the founding of a national newspaper, all of which enhanced their political stature. With their money and property, they were also able to make voluntary sacrifices and thereby to win popular acclaim.

Jawaharlal's sadness at the time of his father's death was deepened by the political scene. Though he was willing to fight for years if necessary, he found the Congress leadership tired and weary and anxious to reach a compromise. He resented Sapru, Jayakar and the rest of the liberal band (who had just returned from the Round Table Conference) for their work in luring Congress into the constitutional arena. The peacemakers were whispering into Congress's right ear that the prospect now existed of acquiring a federal government, comprising the Indian states and the British Indian provinces with a full transfer of power in the provinces. The outlines of the constitution which was in the making, they assured Congress, promised an immediate transfer of substantial power to Indian hands, and also laid down the means by which India could, in due course, attain full sovereign status.

Jawaharlal was fiercely opposed to the principle of gradualness that lay at the foundation of liberal thinking, for he believed more in the conquest than the transfer of power. He was, however, prepared to accept the mode of transfer, provided it was to a position of absolute power. He did not believe that Britain was justified in acting as a self-appointed judge of Indian matters, nor had she any right to withhold India's sovereignty from her. Hence it would be dishonourable, and also contrary to the stand Congress took in 1929, to accept any arrangement whereby Britain conceded only a part and not the whole of India's independence. Jawaharlal argued with Sapru that all the Round Table Conference had yielded was the transfer to India of a mere fraction of power, for the British retained, and intended to retain for ever, their control over the defence forces, foreign policy, and the economic and financial machinery of the country.[46] What was more, this token power would benefit only those with vested interests in the country – the feudal lords, the princely order, the bureaucracy, the industrialists and financiers, and the religious and communal leadership. The people, whether those in the British Indian provinces or in the Indian states, did not come into the picture. What, then, could the Indian Government – having no control over the vital organs of state – do for the masses?

As both politicians started from different premises, there was no real communication or understanding between Jawaharlal and Sapru. This did not particularly worry Jawaharlal, who had little time for Sapru's style of politics. What did concern him was Gandhi's willingness to negotiate for peace. Negotiation and compromise formed a vital part of Gandhi's satyagraha strategy, and unlike Jawaharlal he appreciated the role of Indian liberals as intermediaries in peace negotiations. It seemed to Gandhi an opportune time to call for a truce: the civil disobedience movement had by then spent its force and was nearing the point of extinction. A timely response to peace overtures at this point might turn a defeat into a victory and save the nation from the kind of frustrations it had suffered in the 1920s. Besides, Gandhi was not unequivocally committed to full independence and would be content if the next instalment of reforms transferred substantial power to Indian hands.

Gandhi's overture received a ready response from Irwin, who was anxious to mark the end of his viceroyalty by success in bringing the refractory Congress to the Round Table Conference. Irwin was largely responsible for the first Round Table Conference, its terms of reference and even its composition. He was thus naturally concerned about its success, which seemed doubtful if India's largest party persisted in boycotting it. He was therefore very keen to secure Congress's participation in the second Round Table Conference, which was to be held in the autumn of 1931. The parleys between Gandhi and Irwin thus began on 17 February in the Viceregal Lodge in Delhi with an earnest desire on both sides to come to an agreement. This joint endeavour to find a meeting-point between nationalism and imperialism was frowned on as much by the left-wing nationalists in India as by the right-wing imperialists in Britain.

To Jawaharlal it looked like surrender; the world seemed to have come to an end not with a bang but with a whimper.[47] Winston Churchill foresaw the doom of empire in this 'parley on equal terms between the representative of the King-Emperor and a half-naked fakir of repelling appearance and manners. Paradoxical though it may seem, Jawaharlal and Churchill, though poised on opposite sides of the board, had in common not only an aristocratic family upbringing, an education at Harrow and great literary skill, but also held the view that there could be no joining of hands between nationalism and imperialism, for such a partnership would eventually destroy one or the other. Nehru believed that a continuous war against imperialism would give strength and success to nationalism; it was absurd to think of linking these two forces, for they were incompatible. Churchill believed that the British Empire rested on the superiority of the English people, hence any fraternisation between the ruler and the ruled would undermine the very foundations of the imperial system. If the Empire were to survive, it was therefore necessary to perpetuate or re-create the reality or myth of British superiority. If there were no such thing as the racial superiority of the British, then it must be created. Both men, too, as often happened in their public lives, were obliged under the pressure of expediency and circumstances to concede areas of the intellectual ground they formally occupied in their approaches to political problems. Both had great flair (though Jawaharlal was a greater intellectual and a less ruthless politician than Churchill), which made them excellent critics and formidable leaders in opposition, and both lacked intellectual obstinacy, a lack which not only occasionally saved them from political extinction, but also often brought them into power. Having overcome his initial shock at the idea of peace negotiations, Jawaharlal set himself the task of restraining Gandhi and the right-wingers from striking any humble compromises with the enemy. Likewise, Churchill exercised all his powers in those years to restrain the Labour Prime Minister and the half-hearted imperialists from making any lavish concessions to Indian nationalism.

The Gandhi–Irwin negotiations began in an atmosphere of mixed emotions. The Indian leftists and youth and the British bureaucrats and imperialists were equally hostile, though for different reasons. But a large number of Indian politicians – the rightists, the opportunists and the power-seekers – considered the negotiations as a victory for Gandhi and Congress. In their opinion and in the eyes of the people, the Viceroy's invitation to Gandhi gave legitimacy to the power which the Mahatma had regained through his Dandi march and the civil disobedience movement. The liberal leaders – Sapru, Jayakar and Sastri – suddenly came into the limelight as mediators between Congress and the Government. Dogged by politicians and shadowed by the correspondents of the world press, Gandhi found little time for Jawaharlal, who had moved to Delhi for consultations. Finding that Gandhi – the centre of power – had suddenly moved away from him into the camp of the rightists and liberals, Jawaharlal felt lonely and frustrated. The leaders of the youth organisations and the militant left-wing nationalists looked to him to act as a restraint on Gandhi and to protect socialist objectives from being compromised at the truce negotiations. They also expected that the Gandhi–Irwin parley, no matter what political gains ensued from it, should at least result in saving the lives of three terrorist heroes – Bhagat Singh, Sukhdev and Rajguru – who had been sentenced to death and were awaiting execution in a Lahore prison. Gandhi, however, showed absolute firmness during the peace talks, which symbolised to him a change in the enemy's heart and therefore a success for his satyagraha. Being morally committed against espousing the cause of violence in any form, Gandhi did not make the commutation of death sentences on the Punjab terrorists a necessary part of his bargain with Irwin. The Gandhi–Irwin agreement was signed at noon on 5 March 1931, and the two mahatmas, as Mrs Naidu called them, celebrated the occasion by drinking each other's health; Irwin drank tea and Gandhi sipped lime juice flavoured with a pinch of salt he had manufactured illegally.

The agreement should be considered a victory for Congress if Gandhi's object had been no more than to obtain a temporary truce, during which Congress could, on the one hand, ascertain the extent to which the British Government was willing to transfer power to India and, on the other, revive national energy for a second war of independence. By conceding even qualified relief to people who had suffered during the civil disobedience movement, the truce terms in essence revived the very sources from which Congress drew its war potential. Political prisoners were to be released; pending prosecutions were to be withdrawn; fines which had not been realised were to be remitted; movable and immovable properties, seized or attached in connection with the realisation of land revenue or other dues, were to be returned if they were still in the possession of the Government; government servants and village officials who had resigned their posts during the civil disobedience movement were now permitted to apply for reinstatement; and finally the villages were allowed to collect or make salt for domestic consumption.[48] In turn, Congress agreed to discontinue the civil disobedience movement and attend the second Round Table Conference with the object of considering further the scheme for the constitutional government for India.

The clause relating to Congress's participation in the Round Table Conference was vague, but in the light of various policy statements made by the ministers of the Crown it was fairly clear that the British Government was intent on retaining, during an undefined period of transition, control over defence, external affairs and the economic machinery of India, and on safeguarding during this period the interests of the minorities. The new constitution would thus constitute a further advance towards, rather than full attainment of, self-government for India.

It was this clause, and the fact that no move was made to save the lives of the condemned terrorists, which aroused Jawaharlal's resentment and frustration. But Gandhi was firm in declaring that he would retire from politics if Congress did not endorse the agreement in its entirety. The Congress Working Committee immediately endorsed the terms of the provisional settlement and directed all Congress committees to abide by it. Gandhi tried to soothe Jawaharlal by interpreting the participation clause of the agreement in such a way as to make it fit in with the demand for independence. Jawaharlal was not convinced, but felt there was no alternative but to accept the agreement. In commending the agreement to the nation, however, he emphasised its temporary nature, for no settlement could be final unless it granted full independence.[49] He warned the people not to consider it as 'peace'; it was just a truce – a temporary suspension of hostile activities.[50] He asked them to keep their powder dry, for the truce might be followed by a recurrence of war.

Alarmed by Gandhi's way of springing surprises upon the people and by his manner of interpreting national issues in the vaguest possible terms, Jawaharlal was now intent on getting the socialist objectives clearly embodied in the Congress constitution. Congress must define what was meant by full independence (swaraj) and what kind of social, economic and political system it intended to establish in an independent India. If the theory of the national movement was so set out, Jawaharlal calculated, the individual leaders, no matter how mighty, would be left with very little room for personal manœuvrings and improvisation. The motto he wanted the nation to adopt was: 'Great is Gandhi, but greater still is the organisation which all must serve.' This task, he believed, must be accomplished before Congress sent its delegates to the Round Table Conference. He would put his cards on the table at the annual session of Congress, which from 1931 onwards was to meet in March – a month considered most convenient for the ordinary people to attend it – instead of in December, which had hitherto suited only the professional classes of India.

Under the presidency of Sardar Patel, Congress assembled in Karachi in the last week of March. It met in an atmosphere charged with anger and frustration arising mainly out of the execution of the terrorist heroes on 23 March, despite Gandhi's last-minute plea to Irwin. March 24, which was fixed by Congress as a day of mourning and hartal (strikes), witnessed Hindu–Muslim riots in Kanpur, sparked off by Hindu harassment of some Muslim shopkeepers. Thus when Gandhi arrived at Karachi station he was hooted at by angry members of youth organisations. Disregarding these ill omens, the Mahatma set himself the task of disarming the opposition.[51] He achieved this by impressing upon the radicals that the truce was a necessity because the civil disobedience movement was on the brink of total collapse, and by privately assuring the leaders of the opposition, particularly S. C. Bose, that if the Round Table Conference did not yield satisfactory results, then he would once again take up arms against the Government. To confuse further the left-wing opposition, Gandhi chose Jawaharlal as mover of the main resolution, which endorsed the Gandhi–Irwin Pact and authorised the Mahatma to represent Congress at the Round Table Conference. In return, Gandhi promised to support Jawaharlal's resolution on fundamental rights.

This resolution, on the social and economic policy for an independent India, which was substantially the sum of Jawaharlal's own thinking on the matter, laid the outlines for a secular, socialist and democratic state. The State was to maintain religious neutrality; the economic structure was to be based on the mixed principles of public and private ownership (only key industries and mineral resources were to be state-owned); the gap between the richer and poorer sections of society was to be narrowed through raising taxation on businessmen and landlords, reducing rent and revenue for the peasants, and strengthening the bargaining power of labour; all citizens, irrespective of sex, religion and caste, were to be entitled to fundamental rights, including the right to adult franchise and free primary education.[52] The capitalists – who were making generous donations to Congress funds and to whom Gandhi, in return, was making all manner of promises, including that of securing them industrial monopolies in a free India – raised their eyebrows. But Gandhi, by setting a sad and sorrowful face against the opposition, succeeded in letting Jawaharlal carry his resolution by a majority vote. Jawaharlal thus derived the intellectual satisfaction of having laid down clearly the immediate and distant goals of the national movement.

Thus the Karachi Congress ended on a note of optimism. In early April, India seemed to present a picture of harmony: an alliance had been concluded between the imperialist and nationalist factions, and the latter had brought under its umbrella all kinds of diverse interests represented by landlords and peasants, capitalists and labour, Hindus and Muslims, rightists and leftists. But this concord was illusory. Under the new viceroyalty of Lord Willingdon, who took charge of the administration in April, the very principle of partnership between the imperialist and nationalist forces came under attack.

Willingdon did not believe in parleying on equal terms with the nationalist leaders. He believed this would undermine the prestige of the British Empire and thereby weaken its foundations. He calculated that Gandhi's influence had fluctuated according to the treatment he had received from the Government: it was at its lowest ebb when he was released early in 1931 and reached its high-water mark after the Delhi Pact. He thus determined deliberately to ignore Gandhi, to make no concessions under duress, and to strengthen the repressive machinery of government so that Congress could be ruthlessly suppressed if it chose to go to war again.[53] This policy instantly aroused mutual distrust between the Congress leaders and the Government, each party accusing the other of defying the spirit and breaking the terms of the Gandhi–Irwin Pact. The Government, suspecting that Congress was intent on maintaining intact the defiant mood of the nation, accused it of fostering no-rent campaigns in United Provinces and of indirectly encouraging political assassinations through its unconcealed support for the martyrdom of Bhagat Singh. Congress, while condemning the sporadic acts of terrorism, accused the Government of ignoring the legitimate grievances of the peasants in Gujarat and United Provinces and of applying repressive measures to suppress a non-violent Congress movement in North-West Frontier Province. Congress was particularly sensitive about North-West Frontier Province since, in 1931, for the first time, it had gained a foothold by bringing within its fold the volunteer movement (Redshirts or Khudai Khidmatgars) of Abdul Ghaffar Khan.[54] The Government was equally uneasy about the conversion of this Muslim frontier province to support for Congress.

The Government tried to retrieve the situation by disseminating anti-Hindu propaganda among the Muslims, while at the same time subjecting the defaulting, revenue-paying peasants to severe harassment.[55] A clash seemed imminent in August, when Congress threatened to boycott the second Round Table Conference, but was narrowly averted by Gandhi. Still set on obtaining swaraj by peaceful means, he hastily arranged a meeting with the Viceroy, and a temporary face-saving settlement was reached. He took ship for London on 29 August with an easier mind.

But for Jawaharlal this was to be a time of great worry and strain. Having borne the loss of his father, the suspension of the civil disobedience movement, the compromise of the Delhi Pact, and finally the strains and conflicts of the Karachi Congress – ending with an unsatisfactory settlement that gave no great hopes for a successful outcome to the second Round Table Conference or for a reduction of the troubles in United Provinces, with which he was deeply involved – he became exhausted and was advised by his doctors to take a holiday.

He thus spent a month in Ceylon with his wife and daughter (23 April–23 May), and another fortnight wandering over south India, where he discovered for the first time the southern varieties of Indian culture and civilisation, and also how his own popularity had increased in those distant parts of India: 'Our family has captured the imagination of the millions in this country and "Nehru" has become a magic word with which you can conjure. It is a great honour and a great responsibility.'[56] The holiday was characterised by the growing companionship between Kamala and Jawaharlal. Since her return from Europe in December 1927, Kamala had tried very hard to become a companion to her husband and she had courted imprisonment, to the great delight of her husband, for twenty-six days in January 1931. At Kanya Kumari (Cape Comorin), the southern limit of India, the three Nehrus sat all one day and into the night by the sea, basking in their mutual affection and watching the meeting of the eastern and western waters – the Arabian Sea and the Bay of Bengal seemed to compete with each other in paying homage to 'the old lady', India.[57]

Somewhat restored, Jawaharlal returned to his home province and instantly became involved in the details of peasant politics. The Delhi Pact, whereby Congress had undertaken to stop no-rent campaigns, was difficult to implement in United Provinces, where a great number of peasants, still languishing under the impact of the Depression, were unable to pay their rent and consequently were harassed and ejected from their holdings. Having due regard for the Delhi Pact, Jawaharlal nevertheless considered it almost suicidal for Congress to leave the peasants at the mercy of the landlords and government officials. In his opinion Congress was the labour union for the peasants and therefore in duty bound to negotiate on their behalf.[58] Thus, between June and November, Jawaharlal made various representations to the United Provinces and central governments asking for a large increase in rent remissions, general reinstatement of evicted tenants, and remission of arrears of rent. But while espousing the peasant cause he was cautious to avoid an open class war between tenants and landlords. He proposed that the Government should buy out the big landlords and redistribute their estates among the peasants, thus disclaiming any idea of confiscation. The Government, however, rejected all his demands, and tension increased between tenants and landlords; in the Allahabad district revenue officials were assaulted and landlords killed. Negotiations having failed, the only way Jawaharlal could save Congress prestige was to reintroduce a no-rent campaign. The constraints of the Delhi Pact began to loosen their hold on his conscience when it became clear that the Round Table proceedings were heading, from Congress's point of view, towards total failure.

While Gandhi was on his way to London, the Congress Working Committee despatched a note to him indicating the attitude he should adopt on behalf of Congress at the Round Table Conference.[59] While reminding Gandhi that Congress stood for full Indian control over defence forces, external affairs, finance, and fiscal and economic policy, the Working Committee note stressed that the participation of Indian states in the federation should be conditional on the subjects of the states being given representation in the federal legislature on an elective basis. In the event that the states did not accept these conditions, the Committee suggested that the question of the states' joining the federation should be postponed for the time being and that the Conference's attention should be focused mainly on the future of British India. This suggestion was based on Jawaharlal's assumption that the Indian states could not keep outside the Indian federation and that they could be more conveniently gathered into the federation after British India had acquired a substantial amount of sovereignty. Congress having despatched its directives to Gandhi, Jawaharlal impatiently waited and watched.

Gandhi had scarcely been in England a fortnight before Jawaharlal was complaining of his not 'having got the British government and others to agree to discuss vital matters of principle'.[60] But the prospect of discussing vital matters, especially that of the transfer of substantial powers into Indian hands, seemed to recede further and further into the background. The Conservative-dominated coalition government of Ramsay MacDonald, while emphasising that a self-governing Indian federation remained the ultimate goal of India's constitutional development, maintained that this goal could not be attained in the near future and that the British Raj must remain in India during the transitional period to safeguard the interests of the minorities and of the British Empire. And when at last things could get under way the British Government would only be prepared to grant self-government to the British Indian provinces, to introduce constitutional reforms into North-West Frontier Province, and to separate Sind from Bombay and Burma from India. Even in those areas where power was to be transferred to Indian hands, the minorities – Muslims, Sikhs, Indian Christians, Anglo-Indians, Europeans, and the Depressed Classes (Untouchables) – were to be represented through separate electorates. The unkindest cut of all, for Gandhi, was to give, for the first time, a communal electorate to the Untouchables and thereby to separate them from the main body of the Hindu community.

By mid-October it became clear to Jawaharlal that nothing would be achieved at the Conference.[61] He was also incensed at the insults and humiliations heaped on Gandhi by the British press and politicians. Being variously described by the British press as a 'national joke', a 'simpleton' and a 'humbug'; being patronisingly treated not only by the 'supercilious', 'vain and ill-mannered' MacDonald, but also by the King, who had not forgiven Gandhi for organising the boycott of his son's visit to India in the 1920s; and being constantly opposed and outmanœuvred by some of his own countrymen (Shaukat Ali, the Agha Khan, Dr Ambedkar) Gandhi lost interest in the Conference proceedings.[62] When this was duly reported to Jawaharlal by Devadas Gandhi, he took it as an affront to the nation. Indignant and disillusioned, Jawaharlal ignored the Delhi Pact and fired the peasant movement with a renewed spirit of non-co-operation and defiance.

On 1 December, when the Round Table Conference was concluded, Gandhi warned the British Government that he had come to the parting of the ways and the phase of negotiations was over. On 5 December the United Provinces congress committee licensed four districts – Rae Bareli, Unao, Kanpur and Etawah – in addition to Allahabad to start no-rent campaigns.[63] In mid-December the S. C. Bose faction of the Bengal congress (as against the Sen Gupta faction, which then ruled the Bengal provincial congress committee under Aney's award of August 1931 imposed on Bengal by the Congress High Command), with a view to gaining a power base in the province, resolved to begin satyagraha (boycott and no-rent campaign). The Government instantly introduced repressive measures to deal with the situations in North-West Frontier

Province, United Provinces and Bengal. Applying one repressive ordinance (the United Provinces Emergency Power Ordinance of 1931), the District Magistrate of Allahabad ordered Jawaharlal to remain confined within the municipal limits of the city.[64] Jawaharlal had no intention of complying with the order. He was now determined to launch an individual civil disobedience campaign in the hopes that it would be followed by a mass movement. He informed the District Magistrate that he was not in the habit of taking orders from anyone except Congress, and on 26 December he caught a train to Bombay to meet Gandhi, who was due to arrive there on the twenty-eighth. He well knew that he would not reach Bombay. He was arrested at a wayside station and brought back to Nani prison. He was tried on 4 January 1932 and sentenced to two years' rigorous imprisonment.

Jawaharlal's arrest simply speeded up the inevitable moment of confrontation. On his return to India, the Mahatma found that the two armies were already arrayed against each other. He informed Willingdon that there could be no hope of peace unless the Government withdrew all emergency measures. Gandhi was arrested on 4 January 1932, and by 10 January almost all national leaders were behind bars. Congress was declared illegal.

The second civil disobedience movement began on 4 January 1932, though without leaders and without an elaborately planned strategy, except for a Congress plan (hurriedly drafted in the first week of January) to boycott foreign clothes, picket liquor shops and disregard any law deemed to be immoral. The second-rank national and provincial leaders, who were not immediately imprisoned in January, were now left with the task of improvising plans and strategy. According to one of these plans, which was widely implemented, each provincial congress committee was asked to enroll a certain quota of volunteers. The volunteers were non-violently to raid and occupy those Congress buildings which were now under government occupation, and there to raise the national flag.[65] Observance of national days and weeks, accompanied by strikes and processions, was another feature of the movement. Further, the people were asked to observe the fourth of every month (the day on which Gandhi was arrested and civil disobedience officially began) as a sacred day on which they were required to live frugally on a simple diet, and to abstain from making any purchases.[66] The money thus saved was to be donated to the national fund. But by far the most popular feature of the movement was the picketing of shops selling foreign goods and liquor. In Bombay, where Muslim shopkeepers were encouraged by their leaders (Shaukat Ali, for example) not to co-operate with the Congress movement, a Hindu–Muslim riot occurred in May.[67]

The second civil disobedience movement was suppressed rapidly, and more ruthlessly than the first. The government repressive machinery, strengthened by new emergency ordinances, went into action in a manner which was often cruel. The Redshirt volunteers in North-West Frontier Province were subjected to perhaps the severest humiliation. A village would be surrounded, people would be divided into Redshirts and Whiteshirts (those who took no part in the movement), and the former would be stripped in front of their womenfolk, assaulted and subjected to various indignities. They would then be made to swear on the Koran that they would not participate in the movement again.[68] The government method of realising fines proved ruinous. In Gujarat, for instance, government officials would remove all the contents of a house, including the doors, and all farming implements, and sell them at a low price, and the police would harass the family further.[69]

Although Congress had a greater impact on the masses than the Government thought (the nationalist newspapers had a total circulation of a million and a half copies in 1932),[70] the movement could not long withstand such harsh measures. Ramsay MacDonald even concluded that Willingdon's administration had gone too far.[71] The Government's measures smashed the urban structure of Congress; and, since the Congress organisation, in spite of its large mass backing, was predominantly urban-based,[72] by October 1932 there was no trace of Congress in rural areas.

Gandhi saw that Congress was losing the battle. He also realised that the British Government would now impose on India a constitution of its own making. What he dreaded most in the proposed constitution was the separate electorate for the Depressed Classes. When his fear was confirmed by Mac-

Donald's announcement of 16 August 1932 (commonly called the Communal Award) on the manner in which the minorities, including the Untouchables, were to be represented under the proposed constitution, Gandhi began, on 20 September in Yeravda prison, his fast unto death. His hope was to apply moral coercion to persuade the leaders of both Depressed and Hindu communities to come to an agreement which, while giving to Untouchables more seats in the legislatures than the Communal Award had provided, would not assign to them the status of a separate minority community. Dr Ambedkar (the leader of one faction of the Depressed community), in order to save the Mahatma's life, had reluctantly to renounce what he had gained at the second Round Table Conference. The result was the Poona Pact of 25 September, subsequently accepted by the British Government, which reserved a total of 148 seats for the Untouchables in the provincial legislatures, but provided that the election to these seats was to be through joint electorates. The Poona Pact brought a spark of hope to an otherwise gloomy Congress. To Bengal Hindus, however, the Pact meant enormous political loss: as against the Muslims' 119 seats the Hindus had been given only 80 general seats by the Communal Award, of which they had now, under the Pact, to give 30 to the Untouchables.

The fast and the Poona Pact, followed by anti-untouchability campaigns, diverted people's attention from a stagnating political movement to social reforms. Gandhi found much solace in his harijan works (raising of the Untouchables) and would have felt relieved if, on some grounds or other, the civil disobedience movement could have been officially suspended. But the pride and hopes of many a nationalist rested on its continuance, even though only in name, until the Mahatma could find a miraculous substitute or an honourable way out. The non-conciliatory attitude of the Government gave no room to Congress for compromise, and Gandhi was left with the choice of either surrendering unconditionally or of reviving a battered movement.

Between September 1932 and September 1933 he tried to put life into the movement mainly through a display of his mysticism and charisma. His sudden decision to fast for twenty-one days on 8 May 1933 (the timing and duration of the fast were dictated to him one night by the inner voice) drew world focus on the Yeravda prison and aroused the people's expectations: was the Mahatma about to perform a miracle? Jawaharlal, in Dehra Dun jail, received the news with mixed feelings. He feared that Gandhi's mystical activities would lead people 'inevitably to give up troubling their minds on solutions of problems and wait for miracles'.[73] The fast, however, induced the Government to release Gandhi, who took this opportunity to suspend the civil disobedience movement for six weeks. In July 1933, when Willingdon rejected his peace offer, the Mahatma launched an individual civil disobedience movement. He was duly arrested and brought back to prison on 1 August. The provinces followed his lead, and for a short while the spark of individual satyagraha enlivened the political life of the country. Gandhi played his last hand on 16 August, when he began a fast to the death until certain amenities essential for his harijan work were provided by the prison authorities. He was prematurely released on 23 August. He considered his premature release as providing sufficient moral grounds for his decision, which he took on 14 September, to abstain from civil disobedience till 3 August 1934, the date when he would have been released, had he completed his prison sentence.

His timing of the virtual suspension of the civil disobedience movement coincided with Jawaharlal's third release from prison on 30 August 1933. As before, Jawaharlal had lived an intellectually free and stimulating life in prison, though a touch of pleurisy and occasional bouts of anxiety concerning the political situation had lowered his emotional resistance. The news of Gandhi's fast unto death over the Communal Award puzzled and infuriated him; his feelings about Gandhi were so mixed that he was sometimes reduced to tears. He was intensely irritated by Gandhi's frequent references to the Almighty as if God was his personal adviser.[74] He felt angry and frustrated at Gandhi's temporary suspension of the civil disobedience movement, and was greatly distressed by the Mahatma's apparent confusion in avowing the cause of the poor while leaning on the pillars and beneficiaries of the present social order for counsel and support. Jawaharlal was particularly scandalised by the Indian liberals who, he felt, had shamefully co-operated with the British and endorsed the 'monstrous abortions' which were the outcome of the third and final Round Table Conference of 1932. He felt lost and most reluctant to face the grim political realities that existed outside the prison: 'Perhaps the happiest place for me is the gaol! I have another three months here before I go out, and one can always return.'[75]

Once out of prison, he set himself the task of rebuilding the ideological base of the national movement, which he felt had become lost in the politics of compromise and expediency. He began his ideological crusade by attacking the Round Table Conference as merely an effort to consolidate the vested interests in India which supported the British Government. He condemned each of these interests as reactionary and the enemy of the nation. The princes and the Indian state system could not be reformed; they 'must be and will be ended'.[76] Both Hindu and Muslim leaders came under his heaviest attack, for he thought it was necessary to destroy the bogy of communalism which the British were using as an excuse to perpetuate their rule in India:

> Communalism is essentially a hunt for favours from a third party – the ruling power. The communalist can only think in terms of a continuation of foreign domination and he tries to make the best of it for his own particular group. Delete the foreign power and the communal arguments and demands fall to the ground.[77]

The foreign power and the Indian communalists belonged to the same upper class, hence both wanted to maintain the existing social and economic order. As for the capitalists, he firmly declared that no matter what new social order India might eventually evolve it would certainly not be a capitalist one, for capitalism, shaken by the world war, was now on its last legs and a second world war would see its final extinction.[78] The liberals, who could not be clearly classified in one or another of the economic classes, were condemned for their cowardly, slavish mentality which turned them into traitors to the national cause.

He next scornfully attacked the proposed Indian constitution as a document worthy only of the wastepaper basket. The national movement stood for full independence; there could be no winning of power in instalments: 'People who imagine that they can gradually get the freedom of India, either delude themselves or are thoroughly ignorant of history, because such a thing never happens and will never happen in India.'[79] It was now futile to look to the British Parliament or to the 'sham and lifeless councils and assemblies' imposed on India by an alien authority; the constitution for an independent India must be drawn up by a constituent assembly, made up of Indians elected under adult or near-adult franchise, and thus deriving its sanction from the people themselves.

His verbal demolition of the existing order was followed by a theoretical reconstruction of the new order. Jawaharlal reaffirmed his belief in socialism, particularly in the Marxist view of history. As he saw it, then, the choice before the world was between some form of communism and some form of fascism; his preference was entirely for the former – Gandhism had for him now ceased to be an option.[80] He was bitterly opposed to fascism, the more so after Hitler came to power in Germany in 1933, an event which upset him so much that he even began to dislike the German language, which he had been learning during his imprisonment.[81] In fascism he saw no philosophy, no scientific outlook and no clear goal. By comparison with communist dictatorship, fascist dictatorship was for the possessing classes; working-class and liberal elements were crushed, as he observed was the case in Germany.[82] In principle he was all for the class war, for turning Congress into a peasants' and workers' union, but his theory was tempered by the realisation that a class war might damage the national movement, for 'nationalism hides a host of differences under a cover of anti-feeling against the imperialist oppressor'.[83] Thus an open class war, he anticipated, would have to be deferred until India became free.

It was not so easy for Jawaharlal to implement his policies; both personal and institutional factors stood in his way. Lacking the faith and ruthlessness of a fanatic, he often found his courage and sincerity tempered by compassion and, sometimes, by expediency. Institutional hazards were yet more formidable. As Congress was banned, no formal restatement of policy could be made, and even if Congress could have met it might not have followed Jawaharlal's line. To the liberal 'hangers-on' and the rightists in Congress, the plums of power which the proposed constitution held forth did not seem so sour and repelling as Jawaharlal would have liked. Then there was Gandhi who, though often deliberately vague in his definition of issues and policies, was decidedly opposed to class war and to many of Jawaharlal's prison-chiselled ideas, which he believed had no relevance to Indian conditions. Gandhi firmly reminded Jawaharlal: 'You have no uncertainty about the science of socialism but you do not know in full how you will apply it when you have the power.'[84]

Though critical of Gandhi's style and opposed to some of his ideas, Jawaharlal was still under the Mahatma's spell. Always seeing himself as the political child of Gandhi, he derived a comforting sense of security from his psychological dependence on the Mahatma. Though he was now a powerful, charismatic leader in his own right, even excelling his master in traits of national leadership, Jawaharlal was most unwilling to stand against Gandhi. He was hounded by the fear that Gandhi might die while pursuing one of his ritualistic fasts, leaving India, the national movement, himself, Kamala and his mother in a state of panic.[85] His politics, his household, everything, seemed to rely on Gandhi for survival. He felt that without Gandhi he would become lost in an India which would no longer be familiar; with Gandhi he felt free – free enough to attack all that the Mahatma stood for. He wrote lengthy letters to Gandhi criticising the latter's inconsistencies and vagueness, but would defend him publicly if similar attacks were levelled at the Mahatma from any corner of the world.

While the ideological differences between Jawaharlal and Gandhi were becoming wider, the personal bond between the two had grown stronger in the 1930s, especially since Gandhi had moved into Motilal's place. Gandhi was now consulted on all family matters. It was with his approval and blessing that Jawaharlal's youngest sister Krishna was married in October 1933 – the first instance of an inter-caste marriage in the Nehru family. In his desire to be helpful, Gandhi even found a good match for the sixteen-year-old Indira, though both father and daughter felt disinclination for an arranged early marriage.[86]

But his young leftist colleagues, S. C. Bose in particular, had no such divided loyalties. They wanted Jawaharlal to lead an aggressive socialist movement, to oust Gandhi, and to capture Congress or to split it, but they were much afraid that Jawaharlal might avoid any confrontation with the right wing by deciding to return to jail.[87] Himself an ideologist, Jawaharlal noticed with some alarm the growing prevalence of theoretical and often irresponsible thinking among his leftist comrades. Though unsure how far he himself fully understood the Marxist ideology, he perceived that India's avowed socialists had a very superficial understanding of Marxism. Though he had not freed himself entirely from the burden of Indian tradition, he saw how heavily it weighed on the thoughts and conduct of the so-called revolutionaries. He soon learned to appreciate the dangers of drawing up a neat theoretical programme of little practical value. An effective politician must work from given facts, not from possibilities.[88]

What, then, was he to do, placed as he was between two different groups, each laying its claim to his loyalty? He was too much of an individualist to fit comfortably into either group, yet each contained elements compatible with his own needs. This conflict of loyalty would not have arisen had the civil disobedience movement remained in existence; a mass movement could absorb all manner of people. The communal problem bothered him; and the Muslim demands as represented by Jinnah were, for him, absolutely out of the question.[89] He believed that mass civil disobedience was the only way to divert attention from the 'wretched communal wrangles of today'.[90] But as he saw no immediate prospect for the revival of the movement he decided once more to launch an individual civil disobedience movement. This, he calculated, would revive some defiant spirit among a temporarily much-subdued people, and might enable him to return to what seemed to him the comparative freedom of prison life.

On the family front there appeared to him no cause for special anxiety. Kamala's condition was no worse, and arrangements were made for her treatment in Calcutta. His mother was still bedridden but not as critically ill as she had been in August 1933. Indira was preparing for her matriculation examination, and it was decided that she should go to Tagore's Santiniketan for her higher education. His financial affairs were, however, in a muddle: the family had been spending much more than it could afford, and there seemed to be no obvious way of reducing expenditure. To improve the immediate financial situation, Jawaharlal was obliged to sell off Kamala's jewellery.[91]

Having satisfied himself that all was well at home, Jawaharlal travelled to Calcutta where he made three 'seditious speeches' on 17 and 18 January 1934. Between then and his arrest on 12 February he worked tirelessly on the relief operations in north Bihar which, earlier in January, had suffered severely in an earthquake. He was tried in Calcutta on 16 February, and was sentenced to two years' imprisonment. He was first put in Alipur jail, which was not to his liking, and in May 1934 was transferred to the familiar surroundings of Dehra Dun jail, where he began writing his *Autobiography*.

This time, however, prison did not give Jawaharlal that peace of mind he had enjoyed previously. The Congress politics that he had left behind took what was, for him, a turn for the worse. In collaboration with the liberals, the rightists took full control of Congress and the precarious balance between them and the leftists was entirely upset. Under their pressure, Congress officially suspended the civil disobedience movement in May 1934; they also decided to contest the legislative-assembly elections which were to be held in November that year under the old Act of 1919.

But it was Gandhi's mystical style in politics which caused Jawaharlal the deepest agony. On the very day he was tried in Calcutta, Gandhi publicly stated that the Bihar earthquake was a visitation for the sin of untouchability. Such an irrational statement coming from a man he adored shocked Jawaharlal, and struck him as alarmingly similar to the attitudes of the Spanish Inquisitors. Almost equally irrational was the reason Gandhi offered in April for his decision to suspend the civil disobedience movement. Clearly he was eager to find any excuse to do so, and when a very good friend and fellow satyagrahi confessed to Gandhi that while in prison he had failed as a satyagrahi by not performing the full prison task allotted to him Gandhi publicly declared that he was convinced there were scarcely any true satyagrahis left and that there was thus no point in continuing the civil disobedience movement. Quite apart from the fact that Jawaharlal strongly supported the continuance of the movement, he was enraged by Gandhi's public explanation, which seemed to him 'an insult to the nation, to Congress and to any person with a grain of intelligence'. For in conversation and in private correspondence with his intimates Gandhi had given more logical reasons for his decision: 'The revival of the Swaraj party is a right step; There is no doubt that we have in Congress a body of men who believe in council entry and who will do nothing else if they cannot have that programme.'[92]

From his prison cell he visualised Congress passing into the hands of opportunists and communalists, who had till lately conspired with the Government against Congress and who were now confidently denouncing socialism while not knowing even the real meaning of the term. Jawaharlal noted down his feelings towards Gandhi:

> It is clear to me now that I was mistaken in the hope and that there is hardly any common ground between me and Bapu [Gandhi] and the others who lead the Congress today. Our objectives are different, our ideas are different, our spiritual outlook is different and our methods are likely to be different. It appears that we even understand or interpret the English language differently in so far as it embodies the resolutions of the Congress.[93]

He felt as if something inside him had broken, and felt terribly lonely. But his first spate of disillusion and frustration was in some measure softened with the passage of time, and in August 1934, when he first wrote to Gandhi on the subject, he had adapted himself 'to some extent to the new conditions'.[94]

Despite his disillusionment with Gandhi and his sympathy for his socialist comrades, Jawaharlal would not cast in his lot with the All-India Congress Socialist Party, founded on 17 May 1934 with a view to pressuring Congress into the acceptance of socialist objectives and methods.[95] Even though the programme of the Socialist Party echoed his own ideas and policies (opposition to Congress's falling back on the constitutional method, and promotion of an aggressive labour–peasant movement against British imperialism), Jawaharlal had grave doubts about its ever acquiring the wide mass base such as Gandhi had gained for Congress in the past, and which was so vital for the success of the national movement. He was more inclined towards a middle position, in the hope that he might gain support for himself and the national movement not only from both wings of Congress but also from a large number of people who belonged to neither wing. This middle position could be comfortably maintained provided the two wings did not become involved in a fight to the finish.

However, since the socialist programme was thoroughly uncompromising, a bitter fight seemed more than likely. For the socialists were wholly opposed to Congress accepting office under the new constitution (the Government of India Act), which eventually came out in August 1935. They were also in favour of Congress giving active support to the people's movement in the Indian states through the States Peoples' Conference, founded in 1927. The bulk of Congress rightists, on the other hand, were in favour of office-acceptance, and in September 1935 there was launched a vigorous campaign, particularly by Satyamurti in Madras, against those (for example, Rafi Ahmed Kidwai in United Provinces and Sardul Singh Caveeshar in the Punjab) who were set on dissuading Congress from accepting the new constitution.[96] Congress in fact reached no official decision on this issue at this time, but on the question of the Indian States Congress supported the rightists' stand, which was that of non-interference.[97]

The socialist programme thus stressed the need for strengthening and enlarging the left-wing membership in Congress, though there was some confusion as to how this objective should be achieved. For example, Jayaprakash Narayan, the Secretary to the Socialist Party, cautioned against openly dividing Congress between socialists and non-socialists, while Sampurnanand (a young socialist from United Provinces who was to become the Chief Minister of his province in the post-independence era), emboldened by the fact that the socialists formed one-third of Congress, stood for an open split.[98] The socialist strategy alarmed the rightists, and Sardar Patel and S. K. Patil were driven to advocate disciplinary action against the leftists, but Rajendra Prasad, the Congress President for 1935, advised against such a measure.[99] The socialists, however, waited for Jawaharlal to come out of prison, hoping that he might join their ranks and lead them against the ' reactionaries' in Congress.

While Jawaharlal was in prison, the Mahatma took a clear stand in the right–left controversy by announcing in September 1934 his decision to withdraw from Congress, giving among other reasons his opposition to the socialist programme and strategy which were gaining ascendancy in Congress. Gandhi's theatrical withdrawal was in fact intended to bring Congress more firmly under his control. His original plan had been to seek the support of Congress by proposing some drastic amendments to its constitution, but Rajaji advised him against this course as it contained 'species of subtle violence.'[100] As an alternative, Gandhi chose to stage a self-withdrawal which was to become effective only after he had changed the Congress constitution. Gandhi's amendments were intended to prevent Congress falling under the dominance of the leftists, who did not really believe in non-violence and the spinning-wheel. This was to be achieved by confining the membership of the organisation and the composition of its various committees to the habitual spinners and weavers of hand-spun and hand-woven clothes; for example, no person could be elected to any of the committees unless he had spun for at least six months. To ensure further that the leftist elements did not acquire any ascendancy in the Congress Working Committee, the Congress President was to be empowered to choose his own cabinet. This would make the choice of president a matter of great importance. In view of this, Gandhi had already decided that the next presidency should go to Rajendra Prasad, an ardent Gandhi-ite.[101] The principal amendments put forth by Gandhi were accepted by Congress when it met, after three and a half years, on 26 October 1934 in Bombay. Congress also reaffirmed its faith in Gandhi's leadership.

Still tormented by Gandhi's peculiar strategies, Jawaharlal's anxieties were further increased by domestic crises. Kamala's condition deteriorated, reaching a critical stage in August 1934 when Jawaharlal was temporarily released to see her. The sight of Kamala, 'frail and utterly weak, a shadow of herself, struggling feebly with her illness', afflicted him with the intolerable obsession that she might leave him, and he was weighed down by the nagging suspicion that, in his passion for politics, he had neglected his wife. Should he retire from the political arena? The Government was willing to release him indefinitely if he gave an assurance to abstain from politics for the rest of the period of his sentence. He found the decision an impossible one, and wondered whether his personal conceit and pride were greater than his desire to give Kamala a chance. He was rescued from this predicament by Kamala herself, who forbade him to give any such undertaking to the Government. His temporary release in August lasted for only eleven days, but the Government moved him nearer to Bhowali sanatorium where Kamala was undergoing treatment, by transferring him to Nani prison in Allahabad and then to Almora prison in the United Provinces hills.

Throughout 1934, Jawaharlal was overpowered by a sense of utter loneliness which often compelled him to seek solace and companionship from his daughter. But Indira – herself withdrawn, perhaps because of her poor health (persistent eye, throat and stomach troubles) which made her 'languid and seedy' – was too much occupied with those secretive thoughts that are natural to a young girl and, being generally shy and inhibited in her relationship with her father whose company she had seldom shared in the past, she did not seem to him as responsive as he had hoped.[102] Though there were times when a letter from Indira brought him pleasure and comfort, as often he would impatiently tear open her long-awaited letter only to find what looked to him like a 'hurried note' obviously written to perform 'an unpleasant duty'.[103] He expressed his grievances confidentially to his sister Mrs Pandit:

> If there is one type I dislike it is the languishing type which lounges through life undecided as to what to do, but expecting everybody to minister to his or her comforts. Indu [Indira] has already developed many characteristics of this type. Then again she is remarkably casual and indifferent to others. This is a serious blemish as to teach consideration for others is supposed to be one of the principal objects of modern education. Indu, however, revolves round herself; self-centred, she hardly thinks of others.[104]

Having unloaded his heart in this way, he often admitted that such emotional outbursts were unprovoked and due to his shattered nerves. He occupied himself with writing his *Autobiography*, which was steadily progressing.

Constitutional politics ceased to interest him. Congress obtained a fair victory at the polls in November in spite of large sums of money spent by the Government on propaganda against Congress candidates.[105] Jawaharlal felt comforted, not so much by the victory of Congress as by the defeat of some Congress opponents whom he had come to dislike immensely. His animosity towards these 'undesirable elements' – the liberals and the communalists – can be clearly read in the pages of his *Autobiography*.

The year 1935 brought him more family worries. In January his mother had a paralytic stroke. Kamala was making no progress in Bhowali and it was decided that she should go to Europe for further treatment. In May she sailed from Bombay with Indira and a family friend for Badenweiler in Germany. But her condition continued to deteriorate. Pressure for the release of Jawaharlal was put on the Government by people like Clement Attlee. On 4 September his sentence was suspended and he was released on the understanding that if he returned to India after February 1936, when his term of imprisonment would have ended, he would not have to serve the remainder of his term.[106] Jawaharlal at once flew to Europe.

Indian politics at the time of his release was at the crossroads. On the question of whether Congress should contest the election and accept office under the new Act there was division, not only between the left and right, but also among the rightists themselves. The Madras group, led by Satyamurti and Rajaji and supported by Dr Ansari, stood for office-acceptance; Gandhi and Rajendra Prasad were vaguely against it. Before he left for Europe, Jawaharlal was briefly informed of the controversy by P. D. Tandon, a United Provinces Congressman.[107] Giving his support to those who were against implementing the new constitution, Jawaharlal pointed out that any such co-operation between Congress and the Government would not only be humiliating for the former but would cause its disintegration. Besides, the acceptance of office would hinder the early re-introduction of civil disobedience. It was, however, the question of the Congress leadership rather than the particular issue of office-acceptance which mainly occupied Jawaharlal's mind during his six months' stay in Europe from September 1935 to February 1936.

For reasons both personal and public, Gandhi wanted Jawaharlal to be the Congress President for 1936. Always full of admiration for Jawaharlal's courage and sincerity and his loyalty to Congress, Gandhi had shamefacedly come to realise that his mystical and confused politics of 1934 had not only repelled Jawaharlal's logical and defiant mind but had also given him the false impression that the balance of power had tilted wholly in favour of the rightists and opportunists. Gandhi, too, had been hurt to find that they could not see eye to eye in important matters: 'I can't tell you how positively lonely I feel to know that nowadays I can't carry you with me.'[108] Gandhi was anxious to regain Jawaharlal's loyalty. But there were public grounds, too, for the Mahatma offering the 'crown of thorns' to his political son. Jawaharlal was the hero of the left, representing the policies and aspirations of the socialists, but, as Gandhi had shrewdly observed, he would not necessarily support their methods.[109] As Congress President, Jawaharlal would thus not only be able to keep the right and left united but would also be able to put constraints on the unyielding socialists.

In September 1935, Gandhi thus offered the Congress presidency to Jawaharlal with an assurance that he would be free to follow his own policy and principles and choose his own cabinet. He further assured Jawaharlal that the rightists would not resist him, although they might not be able to follow him all along the line.[110] Gandhi's warning about the rightists was mild to say the least. Rightist opposition to the socialist programme was more severe than it had been in 1929. Rajaji and Sardar Patel were decidedly against Jawaharlal leading Congress. Jawaharlal had declared that if people wanted to elect him as President they should do so knowing his views and policies, which he would not compromise. But what about the right-wing stand on the question of office-acceptance, cried Patel, and what would happen to the money which had already been collected to contest the election under the new constitution?[111] Those capitalists who had subscribed to the election funds would never trust the rightist Congressmen again. The election of Jawaharlal to the Congress presidency seemed to

Patel disastrous to the right-wing cause. He was himself a candidate for the office, and this time was most reluctant to withdraw lest this might imply his endorsement of Jawaharlal's views. The conflict, argued Patel, was one not of personalities but of principles. Patel's chances of winning against Jawaharlal were more slender than in 1929. He was no longer the first choice of the right-wingers, who wanted Rajaji or Ghaffar Khan to come forward for the post, although neither of them was willing to do so. The left-wingers were all for Jawaharlal, and, failing him, for S. C. Bose, who was also then in Europe but less likely to be permitted by the Government to return to India.

Gandhi's verdict as usual carried decisive weight with the right-wingers. Informing Jawaharlal in December 1935 that he was most likely to be elected President, Rajendra Prasad expressed his hope that, in spite of the basic differences between Patel, Rajaji and himself on the one hand and Jawaharlal on the other, they would be able to work together for the country as they had done in the past.[112]

Power fascinated Jawaharlal generally, but it had particular significance for him at that time when, he thought, he could use it to restore the balance between the right and left and to put life back into Congress, which seemed to him to be in a grave state of stagnation.[113] What worried him now, as it had in the past, was not so much the differences of opinion between himself and his right-wing colleagues as the gap between his and their approach and outlook. He had the imagination to put himself into other people's shoes and understand their viewpoints and limitations, but he found his colleagues ever lacking in this ability, making them look rigid, narrow, and insulated from outside influences. How many colleagues of his, he wondered, felt as strongly as he did 'that the Indian problem is part of the world problem and the two must be understood together'?[114] His intellectual perception, his resistance to becoming overpowered by any dogma, made him, particularly, when he was saddled with power and responsibility, more likely to compromise and concede ground than most of his Congress colleagues. Underneath the apparent clarity of his policy-statements and ideological expositions lay always the great question – who can say with absolute certainty which is the correct way?[115] In this attitude lay, in some measure, the secret of his success in public life.

The prospect of his acquiring the Congress presidency came into immediate conflict, however, with his responsibility towards Kamala. His formal election to the presidency in January 1936 (he received 541 out of a total of 592 votes)[116] meant that he had to return to India in March for the Congress session. But Kamala's condition was far from satisfactory. Often her temperature rose to 105°. She was dying and, perhaps knowing this herself, she wanted him to spend as much time as he could with her. Keeping her company most of the time and helplessly watching her suffer was too much for Jawaharlal. He therefore snatched some time away from Kamala and visited England twice, first in November 1935, and later in January–February 1936, soon after his election to the Congress presidency, when a London evening paper said that he was at that time the most sought-after man in London – a remark which did not fail to please his vanity.[117] Political calls as well as his own desire to build new contacts and to revive old ones took him to London. There, during his first visit, he met various Indian groups – the Conciliation Group of Carl Heath and Agatha Harrison, the Friends of India of Reginald Reynolds and the India League of V. K. Krishna Menon, whom he met for the first time. He was deeply impressed by Menon: 'He is very able and earnest and is highly thought of in intellectual, journalistic and left wing labour circles. He has the virtues and failings of the intellectual.'[118] This relationship was to last Jawaharlal's lifetime. He visited Paris, too, mainly for intellectual stimulation, which he derived from meeting and talking to authors whose works he had read (Halide Edib, André Gide, André Malraux, André Viollet).[119] He also managed to meet S. C. Bose, who was then residing in Vienna and, although Bose's leanings towards fascism stood as a barrier between them, they managed to reach agreement on many issues.[120]

Kamala's condition began to worsen in the latter part of January. Her heart grew very weak. In India many voices were raised, mostly by women, in favour of relieving Jawaharlal of the Congress presidency and letting him stay with Kamala. Jawaharlal's conflict of loyalties would have to be resolved:

on the one hand lay India, waiting for him to lead her into the future, and on the other lay Kamala, fast receding into the past. Kamala came to his rescue by telling him to return to India. He booked his air passage for 29 February. But at 5 a.m. on 28 February thirty-seven-year-old Kamala died in the presence of her husband (whom she had married in that very month twenty years before) and her daughter. She was taken to the crematorium in Lausanne, and in a few minutes that face which had borne with dignity so much strain and agony was reduced to ashes. No longer inhibited by her physical presence, Jawaharlal was able to feel a deeper love for Kamala now than ever before.

He left for India, leaving Indira behind in Switzerland to continue her studies. On his way back, during a brief stop at Rome airport, he avoided a meeting with Mussolini for fear that it might be used for fascist propaganda and might also serve to misrepresent his views, which were strongly against Italy's invasion of Abyssinia. From Baghdad he sent a cable to his publishers in London, who were bringing out his autobiography, giving them the dedication for the book: 'To Kamala who is no more'. A chapter in his family life had come to an end; a new and exciting phase in his political life was about to begin.

CHAPTER EIGHT

Farewell to Revolution, 1936–42

We are nearly all – Hindus and Muslims – today somewhere in the 18th or early 19th century. Some are in the 15th or 16th century or even earlier. The Muslim League's attitude can only be understood in terms of the Middle Ages.

Jawaharlal Nehru, February 1942

I do not quite know what I am. I am certainly a socialist in the sense that I believe in the socialist theory and method of approach. I am not a communist chiefly because I resist the communist tendency to treat communism as holy doctrine and I do not like being told what to think and what to do. I suppose I am too much of an individualist.

Jawaharlal Nehru, March 1938

DURING the period from March 1936, when he returned to India, to August 1942, when Congress went into revolt, Nehru acquired and retained popularity and power mainly by avoiding taking sides. Nothing pressed on his mind but the need for national unity, which in the circumstances, so he believed, could be served best by inaction. 'It is something at least to avoid a wrong step although one may not take the right one.'[1] This act of avoidance must not take the appearance of a positive policy, lest the impression were created that one option was rejected in favour of another. Inaction must be performed in slow motion, in drifts rather than jerks. This method may have served the national interest; certainly it enhanced Jawaharlal's popular image. He attained great speed by riding two horses and even greater heights by standing on two stools. And to his own surprise he never fell. Such delicate balancing came to him naturally, but during this period he performed with greater agility and a greater sense of purpose, though with less than usual enthusiasm. Never before had he been so mercilessly torn between idealism and reality. This period also marked for him a comparably long respite from prison (he was in jail for just over twelve months only from November 1940 to December 1941); he was thus obliged to evolve a strategy to enable him to face likely problems as and when they arose.

The general problem that loomed large at the beginning of Nehru's presidency was how to maintain unity between the right and left wings of Congress. The specific issue that threatened a split between the two was whether Congress should accept the Act of 1935. The socialists stood not only for total rejection of the Act but also for an amendment to the Congress constitution which could enable them to increase their strength in the organisation. Rejection of the Act implied immediate resort to civil disobedience, which the socialists believed could be most effectively carried out on a class-war basis with the involvement of peasantry and labour. The rightists, on the other hand, firmly believed that the nation was not ready for another non-violent movement so soon after the collapse of the last one. The alternatives they could visualise were either to remain inactive but watchful, or to accept the Act, in part if not in full, and to enter the constitutional arena with a view not to wrecking it from within (as the swarajists had in vain attempted during the 1920s) but, as Rajaji now urged, to strengthening the prestige and position of Congress.[2]

Arguments against the former course were thrashed out at a meeting of the Congress Parliamentary Board held on 8 February while Nehru was still in Europe. All Congressmen attending the meeting were of the opinion that non-acceptance of office would give the rival parties – the liberals, the Muslim League, the Justice Party in Madras – the chance of entering into office and thereby consolidating their power.[3] Acceptance of office, on the other hand, would place Congress in an advantageous position for striking alliances with the minority parties – the Muslims, the non-Brahmins and the Harijans (Untouchables). Even those like R. A. Kidwai from United Provinces and S. S. Caveeshar from Punjab, who were in principle opposed to office-acceptance, seemed to accept the weight of these arguments.[4]

The general trend towards office-acceptance was as real as the power which the new constitution intended to transfer into Indian hands. The Act of 1935 provided for the establishment of almost full responsible government in the eleven provinces of British India. Based on the British parliamentary system, government in these provinces was to be conducted by Indian ministers who were to be responsible to the elected legislatures of the provinces. The Provincial Governor was essentially a nominal head, though he was invested with certain special powers. The federal part of the Act, which was never implemented, transferred only a portion of central power into Indian hands; the Governor-General was still to retain exclusive control over defence and external affairs. In addition, the federation, consisting of British India and 562 Indian states, was to come into existence only when a certain number of states, including at least half of the total population of all states, had voluntarily acceded to the federation. Thus the princes, not the people, were given the chance to choose.

The federal provisions were not attractive to any of the major political parties, though for widely divergent reasons. For Congress, the federal scheme was designed to perpetuate indefinitely the British hold on India through an alliance between a decadent imperial and an outdated feudal order. All party members kept their eyes on the provincial capitals where, for the first time, real power was available for use by Indians. Would this power corrupt rather than strengthen the Congress movement? This was the question at the back of Rajendra Prasad's mind. But an overwhelming number of rightists – particularly the provincial leaders who would, in the eventuality of office-acceptance, actually wield the power – were prepared to take this risk rather than let Congress stagnate in isolation. The young socialists, on the other hand, who were far removed from the power zones in the provincial and central organisations of Congress, and consequently least likely to enjoy power under the new constitution, were, more by virtue of their weak position than by strength of conviction, emphatic in demanding a total rejection of the Act. Their only hope lay in the leadership of comrade Nehru. Some among them, however, had misgivings about Nehru. Would he stand by them? Or would he succumb to right-wing pressure?

M. R. Masani, one of the joint secretaries of the Congress Socialist Party, conveyed to Nehru in Europe the general impression that the rightists, in making him President, expected him to impede the advance of the socialist movement in India;[5] even among the liberals it was commonly understood that Gandhi was hiring Nehru to kill the socialist cobra.[6] Nehru was thus put on his guard against easily conceding ground to the rightists. Further, just before he left Europe for India, S. C. Bose entreated him to lead Congress 'in a progressive direction', to prevent office-acceptance by all possible means and to broaden the composition of the Congress Cabinet: 'If you can do that, you will save the Congress from demoralisation and bring it out of its rut.'[7]

Nehru's arrival in Lucknow in April for the Congress session was eagerly awaited; the socialists looked to him with hope, and the rightists, liberals and Government with apprehension. Many questions faced the Congress President, the most pressing being whether it was worthwhile to maintain Congress unity. He resolved this problem with surprising speed. His earlier feeling that the national movement might achieve greater solidarity if run on a class-war basis now seemed risky and impractical. He became conscious not only of the strength but also of the value of the rightists in Congress. They were experienced politicians with prestige and influence among the masses.[8] They were in any case misnamed rightists, for politically they were far to the left and confirmed anti-imperialists. Besides, they were supported by Gandhi, without whom the national movement could not, he was convinced, function effectively. As compared with these old guards of Congress, the socialists seemed to him politically immature, ill at ease with their borrowed Marxist terms and unintelligible to the masses – particularly to the vast middle groups of Congress, who looked askance at the new type of socialist propaganda which attacked the Congress leaders: 'Thus the very people to whom socialism should have appealed were pushed away and made hostile.'[9] Besides, the socialists, instead of being crusaders, seemed to be fully occupied in seeking positions of authority in Congress through petty manœuvrings.[10] The fact that they appeared to be an organised force, that their militancy had a definite appeal among the young men of India, and that he shared with them the image of a socialist India ranked second in importance to his first priority of nationalism, for the furtherance of which he needed right-wing support. He thus adopted the objective of preserving Congress unity at all costs.

This objective determined the nature of his role from April 1936 to March 1937. It was essentially a conciliatory role, though he took pains to conceal the fact. While allowing the rightists to win on all major issues of contention, he continuously reinforced his credentials in the socialist camp by strongly affirming his commitment to socialism. By assuming the role of a helpless socialist, he neutralised any concerted action on the part of his socialist comrades and led them into reluctantly accepting Congress decisions as he himself appeared to have done. Then again, he worded his socialistic proclamations strongly, which created a stir among his right-wing colleagues and occasionally made them concede some ground to the socialists. In this way a delicate balance was maintained.

The Lucknow Congress witnessed the beginning of the process of indirect decision-making. The main question of whether the Act of 1935 be accepted or rejected was split into two parts – contesting the elections, and forming ministries in the provinces. As the elections were due to be held early in 1937, a decision on the first part of the question could not be postponed. It was decided that Congress should contest the elections, but this was to be done, so Nehru explained, with the object not of implementing the new constitution, but of wrecking it from within.[11] If Congress did not contest the elections its enemies would, and the Government would be given the chance of showing the outside world that it was ruling India with the co-operation of Indians. Congress must therefore win the elections and oppose the Government from within the provincial legislatures. Nehru had another, private, reason for wanting to contest the election. He believed that a European war was imminent and that in the event of hostilities breaking out Congress should be able to wring further substantial concessions out of the Government; hence the gate for negotiation must not be closed.[12] As the ostensible reason for contesting the election was to destroy the Constitution, it seemed inevitable that Congress should make a negative decision on the second part of the question, that is whether, in the event of its winning at the polls, it should accept office.

On this second issue the confrontation between right and

left was relentless. The rightists banked on political realities, the socialists relied on principles and ideologies. Nehru himself was for an immediate decision against office-acceptance, which seemed to him inconsistent with Congress policy. But perhaps the real reason for his stand against office-acceptance lay in his doubts as to whether Congress would sweep the polls and gain the majority of seats – even in the legislatures of Hindu-dominated provinces. Even in his own province, United Provinces, the odds seemed to lie against Congress. By all estimates (including those of many Congressmen), the non-Congress elements in United Provinces – the liberals under C. Y. Chintamani, the landlords through their Government-patronised party, the National Agriculturist Party – were a formidable enough force to capture the majority of seats.[13] Madras was still in the grip of the Justice Party. Congress was divided and weak in Bengal and Punjab, and the Hindu communal parties, such as the Hindu Mahasabha, were likely to divide Congress support in most provinces. Without a majority, the only way Congress could enter office would be through coalition with other parties, a possibility which seemed repugnant to Nehru.[14] The rightists, however, persuaded Nehru to postpone any decision on this question until after the election. This implied defeat for the militant socialists, whom Nehru tried to placate in his presidential speech:

> I am convinced that the only key to the solution of the world's problems and of India's problems lies in socialism, and when I use this word I do so not in a vague humanitarian way but in the scientific, economic sense.[15]

At the same time he made it clear that, much as he wished for the advance of socialism in India, he had no desire to force the issue in Congress and thereby create difficulties in the way of India's struggle for independence. His speech contained tirades against imperialism and feudalism, against landlords and capitalists, but no glimpse of an immediate course of action, of a definite plan. It was a good illustration of his high-flown oratorical style, full of fine principles but carrying little real weight. Even on the question of the affiliation of labour and peasant unions to Congress, which the socialists wanted and to which the rightists were opposed, Nehru merely offered the feeble advice that it would be advisable for Congress to broaden its mass base by offering corporate membership to such unions. Though he had definite views on the much-debated subject of whether India should opt for large-scale industrialisation – whether she should enter the modern world with Gandhi's spinning-wheel or with tractors – he carefully avoided taking sides by emphasising the economic and political value of cottage industry, particularly of khadi, till India became fully industrialised.[16]

At the Lucknow Congress, Nehru thus succeeded in averting the imminent danger of being specifically classified in any way. All groups and factions were to claim him, but to none did he exclusively belong. He also succeeded in keeping Congress precariously united. He had retained the confidence of the socialists while keeping the rightists on their toes. The latter banked on Gandhi to keep Nehru in order.

Gandhi was at first puzzled by Nehru's presidential address: 'I would strain every nerve to prevent a class war. So would he [Nehru], I expect. But he does not believe it to be possible to avoid it. I believe it to be perfectly possible especially if my method is accepted.'[17] But he recognised that, despite the apparent implications of Nehru's speech, if it came to action he would be careful and moderate: 'But though Jawaharlal is extreme in his presentation of methods, he is sober in action. So far as I know him, he will not precipitate a conflict nor will he shirk it if it is forced on him.[18] The Government, however, had no such understanding of Nehru, and took his speech at face value – so much so, in fact, that the question arose whether Nehru should be prosecuted. The provincial governors advised the central government not to take any action. Nehru's speech, it was argued, would not only galvanise the landlords and propertied classes into action but would also most certainly split and weaken the Congress movement. One of the provincial governors went so far as to suggest: 'Indeed we should keep him in cotton wool and pamper him, for he is unwittingly smashing the Congress organisation from the inside.'[19]

For a while it seemed that the government prediction might come true. In one of his many speeches made during the summer of 1936 – generally to exculpate himself from the responsibility of curbing the socialist influence on Congress –

Nehru, while explaining to a women's gathering on 18 May why not a single woman was included in his Cabinet, tactlessly remarked that he had no hand in forming his own Working Committee, implying that all its members – including his old colleagues like Rajaji, Patel and Prasad, and excluding the four socialists (Subhas Bose, Narendra Dev, Jayaprakash Narayan and Achyut Patwardhan) – were imposed upon him irrespective of whether he liked them or not.[20] His remark offended the rightists. To Gandhi it seemed uncharitable; Patel found it downright humiliating to be subjected to such a display of 'injured innocence' on Nehru's part.[21] As the right wing closed their ranks against him, Nehru persisted in teasing them and appeasing the socialists. On 2 June in Lahore, while commenting on a journalist's remark that his preaching of socialism might split Congress, Nehru mentioned, rather as an academic point, that a split would be beneficial to the organisation, for whereas it would lose only two per cent of its present support it would gain eighty per cent of mass support in consequence of the split.[22] Nothing was then further from his mind than the determination to cause a split in Congress; on this, as on other occasions, he said more than he meant.

The reactions to his speech varied. The socialists were encouraged by what they took to be an open renunciation of Gandhism and a declaration of war against the Patel–Prasad hegemony in Congress.[23] The liberals interpreted his outburst as an outcome of his acute egocentricity, which was the natural result of his 'long confinement and withdrawal from affairs'.[24] Some of Nehru's friends were alarmed and cautioned him to steer a middle course.[25] The rightists, however, could take no more, and with Gandhi's blessing (which was given with the intention of restraining rather than isolating Nehru) seven of them, including Prasad, Patel and Rajaji, tendered their resignation from the Working Committee.[26] Nehru realised he could no longer lash out at the rightists to placate the leftists. The Mahatma's intervention was sought. He reminded both parties that the country should not be made to suffer for their mutual intolerance.[27] The letter of resignation was withdrawn two days after it was submitted on the understanding that Nehru as President was to act as the mouthpiece of the majority and not of the minority in Congress.[28] The fact that Nehru could, at least temporarily, keep the right and left united obliged the rightists to elect him to office for another term. But, to make the point quite clear to Nehru, Patel, in withdrawing his candidature, said: 'We know him to be too loyal to the Congress to disregard the decision of the majority, assuming that the latter lays down a policy repugnant to him.'[29] Nehru chafed at the manner in which the condition was laid down but did not decline the presidency.

It was obvious that the majority of Congress was still in favour of office-acceptance – an attitude which still seemed to Nehru inconsistent with Congress policy. A decision on this matter was scheduled to be made at the annual session of Congress, to be held in Faizpur in the last week of December 1936, but this was postponed until February–March 1937 when the election would be over. Had the question been openly debated at the annual session the socialists would have made noisy opposition to office-acceptance, whereas deferment meant that the decision would be virtually taken by the Working Committee and the All-India Congress Committee, in both of which the rightists predominated; in addition, it seemed advisable to present an apparently united front at the Faizpur session.

At the annual session, the socialists, communists and the Royists (followers of M. N. Roy's brand of communism) all seemed to converge in a central policy, each with the hope of eventually destroying its right-wing core and of capturing the entire organisation. The rightists showed surprising tolerance in letting M. N. Roy be appointed organising secretary of the primary committees, but their apprehension regarding Nehru persisted. Office-acceptance now seemed to them the only effective way of protecting Congress from the steadily rising tide of socialism. The alternative lay in declaring war on the Raj, a war which they feared would enable the militant elements to come to the fore and disrupt, possibly destroy, the Congress movement. Nehru thus had to be forced, if need be, into endorsing the majority decision. Though he continued until the last hour formally to express his opposition, Nehru did in fact accede to the majority vote. The election results were chiefly responsible for this change of heart, for, to his great surprise, Congress gained the majority vote in all the provinces of British India except the Punjab.

Nehru himself was largely responsible for the Congress victory. His electioneering was a monumental achievement. Between July 1936 and February 1937 he toured every province, visiting many small villages. Altogether he covered over 50,000 miles, using every conceivable form of transport – including a bicycle. He addressed literally thousands of meetings and came in direct contact with ten million people.[30] It was for him also a voyage of discovery. India looked like 'some ancient palimpsest on which layer upon layer of thought and reverie had been inscribed, and yet no succeeding layer had completely hidden or erased what had been written previously'.[31] It was in this complex and mysterious personality of India that he found his own identity; its diversity and variety echoed his own multiple personality. In identifying himself with India he rationalised his all-inclusive style of leadership. Would not the soul of India be smothered if it was tightly and exclusively dressed in the garb of communism, socialism or even Gandhism? The Soviet system, for which he had so often publicly expressed his admiration, now stood somewhat discredited in his eyes on account of Stalin's Moscow trials. He revolted against the violence that lay at the root of revolutionary socialism. Socialism still remained an ideal for him, but he was convinced that it should not be implemented otherwise than in a democratic framework. Democracy based on a rule of law was the only safeguard against such organised violence as the Moscow trials: 'I cannot conceive of independence without democracy in India. The two hang together.'[32]

The election results were most gratifying to Nehru. Congress obtained a clear majority in six of the seven Hindu-majority provinces – Bihar, Bombay, Central Provinces, Madras, Orissa and United Provinces; though it did not capture the majority of seats in Assam, it turned out to be the largest single party. By securing more than one-third of the seats, it virtually became the strongest party in the North-West Frontier Province – one of the four Muslim-majority provinces. In Bengal and Sind it acquired a moderately strong footing for bargaining, if it wished, with other parties; in Punjab, however, it made no headway against the entrenched strength of the Unionist Party. Congress thus could form governments, as it eventually did, in eight of the eleven provinces of India.

The question of office-acceptance now came to acquire a real significance. Congress could now reform the system of land tenure and give immediate relief to the smaller peasantry, as promised in its election manifesto.[33] It could also fulfil its policy of obstructing the implementation of the federal provisions of the new Act, for the provincial assemblies were to form the electorate for the proposed lower house of the federal legislature. Such prospects, together with Gandhi's gentle persuasion, tempered Nehru's resistance to office-acceptance and he endorsed the All-India Congress Committee resolution of 18 March. This authorised formation of ministries by Congress in provinces where it commanded a majority in the legislature, provided that the governor of a province was not to use his special powers of interference or to set aside the advice of ministers in regard to constitutional activities. This proviso, which was laid down not only to make the idea of office-acceptance palatable to the leftists but also to strengthen the control of Congress High Command over provincial congress committees, delayed matters for nearly three months because the Government did not consider itself empowered by the Constitution to give any such undertaking. In fact Lord Linlithgow's administration was unwilling to take any steps which might strengthen the position of the central Congress party machine *vis-à-vis* the provinces, and so help to extricate Congress from the difficulties in which it found itself and which, in the government view, were of its own creation.[34] The deadlock, however, was resolved by Gandhi, who was prepared to accept simply a gentleman's agreement between the governors and their Congress ministers that the special powers would not be used so long as the ministers acted within the Constitution. This was soon followed by Linlithgow's statement that it would not be easy for the governors to use their special powers.

On 8 July 1937 the Working Committee of Congress authorised the provincial congresses to form ministries. Within a few days Congress governments were formed in all the Hindu-majority provinces except Assam (where Congress was able to form a coalition ministry in March 1938), and in the Muslim-majority province of the North-West Frontier. Nehru reminded the Congress ministers that this was just a period of respite during which Congress was expected to strengthen its forces to face a larger movement, and possibly greater conflicts and changes. Thus began the Congress Raj in seven of the eleven provinces of British India.

The Congress victory symbolised for Nehru the triumph of secularism and socialism over communalism, feudalism and capitalism. All political parties – local or national, run by communalists, landlords and capitalists – fared very poorly at the election. The Muslim League won only 109 of the 482 seats allotted to the Muslims, securing only 4·8 per cent of the total Muslim votes. It failed to capture power in any of the four Muslim-majority provinces; though predominantly Muslim, the Unionist Party came to power in the Punjab with some support from the Sikhs and Hindu communalists. The Muslim League also failed to achieve perhaps its most important objective – that of driving out all local Muslim parties from the political arena. Muslim politics remained divided between locally entrenched parties – two each in Bengal, Bihar, Central Provinces and Madras, and three in Sind. Nehru attributed the defeat of these parties to the fact that the electorate – which numbered about thirty million as a result of the new Act – was more concerned about such questions as poverty, unemployment and independence, for which Congress had an answer, than about religion, which had hitherto been the battle-cry of self-seeking communal leaders.[35] The election results convinced him that the masses were capable of forming class and economic alliances across caste and communal barriers; indeed, in his own province of United Provinces, Congress had inflicted a crushing defeat on the Government-supported National Agriculturist Party of feudal barons, both Hindu and Muslim. He calculated that communal politics could be completely destroyed by appealing further to the masses and bringing more of them within the Congress orbit.

With this end in view Nehru instigated, soon after the election, a vigorous campaign for mass contact. A central Muslim Mass Contact Committee was founded at Congress headquarters, Allahabad, and the provincial congresses were asked to organise similar committees for establishing direct contact with the Muslim masses and enrolling them in Congress. Usually Congress Muslims (also called nationalist Muslims) were chosen to run this movement at national and provincial levels. Nehru and Abdul Ghaffar Khan made extensive tours to popularise this movement, and by mid-1938 nearly a hundred thousand Muslims were enrolled as primary members of Congress.[36] The movement, however, declined as the Muslim League intensified its opposition to it, and in the early summer of 1939 Congress scrapped its Muslim Mass Contact committees.

Despite an increase in their numbers, the Congress Muslims, forming as they did a minority in the organisation, had little prospect of election to the various Congress committees. As most of them lived in towns and cities in Hindu-majority provinces, their prospects of representation on the Congress committees became slimmer when, in June 1939, the Congress constitution was amended to give more representation to rural than to urban areas.[37] Thus the only way Muslims could be brought into Congress bodies was either through co-option or through reservation of seats. Being in principle opposed to the latter mode of representation as practised in the government sector, Nehru could not adopt it for Congress. So in the summer of 1939 he endorsed co-option as the method for associating Congress Muslims with the various provincial and central committees of Congress. A co-opted member, however, rarely had the same rights as an elected member. He usually regarded his seat merely as a reward for his loyalty to Congress rather than as a well-earned promotion. He thus lacked confidence and a sense of identity, and, no matter how senseless the anti-Muslim prejudices expressed by some Hindu communalists – for example, Dr Moonje, who even in 1939 was fearful of an Afghan invasion of India, in the event of which, he believed, the nationalist Muslims of Khaksars and Redshirts kind would turn against the Hindus[38] – they still wounded his sensibilities. Being in such a weak position, the Muslim members of Congress appeared unreliable. It was a vicious circle, only occasionally broken by integrated secularists like Nehru who inspired a nationalist Muslim's confidence and protected him from excessive right-wing suspicion.

Congress entry into office not only drew into its organisation a large number of opportunists and job-seekers but also created in its provincial leadership a scramble for power. Congress High Command was forced on occasions to intervene in disputes between rivals for premiership (as in Bombay, where K. F. Nariman was forced to step down for B. G. Kher), or to reprimand unruly Congressmen – as in the case of Dr N. B. Khare, who was suspended from Congress for disobeying the Working Committee's command to stand down from the premiership of Central Provinces; or that of S. C. Mitra, President of the Bengal legislative assembly, who would not abide by the Congress ruling which required all Congress legislators and office-bearers to take only a certain percentage of their total government salary and to transfer the rest to the Congress fund. In spite of the vigilance of the Congress High Command, there persisted in Congress governments all manner of individual and factional rivalries which weakened Congress prestige and worked against a uniform policy and programme.[39] Within a year of taking office, Nehru warned Gandhi: 'We are sinking to the level of ordinary politicians who have no principles to stand by and whose work is governed by a day-to-day opportunism.'[40]

Indeed, some of the provincial governors, who had established cordial relationships with their Congress ministries, openly regretted the gradual disintegration of Congress. To Haig, Governor of United Provinces, nothing seemed so effective in disintegrating a party as the taking of office;[41] he was convinced that if the Muslim League were to take office in United Provinces it, too, would soon lose its solidarity.[42] Congress government in United Provinces declined to the point where it was thought that nobody but Nehru could save the situation, and Gandhi even asked Nehru to become premier of the province.[43] Hand in hand with internal disintegration went the opposition to Congress governments from without – opposition not only from the Muslim League, which was expected, but also from peasant and labour leaders who, according to Patel, were deliberately destroying the prestige of Congress and 'waiting for a time when they could displace us'.[44] Congress had to take special measures to dissociate itself from the Kisan Sabha movement and its leadership in provinces like Bihar, where peasant leaders threatened Congress government with violence.[45]

The Congress standard seemed to be falling also in provinces where Congress formed the opposition party – Bengal, Sind, Punjab. Irrespective of the High Command directive that Congress legislators in these provinces should behave honourably, the Congressmen indulged in all manner of manœuvres with a view to winning over members of the government party, thereby replacing the Government with a Congress-dominated coalition ministry.[46] Almost every Congress legislator, as Rajendra Prasad observed, seemed more anxious to become a minister than to get the Congress programme adopted by the Government. Congress High Command could not impose a uniform code of conduct on the Congressmen in these Muslim-majority provinces partly because the High Command itself became divided on this issue during S. C. Bose's presidency. For Bose stood for coalition ministries in the provinces:

> The position today is such that a coalition ministry in Sind, Bengal and Punjab is within the domain of practical politics. If this change could be brought (and in my humble opinion it can be) – the Congress will be in a position to speak to the British government on behalf of eleven provincial governments. This will mean that even without a Hindu–Muslim settlement, the Congress will be able to officially represent the people of British India while dealing with the British Government, and we shall not be seriously handicapped because there has been no settlement with the Muslim League.[47]

Bose was thus all for pulling down Fazl-ul-Huq's ministry in Bengal and Sikandar Hyat Khan's ministry in Punjab. All he succeeded in doing, however, was to awaken the wrath of the Muslim League, and of Huq and Khan, who were not at that time fully committed to Jinnah's League.

Congress entry into office also created tension and division at the central command level. In implementing one-half of the Act of 1935, Congressmen were also tempted to accept the federal provisions of the Act, provisions which Congress had emphatically rejected before coming to power. With their experience in provincial governments, many Congressmen had come to realise that the 'safeguards' and 'emergency powers' as laid down in the Act were after all not so stifling and arbitrary as they appeared on paper. Then there was the Muslim League to reckon with. It was becoming strong and uncompromising, and talking in terms of a lion's share of power at all levels. Might it not restrain them if the Muslims were allotted one-third of the reins, as laid down in the Act? Though Nehru and S. C. Bose remained uncompromisingly opposed to the federal provisions of the Act, there was a distinct swing in Congress towards exploring the possibility, or at least keeping the option open.

The possibility of federation brought the question of what should be Congress policy towards the Indian states to the fore. Since federation appeared on the horizon, the people had become restive in several Indian states – in the Orissa region, in Rajkot, Jaipur, Travancore, Mysore – and their struggle for liberty was firmly repressed by their rulers. Congress, which was fighting for the people's rights in British India, could not in principle apply a different standard in formulating its policy towards the Indian states. Yet open support for the struggles of the people and condemnation of their princes was bound to turn the latter against Congress and the idea of federation at a time when the coming into being of the federation entirely depended on their voluntary accession. This problem came to the fore in 1937 when the All-India Congress Committee, which met in Calcutta under Nehru's chairmanship, passed a left-wing resolution condemning repression of civil liberties in Mysore state and appealing to the people of the Indian states and British India to give support and encouragement to the people of Mysore in their struggle for self-determination. Gandhi, who was not at the meeting, subsequently declared the Mysore resolution *ultra vires*. Sardar Patel and Rajendra Prasad convinced Nehru, much against his will, that the resolution was inconsistent with the official Congress policy, pursued since 1928, of non-intervention in state affairs.[48] They tactfully imposed upon Nehru a policy of expediency and caution. Prasad confided to Patel that 'Nehru had been lately veering round to our view' and nothing harsh should be done 'to drive him away from us'.[49] For Nehru it was as hard a compromise to accept as that of office-acceptance.

Thus, in the eyes of the Congress old guard, office-acceptance had produced many undesirable results. They recognised that the longer Congress stayed in power the more damaging would be the results. This was the principal reason for the High Command's anxiety to withdraw Congress from the Government. Congress went out of office in October 1939 more with a view to regaining its stability than to commencing an immediate war with the British Raj.

As with Congress acceptance of office, Nehru's policy of non-alignment, or calculated indifference towards the Muslim League, produced results contrary to what had been intended. He had mistakenly attributed the failure of the Muslim League in the election more to a shift in mass interest from communal to economic issues than to the fact that at the time of the election the League lacked leadership, organisation, a sense of purpose and a determination to exploit to the full the religious fear and prejudices of the Muslim masses. Not only had Muslim politics been divided into a number of provincial parties and factions, but also the only effective all-India party of the Muslims – the Muslim League (the other being the inactive All-Parties Muslim Conference of the Aga Khan) – had since 1928 existed only on paper with an annual income of less than fifty pounds and a total of about 300 council members. The League's leadership lay in abeyance from 1929 to late 1935, when the fifty-nine-year-old Jinnah returned to India from London, where he had previously settled down to practise law, having become thoroughly disillusioned with politics. The Act of 1935 and a promise of co-operation from his Muslim friends induced Jinnah to return to India for one last show. He had then less than a year to mobilise the League for the election. Besides, he was at that time reluctant to give an overtly communal flavour to the League's election manifesto, which – as it finally emerged in June 1936, with its emphasis more on economic, administrative and educational issues than on religious and communal problems – seemed almost like a copy of the Congress manifesto. The League was not yet fully committed to an anti-Congress policy and came to an understanding with Congress, particularly in United Provinces where both parties joined hands in fighting their common foe – the National Agriculturist Party.

However, circumstances arising soon after the general election destroyed the mutual tolerance that had existed between

Congress and the League. The first breach took place in United Provinces where the League leaders, on the refusal of Congress to accept office until a certain undertaking was given by the governors, formed an interim government. This angered not only the Congress leaders but also some Muslim leaders who immediately shifted their loyalty to Congress. Finding itself in a weak position, the League contested the by-election in Bundelkhand, United Provinces, raising the cry of Islam in danger and adopting various devices, including the bribery of Muslim voters on an extensive scale. The League won the election, and the distance between the two parties was further widened.

It was against this background that in July 1937 (after Congress had agreed to form a government) negotiations began at Lucknow (the capital of United Provinces) between Nehru, A. K. Azad and G. B. Pant (now the premier of United Provinces) on the one hand and Choudhry Khaliquzzaman on the other; the last named asked for the inclusion of two Leaguers, including himself, in the Congress ministry in United Provinces. Congress, having won an absolute majority in the United Provinces legislature, was not obliged under the terms of the new constitution to form a coalition government with the League. But Nehru seized this apparent opportunity to obliterate the League in his own province, hoping that this would lead to its ultimate disappearance from the rest of India. In the face of opposition from Congress Muslims, Nehru was prepared to take two Leaguers into the Congress ministry provided that the League agreed to wind itself up in United Provinces, dissolve its Parliamentary Board and allow its members to become full members of the Congress Party. In addition, it must undertake never to submit a separate candidate at any by-election. Acceptance of these conditions by the League in United Provinces, Nehru calculated, would mean the solution of India's greatest problem:

> This would have a great effect not only in the United Provinces but all over India and even outside. This would mean a free field for our work without communal troubles. This would knock over the British Government which depended so much on these troubles.[50]

Nehru was himself both advocate and leading critic of this strategy. Against a background of opposition to the deal from the Muslim group in Congress, the whole affair began to acquire for him the appearance of market-place bargaining and his enthusiasm began to subside. The League leaders – Khaliquzzaman and Nawab Ismail Khan – eager to become ministers, accepted all but two conditions – the winding-up of the Parliamentary Board and the undertaking not to submit separate candidates at by-elections. In spite of the fact that Congress's Muslim Mass Contact Committee had aroused Muslim fears and enabled Jinnah to restrain the League from a total merger with Congress, there was still rivalry between Khaliquzzaman and Jinnah, and the former might even have accepted all conditions if Nehru had dealt with him more tactfully.[51] But Nehru had by then lost interest in the matter and actually discouraged Khaliquzzaman from pursuing the negotiation any further.

It was not so much the failure of the Lucknow negotiations as a general sense of being permanently in opposition in a situation where roles could be reversed that set the League on the war-path. In 1937, Nehru believed that there was no 'real strength behind the Muslim League or its new fangled supporters', and Jinnah seemed to him to have 'lost all idea of perspective and balance'.[52] As he saw it Jinnah, who had 'no conception of numbers or the big issues at stake', was treating Indian politics just as 'a background for being notable himself'.[53] But Nehru had not bargained for Jinnah's ruthless ambition, nor for his organisational powers.[54] Jinnah was determined that the Muslim League should be revived with the support of the Muslim masses and brought back into the political arena as a third party – a party which Congress must be forced to recognise as its equal. Muslim support was to be gained by creating among Muslims a fear of the Hindu Raj, by pointing out how the Hindu governments of the eight Indian provinces were threatening to destroy their religion, their culture, their language – indeed their whole identity.[55] In fact no such threat was ever posed by Congress governments during their twenty-seven months' rule, but Congress's growing vulnerability and the symbols the Hindu Congressmen used (which could be given a religious colouring) gave Jinnah's lieutenants sufficient ground for manœuvre and effective weapons with which to attack.

The League leaders began their attack on all fronts. The Muslim Mass Contact movement was branded as a 'Muslim Cutter' movement, and Muslims were warned to keep away from it.[56] Muslim sensitivity was aroused against the Bande-mataram song which Congress had adopted at the beginning of the century as the national anthem. Although the song had been sung for decades at each session of Congress, Jinnah now condemned it as a Hindu song with strong anti-Muslim under-tones.[57] Objections were also made to the Congress flag – saffron, white and green horizontal stripes with a spinning-wheel in dark blue in the centre of the white stripe. This new flag was adopted by Congress in August 1931: saffron represented courage and sacrifice, white stood for peace and truth, green symbolised faith and chivalry, and the spinning-wheel represented the hope of the masses.[58] Their religion, the Muslims were told, forbade them to bow to a flag. At Jinnah's behest a campaign was launched on the language issue, raising the alarm that the future of Urdu was at stake because Hindustani, which Congress proposed as the future national language of India, was essentially Hindi with just a veneer of Urdu. Even the Congress scheme for basic national education (devised to educate children from six to fourteen years of age through some suitable form of productive work) was so interpreted as to imply a cultural threat to Muslim children.

With a rise in the intensity of the League's opposition campaign there was an increase in Muslim assertiveness, filtering as far down as primary and secondary schools where Muslim children insisted on observing prayers during school hours.[59] This caused reactions among the Hindu children, who claimed similar rights to observe their own rituals. Within the legislatures of the Hindu-majority provinces, League members vehemently attacked the Congress governments. All legislative measures were condemned as being reactionary or discriminatory. In United Provinces, for example, a generous Congress Bill for the relief of agricultural and other poor debtors was criticised by the League members as being quite inadequate.[60] This was an easy line for them to take as the creditor class in United Provinces consisted mainly of Hindus.

Ignoring the fact that there were more Hindus than Muslims qualified for government jobs, the League accused the Government of patronising Hindus. While Congress was handicapped by being in the position of a responsible government, the Muslim League was free to advocate and promise far more sweeping measures. The League appointed committees to enquire into the 'misdeeds' of Congress governments, and the reports of such committees (the Pirpur and Shareef reports) were widely circulated among literate Muslims with a view to further strengthening the League's hold on them. Attack was also mounted on all Congress Muslims, who were branded as traitors and were socially boycotted and victimised.[61] Congress Muslims, Jinnah asserted, could not represent the Muslims of India, 'for the simple reason that their number is very insignificant and that as members of the Congress they have disabled themselves from representing or speaking on behalf of the Mussulman community.'[62]

The League's propaganda campaign created communal tension, resulting in Hindu–Muslim riots and, in turn, further strengthening the League's hold on the urban Muslim masses. In fact the League came to consider its capacity to cause communal riots its most effective weapon. For example, when Congress went out of power in October 1939 and the British Government consequently leaned on the League for support, the League leaders (particularly Khaliquzzaman and Jinnah) gave an assurance to the British administrators that if Congress launched an attack on the British Raj the League would fight Congress from the rear by causing communal riots.[63]

By the end of 1938 the League had succeeded in winning a number of by-elections, even one in the Hazaribagh district of Bihar which Congress seemed sure to win as there was no sign of any League activity in that area on the eve of the election.[64] Congress was forced to recognise the existence of a third national party. From this position of strength Jinnah emphatically demanded in August 1938 that both Congress and the British Government must recognise the Muslim League as the 'only authoritative and representative political organisation of the Mussulmans in India'.[65] Congress was not prepared then or later to concede this status to Jinnah's League, for it could not disown its Muslim members, which an acceptance of Jinnah's demand implied. Nonetheless, Congress was now willing to negotiate with Jinnah with a view to re-establishing the communal harmony which had been seriously disrupted.[66] Congress was further willing to form a coalition ministry with the League, at least in United Provinces, but Jinnah would not agree unless this was done on an all-India basis.[67]

Since June 1938,. Nehru's interest had gradually shifted from domestic to international problems and he had more often ignored than faced India's communal problem. The rise of Jinnah and the League was a reality which he recognised, but which he could not understand. He confessed to Jinnah:

> My own mind moves on a different plane and most of my interests lie in other directions. And so, though I have given much thought to the problem and understand most of its implications, I feel as if I was an outsider and alien in spirit.[68]

Yet the communal problem, he realised, had become a great drag on national politics at a time when, as it seemed in the autumn of 1939, not only India's future but that of the whole world was in the melting-pot.

On 3 September 1939, India was dragged into the world war, as Nehru saw it, without her people's consent. He had returned from a visit to China just in time to draft the Working Committee resolution of 14 September, declaring that Congress would not support the British in war unless the British Government, while giving a clear assurance that it was fighting the war for democracy and the people's right of self-determination, made immediate arrangements for the transfer of those rights to India. He was dissatisfied with the Viceroy's statement of 18 October vaguely promising dominion status to India at an undefined future date and assuring the minorities, particularly the Muslim League, that no constitutional advance for India would ever be contemplated without their consent and co-operation. That same day Nehru implored Jinnah to join hands with Congress and present a united front against the British Raj:

> I do not know what you and your colleagues in the Muslim League will decide, but I earnestly trust that you will also express your strong disapproval of the viceroy's statement and refuse to co-operate with him on the lines he has suggested.

> I feel strongly that our dignity and self-respect as Indians have been insulted by the British Government. They take us for granted as hangers-on of their system, to be ordered about when and where they will.[69]

Jinnah was unmoved. Yet he was not certain about his next step. The Viceroy's statement of 18 October, though gratifying, was not indicative of firm support. The Viceroy was, in fact, still under the impression that the Muslim League, having no positive plan and lacking in decisive leadership, might not be of much help to the British against Congress.[70] Besides, Congress still held office. But the situation changed most favourably for Jinnah when on 23 October the Congress Working Committee, as a result of the Viceroy's statement of 18 October, asked all the Congress ministries to resign.

There was hardly any division of opinion in the Congress High Command on the consequences of Congress's resignation. Nehru, who had wanted all Congress governments to resign for the last six months, was immensely pleased at the Working Committee decision and remarked proudly that there was more statesmanship in Congress than there was in most of the big cabinets in Europe put together.[71] It was believed that the measure would strengthen the organisation and establish the control of the High Command over the provincial congresses. Indeed, the provincial Congressmen instantly bowed to central command, albeit occasionally with reluctance, and Congress stepped down in seven provinces, in each of which governor's rule was imposed. But this measure, in the British view, weakened Congress's hold on the people, and when faced with the question of whether to placate or ignore Congress the Viceroy decided to ignore Congress and lean on the Muslim League, not so much in Britain's war against Germany (for India's war effort was then considered comparatively negligible) as in the event of a possible showdown with Congress if the latter launched a civil disobedience movement.[72] Jinnah was now emboldened not only to refuse to negotiate with Congress until it recognised the Muslim League as the only 'authoritative and representative organisation of the Muslims' but also to abandon his hitherto negative role in politics and give to the Muslim League movement a definite impulse towards a still somewhat vaguely conceived objective.[73]

With the Government's virtual abandonment at the outbreak of war of the idea of implementing the federal provisions of the Act of 1935, and reassured by Linlithgow in November 1939 that the British Government would not make any further constitutional arrangement for India without the consent of the Muslim League, Jinnah now gave serious consideration to the idea of having separate autonomous Muslim states in India. This idea, which was first propounded by the Muslim poet and philosopher Muhammad Iqbal in December 1930, had, during 1938 and 1939, captured Muslim political thinking. Were not the Muslims a nation separate from the Hindus, and as such entitled to have a separate homeland? At the suggestion of the Muslim League, a number of Muslims had since March 1939 attempted to give the idea practical shape, and had produced a few constitutional schemes, each based on the separation of Muslim from Hindu India and the organisation of the former into two or more independent states. On the one hand Muslim political thinking, as manifested through these schemes, totally rejected the idea of a secular and federal democracy and, consequently, the Act of 1935 which, while introducing autonomy in the provinces, aimed at creating a federal centre where Hindus, being in the majority, were certain to occupy all important offices and to wield overriding power over the provinces. On the other hand, Muslim thinking was vague and divided on the question of whether Muslim India should be fully separate and independent. While some conceived of a Muslim joined with a Hindu India in a federation which possessed minimal powers, others foresaw that the Muslims would lose their identity in a federation of this kind.

Various factors induced Jinnah to take an extreme position, the chief of these being a marked change in Congress policy towards Jinnah. Assuming that the resignation of its ministries had put Congress in a position of strength and enhanced its dignity, the Congress leaders, particularly Nehru, believed that Jinnah, having now no bones to pick and existing as a mere hanger-on to the Raj, would soon lose his hold.[74] Sardar Patel was against making any persistent approaches to Jinnah: 'I have a strong conviction that there can be no settlement of the communal question till Mr Jinnah feels that he cannot coerce the Congress.'[75] Rajendra Prasad warned Nehru against falling into Jinnah's trap and placing in his hands the power of veto:

> Mr Jinnah has been saying that he is ready to make up with the Congress and Hindus on the basis of equality. People generally take this basis of equality to mean equality in the matter of negotiations, etc. But I should not be surprised if Mr Jinnah's meaning, when he explains it, comes out to be division of power in equal shares between the Congress and League or between Hindus and Muslims, irrespective of population or any other consideration.[76]

Prasad's suspicion was based on Jinnah's support for the new constitution of the Hyderabad state which gave an equal number of seats in the legislature to Hindus and Muslims, although the latter formed only ten per cent of the population of that state. Nehru, who was optimistic about winning India's struggle against British imperialism more with the support of American public opinion (which he believed was building up in favour of Congress) than with the co-operation of Jinnah and his League,[77] duly held aloof. The stiffening of Congress's attitude towards him and the fear that he might lose his followers by standing still galvanised Jinnah into action. He asked the Muslims to observe 22 December as a day of deliverance and thanksgiving and as a mark of relief that Congress governments had at last ceased to exist. Nehru immediately abandoned the idea of having any further discussion with Jinnah. The 'Day of Deliverance business', in his view, did a good deal of injury to the Muslim League:

> Essentially the conflict between the Congress and the League is a conflict between the lower middle classes with a large mass following and the Muslim feudal and middle classes. Of course the religious element confuses the issue and excitement can be roused up in the name of Allah and Islam.[78]

Jinnah moved fast towards finding a goal and vision that could capture the imagination of Muslim India and strengthen his bargaining position. On 22 March 1940, at the Lahore session of the Muslim League, Jinnah, while asserting that Hindus and Muslims were poles apart and could not be yoked together under a single state which would necessarily have a Hindu-majority government, demanded that the Muslim-majority provinces in the north-western and eastern zones of India be grouped to constitute independent states. It was not made clear whether these two Muslim states, separated from each other by a long stretch of Hindu territory, were to exist independently of each other or to form a union. Perhaps Jinnah's move, though based in some measure on his genuine passion for a separate Muslim homeland, was essentially a part of his game of party politics, leaving room for compromise. But the vision of a separate homeland swept the politically conscious Muslims off their feet and the gospel of Pakistan spread rapidly among them, both in areas where they were in the majority and also in areas where they were in a hopeless minority and least likely to benefit from the vision if it ever came true.

Both in his policy towards Jinnah and the Muslim League and in his stand on the war issue (as expressed in the Working Committee resolution of 14 September 1939), Nehru was greatly influenced by his own reading of the domestic and international situations. In taking a hard line against British imperialism at a time when it seemed to be fighting a global war for democracy and people's right of self-determination, Nehru was torn between conflicting urges and considerations. His great regard for democracy, his sincere sympathy for the countries and systems that had already fallen prey to Hitler's fascism, and his passionate desire that India should play a role in the war were all outweighed by his suspicions of British government war-aims, by his distrust of British promises made to India and by his consideration for Congress unity which, he feared, would be threatened by the leftists if the organisation took a less uncompromising stand on the issue. Nehru's inner conflicts were perhaps, in September 1939, understood by none except his sister Mrs Pandit, who was then a minister in the Congress government in the United Provinces. She told the Provincial Governor that her brother might eventually come down in favour of supporting the war provided the British dispelled his suspicions by making a definite statement on the future status of India while, in the interim, making practical arrangements for associating Congress leaders with war activities at the centre.[79] The Government of India, however, felt more inclined to ignore than to placate Nehru.

Nehru's lack of faith in British leadership had been strengthened and his awareness of Asia's importance in the world intensified by his visits abroad – to Burma and Malaya in May–June 1937, to Europe (including Britain) from June to October 1938, to Ceylon in July 1939, and to China in August–September 1939. Of these, his visit to Europe was the most significant in terms of the distressing impressions he gathered about Britain's role in world politics.

He also spent nearly two days in Egypt, at the invitation of Nabhas Pasha and his colleagues of the Wafd Party. Nehru used this opportunity to cultivate the friendship of the Wafdist leaders and to bring the Indian National Congress and the Wafd Party into a closer relationship.[80] He was, of course, generally drawn towards nationalistic forces whether in China, Egypt or Spain, but to have a big Muslim country like Egypt as an ally of Congress, he calculated, might strengthen the faith of Indian Muslims in the secularity of Congress and prevent the Muslim League from acquiring the image of the sole guardian of Muslim interests.[81] He thus laid, for tactical as well as ideological reasons, the foundation of Congress's pro-Arab policy, which Nehru was to pursue more vigorously in the post-independence era in order to isolate Pakistan from the Muslim world. A further manifestation of this technique was to be seen in 1955 when Nehru befriended the Russian leaders in order, among other things, to undermine the growing strength of Indian communists. Nehru had already established his credentials as an ardent supporter of Arab nationalism when, in 1936, he had come out openly in support of the Palestinian Arab revolt against Jewish immigration into Palestine, which had begun under the Balfour Declaration of a national home for the Jews.[82] Under his direction Congress had since then observed a Palestine Day as a gesture of India's support for the cause of the Palestinian Arabs. For Nehru, however, there was no racial or religious issue involved in the Jew–Arab confrontation in Palestine. He regarded it as essentially a nationalist movement against British imperialism, which he believed was the source of all Palestinian problems. He was in fact most sincerely distressed at the plight of the Jews and, when in Europe during the summer of 1938, he seriously thought of inviting Jews to India to serve in government and private industry. He wrote to the Congress premiers suggesting the idea and pointing out that Turkey had immensely benefited from Jewish labour and that there was no reason why India could not do the same.[83] But the British governors and some Congress ministers opposed the idea on the grounds that there were not enough jobs even for qualified Indians.

Nehru was generally treated with more respect than on his previous visits to Europe, mainly because Congress was then in power and he virtually occupied the position of a 'super prime minister'. Before he left India, he received invitations to meet British politicians from both parties, and the German consul in India had extended to him an invitation to meet high officials, including Ribbentrop. He was not inclined to call on any German leader, Hitler included, though he kept his door open, when in Munich and Berlin, for all those who wished to call on him. He declared himself willing to meet all British visitors provided, as he told his English friend, they had by now learned 'how to behave themselves before decent Indians can go anywhere near them'.[84] Soon after his arrival in Europe he flew to Barcelona with Krishna Menon. There he met ministers of the Republican government and witnessed the civil war that had been going on for nearly two years. He promised his support for the Republicans, and condemned the Anglo-French policy of non-intervention which had virtually enabled the fascist governments of Germany and Italy freely to support the rebels against the loyalists. His later appreciation of the Soviet Union arose out of the support it was offering to the Republicans. From Barcelona he went to Paris, where he tried to grasp the European situation, and then to Britain where he spent almost the whole of July and met everybody who counted in regard to India except the Prime Minister, Neville Chamberlain, and Winston Churchill. He met Linlithgow, who was there on a short visit from India, and all the important Labour leaders including Attlee, Cripps, Laski and Morrison.

The Indian problem was on everybody's mind, partly because of the world situation, but he noticed a marked difference between the approach of the rightists and leftists. Whereas the rightists were still not prepared to end the empire in India, the Labour leaders, to his surprise, were all for giving India the fullest opportunity for self-determination by means of a constituent assembly elected on the principle of adult franchise. They went so far as to suggest that the British Government should immediately scrap all treaties with the Indian princes, but Nehru pointed out that this should not be done before the constituent assembly was created otherwise many Indian states might declare for independence.[85]

The respect and cordiality with which he was received in Britain softened his bitterness and subdued his suspicions. He even found himself willing to accept, on few conditions and as a temporary measure, the federal provisions of the Act of 1935.[86] But the Munich Pact of 30 September destroyed Nehru's new-born trust in British leadership. It was not just that the Pact permitted the occupation by Germany of the Sudetenland which shocked Nehru, but also the manner in which this agreement had been concluded by Hitler, Mussolini, Daladier and Chamberlain. He felt as if he were helplessly witnessing the rape of Czechoslovakia by Germany with England and France forcibly holding her down. He hoped that Britain would publicly express her shame of Chamberlain, who now looked to him like a man with no 'nobility in his countenance', 'a man not big enough for the tasks he undertook', certainly 'not a man of destiny'.[87] But he found no serious opposition to the Munich Pact, and *The Times* even sang the praises of Hitler and Chamberlain, which to his amusement actually annoyed *Punch* – that very respectable organ of the British middle class. The right course for Britain and France to take was, as he visualised it, to join hands with the Soviet Union in creating a front against Nazi aggression. By refusing to co-operate with the Soviet Union, the British Government had allied itself with fascism. He saw no effective leadership in the Labour Party and expected little from it in the future. India, he realised, could not now rely on Britain for her own emancipation:

> We have long experience of promises broken and betrayals by the British Government. Yet it is well that this new experience has come to us also, lest we forget. None so poor today as would care to have the friendship of England or France, for open enemies are safer and better than dangerous friends who betray.[88]

Nehru now firmly blamed the British Government for the tragedies in Palestine, Spain, Czechoslovakia and even Manchuria, which by 1933 had been snatched away from China by Japan. Disillusioned and agitated, Nehru returned to India in November 1938 with plans to organise relief for Spain and China, and to prepare India to face the second world war which, he was almost certain, would break out in the following year.

Soon after his return he was faced with a domestic crisis which was to shake Congress to its core, and to hurt him deeply. The crisis arose out of S. C. Bose's decision to seek re-election to the Congress presidency for 1939. For the entire right wing of Congress he had been, during 1938, an irresponsible, inefficient and unmanageable president. He had shown more interest in making a dent in Patel's hold over Congress machinery than in carrying out routine work at Congress headquarters. With Nehru in Europe, Patel had found it almost impossible to contain Bose.[89] Nehru was asked to cut short his stay in Europe, but when he returned Bose's term had nearly run out and Patel was looking forward to a new president. Political conditions surcharged with Congress–League tension dictated the choice for the presidency, and Gandhi selected A. K. Azad – the nationalist Muslim – to wear the Congress crown.[90] But Azad declined, and the nationalist Muslims and leftists, fearing that the next choice might be Patel himself, veered towards Bose.[91] Gandhi's next choice was Pattabhi Sitaramayya who, though an old member of the Congress Working Committee, lacked the status of a continental leader and was scarcely known outside his province. The rightist members of the Working Committee, including Patel and Prasad, urged Bose to withdraw, but he was adamant. The contest that followed essentially symbolised Bose's struggle to capture power from the Gandhi group in Congress.

There were many reasons – ideological and personal, noble and shallow – behind Bose's determination to seek re-election. The year 1939 was going to be crucial. The war might break out, in which case, he believed, Congress must take advantage of Britain's plight, give the Raj an ultimatum and begin a mass civil disobedience movement with support from foreign powers hostile to Britain, particularly Nazi Germany. He suspected that the rightists might instead decide to co-operate with the British and work out the federal provisions of the Act.[92] He went so far as to suspect, wrongly, that Patel had already decided who should be the ministers in the federal government. This hurt Patel, who sadly remarked: 'our enemies have also given credit for our honesty, but not our President'.[93] Bose therefore considered it necessary to remain at the helm in 1939.

The election was held on 29 January 1939. Sitaramayya was defeated by nearly 2000 votes.[94] His defeat, however, did not imply Bose's supremacy. The right wing rose against Bose and at the annual session of Congress, held on 7 March in Tripuri in Central Provinces, it asserted the supremacy of Gandhi over Congress through a resolution moved by Govind Ballabh Pant, the premier of United Provinces, which asked the President to appoint the members of the Working Committee 'in accordance with the wishes of Gandhiji'.[95] Bose's intention to bring young radicals into the Congress Cabinet was defeated. He was in fact entitled to defy the Pant resolution, but he could not run Congress without right-wing co-operation since the Gandhi group had firm control over Congress machinery and also held the purse strings. Though Bose accepted the resolution and asked Gandhi to form a Working Committee for him, he insisted that his own men must be included.[96] Gandhi would not co-operate on these conditions. He asked Bose to form his own Cabinet, formulate his own policies and put them for approval to the next All-India Congress Committee meeting. If they were not approved, then he must resign from the presidency.[97] Bose knew perfectly well that the All-India Congress Committee was the rightists' stronghold and that the right wing was determined to oust him. He therefore resigned at the All-India Congress Committee meeting held in Calcutta in April 1939.

Nehru attempted to save the situation at the last minute by offering two seats on the Working Committee to Bose's men and letting the rest be occupied by the old guard. Bose declined the offer. His resignation was accepted, and Rajendra Prasad was elected to the Congress presidency. In the first week of March 1939, Bose formed his own party – the Forward Bloc – within Congress with a view to rallying all radicals in the party in the hope of capturing power in Congress. Though Nehru believed that both rival groups were in the wrong,[98] he believed that Bose and his followers constituted the greater evil. It was not easy for Nehru to align himself against Bose, who had been his socialist comrade since 1927. On his return from Europe he had been urged by the poet Tagore to support Bose's re-election.[99] But he distrusted Bose.

It was not Bose's crudity which obviously distressed Nehru, nor even his ruthless crusades against the rightists in Congress. Nor was it Bose's political inconsistency. Nehru was even prepared to ignore Bose's inefficiency, which he thought was compensated by his modern ideas, one of them being the All-India National Planning Commission which he had founded in October 1938 with Nehru as its chairman. It was Bose's political ideas and methods which Nehru most distrusted. Both had travelled widely in Europe in the 1930s but each had acquired different political leanings. Bose had a definite leaning towards fascism and he shed no tears for lost causes like those in Spain and Czechoslovakia. This was Nehru's main indictment:

> The fact that in international affairs you held different views from mine and did not wholly approve our condemnation of Nazi Germany or Fascist Italy added to my discomfort, and looking at the picture as a whole, I did not at all fancy the direction in which apparently you wanted us to go.[100]

Bose's methods, it seemed to Nehru, involved a break with Gandhi which he thought might prove fatal to the national movement. Besides, the left was not strong enough to shoulder the burden by itself and when a real contest came in Congress it would lose. Bose was therefore a threat not only to Congress and the national movement but even to the left.

Bose wrote a long letter of twenty-seven typed sheets indicting Nehru. He accused Nehru of not making up his mind in a time of crisis and riding two horses. How could he be a socialist and an individualist at the same time? He saw no depth or vision in Nehru's foreign policy, which seemed to him nebulous and based on a superficial understanding of international affairs:

> I was astounded when you produced a resolution before the Working Committee some time ago seeking to make India

> an asylum for the Jews. You were mortified when the Working Committee (with probably Mahatma Gandhi's approval) turned it down. Foreign policy is a realistic affair to be determined largely from the point of a nation's self-interest. . . . Now, what is your foreign policy, pray? Frothy sentiments and pious platitudes do not make foreign policy. It is no use championing lost causes all the time and it is no use condemning countries like Germany and Italy on the one hand and on the other giving a certificate of good conduct to British and French Imperialism.[101]

Bose believed that Germany would win the impending war. Nehru was certain of Hitler's defeat. Perhaps both were letting their beliefs be influenced by their wishes. This was the parting of the ways for India's two most popular heroes. The young Indians, in India and abroad, felt sad and surprised, and bluntly put the blame on Gandhi for setting Nehru against Bose. But they over-simplified matters.

It was more the domestic situation than his distrust of British intentions as formed during his visit to Europe which obliged Nehru to take an uncompromising stand against the British Government on the war issue. A less uncompromising stand would have provided the Forward Bloc with a weapon with which to attack Congress. The period between October 1939 and October 1940 was a confused one for Congress and Nehru. Congress lay low during this period and was frequently attacked by the leftists – by Bose and his Forward Bloc, Royists, communists, socialists, all officially belonging to Congress and each group trying to overpower it. Congress was paralysed both by its awareness of the fact that the moment it declared a mass civil disobedience movement anarchy and violence would follow and it would, in consequence, be crushed and destroyed, and by its knowledge that the Muslim League would incite communal riots the moment Congress went to war against the Raj. Congress thus looked to the British Government for a conciliatory offer. The Government, however, was aware of Congress's predicament. The international press and British politicians were convinced that Gandhi would stand out against any direct action.[102] The British Government was under no real pressure and there seemed no need to placate Congress.

But the situation began to change after the fall of Norway, Holland and Belgium in May and of France in June 1940. The Battle of Britain began in July, and within a month the Viceroy made a move to win Congress support. But the offer Linlithgow made on 8 August was instantly rejected by Congress. Though the Viceroy conceded that India's constitution would be framed by Indians themselves, he assured the Muslim League at the same time that without its consent Britain would not transfer power to any system of government in India. This placing of the power of veto in the hands of Jinnah, as Nehru saw it, meant that Britain had no intention of granting independence to India.

In September the All-India Congress Committee reasserted its faith in Gandhi's leadership and the Mahatma was given a mandate to take necessary action. The Congress leaders expectantly assembled in Wardha in Central Provinces in the second week of October for the Working Committee meeting at which Gandhi was to disclose his plan of action. The meeting was scheduled for 13 October but private conversations between the Mahatma and his close associates began a few days earlier. Notes of these conversations were taken by Miss R. A. Kaur, a disciple and secretary of Gandhi. During these meetings Gandhi revealed his programme. A mass civil disobedience movement was out of the question, as it would be too risky. He therefore proposed an individual civil disobedience coupled, if need be, with his own fast. All accepted his proposal except A. K. Azad (the Congress President for 1940) and Nehru, who instantly exploded:

> For me I may have to rebel. Oppose aggressively. Can give you no undertaking of any kind. I do not understand your thoughts, your line of action. I see gloom. I have to think what I am to do. Rebel or not rebel. I feel you are leading the country to destruction. I don't fit into the Congress. I left it but returned because of the impending fight. This is my last W.C. [Working Committee] meeting. I can not subserve my mind. I look upon it as murder. I think you are unreasonable.[103]

Gandhi firmly pointed out that the Working Committee was entitled to ask for their resignation. This calmed Nehru who, realising that a wrong action was better than inaction, decided reluctantly to go along with Gandhi's plan.

The plan was duly endorsed by the Working Committee, and Gandhi selected Vinoba Bhave – an inmate of Gandhi's ashram and a true satyagrahi in his estimation – to offer the individual civil disobedience. This Bhave performed on 17 October in a village near Wardha by delivering an anti-war speech. He was duly arrested and sentenced to three months' imprisonment. But the Government frustrated Congress plans by banning publication of Bhave's speeches in the press. The Mahatma seriously considered fasting, in the hope of acquiring the necessary publicity, but Nehru dissuaded him on the grounds that this would only confuse the people, and might be interpreted by the Government as a failure of the individual civil disobedience movement.[104] Nehru himself was chosen to follow Bhave and was due to offer the satyagraha on 7 November in a village near Allahabad. But he was arrested on 31 October while on his way to Allahabad. In the government view Nehru was in 1940 'the most disruptive single force in the politics of the country',[105] and grounds were being sought for his imprisonment. The two speeches which he delivered on 6 and 7 October in the district of Gorakhpur, United Provinces, were considered by the Government as containing enough grounds for his conviction. He was thus tried at Gorakhpur and sentenced to four years' imprisonment. He settled down in the familiar environment of Dehra Dun district jail.

Nehru returned to prison after five long years of active political service. In these years he had acquired great popularity and prestige. He retained, however, the ability to view himself fairly objectively and with not a little humour. In 1937, when he was Congress President for the second term, he wrote his own portrait and published it anonymously in an Indian journal – the *Modern Review* – under the name 'Chanakya'. He wrote it, as he admitted later, mainly to study and enjoy people's reactions to it.[106] There was a trace of malice in the article, but he admitted that he had dwelt on some of his real qualities and his public style:

> Jawaharlal cannot become a fascist. And yet he has all the making of a dictator in him – vast popularity, a strong will directed to a well-defined purpose, energy, pride, organi-

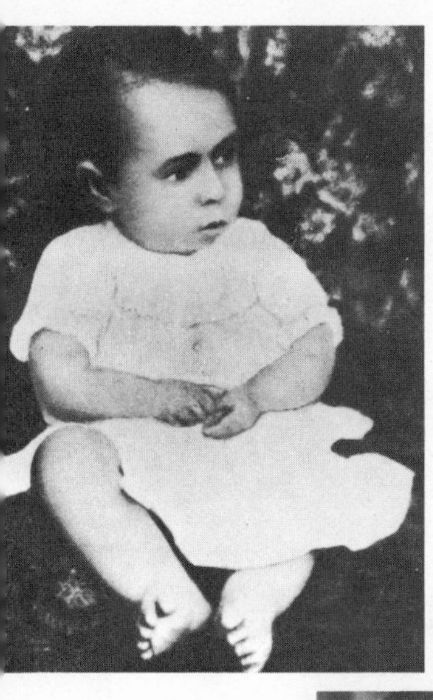

Nehru aged 2. *Below*, a family group taken in 1909 when Nehru was 20. His father, Motilal, was the first important influence in his life; his sister Nan, later Mrs Pandit, for whom he always had a deep affection became his chief confidante.

New Anand Bhawan, built by Motilal, was the Nehru family home from 1928

Nehru in prison; his long periods in jail enabled him to read widely and generally to prepare for the moment when India became independent. *Below*, a return to his 'alma mater'. He is cheered by the boys of Harrow School.

Nehru with his two sisters and his daughter
Mrs Indira Gandhi. *Below*, negotiating with
Lord Mountbatten for the partition of India in the
summer of 1947. Jinnah sits on Mountbatten's left.

Above, Nehru and Chou-En-Lai seemed friendly in 1954. *Right*, Nehru cuts the cake for Khrushchev and Bulganin during their visit to India in 1955.

CUPID: "GET A MOVE ON! I CAN'T STAY HERE FOR EVER"

Nehru wooing Jinnah; Clement Atlee plays Cupid. Low, 5 March 1947. *Below*, Nurse Brittania leaves Nehru with howling babies—the Princely States. Low, 18 July 1947.

"YOUR BABIES NOW"

"H'M... DON'T LIKE HIS ATTITUDE"

Nehru kneels to Ike—the Republican 'Old Guard' look on. Low, 10 December 1954. *Below*, Nehru and the Chinese Dragon. Low, 9 October 1962.

BIT BY BIT.

Nehru converted Nasser to non-alignment in 1955.
Below, he talks with Jinnah between meetings at a
conference in London in December 1946.

India. He saw in this same war, however, the end both of Hitler's Nazism and the British Empire, and was astonished to find that the British did not regard their empire as already a thing of the past.[113] He was convinced that there could be no successful settlement of world problems unless India and China were included in that settlement as free nations.[114]

However, during the course of his imprisonment the nature of the war began to change for him. When Germany invaded Russia in June 1941 and Churchill pledged his support for the Soviet Union the war ceased to be an imperialist charade. In the following month Japanese troops landed in Indo-China bringing the war to the doorstep of South Asia. Mobilisation of India's vast resources and manpower, and assurance of India's co-operation became necessities for Britain. As a conciliatory gesture towards Congress, the Viceroy announced on 3 December 1941 that all political prisoners who had courted imprisonment since October 1940 under Gandhi's individual civil disobedience movement would be released. Nehru's premature release on 4 December was followed on 7 December by the Japanese attack on Pearl Harbor and on 11 December by the declaration of war on Japan and Germany by the United States and China. Almost simultaneously, Germany and Italy declared war on the United States. The war assumed a real global dimension.

The involvement of Russia, America and China and the steady advance of Japan towards India's eastern frontiers (Rangoon and Singapore fell to the Japanese in February–March 1942) had a great impact on Nehru's attitude towards the war. Though still highly critical of British imperialists, whom he considered arrogant and inefficient, and though persisting in his view that lack of co-operation between the Army and the people was mainly responsible for British reverses in Malaya and Burma, Nehru was now open to considering terms for Congress support for Britain in her war effort. A corresponding change in British policy towards Congress was, at this time, perhaps brought about more by American pressure than by the imminent Japanese threat to the British Empire in India. Much to Roosevelt's puzzlement, Churchill had declared, on 9 September 1941, that the Atlantic Charter did not apply to India and Burma. This meant that India was excluded from the category of peoples who were assured of their right to choose their own government. Churchill's statement had deeply humiliated Indian politicians of all parties. When Churchill met Roosevelt again in mid-December 1941 in Washington, and the idea of the United Nations was conceived, the American President emphasised the importance of China and India. At his insistence China was brought into the group of the Big Five (the others being America, Britain, France and the Soviet Union), an event which foreshadowed the predominance of these powers in the post-war United Nations Organisation. Roosevelt also impressed upon Churchill the need for a reorientation of British policy towards India.[115]

Two events of considerable significance for the future of India occurred soon after the Roosevelt–Churchill meeting in Washington. Generalissimo Chiang Kai-shek (President of the National Supreme War Council of China) and his wife visited India in February 1942. And almost at the same time Churchill's War Cabinet and its committee on India began framing a constitutional plan for India. The plan was completed by 9 March, and Sir Stafford Cripps – the Lord Privy Seal and Leader of the House of Commons – was chosen to take the plan to India. Cripps arrived in India on 22 March. Meanwhile, Roosevelt had on 19 March appointed Colonel Louis Johnson to be his personal representative in India with the rank of minister.

Generalissimo and Madame Chiang Kai-shek exercised considerable influence on Nehru from February to May 1942. During their visit to India they prepared Nehru for giving favourable consideration to any terms of settlement offered by the British. The fact that China and the Soviet Union were involved in the war, coupled with Madame Chiang Kai-shek's assurance of securing Roosevelt's firm support for India's cause, disposed him favourably towards the Cripps Mission. Even though the long-term constitutional plans were unacceptable to Congress, he strove hard to come to an interim settlement with the British under the Cripps proposals with a view to letting India play her role in the war. After the failure of the Cripps Mission, Madame Chiang Kai-shek promised Nehru to secure Roosevelt's intervention in resolving the Indian deadlock and entreated him to prevent Congress from taking militant action against the British while she was pursuing India's cause in Washington during the summer months of 1942:

> Regarding your suggestion in answer to the Generalissimo's enquiry how we can help India, I have translated it to him in full. He is most anxious to do everything he can to help, and is now taking up the matter with Roosevelt. What answer Roosevelt will give, we do not know of course but you can count on us to press India's interest to the utmost.[116]

Stafford Cripps arrived in India with a two-part plan. The long-term plan envisaged the creation of a new Indian union with dominion status. The constitution for the Indian union was to be framed soon after the end of the war – by Indians representing both the British Indian provinces and Indian states; the representatives of the Indian states, however, were to be appointed by the rulers. Any province of British India that did not accept the new constitution and in consequence did not want to join the Indian union was entitled to retain its separate existence and frame its own constitution. Under the interim proposals, which were intended to be operative during the continuation of the war and until a constitution-making body was formed, the leaders of the principal sections of the Indian people were invited to join the Viceroy's Executive Council and to give their advice and support to the British Government in the prosecution of the war. The defence portfolio, however, was to remain the charge of the British Commander-in-Chief and would not be entrusted to an Indian member of the Government.

Congress reacted vehemently against the long-term proposals, which seemed to pave the way for the partition of India into several sovereign states. Not only the Muslim provinces of British India but also some large Indian states might well bid for sovereign status. This was particularly likely in the case of Indian states whose rulers, and not the people, were given the right to opt out of the proposed Indian union. Congress High Command did not exclude the possibility of such a separatist movement becoming strong even in Hindu provinces of British India. The Justice Party of Madras was already asking for the formation of a separate state of south India, to be called

Dravidastan. In the Congress ranks themselves a leader of great standing – Rajaji – was inclined to accept the idea of Pakistan. Congress therefore rejected the long-term proposals, leaving the door open for further negotiations on the interim proposals.

These negotiations were almost entirely conducted by Nehru, who even drafted the formal letters of Congress President Azad to Cripps. Nehru's mood was conciliatory throughout, which was due not only to Madame Chiang Kai-shek's intervention but also to the fact that Cripps had been a close friend since 1938. When, during the course of the Cripps Mission, the editor of a nationalist newspaper condemned the Cripps proposals under the headline 'Put it in your pipe and smoke it, Cripps', Nehru reprimanded him severely for such a vulgar remark.[117] Nehru held Cripps in high regard for his unquestioned abilities and straightforwardness but believed that his judgement was 'not always to be relied upon'.[118] Nehru was even willing to consider favourably the long-term proposals, provided the scheme was amended so as to give to the Muslim provinces of British India the opportunity to opt out of the Indian union only five or ten years after the promulgation of the new constitution. Cripps ruled this out as being 'a far more disruptive method of deciding the matter than doing it in the making of the constitution'.[119] In four years' time Nehru's view was to find a place in the Cabinet Mission Plan of 1946, of which Cripps was a member.

The negotiations between Nehru and Cripps, with the aid or intervention of Colonel Johnson, mainly focused on the interim proposals. The British War Cabinet sought Indian collaboration with the central government in the existing imperial framework, where the Governor-General was to retain his supreme powers, the important portfolios like Home Defence and Finance were to remain in British hands, and the Indians were to function as members of the Viceroy's Executive Council. Nehru, on the other hand, asked for the immediate establishment of an interim national government wherein the Viceroy would play the role of a titular head and all portfolios including Home, Defence and Finance would be placed in the hands of Indian ministers. The very idea of a national government put Churchill on his guard, and Linlithgow and

Lord Wavell (now Commander-in-Chief) were opposed to surrendering the powers of their respective offices into Indian hands. Cripps, however, was willing to meet Nehru halfway.

On his own initiative he offered on 7 April to modify the original plan so as to let the Commander-in-Chief and an Indian member function on the Executive Council as War and Defence ministers respectively, the former retaining full control over all the war activities of the armed forces in India and the latter taking over certain sections of the Department of Defence which could be immediately separated from the Commander-in-Chief's War Department. This division of powers between the War and Defence ministers seemed to Nehru uneven and he asked for more powers to be transferred to the Indian Defence Minister in order to make it appear that there was a real transfer of responsibility for defence to Indians in the national government.[120] Colonel Johnson intervened at this point, and the result was the Cripps–Johnson formula of 9 April which transferred a few more departments to the Defence Minister, but not enough to satisfy Nehru. On the same day Churchill warned Cripps against committing the British Government in any way until his plan was approved by the War Cabinet. He further requested Cripps not to let Johnson intervene in political matters. On 10 April, Churchill cabled Cripps: 'We feel that in your natural desire to reach a settlement with Congress you may be drawn into positions far different from any the Cabinet and ministers of cabinet rank approved before you set forth.'[121]

This was in essence a show of Churchill's lack of confidence in Cripps' mission to India. The same day – 10 April – Azad, the Congress President, wrote to Cripps expressing Congress's dissatisfaction with the Cripps–Johnson formula. Azad's letter, drafted by Nehru, was not a total rejection of the formula, however. Nehru hoped that the situation might be improved through further negotiation. Realising that he had gone too far for the War Cabinet and not far enough for Congress, Cripps lost enthusiasm and returned to London on 12 April. Churchill was relieved; the purpose of the Cripps Mission, so far as he was concerned, was primarily to impress upon Roosevelt that Britain had done all it could to resolve the Indian problem.[122]

But Roosevelt was not convinced. On 12 April he asked Churchill to encourage Cripps to put one last effort into resolving the deadlock:

> The feeling is held almost universally that the deadlock has been due to the British Government's unwillingness to concede the right of self-government to the Indians notwithstanding the willingness of the Indians to entrust to the competent British authorities technical, military and naval defence control. It is impossible for American public opinion to understand why, if there is willingness on the part of the British Government to permit the component parts of India to secede after the war from the British Empire, it is unwilling to permit them to enjoy during the war what is tantamount to self-government.[123]

Fortunately for Churchill, Cripps had already left India.

The failure of the Cripps Mission was mainly due to Churchill's unwillingness to concede to India even the semblance of a national government. Nehru was disappointed. He had gone against Gandhi's wishes in negotiating conditions for India's participation in the war. Gandhi was all for India offering non-violent non-co-operation to the Japanese aggressor, and he even asked Britain to offer a non-violent satyagraha against the German invaders. Nehru was decidedly against introducing non-violent techniques into an international war and was all for fighting Japan with the bayonet rather than the spinning-wheel. Nehru, however, seemed to be losing ground with the Mahatma on the question of non-violence. The Cripps Mission offered him a chance. Its success would have enabled him to stand against the Mahatma. But the Mission failed.

Disarmed by the failure of the Cripps Mission, Nehru gradually veered towards the Gandhian alternative of mass action. For a couple of months there lingered in his mind a hope that a settlement might be made under the pressure exercised on Britain by America and China. But nothing happened. In the meantime the British reverses in Burma, and the racial discrimination allegedly applied by British officers in their treatment of Indian refugees from Malaya and Burma, revived Nehru's resentment against the Raj:

> It is the misfortune of India at this crisis in history not only to have a foreign Government but a Government which is incompetent and incapable of organizing her defence properly or of providing for the safety and essential needs of her people.[124]

His concern to preserve the goodwill of the Allied powers towards India, particularly of Russia, China and America, gradually subsided under the pressure of the national demand. Cripps' long-term proposals had already done damage to Indian unity. To both Gandhi and Nehru the Cripps Plan foreshadowed the policy Britain would most assuredly adopt towards a settlement of the Indian problem after the war. She would insist on a prior agreement between all parties, particularly between Congress and the League, before transferring power to India. This agreement would never be reached, for the parties would never come together as long as they had to look not to one another but to the British for support and sustenance.[125] As a result of this India would either be partitioned into two or more sovereign states or her independence would be delayed indefinitely. Neither of these alternatives was acceptable to Gandhi and Nehru. Britain must, therefore, transfer power to India unconditionally. Communal problems would resolve themselves as soon as the British withdrew from India leaving the country to its own fate. The year 1942 provided an opportune time for putting pressure on the British through a mass movement.

During the months of May and June, Gandhi occupied himself in preparing Congress to give the British an ultimatum to quit India. Nehru waited and watched and took a short holiday in the Kulu Valley. In June he began to realise that there was probably no alternative to Gandhi's plan of action.[126] The Congress Working Committee met in Wardha from 6 to 14 July and passed the 'quit India' resolution, asking the British to transfer power to Indian hands immediately. While affirming that it was not the intention of Congress to embarrass the war effort of Britain and her allies, it offered them bases in India for the duration of the war. If this ultimatum was not heeded by the British, then Congress was to declare a non-violent mass movement against the Raj. An All-India Congress Committee was summoned to meet in Bombay on 7 August to endorse the 'quit India' resolution. Nehru was now fully committed to starting a mass movement:

> I have been worried and disturbed beyond measure. Yet gradually I have come to this conclusion that there is no other way out. I am convinced that passivity is fatal now. Our soldiers will largely surrender to the Japanese, our people will submit to them. There is only one chance of changing this and that is by some actions now. The risk is there. I hate anarchy and chaos but somehow in my bones I feel some terrible shake-up is necessary for our country. Otherwise we shall get more and more entangled in communal and other problems, people will get thoroughly disillusioned and will merely drift to disaster.[127]

On 24 July, Nehru wrote confidential instructions for the Congress workers: the proposed movement was likely to be of a far more intense and widespread character than previous movements; it was not Gandhi's intention to fill the jails. The movement would include non-payment of taxes, hartals, resignation from government service, and refusal to obey government orders. As it would be difficult to have central or provincial control over the movement, work must be carried on through local initiative; in the course of the movement there should not be destruction of property.[128]

The Wardha resolution was condemned by leaders of almost all political parties – by Jinnah, Savarkar of the Hindu Mahasabha, Sapru and Sastri of the Liberal Party, P. C. Joshi of the Indian Communist Party. In his broadcast to the Americans on 27 July, Stafford Cripps directly attacked Gandhi for asking the British to walk out of India, leaving the country with its deep-rooted religious division, without any constitutional form of government and with no organised administration. Congress, however, was now firmly set on the war-path. Moved by Nehru and seconded by Sardar Patel, the 'quit India' resolution was passed by the All-India Congress Committee on 8 August. A mass civil disobedience movement began and millions of Congress supporters were galvanised into action. On 9 August all members of the Congress Working Committee were arrested in Bombay. Gandhi was detained at the Aga Khan's palace in Poona, while Nehru, together with other Congress leaders, was taken to the Ahmednagar Fort. This was to be Nehru's last and longest period of imprisonment. It was also to be Congress's last, and most widespread, revolt against the Raj. Congress embarked on the contest mainly to circumvent the communal obstacle that lay in India's path to freedom. This it was not destined to achieve.

CHAPTER NINE

The Defeat of a Nationalist, 1942–7

We are all, individuals as well as nations, products of our past (call it heredity or the cumulative effect of action) and our environments. To that extent, and it is a great deal, we are children of destiny, bound in many ways to walk along a pre-determined path.

Jawaharlal Nehru, November 1943

How have we played our part in this brief interlude that draws to a close? I do not know. Others of a later age will judge. By what standards do we measure success or failure? That too I do not know. . . . In spite of all the mistakes that we may have made, we have saved ourselves from triviality and an inner shame and cowardice. That, for our individual selves, has been some achievement.

Jawaharlal Nehru, September 1944

We are little men serving a great cause, but because the cause is great something of that greatness falls upon us also.

Jawaharlal Nehru, 3 June 1947

NEHRU began his sentence of 1041 days with a sense of frustration and uncertainty: frustration because he had been denied the opportunity to play an active role in a world war from which, he believed, a new world was bound to emerge; uncertainty about the results the 'quit India' movement might achieve. Several leading Congressmen then believed, though they did not say to Gandhi, that the 'quit India' resolution was a greater blunder even than the resignation of the Congress ministries in 1939.[1] Nehru had revolted at a time when he knew it would most assuredly be misconstrued by the British as a stab in the back. Much of his conduct seemed to him to be determined 'by the past complex of events which bear down and often overwhelm the individual'.[2] Likewise, the Congress revolt seemed to him inevitable; no matter how futile in terms of major results, it was, he believed, a manly, courageous and noble course for Congress to follow. The 'quit India' movement might not compel the British to withdraw from India but he hoped that at least it would succeed in arousing among the Muslim masses sympathy and admiration for Congress and would win them away from Jinnah's Pakistan movement.

There was also at the back of his mind a deep concern for the people. Gandhi's last message to the nation – do or die – was certain to rouse the people to violence and bring upon them the scourge of repression. Would the people suffer and die knowing that they were fighting for freedom, dignity and honour? Or would they behave like a herd of animals? As if to clear his own conscience, Nehru persuaded himself that, no matter how ignorant, poor and superstitious, the people had a godlike quality which would induce them to sacrifice their lives for 'an ideal, for truth, for faith, for country and honour'.[3] This romantic view of the people helped to calm him, and he resigned himself to his prison existence.

Ahmednagar Fort was a medieval fort with a long and exciting history. Nehru took to gardening there, but his digging soon developed into a minor archaeological exploration. He was fortunate at this time to have the company of the members of the Working Committee, who formed an interesting cross-section of Indian society, and included several scholars. He thus had a good store of knowledge upon which to draw. His decision to study India's past was mainly inspired by his urge to understand the India of the present. After twenty months of exploration and research, he put away his spade and took to his pen. He finished his *Discovery of India* in September 1944, a job of less than five months.

Did he find the genius of India he had set out to discover? Did he discover what impact 5000 years of Indian history had had on the attitudes and character of the Indian people? He realised that it was presumptuous to imagine that he could unveil India, yet he recognised that the 400 million individual men and women who represented India were bound together by some invisible thread he could feel but not see. India remained for him a myth, a dream and a vision, and yet very real for all that.[4] Was there, then, anything particular about India and Indians? Nehru concluded that India from the earliest days had searched for basic principles – for the unchanging, the absolute. The very thing India lacked, the modern West possessed to excess. The West was dynamic: it was engrossed in the changing world, cared little for ultimate principles, emphasised rights and paid little attention to duties and obligations; it was active, aggressive, acquisitive; it was full of life, 'but that life was a fevered one and the temperature kept on rising progressively',[5] so that periodically the West indulged in self-destruction on a colossal scale. Indians, on the other hand, loved humanity and were more tolerant and forgiving. Any hatred the Indians might have for the British existed because a proud race did not easily forget repeated affronts to its dignity, but fortunately 'Indians do not nourish hatred for long; they recover easily a more benevolent mood'.[6]

His mind ran often, too, on India's role in the world of the future. The Pakistan movement still seemed disastrous to him. He believed that the sentiment of regionalisation had been artificially created and had no real roots in the Muslim mind. Humanity was at the end of an age of fragmentation – the future belonged to world organisations and large multinational states or federations. Pakistan therefore had no place in the logic of world progress and, besides, she would not be economically viable. If these considerations failed to impress the advocates of Pakistan, he was then willing to concede them the right to secede, with the advice that they ought to exercise this right ten years after the withdrawal of British power from India and the establishment of the free Indian state. During this period, he hoped, their emotionalism would subside and the need for a Pakistan might be seen to be illogical. It was not so much the image of Pakistan that tormented Nehru as the further balkanisation of India which might follow in its train. If India were divided into two or more parts, then the amalgamation of the major Indian states would become more difficult, for those states would find an additional reason 'for keeping aloof and holding on to their authoritarian régimes'.[7]

He visualised India playing a great role in world affairs. The Pacific and Indian oceans would take the place of the Atlantic as the nerve centre of the world. India's position gave her an economic and strategic importance in a part of the world which was going to develop rapidly in the future. There might come into being a regional grouping of the countries bordering on the Indian Ocean, including those of the Middle East and South-East Asia, in which case existing minority problems would disappear, and separatist movements like that for Pakistan would become an anachronism.

Nehru believed that India, constituted as she was, could not play a secondary part in the world. Though Indians did not show the same degree of vitality as he observed among Americans, Russians and Chinese, he believed it lay dormant within them, needing only to be recharged. Behind the struggles of the past quarter of a century lay the desire to revitalise India:

> We felt that through action and self-imposed suffering and sacrifice, through voluntarily facing risk and danger, through refusal to submit to what we considered evil and wrong, would we re-charge the battery of India's spirit and waken her from her long slumber.[8]

In that summer of 1944 he visualised the emerging new world being dominated by two super-powers, America and Russia. In spite of the differences in their political structures, the two great countries seemed to have much in common – 'a dynamic outlook and vast resources, a social fluidity, an absence of a medieval background, a faith in science and its applicaions and widespread education and opportunities for the people'.[9] Should these giants fail to co-operate, was India to ally herself with one or the other? Nothing was further from Nehru's mind: though he appreciated the power and resources which both countries possessed, he was not enamoured of either. Drawn as he was towards the frank American way of looking at things, he often felt that America was too obvious, too superficial: 'That obviousness has its own attraction for it is accompanied by a certain frankness and forthrightness, but it is not too interesting as it is apt to bore after a while.'[10] Though his view of the Americans was mainly based on personal relationships – especially that with Frances Gunther, who was very outspoken, embarrassingly frank, and obviously very fond of Nehru – he was to persist in holding this view even after his first visit to the United States as India's Prime Minister. It was not, however, his personal dislike for the capitalist American system and the autocratic Soviet structure, but his ambition for India – that she should rise on the world horizon, preferably hand in hand with China, as the leader of the Third World – that resolved him against an alliance with any of the super-powers. At the root of Nehru's world outlook lay the passion and romance of a nationalist, and of this he was himself aware: 'We are all, or nearly all, internationalists today, but for each one of us internationalism has its own particular significance. It is really nationalism in a new garb.'[11] Ahmednagar Fort was the last caravanserai in his long political journey and Nehru devoted those peaceful days to stocktaking. He believed that ideas were more powerful than realities; that, if only an individual or a group pursued the right set of ideas, the dark realities would eventually disappear like shadows. But had he himself always pursued such ideals? Had he not made compromises? Had he not forsaken revolution when that seemed to be the only true course? He was troubled by self-doubt:

> Every virtue is inextricably intertwined with vice, every vice has something of good in it. And so good and evil march together. Are they opposites or just different sides of reality? I become introspective in jail, and I see a long procession of strangers calling themselves by my name, rather like me and yet different, with something about them that attracts and something that repels. And this long procession of past selves gradually merges into the present ever-changing self. Which of these innumerable shadow selves is me? Or am I all this multitude?[12]

Such constant introspection made him uneasy for a while, but gradually he came to accept the many facets of his personality. He sought consolation in the thought that after all he was what his heredity and environment had conditioned him to be.

In January 1944, Nehru's brother-in-law Ranjit Pandit – a keen scholar who had turned politician – died from pleurisy, leaving behind a widow and three talented and beautiful daughters. Nehru came to the rescue of his sister, whose loneliness was increased by the absence of her daughters who were studying in America. He consoled her through his letters, and begged her not to lead the life of a conventional Hindu widow, but to work hard and write a book – to do anything to keep her mind occupied – for hard continuous work was the best occupation and antidote for a disturbed mind. He advised her to become attached to ideas, for personal sorrows were always greater for those who had nothing but personal attachments to sustain them.[13] He offered her emotional and financial security, and the great affection which had always flourished between the two now grew even stronger.

Then, in August 1944, Nehru became a grandfather: Indira gave birth to a son – Rajiv. Since Indira's marriage in 1942 a mutual understanding had developed between father and daughter. He had come to realise more clearly that Indira was born 'in the days of storm and stress' and had grown up with a feeling of physical and emotional insecurity which often made her seem inhibited, sad and assertive.[14] Marriage had matured her, and she had begun to cope courageously with new horizons and puzzling questions.[15]

Madame Chiang Kai-shek agitated for Nehru's release. In April 1943, while she was in America, she deplored the situation in which a statesman like Nehru, with a world vision, should be languishing in British detention at a time when he could be so useful for the United Nations cause.[16] Lord Linlithgow deeply resented China's first lady's interference in India's internal affairs. He pointed out to the Secretary of State that such open support for a rebel like Nehru would have disastrous effects in India, for it would revive Congress hopes and depress those of the Muslims who had 'supported us in the rebellion and on whose help we must depend'.[17] British policy towards the 'Congress rebels' did not change until June 1945, by which time Germany had surrendered and the new viceroy Lord Wavell had succeeded in breaking new ground on the Indian scene.

When Nehru, together with other Congress leaders, came out of prison on 15 June 1945, he faced a political situation very different from that of August 1942. The 1942 revolt of Congress, the appointment in October 1943 of Lord Wavell as Viceroy of India, the abortive Gandhi–Jinnah negotiations of September 1944 – these events had made the political situation more complex and fluid and, in addition, given to it the appearance of a market-place where the capacity to bargain had become a mark of statesmanship and adherence to principles a distinct handicap.

The August revolt of Congress had led to an instant and spontaneous mass uprising which raged most fiercely in Bihar, United Provinces and Bombay. In Punjab and Sind it gathered but little strength. Rural involvement in the movement was most intense in the eastern districts of United Provinces and western parts of Bihar, where country folk attacked police and railway stations, post and telegraph offices, government buildings, and looted goods trains and public property – activities in which Hindu and Muslim villagers participated equally. The movement in the urban areas was more politically orientated and was organised by militant elements in Congress – the young socialists and terrorists – who tried, though not with much success, to turn the movement into a disciplined guerilla war. In this the lead was taken by Jayaprakash Narayan. He had escaped from prison in November 1942 with six other political prisoners. Bombs were manufactured in his hideout, and there was a total of 664 explosions by December 1943. A 'Congress' broadcasting station was secretly established to give progress reports on the revolution to the people. Students, as usual, played a leading role. The Banaras Hindu University turned into a citadel of revolutionaries; Ballia, an eastern district of United Provinces, virtually became an independent state with no traces of British authority. Over many more areas, rural and urban, British authority ceased to function.

It was all short-lived, however. Armed with a special ordinance and supported by the military and a special armed constabulary, the Government lost no time in setting into motion the machinery of repression and reprisal. Figures vary from the official thousand or so to the unofficial 25,000, but perhaps about 10,000 people lost their lives as a result of police and military attacks and the aerial bombardment of certain rebel areas.[18] Many thousands more were subjected to collective or punitive fines. Students were whipped – a method of breaking student resistance which Linlithgow valued despite the sensitivity of the War Cabinet on the subject.[19] The Government succeeded in suppressing the movement by the end of September 1942. This was perhaps the biggest uprising that the British Raj had had to face since the Mutiny of 1857. But the Government had been fully prepared, a situation which was in no small measure due to the fact that Gandhi had publicised the proposed 'quit India' movement long before it actually began.

The Congress revolt of 1942 failed to achieve any political ends. Nehru's hope that the Congress movement might make an impact on the Muslim populace proved empty, for at Jinnah's behest the Muslim League stood aloof and on the whole Muslims in urban areas did not participate in the movement; they were told that it was but a shameful attempt on Gandhi's part to capture power from the British and establish a Hindu Raj. In extending and strengthening his hold on the Muslims in the Muslim provinces (Punjab, Sind, Bengal and the North-West Frontier Province) Jinnah was as much helped by the circumstance of Congress being in voluntary exile as by any positive support shown by the British. Lord Linlithgow and Winston Churchill not only took the Congress revolt as a stab in the back but mistakenly believed that the Congress leadership lacked real ability and that Gandhi was either senile or at best a naughty child whose main concern was to remain a focus of attention. Linlithgow firmly assumed a protective role: all those groups and interests which had dissociated themselves from the Congress movement must be protected against Congress. In this protective role the British Raj, so Linlithgow believed, would last for at least thirty years.[20] This strong reaffirmation of an old role at a stage in Anglo-Indian history when the British administration was faced with a new problem – the unity or division of India – was to have significant consequences. It meant that the British administration, anxious though it was to maintain the unity of India, would not do the only thing which could maintain the unity of India: it would not transfer power to Congress alone.

It was their suspicious and hostile attitude towards Congress which determined the British role in the period between 1942 and 1946. In June 1943, Linlithgow remarked to Leo Amery, the Secretary of State: 'But Jinnah is not in as strong a position as Gandhi and Congress, and he is never likely to be, in the near future, since he represents a minority, and a minority that can only effectively hold its own with our assistance.'[21] At the end of his viceroyalty Linlithgow remarked that the Indian problems were the product of Indian stupidity and

British dishonesty.[22] For his successor, Lord Wavell, British dishonesty and Indian stupidity were represented respectively by Winston Churchill and Gandhi. But, although he understood the ways of the 'fraudulent' Churchill, he lacked any insight into the mind of the 'malevolent' Mahatma.

Gandhi had always been an enigma to the British, but during the 1940s he became a puzzle and sometimes an embarrassment and a liability, even to his close associates. For his saintly style of leadership had failed to convert the British and the Muslim League to the Congress faith, and had also inhibited his colleagues and followers in Congress from fighting their foes with the usual political weapons. Gandhi himself was torn between the roles of saint and politician, and in desperately trying to include both often lost his own identity and sought reassurance from both the British and his own colleagues. He was – to his own satisfaction – increasingly ignored by both sides, and he was to resume, during the last phase of his life, a state of detachment or non-involvement in which he sought his own salvation and identity.

In February 1943, when he was in his early seventies and in very fragile health, he went on a fast for three weeks in his detention camp in the Aga Khan's palace, near Poona. The fast was partly the consequence of a correspondence between Gandhi and Linlithgow, in which each had tried to put the blame on the other for the outbreak of violence that had followed the Congress resolution of August 1942, but mainly to put life back into the Congress movement. He also wanted to atone for any violence. World attention was drawn towards him, and countrywide agitation for his release began in India. Three Indian members of the Viceroy's Executive Council resigned. Linlithgow offered to set Gandhi at liberty for the duration of his fast, but Gandhi declined the offer. In spite of the alarm raised by the Indian doctors attending Gandhi, the Mahatma survived his three-week fast. Winston Churchill was surprised that Gandhi did not die and suspected the *bona fides* of Gandhi's fast. It would be most valuable, Churchill told Linlithgow, if any fraud could be exposed, as this might disenchant Gandhi's supporters in America: 'Surely with all those Congress Hindu doctors round him it is quite easy to slip glucose or other nourishment into his food.'[23] But Linlithgow sadly admitted the difficulty of collecting such evidence.[24]

Lord Wavell began his viceroyalty in October 1943 with a sense of purpose and sincerity, though he lacked imagination and had little sympathy for India and her leaders. He had served India as Commander-in-Chief since January 1941 and saw the country and her people through a soldier's eyes. As far as he was concerned, India was docile and inefficient, and would remain so. He felt that Indian leaders had singularly failed to produce a sense of nationhood, for only a few saw beyond their own personal or sectional interests. His view of Indian leadership grew more unfavourable with the passage of time. He found in Gandhi nothing but hypocrisy and malevolence; Jinnah was chronically conceited and vain; Nehru was honest, sincere and charming but too much of an idealist. In Patel alone he found something of himself. But Gandhi (just on seventy-five), Jinnah (sixty-eight) and Churchill (nearing seventy) were the ones who mattered, and Wavell wondered whether there was any chance of a solution of the Indian problem 'till the three intransigent, obstinate, uncompromising principals' were out of the way.[25] In due course his own defeatism was to overpower him, but at the beginning of his viceroyalty Wavell was determined to impress upon Churchill the propriety of being honest towards India for once.[26] The British Government must convince the educated Indians that it was sincere and friendly towards India, and it must decide to transfer power to India soon after the war otherwise India would pass into chaos and probably into other hands. Wavell argued that it was no longer possible to hold India by force alone. In the meantime a provisional government representative of the main political parties should be formed at the centre, and he asked for cabinet permission to call a small conference of political leaders with this object in view.

Imbued with this new approach towards the Indian problem, Wavell took the earliest opportunity to release Gandhi on humanitarian grounds. Since the conclusion of his fast in March of 1943, Gandhi had been in very poor health. The death of his wife Kasturba in February 1944 had deeply upset him, and in the following month he suffered from malaria and was believed to be at death's door. He became more anaemic and there was a progressive deterioration in his blood pressure and kidney functions. Both his Indian and English doctors believed that the Mahatma was failing and that, even if he survived, his further participation in active politics was improbable. Having obtained Churchill's go-ahead, Wavell released Gandhi in May 1944, hoping that the Mahatma would die peacefully outside a British prison. Gandhi, however, did not die, nor did he retire from politics. In fact, soon after his release the Mahatma began to occupy himself in finding ways of resolving the political deadlock. Pressed by Churchill, who wished to know why Gandhi was not yet dead, Wavell felt rather as if he had been betrayed by the Mahatma.

The one political move Gandhi made during the summer of 1944, however, turned out to be significant and, in the opinion of some Congressmen, disastrous for Congress. This was his meeting with Jinnah at the latter's house in Bombay to seek an agreement on the basis of a scheme formulated by Rajaji – the only Congress Leader who had opposed the Congress movement and had consequently remained free while his colleagues were in prison. Since the early forties Rajaji had been urging Congress to give token acceptance to the principle of a separate Pakistan. Rajaji published his formula in July 1944 and discussed it with Gandhi, arguing that if the principle were accepted and the details worked out, then the idea might not seem so impossible to Congress or so attractive to the Muslim League. According to his scheme, the Pakistan areas were to be demarcated not by provinces but by districts: only those districts in Muslim provinces wherein the Muslim population was in an absolute majority were to decide, through a plebiscite of all their inhabitants (Hindus and Muslims), on the question of separation from India. This demarcation line would exclude the predominantly Hindu districts of Bengal, Assam and Punjab. Jinnah would thus be left with a moth-eaten, truncated husk. Furthermore, the scheme did not provide for complete separation from India even of this truncated Pakistan. It conceived of a central or federal authority to look after the defence, commerce and communications of both countries.

Gandhi approved the scheme, knowing that Jinnah would find it unpalatable. He asked Jinnah for an interview more with a view to publicising among the Muslims the hollowness and unreality of the Pakistan ideal than of striking a final agreement between Congress and the Muslim League. Gandhi's move was reasonably shrewd, but his direct approach to Jinnah and the timing of the negotiations were beset with risks which he could not have visualised. Though, since 1942, Jinnah had in some measure strengthened his leadership over the Muslim provinces, he was still far from feeling secure, and in the summer of 1944 he was desperately trying to gain ground for himself and the Muslim League in the Punjab against Khizar Hyat Khan Tiwana – premier of the Punjab since 1942 – and his Unionist Party. Jinnah had not yet succeeded in bringing all Muslim groups and areas under his control. He could not claim to be the only spokesman of the entire Muslim community – a status which he desperately needed in order to enter the political arena as Gandhi's equal.

The status for which Jinnah was struggling was unwittingly accorded to him by Gandhi when the latter expressed his willingness to negotiate with him on equal terms. Gandhi's invitation suddenly raised Jinnah's shares in the political market, and he first cashed in on his added prestige by attacking his rival Tiwana and the Unionist Party.[27] Next, Jinnah used his long-drawn-out meeting with Gandhi, from 9 to 27 September, to publicise his newly acquired status rather than to discuss the details of Pakistan. And finally Jinnah rejected Rajaji's scheme and reasserted the claim to include in Pakistan the whole of Bengal and Assam in the eastern zone and the whole of Punjab, North-West Frontier Province, Baluchistan and Sind in the western zone, possibly with a corridor through the heart of Hindu India which would join eastern and western Pakistan. He also rejected the idea of a central or federal authority.

The Gandhi–Jinnah talks might have enhanced Jinnah's prestige, but of more consequence was the tone and style which they imparted to Congress thinking on the Pakistan issue. From then onwards Congress was to use Rajaji's formula as a threat against rather than as a concession to Jinnah, for it was convinced that Jinnah would rather have nothing than a truncated Pakistan. As it turned out, when faced with the option between a truncated Pakistan or none at all, Jinnah in fact opted for the former. Had Rajaji's scheme, including its provisions for a central authority, been forced upon Jinnah by a viceroy of Mountbatten's calibre in the summer of 1944 or even in 1945, Jinnah would probably have accepted it (though Congress might have wavered, as it did when accepting the Cabinet Mission Plan in 1946), and the unity of India might have been maintained. Perhaps this formed the basis of Mountbatten's belief that he might have succeeded in averting the division of India if he had been asked to replace Wavell earlier (in August 1945) than was the case.[28]

Wavell would have been surprised and even jealous if the Gandhi–Jinnah parleys had resolved the Indian problem. He was, however, shrewd enough to expect nothing out of them. Anxious as he was that the initiative should come from the Government, he visited London in March 1945 to get his plan for the provisional government approved by the Cabinet. Churchill kept Wavell waiting for over two months and then endorsed his plan for the simple reason, as he himself revealed to Wavell later, that it was bound to fail.[29] Wavell returned to India in the first week of June, and the plan was announced on the fourteenth by the Secretary of State in the House of Commons and by Wavell in India. The plan was essentially the same as Wavell had proposed to the Cabinet in September 1944. It envisaged the immediate formation of a provisional government at the centre, in which the Muslims and caste Hindus were to be represented in equal proportions. All members of this reconstituted Viceroy's Executive Council were to be Indians, except for the Commander-in-Chief and the Viceroy. Similar coalition governments were to be established in the provinces. With a view to striking an agreement between the major political parties on the composition of the central government, the Viceroy was to meet the Indian leaders in Simla.

For Jinnah, as it turned out, the most intriguing feature of the plan was the hope it expressed that the proposed provisional government might also work out a permanent constitution for India. For Jinnah realised that the provisional government, in spite of its being composed on the principle of parity between the caste Hindus and Muslims, was going to be dominated by Congress. The government was to include, in addition to caste Hindus and Muslims, at least two members representing the Sikh and Untouchable communities, who would invariably support the Congress group. In addition, the Muslim seats would not necessarily all be filled by the Muslim League since Wavell, in fairness to the Unionist Party of Punjab, wanted to give at least one Muslim seat to a Unionist Muslim who would be unlikely to toe Jinnah's line. Further, Congress itself might claim, as it did, to nominate one or two Congress Muslims on the Muslim quota in the government. As Jinnah saw it, such a Congress-dominated government would certainly work for an all-India Union and as a result the Pakistan issue would be put in cold storage for ever. Jinnah thus faced the Simla conference (June–July 1945) in a great dilemma.

On being released the day after the Wavell plan was announced, Nehru found it a little difficult to understand and to adjust himself to the new political environment. It took him some time to realise that Congress's voluntary exile had strengthened, not weakened, Jinnah's Pakistan movement. He longed to escape to Kashmir, but the impending conference at Simla pulled him straight into the vortex of politics. The Congress Working Committee drew up a strategy for the conference. The principle of parity (between caste Hindus and Muslims) was to be accepted, but only for a temporary period and in relation only to the composition of the central government; the idea of coalition or composite government was not to extend to the provinces.[30] Congress was in no event to recognise the right of the Muslim League to nominate all the Muslim members of the central government.

When the Simla conference began on 25 June, Britain had decided to go to the polls. Germany had surrendered in May, and Churchill had formed a caretaker government, predominantly of Conservatives. During the electioneering the Labour Party stressed the urgency of resolving the Indian problem as soon as the war with Japan was over. It was generally expected in India that the Conservatives would win. The voting took place on 5 July. The results were not announced until 26 July, to allow time for the services to vote. In the meantime, on 11 July, Wavell acknowledged the failure of the Simla conference.

The principal reason for the failure of the conference was

Jinnah's fear of the adverse influence the proposed provisional government would have on the prospect of Pakistan. All his moves during the conference were designed to secure for the Muslim League a position of strength in the provisional government equal to that of Congress. He demanded that the Viceroy should exercise his veto if ever the majority decision of the government went against the wishes of its Muslim League members; and insisted that all Muslim members of the government were to be nominated by the Muslim League. Wavell refused to concede either of his demands and decided to go ahead even without Jinnah's co-operation. He sent to the Cabinet a list of names chosen from the lists submitted to him by Congress and the Unionist Party. Churchill's Cabinet approved Wavell's shadow council, but only on condition that it was acceptable to Jinnah and other leaders.[31] This meant giving Jinnah a veto on the constitutional development of India. Knowing very well that Jinnah would not approve of the proposed shadow council, Wavell accepted the failure of the Simla conference. Some Congress leaders (Azad, Pant, Rajaji) were disappointed, for they thought Congress had gone further than ever before in its effort to reach an agreement. But Wavell was helpless. In the last few days of its existence Churchill's Cabinet succeeded in retrieving Jinnah from what he called the snare of Wavell's plan. The situation became less secure for him, however, when on the afternoon of 26 July 1945 Attlee became Prime Minister with 393 Labour seats against 213 Conservative.

Nehru was not in the least perturbed by the failure of the Simla conference, and was even relieved that Congress had escaped the position of being treated equally with the Muslim League. The British Government had at last conceded the idea of a constituent assembly. Once this body was set up, Nehru calculated, the question of forming a provisional government was bound to arise again.[32] And when it arose Congress must be in a stronger position to take full advantage of it. His strategy thus mainly lay in strengthening Congress; his hope for the unity of an independent India now rested on the constituent assembly.

Between July 1945 and March 1946, Nehru nourished his optimism on hopes, visions, and contact with the masses. His hope of India becoming free in the immediate future rested on his firm belief that colonialism had to retreat from Asia soon after the conclusion of the war. The coming of the Labour Government did not arouse in him undue hopes but the event did assure him that, unlike Churchill, the Labour Prime Minister would not stand against the tide of decolonisation. The events in Syria and the Lebanon, where even Churchill's Cabinet had been obliged to recognise the independence of these countries against the wishes of the French Government, were to Nehru a pointer in the right direction. He witnessed the disintegration of colonialism in South-East Asia soon after the Japanese surrender of 14 August 1945. He was not shaken in his belief by the support Britain was giving to Holland and France in recovering their hold respectively over Indonesia and Indo-China. He saw the inevitable happening in the virtual recognition of the Indonesian Republic by Lieutenant-General Christison, commander of the British force which arrived in Jakarta in September to take the Japanese surrender. The British, the Dutch and the French could delay but certainly not stop the process of decolonisation. And Nehru was determined to see that it was not delayed any longer. The Indonesian leader Mohammad Hatta assured Nehru that the freedom of Indonesia would follow soon after the withdrawal of the British from India, for then the British would have no interest in supporting the Dutch claim over Indonesia and, without British support, the Dutch could not hold Indonesia any longer.[33] This was an opportune moment, Nehru felt, to win the friendship of the Indonesian people and their leaders – Sukarno and Hatta. In his ideological warfare against the Pakistan movement, Indonesia, like Egypt, had a strategic significance as a predominantly Muslim country. He vouched his support for the Indonesian war of independence and mounted his opposition against the use of Indian soldiers by the British in South-East Asia.

Nehru also derived inspiration from his vision of the new world. As observed earlier, he visualised large federations of countries emerging on the map of the world. India had the potential as well as the strategic advantage of being the centre of South Asia and South-East Asia, at least for defence and trade purposes. Even if this development did not take place, he saw no future for a small country like Ceylon (Sri Lanka) outside the Indian federation:

> Admission into the Indian Federation should not limit Lanka's freedom except in regard to certain minimum federal subjects, such as defence. I am in favour of having a compulsory minimum of federal subjects, as well as, in addition, optional federal subjects.[34]

His expectations were not to materialise, except for the formation, in the post-colonial era, of short-lived Asian and Afro-Asian blocs but, enamoured as he was by such a vision in the mid-forties, he gave no serious thought to the threat of Pakistan, which now seemed to him not only reactionary but unfeasible.

His greatest inspiration and enthusiasm, however, Nehru derived from his contact with the masses, the opportunity for which arose with the holding of the Indian general election in the winter months of 1945–6. The election – none had been held since 1937 owing to the war – was called by the Labour Government primarily to ascertain the strength of the political parties. In August 1945, Wavell was called to London to advise the Government on the next move. He found the Cabinet keen to take early action mainly to show to the United States and the Soviet Union that progress was being made in India.[35] Wavell also remarked that the Labour leaders were 'bent on handing over India to their Congress friends as soon as possible'.[36] A plan was formulated and announced by Wavell in Delhi on 19 September. The announcement affirmed the determination of the British Government to grant self-government to India as soon as possible after the general election. A constituent assembly was to be set up to frame the constitution of an independent India. In the meantime the Viceroy was to re-attempt to form a provisional government with the support of the main Indian parties.

Much depended on the outcome of the Indian election for all parties concerned, including the British. The election was to be held under the old regulations with limited franchise, and on the basis of general constituencies for all non-communal seats and Muslim constituencies for Muslim seats. If Congress, Nehru calculated, besides winning all the general seats in the provincial and central legislatures could also win a substantial number of Muslim seats, then the claim of the Muslim League to be the sole representative of the Muslim community would fall flat and the Pakistan movement would collapse. Jinnah's Muslim League would lose all its bargaining power if it failed to capture the majority of Muslim seats in the central and provincial legislatures. Wavell's next move regarding the composition of the provincial government depended on how the Muslim League fared in Punjab. If the Punjab elections went well for the Muslim League, then he would assure Jinnah that the Muslims would have parity with the Hindus (other than scheduled castes) in the government, and also that the Muslim seats in the government would be filled by Muslim Leaguers only.[37] He was also, in December 1945, determined to make it clear that if any party refused to co-operate he would go ahead and form the government without them. Every party thus had a high stake in the election.

Nehru, as usual, left the politics of management and manœuvre to Patel and Prasad, but never permitted them, or even Gandhi, to compromise what he held to be the essential principles and ideals of the Congress Party. His election strategy had two main features: winning seats for Congress Muslims in Muslim constituencies; and presenting to the masses an economic plan for a better standard of living. In order to achieve the first objective, it was necessary, he felt, to project to the Muslim masses the secular image of Congress. With this in view he ruled out Prasad's proposal that Congress should make pacts with the Hindu Mahasabha;[38] any alliance or understanding with the Mahasabha would make the Congress Muslims suspicious. Congress must disprove the allegation that it was a Hindu organisation. He also overruled Patel's objection to Congress support for non-League Muslims in areas, particularly in the Punjab, where no suitable Congress Muslim candidates were available. Patel gave way, though he was convinced that Congress was going to waste a lot of money in the Punjab in supporting insignificant Muslim candidates (Ahrars, for example) against the Muslim League. Patel's calculations proved to be right: non-League Muslim candidates fared very poorly in the Punjab, and one candidate on whom Congress had spent nearly £2000 even lost his deposit.[39]

On the question of alleviating India's poverty through massive industrialisation, Nehru clashed with Gandhi when the Mahatma declared in October 1945 that he stood against industrialisation and 'massification' of society and that he still firmly believed in what he had written in his *Hindu Swaraj* over thirty-seven years ago.[40] Nehru reminded Gandhi that his thesis against industrialisation had never been officially accepted by Congress. India could not provide the basic necessities of life for her people in any other way but through industrialisation. While admitting that industrial civilisation had many evils, Nehru affirmed that it would be possible for India to avoid those evils through a planned economy, which left little room for acquisitiveness and competition. He challenged Gandhi's idealisation of village India:

> I do not understand why a village should necessarily embody truth and non-violence. A village, normally speaking, is backward intellectually and culturally and no progress can be made from a backward environment. Narrow-minded people are much more likely to be untruthful and violent.[41]

Gandhi did not persist in his opposition, though he did not abandon his prophecy that one day industrial civilisation would collapse and the world would return to a village society. Nehru ignored Gandhi, wondering, perhaps for the first time, whether the Mahatma had outlived his usefulness.

Purging Congress of anti-national elements had become an important issue before the electioneering commenced. The Indian communists, who had joined Congress in 1937 but who, since 1942 when the Soviet Union joined the war, had gone against Congress policy and supported the British in their war efforts, were now considered anti-national elements in the Congress organisation. In September 1945 the Congress Working Committee appointed a sub-committee, consisting of Nehru, Patel and G. B. Pant, to enquire into the charges against the communists. In December the sub-committee recommended that the communists be expelled from Congress. Though he had no regrets for the Indian communists, Nehru differentiated between them and communists of the Soviet Union, and sincerely hoped that the Congress action would not damage relationships with Russia, with whom he looked forward to closer relations when India became independent.

On this issue there was full agreement between Patel and Nehru, but the former wanted to go further and deal similarly with the Indian socialists, whose Congress Socialist Party had been functioning within Congress since 1934.

Patel had always disliked the socialists both on ideological and personal grounds, and was severely critical about some of them, notably Mrs Aruna Asaf Ali and her group who, in his opinion, were behaving hysterically and gaining cheap popularity by making wild speeches.[42] Patel held them responsible for inciting the ratings of the Royal Indian Navy in Bombay and Karachi to revolt. In February 1946 the Indian sailors, complaining of low pay, bad food and racial discrimination, hoisted the Congress and League flags on their ships and shouted 'Jai Hind' ('Hail India'), the national slogan of S. C. Bose's Indian National Army.* When troops were called in to suppress the revolt, they openly defied them. Patel had to intervene, and it was at his call that the Bombay ratings laid down their arms. The rebel sailors (who further convinced the soldier-viceroy Wavell that India could no longer be held by the Indian military and naval forces) were in some measure influenced by the trial and conviction in Delhi of Bose's Indian National Army officers (who had been captured by the British force after the Japanese surrender in South-East Asia), and the commutation, in January 1946, of the sentences passed on them. The sailors had reason to believe that they would receive similarly lenient treatment. Patel feared the revolutionary flavour with which the political atmosphere was surcharged in the winter of 1945–6, and forecast chaos if the socialists were not restrained in time. But Nehru would not let him use the stick against the socialists. In Nehru's eyes they were first-rate nationalists, no matter how irresponsible and misguided; besides, some of them, including Mrs Asaf Ali herself, were his friends.[43]

Nehru began his election tours with his usual zest and vigour.

*After the fall of Malaya and Burma the Japanese recruited the Indian National Army from the captured Indian soldiers and from Indian civilians. This army, the Japanese proclaimed, was to liberate India. In 1943 the command of this combat army of over 20,000 men was taken over by S. C. Bose, who in October of that year set up his headquarters in Singapore.

He visited every province, penetrating far into the interior and drawing enormous crowds. He praised the people's bravery and patriotism during the 'quit India' movement and asked them to look forward to a bright era in their country's history which was about to begin with their freedom from British rule. When, in November 1945, the Indian National Army trials began in the Red Fort in Delhi, he donned his barrister's gown and appeared as one of the defence counsel. This was not just for show. Nehru's support for the Indian National Army had a firm political basis. The Indian National Army had become a symbol of unity among the various religious groups in India, for Hindus, Muslims, Sikhs and Christians were all represented in that army. They had solved the communal problem amongst themselves, and why should Indians in India not do so? Their trial by court martial aroused the country as nothing else could. In defending them just on the eve of a general election, a political party was sure to find popular support. Nehru was also, in the beginning, emotionally drawn towards them. They represented, for him, India's fight for freedom. He somewhat changed his view, however, when he visited Malaya in March 1946 and met Lord Mountbatten. The latter, while dissuading him from laying a wreath on the Indian National Army memorial, told him:

> The I.N.A. were not politically conscious heroes fighting for their country but cowards and traitors who betrayed their loyal friends. The people who will serve you well in your national army of the future are those who are loyal to their oath; otherwise if you become unpopular a disloyal army may turn against you.[44]

Nehru took the point and, though for political reasons he continued to oppose the trials, he was on his guard against ever permitting the Indian National Army men to rejoin the army of an independent India.

What agitated Nehru during those election months and after was not so much the danger of the division of British India but the disintegration of Indian India (the Indian states) when the British withdrew from the sub-continent. He feared that the British Government would encourage the princes to seek an independent existence, a balkanisation of

India which he was determined to prevent. But how? Gandhi's method of persuading the princes to join the Indian union might not work so long as the princes had the option of retaining their autocratic powers and privileges. The alternative seemed to be for the people of the states to exert pressure upon their rulers. The states' people and their leaders were with Congress, and it was on them that Nehru relied.

His entire thinking on the future of the Indian states came out clearly in his presidential address to the All-India States Peoples' Conference, which met on 31 December 1945 in Udaipur. 'It is our basic policy', he asserted, 'that there should be full responsible government in the States as integral parts of a free India.'[45] Of nearly 600 Indian states, he pointed out, scarcely fifteen to twenty were large enough to form autonomous units in the Indian federation. He conceded that the rulers of these states could remain their constitutional heads under the federal structure of a free India. The other states would have to be absorbed in the provinces of British India. Excepting Kashmir, the large states were predominantly Hindu. The leader of the Muslim populace of Kashmir was Sheikh Mohammad Abdullah, who was then and afterwards totally opposed to the idea of Pakistan. If Pakistan was supposed to rescue Muslims from Hindu domination, Abdullah argued, then the Muslims who needed to be rescued and who would be kept out of the orbit of Pakistan were the Muslims in the Hindu-majority provinces, and not the Muslims in the Muslim-majority provinces where they had no fear of Hindu domination.[46] Nehru thus had good reason to rely on what seemed to him the progressive outlook of the states' people as opposed to that of their reactionary rulers.

The election results, however, did not quite come up to Nehru's expectations; neither did they contain the clear verdict in favour of Pakistan which Jinnah claimed. The real contest between Congress and the Muslim League lay in Muslim seats, for Congress was sure to win, as it did, a majority of the general seats. In the central assembly Congress won fifty-seven general seats but it failed to secure any Muslim seat, all thirty of which were won by the Muslim League. At an All-India level the League thus acquired a substantial stature. But what mattered to the League in terms of Pakistan was not its position in the central but in the provincial legislatures, particularly those of the provinces which Jinnah claimed for Pakistan. In the provincial assemblies of the Hindu provinces the Muslim League secured most and in some cases all of the Muslim seats but it failed to secure all the Muslim seats in the Muslim (or Pakistan) provinces. In Punjab it secured 79 out of 86 Muslim seats, in Bengal 113 out of 119, in North-West Frontier Province 17 out of 38, and in Sind 28 out of 34. It failed to obtain an absolute majority in Sind, Punjab and Bengal, though in each of these provinces it secured more seats than any other party. The North-West Frontier Province, where Congress won more Muslim seats than the League, still remained outside its pale of influence. In Assam – which Jinnah claimed for Pakistan, even though it was a Hindu province – the League secured 31 out of 34 Muslim seats, but Congress retained an over-all majority by winning 58 seats. In the Punjab the League's hope of success lay in weakening its rival party – the Unionist Party – but it could not form a ministry there because of the Unionist–Congress–Sikh alliance. The League thus succeeded in forming ministries only in Bengal and Sind; Congress formed ministries in the rest of the provinces except Punjab, where a coalition government was formed under Khizar Hyat Khan Tiwana. Though the election results did not clearly support what Nehru claimed for Congress and Jinnah for the League, they did indicate explicitly that there were only two political parties in India that mattered – Congress and the Muslim League. Nehru's strategy had succeeded in one respect: it had uprooted and demolished the Hindu Mahasabha.

Nehru's election speeches had unnerved Wavell, who was somewhat relieved when Nehru left Delhi on 17 March 1946 on an eight-day visit to Malaya to study the conditions of Indian labour and the Indian National Army foundations and assets in Singapore. The visit gave Nehru an opportunity to think further on the problems of Indians living outside India. Should they return to India? Or should they be asked to renounce Indian citizenship for their country of adoption? Nehru's thinking was then geared towards a federation of the countries of South and South-East Asia and he hoped that one day the people of these countries (India, Ceylon, Indonesia,

Malaya and Burma) would come to acquire a common nationality and common citizenship.[47] Pan-Asianism was very much on his mind, and he found a definite response to his idea from the Burmese leader General Aung San, whom he met in Rangoon on his return journey to India. It was Aung San who suggested to Nehru a conference of the representatives of Asian countries. Nehru warmly accepted the proposal, and the first Asian Relations Conference was held in Delhi in March 1947.

But the real significance of Nehru's visit to Malaya lay in his meeting with Vice-Admiral Lord Mountbatten, then Supreme Allied Commander in South-East Asia. Mountbatten had long wanted to meet Nehru, and was delighted when he was officially informed of Nehru's impending visit to Singapore. Here was the opportunity to meet 'a high class man' with an attractive personality who might indeed become the first prime minister of an independent India. He considered it of the highest importance not to antagonise Nehru, and accordingly reversed the official plan to play down Nehru's visit to Malaya. He made all arrangements appropriate to Nehru's dignity, and enabled him to address large gatherings of military personnel as well as civilians. The two men took an instant liking to each other. It was refreshing for Nehru to meet, perhaps for the first time, a high-ranking British official, with royal blood in his veins to boot, who was uninhibited, above the pettiness, prejudices and racial arrogance of so many colonial officials, and, above all, so eager to understand and befriend him. They were alike in some ways, for they had in common a sense of detachment, an aristocratic outlook, and enormous pride and sensitivity which occasionally made them susceptible both to flattery and frustration. Each felt naturally entitled to the highest degree of power but, whereas Mountbatten revelled in its exercise, Nehru felt happier in its possession than in its use.

Nehru's gentility and the way in which he had risen to power perhaps conditioned him against the ruthless exercise of power. He considered such behaviour ostentatious and vulgar, and would rarely make full use of the enormous powers he in fact possessed. He relied on others – Mountbatten, Patel, Pant, Kidwai – to play the power-game for him, and to be his trouble-shooters. Himself an idealist and an intellectual, he yet had the redeeming quality of using the skill of those who were more practical, worldly-wise and self-confident. However, he rarely accepted advice which went against his sentiments without at least a token protest. He manifested this trait during his brief visit to Malaya: he accepted Mountbatten's advice not publicly to place a wreath on the Indian National Army memorial, but he privately visited the monument and placed some flowers there. This was his way of bridging the gulf between the real and the ideal world and of keeping his own conscience clear. But there were times when this inner conflict reduced Nehru to a state of inaction and ineffectiveness. Such was the case during the Cabinet Mission negotiations (March–June 1946), with which Nehru was closely involved from the outset.

Nehru was still in Malaya when the Cabinet Mission, consisting of Sir Stafford Cripps, Lord Pethick-Lawrence and A. V. Alexander, arrived in New Delhi on 24 March. The ministers arrived in a mood of goodwill but without any ready-made plan. The decision to send the Cabinet Mission soon after the elections were over had been made in January. An all-party British parliamentary delegation (consisting of ten members and headed by Professor Robert Richards) had visited India in January and on its return to England on 12 February unanimously recommended to the Cabinet an immediate grant of independence to India. Attlee's government, however, needed no such recommendation, for it was already determined to transfer power to India. The Cabinet Mission thus represented the true intention of the British Government finally to resolve the Indian problem. Drawing on their past experiences with the British Government, the Congress leaders were at first reluctant to trust the British. Their suspicions, however, were short-lived. Once Congress became convinced that the Labour Government meant business, there began, during the summer months of 1946, the real scramble for power – not between Congress and the British Raj but between Congress and the Muslim League.

During the last year of its existence, the British Raj was involved in the impossible task of maintaining the unity of India while remaining impartial towards the contending parties –

the League and Congress. There were occasions when the British might have changed the course of subsequent history had they chosen to back Congress against the Muslim League. Pethick-Lawrence and Cripps would, in fact, have done so, but they were held back by Wavell and Alexander. Congress and the League were thus left to fight it out between themselves. In this final contest the victory was to come to the party which was more united, more organised and more flexible. Congress was at an obvious disadvantage: pulled in two different directions by its right and left wings, it could not act decisively and swiftly. Attached as Congress was to the ideals it had espoused for so long, it could not always look reality full in the face. As a result Congress made more mistakes than the League. Though neither party obtained complete victory, India nonetheless had to be divided. Temperamentally, Nehru was most unsuited to planning the strategy for such warfare, yet he had to take command. Gandhi was now too old and had virtually renounced the leadership of Congress. Patel had grudgingly come round to accepting second place. In May the Congress presidency fell on Nehru's shoulders: Azad had declined to continue for a second term, and Patel and Kripalani – two of the five proposed candidates – had withdrawn their names.

The cabinet ministers had not arrived in India with a cut-and-dried plan. The plan grew during their negotiations with the leaders of Congress and the League. On 16 May, in the absence of an agreement between the two parties, the Cabinet Mission offered a constitutional award. While rejecting the possibility of a partition of India, the award provided a three-tier constitutional scheme for India. The cabinet ministers decided that a sovereign state of Pakistan could not solve the communal problem. A large Pakistan (consisting of Punjab, North-West Frontier Province, Sind and Baluchistan in the north-west and Bengal and Assam in the north-east), as demanded by Jinnah and the League, would contain a large percentage of non-Muslims (37·93 per cent in West Pakistan and 48·31 per cent in East Pakistan). Even after the creation of a larger Pakistan some 20 million Muslims would be left amongst India's 188 million. The demand for a larger Pakistan thus seemed unjustifiable. A smaller or truncated Pakistan seemed unfeasible on administrative, economic, geographical and military grounds. Besides, it involved the partition of Punjab and Bengal, which the people of those provinces would not like.

Pakistan within a union of India, embracing both British India and the states, was the alternative compromise solution which the three-tier system offered. This would deal with foreign affairs, defence and communications, and would have the power to raise the finances required for its functioning. The union would have an executive and a legislature. The provinces and states were to retain all subjects and powers other than those ceded to the union. The provinces were grouped into three sections, of which A was to consist of all Hindu provinces, B of the Muslim provinces of the north-western region, and C of Bengal and Assam. To frame a constitution for the union of India, for the provinces and, if so desired, for the groups or sections, a constituent assembly was to be immediately formed. The assembly would include about 385 representatives, of whom 93 were to be from the states and the remainder to be elected by the existing provincial legislative assemblies (in accordance with a quota allotted to each province). These representatives were to hold a preliminary meeting at New Delhi and then the provincial representatives were to divide up into three separate sections in accordance with the grouping of the provinces (for example, the representatives from Bengal and Assam were to form one group). The three sections were then to proceed separately to draft provincial constitutions for the provinces included in their own section and were also to decide whether any group constitution was to be set up for these provinces and, if so, with what provincial subjects the group was to deal. No directive was laid down for the states' representatives. They were to reassemble with the provincial representatives, after the latter had framed their provincial and group constitutions, for the purpose of settling the union constitution.

Only after the union constitution had been framed and elections to the union and provincial legislatures had taken place under the new constitutional arrangements would it be open to the newly elected legislature of a province to elect to withdraw from any group in which it had been placed. For example, if Assam, a Hindu-majority province, wanted to opt out of Section C it could do so only after its constitution had been settled at the sectional meeting (where the majority of the representatives was bound to be Muslim and pro-Pakistan) and an election had been held under the new constitution. After an initial period of ten years, and at ten-yearly intervals thereafter, any province, by a majority vote of its legislative assembly, could call for a reconsideration of the terms of the union or group constitution. This provision of the scheme, like the one on the compulsory grouping of the provinces, was to be interpreted differently by the League and Congress.

While constitution-making proceeded on these lines, the Viceroy was to form an interim government in which all portfolios, including that of war member, were to be held by Indian leaders. This government was to function under the existing constitution which gave the Viceroy overriding powers over his councillors. It thus could not function free from British control, for independence, as the Cabinet Mission stated, could not precede the bringing into operation of a new constitution.

With the Cabinet Mission announcement of a long-term constitutional scheme for India began the second phase, during which members of the Cabinet Mission and the Viceroy carried on negotiations with Jinnah and Congress leaders on the composition of the interim government. As the Indian leaders could not reach agreement among themselves, the Cabinet Mission was once again forced to offer an award. On 16 June 1946 the ministers announced the composition of the interim government. This was to consist of fourteen members, comprising five Hindus from Congress, five Muslims from the Muslim League, and one representative from each of the four minority communities – the Sikhs, Indian Christians, Parsis and the Untouchable Hindus (the scheduled castes). The composition of the government was thus based on the principle of parity between the Muslim League and Congress – a principle which dismayed Congress leaders even though they were assured by the Cabinet Mission that it was only a temporary arrangement and was in no way to be taken as a precedent.

The Cabinet Mission awards, overruling as they did the creation of a sovereign state of Pakistan, should have frustrated

Jinnah more than Congress. In fact, however, the Congress leaders' distrust of Jinnah and his League was so intense that they wavered between acceptance and rejection of the awards. Indeed, Nehru's outburst of 10 July against compulsory grouping of provinces (page 267) seemed largely responsible for Jinnah retracting his acceptance of the Cabinet Mission Plan. Would the partition of India have been averted and millions of lives saved if Congress had unequivocally accepted the Cabinet Mission Plan? Such a question is perhaps unjust, since no one was to know in the summer of 1946 that Jinnah was to die within a year of the partition of India.

At the time, the constitutional scheme seemed to the Congress High Command to offer on the one hand the semblance of an Indian union and on the other to provide, through the compulsory grouping of provinces, a great opportunity for the Muslim League to consolidate its position in provinces placed under Sections B and C. Congress feared that Punjab and Bengal, by dominating respectively Sections B and C, might frame a provisional constitution which was entirely contrary to the wishes of Sind, the North-West Frontier Province or Assam, and might also lay down rules for elections which could nullify the provision that a province could opt out of a group.[48] What if these federations then decided to break away from the Indian union? Jinnah would achieve his larger Pakistan, comprising the Hindu areas of West Bengal, Assam, East Punjab, and the pro-Congress Muslim province of the North-West Frontier Province.

Congress's fears were fed by Jinnah himself, for he publicly interpreted the provision relating to the right of a province or group to ask for a reconsideration of the whole constitution after an initial period of ten years to imply that the groups had the right to secede from the Indian union. In accepting the Cabinet Mission Plan on 6 June 1946 the Muslim League stated that it was doing so in the hope of ultimately establishing a fully sovereign Pakistan.[49] Were Jinnah's intentions serious, or was he simply trying to keep intact the morale of his constituents by not letting the dream of Pakistan dissolve too suddenly? His motives were never clear, even to his closest colleagues, though he was consistent in his pursuit of political power. His main object was to get the Muslim League entrenched in the interim government and to obtain for himself the defence portfolio.[50] When privately told by Wavell that if the Muslim League accepted the Plan and Congress did not the League would be allowed to go ahead, without Congress, with the implementation of the Plan, particularly with the formation of the interim government, Jinnah hastened to get the Muslim League formally to accept the Plan. He wanted to get as much power for the League as he could before the British left India, as he knew they would. His main concern was to prevent a situation where Congress was in control of the interim government while the British were packing. A firm 'no' from the Cabinet Mission to his Pakistan demand had forced him to abandon the attitude which had served him so well for so long. He was now prepared to make compromises to avoid complete defeat. In this he had the advantage of having as a rival a body whose movements were slow and predictable.

Congress leaders were reluctant to gamble on the grouping of the provinces. They persisted in their opposition to the compulsory grouping of the provinces, an attitude which implied that, if the worst came to the worst, they would rather let Jinnah have a truncated Pakistan than gamble with the future of a Hindu Assam, West Bengal and East Punjab. The firm refusal of the Cabinet Mission to concede ground on this issue made them even more apprehensive about the implication of the compulsory grouping of the provinces. There thus occurred a change in Congress strategy. It seemed possible that the compulsory grouping might be demolished through the proposed constituent assembly. Congress thus claimed full sovereign status for the constituent assembly. In other words, it held that the constituent assembly was entitled either to scrap or to modify the Cabinet Mission Plan relating to the grouping of the provinces. This strategy suited Nehru, who had for so long espoused the cause of a sovereign constituent assembly. The Cabinet Mission pointed out, however, that the constituent assembly could not alter the arrangements which had been made for the protection of minorities.[51]

Congress then shifted its attention to the interim government, though without abandoning its stand on the long-term plan. Nehru believed that all problems could be resolved if

Congress captured immediate control of the central government. Congress could then deal with the Muslim League and the princes, and at leisure make a constitution consistent with its ideals.[52] Nehru had been particularly worried about the Indian states. The provisions of the Mission Plan relating to the states seemed to him vague, and also undesirable to the extent that they empowered the rulers, and not the people, to appoint representatives to the constituent assembly. What if the rulers decided to remain outside the Indian union? In that case the territorial loss to India would be greater than if Jinnah ran away with a truncated Pakistan. But if Congress controlled the interim government it might keep the princes under control.

But here again the odds stood heavily against Congress. First there was the principle of parity with the Muslim League – a sour pill for Congress to swallow. Patel would have preferred civil war to partnering the League in the administration of the country. Congress might, however, upset that balance if it could gain the support of at least three of the four minority members (the Sikh, Baldeo Singh, the Parsi, N. P. Engineer, the scheduled-caste representative, Jagjivan Ram, and even the Indian Christian, Dr John Mathai), all of whom were more likely to be Congress supporters. But then there arose a matter of principle which held Congress back: the list did not include a Congress Muslim. Gandhi and Nehru wanted a Muslim on the Congress list, but Jinnah was opposed to any Muslim other than a Muslim League nominee being included in the government. Jinnah would not have persisted in his stand against a Congress Muslim (which seemed unreasonable even to the cabinet ministers) without Wavell's support. Wavell had come to distrust Congress intentions and dislike its leadership. Once the Congress leaders recognised Wavell's bias towards the League they reacted by taking a firmer stand on the Congress Muslim issue, and rejected Patel's advice to compromise. In adopting a negative attitude towards the interim government Congress was influenced by another consideration. Of what use to Congress would be the interim government if it were not allowed to function independently of the Viceroy? Wavell had made it very clear to Congress leaders that he was not going to function as a mere titular head of the government. There thus existed no clear prospect of Congress using the machinery of government to control the Indian princes or curb the designs of the Muslim League.

Indian politics had taken a turn which was not to Nehru's liking. It was no longer the British Raj, but the despised Muslim League, which stood in the way of the national movement. The alternative to power-sharing with the League lay in civil war, which to Nehru was unthinkable. Struck with a sense of helplessness, he longed to escape from New Delhi. At this point the political development in Kashmir offered him an opportunity to plunge into the politics of an Indian state. His friend Sheikh M. Abdullah, the president of the people's party – the Kashmir National Conference – was arrested on 20 May 1946 by the Kashmiri Government in consequence of the Quit Kashmir Movement which he had launched earlier in March against the autocratic princely government of the state. The situation was a delicate one, since the ruler of the state was the Hindu Hari Singh, the population of the state was predominantly Muslim, and the leader of the mass movement was a Muslim. For Nehru, however, the situation in Kashmir represented a straightforward fight between an autocratic government on the one hand and a democratic people's party on the other. Being a Kashmiri himself, and at the time the President of the All-India States Peoples' Conference, Nehru was drawn towards the movement. Besides, Congress support for the states' people, whether in Kashmir or any other state, was in Nehru's thinking the only effective means of preventing the princes withdrawing from the Indian union.

However, Nehru's view of the Kashmir situation and his confidence in Abdullah were not shared by the leaders of the Hindu Mahasabha, who suspected that Abdullah was trying to drag Kashmir ultimately into the north-western Pakistan zone. Even the rightists in Congress were not happy about Nehru's intervention in Kashmir affairs at a time when the future of India and the states seemed to be in the balance. Nehru was adamant, however, and on 19 June, against the wishes of Wavell and some of his colleagues, he decided to fly to Kashmir with a view to supporting and defending Abdullah. He was stopped at the border by the state police and offered the choice of either returning to India or courting imprisonment. He defied the ban, marched on foot with his party into Kashmir territory, and on 20 June was duly put under house arrest. It was at this time that Congress High Command had to decide on the Cabinet Mission's award of 16 June. Azad and Patel implored Nehru to return immediately. Wavell sent a special plane for him, and Nehru returned to New Delhi on 22 June, perhaps a little refreshed by his brief adventure.

Within two days of Nehru's return Congress half-heartedly decided to accept the 16 May award with reservations and to join the proposed constituent assembly, but it rejected the 16 June award and consequently declined to join the provisional government. If left to themselves the Congress leaders would probably have deferred making any decision for some time, but the cabinet ministers were about to leave, and Pethick-Lawrence and Cripps privately impressed upon the Congress leaders the propriety of accepting at least the 16 May award, otherwise the Viceroy would be obliged under the terms of the Cabinet Mission Plan to form a provisional government with the co-operation of the Muslim League.[53] To gain a tactical advantage over the League regarding the interim government Congress thus accepted the 16 May award, but it was an equivocal acceptance amounting only to a decision to enter the constituent assembly with a view to framing the constitution of a free, united and democratic India. It still maintained its opposition to the compulsory grouping of the provinces. But the Congress decision was consistent with Nehru's thinking on the Mission's plan. He asserted that Congress was entering into a constituent assembly for which he claimed sovereignty absolute enough to modify the arrangement made by the Cabinet Mission regarding the grouping of provinces.

Jinnah misunderstood the implications of the Congress decision. He believed that Congress's rejection of the 16 June award had left the field open for the League. On 25 June he thus summoned a meeting of the League's Working Committee and passed a resolution accepting the 16 June award and agreeing to join the interim government. Jinnah was now certain that the Viceroy would call him to form a government without the Congress representatives. He was bitterly frustrated the following day when the Cabinet Mission made it clear that both parties, having now accepted the 16 May plan, stood in an equal position. As Congress had declined to co-operate with the 16 June plan for an interim coalition government, it would remain suspended. The cabinet ministers hoped that talks between the leaders of the two parties regarding the formation of an interim government would be resumed after a brief interval. In the meantime the Viceroy was to form a caretaker government, and the election of representatives to the constituent assembly was to go ahead. Jinnah complained of a breach of promise and asked the Viceroy on 28 June either to let the League form a government or to postpone the elections to the constituent assembly. As the two awards of the Cabinet Mission formed one whole, he argued, it was undesirable to proceed with one part (the election to the constituent assembly) and to postpone the other – the formation of the provisional government.[54] But, with all his sympathy for the League, Wavell had to bow to the Mission's ruling and reject Jinnah's argument. The cabinet ministers left for home on 29 June.

Jinnah was left in the lurch. The prospect of capturing control over the central government having vanished, he was no longer interested in the long-term plan which, in the face of Congress's continuing opposition to the compulsory grouping of provinces, seemed unlikely to yield a large Pakistan either within or without the Indian union. The proposed constituent assembly seemed to him a trap. He suspected that Congress might use it not only to destroy the idea of Pakistan but also to create a strong central government for India. He thus sought an excuse to retract the League's acceptance of the 16 May award, and found a sufficient excuse in Nehru's statements of 10 and 22 July, made respectively to a press conference in Bombay and at a public meeting in Delhi.

On 10 July, soon after taking over from Azad the presidency of Congress, Nehru explained Congress thinking on the Cabinet Mission Plan. In accepting the plan of 16 May, he stated, Congress had agreed only to join the constituent assembly.[55] While asserting Congress opposition to grouping, he pointed out that it was highly likely that North-West Frontier Province and Assam would decide against grouping, in which case sections B and C would certainly collapse. On 22 July he expressed similar arguments against compulsory grouping with special reference to Assam. The legislative assembly of Assam had by then passed a resolution at the instance of the Congress premier Gopinath Bardoloi boycotting Section C in which the province was placed.[56] At the same time Nehru impressed upon the elected representatives of the constituent assembly its sovereign character.[57]

Nehru's speeches revealed nothing new to Jinnah, nor were they inconsistent with the Congress interpretation of the 16 May plan, but they placed Jinnah in an embarrassing position in relation to his followers. Nehru was after all publicly destroying the very prospect of Pakistan by claiming for the constituent assembly the sovereign right to scrap the compulsory grouping of the provinces. On 29 July the Muslim League, after making due reference to Nehru's speeches, withdrew its acceptance of the Cabinet Mission Plan. That very day the Council of the League further resolved to resort to direct action to achieve Pakistan. It was a virtual declaration of civil war.

Jinnah was aware of the possible consequences of his decision, but violence was the only threat he could now use. Congress was not unduly alarmed, though it lowered its tone, and Nehru even expressed regret for his hasty and intemperate statements. But Congress was still unwilling to concede any ground to the League and, during his abortive negotiations with Jinnah, Nehru insisted on Congress's right to include a non-League Muslim in its quota for the interim government – which Congress was now entitled to form, if it wished, without the League, as the latter, having withdrawn its acceptance of the 16 May plan, was no longer legally qualified to be included in the government. Congress in fact took the League's decision of 29 July as a blessing in disguise. When Jinnah learnt that Nehru was now willing to form a government without the League's representatives, he realised that direct action was the only possible means of retrieving the ground he had inadvertently lost.

The action was launched on 16 August. Over 5000 lives were lost between 16 and 20 August in Calcutta, where, to celebrate the day, the Muslim League premier Suhrawardy had declared a public holiday. The civil war was soon to spread over the whole of northern India from Bengal to Punjab. The antagonists were Hindus and Sikhs on the one hand and Muslims on the other, and the war was to take a toll of at least a quarter of a million lives – men, women and children – by November 1947. But in August 1946 the situation did not seem particularly severe to Congress. While blaming the League for the Calcutta massacres (which might have cost more Muslim than Hindu lives, as the Muslims were in the minority in Calcutta), Congress hoped that Jinnah would realise the folly of declaring civil war. Nehru went ahead with his plan for the formation of the provisional government. Wavell wanted to keep five of the fourteen seats in the government vacant for the Muslim League but Nehru insisted on filling them with neutral Muslims to maintain government stability. The government was duly inaugurated on 2 September with twelve members (six Congress representatives, three neutral Muslims, three minority members – two more Muslim members were to be appointed later), with Nehru as Vice-President. Congress now held power at the centre as well as in the eight provincial governments.

The tide of events leading to the installation of Congress in the interim government dismayed Wavell. He had been overtaken by a feeling of defeatism while the cabinet ministers were still in India, and since May he had been working on his own scheme for the withdrawal of British power from India.[58] The breakdown plan, as he called it, was based on his assumption that Congress and the League would never come to an agreement, and on his determination never to let Congress wield single-handed the powers of central government. Under his scheme the British were to hand over the Hindu-majority provinces to Congress and to retain control over the Muslim-majority provinces (North-West Frontier Province, Punjab, Sind, Bengal and Assam) until these provinces were able to evolve a constitution and arrive at an agreement with Hindu India. He modified his plan on 1 September – one day before the interim government was inaugurated. Under his revised plan the British would retain control over two north-Indian Hindu provinces (United Provinces and Bihar) to avoid the impression that control was being retained only in Muslim-majority provinces. With the withdrawal of British power paramountcy was to lapse and the Indian states would be left to decide their own futures. Though his plan was considered too drastic, and was rejected on each occasion, Wavell never gave up, and he was still pleading for its acceptance in December 1946, not knowing that the Prime Minister had decided to terminate his viceroyalty.

On the eve of Nehru's formation of the interim government Wavell felt he had been cheated and out-manœuvred by Congress. He did not believe that the Congress acceptance of the 16 May award was genuine, and with a view to proving this he insisted that Congress should give a firm assurance that it would abide strictly by the scheme of compulsory grouping of provinces. Though the Secretary of State prevented Wavell from pressing too hard on this point, Nehru made, in his broadcast of 7 September, what seemed to Wavell a conciliatory reference to 'grouping'. There was in fact no substantial change in Nehru's thinking on this issue. All Nehru said was that Congress had accepted the position that provinces should sit in sections in the first instance.[59] But on the vital procedural question as to how the voting was to take place in the sections Nehru remained firmly opposed to the Cabinet Mission interpretation that the decisions of the sections were to be taken by a simple majority vote of the representatives in the sections. Nehru insisted that in sectional meetings each province should vote as a province. This would not only be consistent with the principle of provincial autonomy but would also ensure the retention by a province of its right to form its own constitution and of the option to withdraw itself from the group in which it was initially placed.

As it did not seem possible to force Congress out of the government, Wavell hoped to redeem the situation by bringing in the Muslim League. He read much more into the Calcutta killings than was perhaps warranted, and saw nothing but complete disaster for the country unless a Congress–League coalition government was formed at the centre and, if possible, in the provinces. As violence spread in East Bengal and Bihar the intensity of Wavell's pleadings for the inclusion of the Muslim League in the interim government increased. To permit this would, in the Congress view, amount to surrendering to Jinnah, whom it held entirely responsible for the outbreak of violence. Patel, now the Home Member, was fully confident that violence could be suppressed by effective use of the police and military forces. But Wavell kept on insisting and at the same time negotiating, almost behind Nehru's back, with Jinnah.

It was perhaps another crucial moment in Indian history. On both moral and practical grounds the Congress leadership was opposed to the Muslim League being drawn into the government. The longer the League was kept out of the government the greater the opportunity for Congress to strengthen its hold over the civil and military administration of the country. If Nehru had put his foot down, Wavell might not have succeeded in his attempts, for at this time the Secretary of State in all probability would have backed Nehru against the Viceroy. But Nehru, no matter how much he wished that the League should be excluded from the government, could not take a stand, for it was not in his character to disregard his own conscience and ruthlessly to seek political gains at the cost of his public image. The League was entitled to enter the interim government provided it accepted the 16 May award and joined the Constituent Assembly. Thus, while resenting the Viceroy's overtures to Jinnah, the most he could do was to insist that the League first complied with that vital condition. This he did, and was assured by Wavell – who in turn was assured by Jinnah – that as soon as the Council of the Muslim League met it would formally accept the 16 May award. As it turned out Jinnah, having secured on 25 October the entry of five League nominees into the interim government, never called the League's council meeting to endorse the Cabinet Mission Plan. Nehru had been tricked. However, a formal acceptance on the part of the League would really not have made much difference. Jinnah would have subsequently found some excuse to prevent the League from entering the constituent assembly. His main objective was to get the League into the government, and no one could stop him from doing so once Wavell had made overtures to the League. Set as he was in his views and prejudices, Wavell believed he had no other option.

The government which was reconstituted on 25 October (with five nominees from the League, five from Congress, four from the minority communities) lacked from the very beginning the spirit and appearance of a coalition. The League's team of five (including a scheduled-caste Hindu as a counter to Congress's inclusion of a Muslim on its list) entered the government with a view to dividing it, and to harassing the Congress team. It is most unlikely that the League's team would have set off in a less antagonistic tone if Jinnah himself had joined the government. Jinnah was willing to join the government provided only that he was given an important portfolio and the vice-presidency was within his reach. But Nehru was most unwilling either to give up the vice-presidency or to let it rotate between Congress and the League. He considered the post as comparable with that of a prime minister and believed that a Congress leader alone should be entitled to hold it then, as in the future central government of a fully independent India. Jinnah, conscious as he was of his prestige and position, would not occupy a position in government which was subordinate to Nehru's. Distrusting the League's intentions the Congress leaders decided to keep the most important portfolios in their hands: Nehru retained External Affairs, which was his special interest; Patel made it known that he would rather resign than hold any portfolio other than that of Home Affairs; Defence was considered safe in the hands of Baldeo Singh, a Sikh representative of Congress choice. Only Finance, the last of the four key portfolios, was given to Liaquat Ali Khan – the leader of the League team. Nehru and Patel considered this a fairly safe arrangement – and so it would have been but for the League's determination to harass Congress by whatever means it had at its disposal.

In February 1947, Liaquat Ali Khan produced a budget containing many new taxes, all designed to fall heavily on the Hindu industrialists and businessmen from whom Congress derived its main financial support. Nehru and Patel did not realise the implications of the budget until it had gone into committee stage. The League members of the government also caused personal annoyance and frustration to Nehru in not acknowledging him as a *de facto* prime minister and in boycotting his tea parties which he periodically arranged with a view to meeting the ministers informally. They pursued their obstructionist policy further and often opposed Nehru's proposals in cabinet meetings.

Outside government the League's activities were even more distressing to Congress. The League set out to capture those 'Pakistan provinces' – North-West Frontier Province, Punjab and Assam – where its position was weak. This aim increased in urgency as a result of Attlee's statement of 20 February 1947 in which, with a view to forcing the League and Congress to come to an agreement, he made it clear that Britain wanted to transfer power to India by a date not later than June 1948. If by that time no constitution was worked out by a fully representative assembly, then Britain would be obliged to consider to whom the powers of the central government in British India were to be transferred on the due date, whether as a whole to some form of central government or, in some areas, to the existing provincial governments. The statement implied that, in the event of a constitution not emerging by the due date, Britain might transfer power over the Hindu provinces to Congress, and to existing governments, individually, in the Pakistan zones – in which case the Muslim League might get only Bengal and Sind.

The League took to all kinds of measures – armed conspiracy, propaganda, even Gandhian-style civil disobedience – to overthrow Khizr Hyat Khan's coalition government in the Punjab. The premier succumbed to the League's pressure and resigned on 3 March 1947. The Hindus and Sikhs, fearing that the League might be allowed to capture the government, resorted to communal riots, and the scramble for the Punjab began. The League, however, could not form a ministry and on 5 March the province passed under governor's rule. But the civil war, once begun, continued to thrive on mutual suspicion and fear between the Muslims on the one hand and the Sikhs and Hindus on the other. In Assam, a predominantly Hindu province, the Muslim League campaign took the form of an attempt to swell the Muslim population of the province with Muslim emigrants from East Bengal. However, G. N. Bardoloi, the Congress premier of Assam, succeeded, with Patel's firm support, in evicting the Muslim squatters and thereby foiling the League's plan.[60] The League's movement in North-West Frontier Province similarly failed to dislodge the Congress ministry headed by Dr Khan Saheb. It did succeed, however, to some extent, in tarnishing Nehru's (and, by implication, Congress's) image in the frontier province by organising a hostile reception for him when he visited the province in October 1946.

The League's success in harassing Congress from October 1946 to March 1947 was in no small measure due to Wavell. Wavell ignored Nehru's persistent demand that the League, having deliberately avoided accepting the Cabinet Mission Plan of May 1946, be dismissed from the interim government. Legally the Muslim League members were not entitled to remain in the government. But Wavell not only dismissed the technicalities of the matter but also was vastly impressed by Jinnah's repeated pleas that Congress acceptance of the 16 May award was not genuine as the Congress leaders continued to put their own interpretation on the grouping clause of the award – an interpretation which according to Jinnah was contrary to the spirit and meaning of the Cabinet Mission Plan. Jinnah thus demanded that the first meeting of the Constituent Assembly (which the League had not joined) scheduled for 9 December 1946 be either postponed or cancelled.

To resolve the difference between the League and Congress interpretations of the 'grouping clause', Attlee convened a conference in London of the Indian leaders (Nehru, Baldeo Singh, Jinnah, Liaquat Ali Khan) on 3–6 December. Nehru accepted the invitation with great reluctance, for he feared that Jinnah might succeed in getting further concessions at a time when his technique of violence was beginning to pay smaller dividends. As he had anticipated, the cabinet ministers stood by their original interpretation of the 'grouping clause' (which went against the Congress stand on the voting procedure in the sections) but conceded, as a consolation to Congress, that further questions of interpretation might with the consent of the League and Congress be referred to the Federal Court. Nehru returned to India disappointed but in time for the opening of the Constituent Assembly, which met on 9 December. On 15 December, while Wavell was still in London, Patel wrote privately to Cripps accusing Wavell of partiality towards the League: 'The Viceroy here took the contrary view, and every action of his since the "Great Calcutta Killing" has been in the direction of encouraging the Muslim

League and putting pressure on us towards appeasement.'[61] During his brief stay in London, Nehru, too, had made it clear to the cabinet ministers that Congress disapproved of Wavell's partiality towards the League. Wavell's defeatist attitude and his unpopularity with Congress must have weighed heavily on Attlee's mind when on 18 December 1946 he decided on a change of viceroy. Wavell, however, functioned for three more months till 22 March 1947, and in those crucial months events in India took a decisive turn towards the partition of the sub-continent.

The history of these months was characterised by a war of succession. Congress went ahead with the opening of the Constituent Assembly, claiming sovereign power and hoping that the League and the Indian states would soon join it. But the prospect of the League joining the Constituent Assembly became more remote when Congress insisted (as manifested in the All-India Congress Committee's resolution of 6 January) that no province or part of a province could be compelled against its wishes to remain in a particular group. The Congress resolution, in the Muslim League's view, constituted a complete repudiation of the final interpretation put on the Cabinet Mission Plan by the British Government at the London conference held in December. On 31 January 1947 the League formally decided to boycott the Constituent Assembly; it also demanded that the meetings of the Assembly be declared invalid. The League's resolution, in Congress's view, constituted the League's non-acceptance of the 16 May award, and on 5 February Nehru firmly asked Wavell to dismiss the League members from the government.[62] Wavell took no action. Then on 20 February came Attlee's announcement (which was in fact drafted by Lord Mountbatten) putting a time-limit on the British Raj and thereby setting in motion a war of succession between India and Pakistan, fought mainly over Bengal, Assam, Punjab and North-West Frontier Province.

Communal violence erupted in the Punjab causing the loss of more Hindu and Sikh lives than Muslim, for the League volunteers were better armed and organised than their opponents. Bengal and Bihar remained relatively peaceful, mainly because Gandhi spent his time, from October 1946 to March

1947, touring these provinces as a healer and peace-maker, a task for which he was well suited. He was not missed in New Delhi where Nehru and Patel had taken upon themselves the sole responsibility for making political decisions and planning strategy.

It was thus in Gandhi's absence and without any prior consultation with him that the Working Committee of Congress made its momentous decisions between 6 and 8 March. While affirming that the constitution framed by the Constituent Assembly would apply only to those areas which accepted it, the Working Committee made it clear that any province or part of a province which accepted the constitution and desired to join the Indian union could not be prevented from doing so. As if to leave no illusion in Jinnah's mind as to the size of Pakistan he would get if he continued chasing his 'mad dream', the Working Committee proposed the partition of the Punjab into two provinces – a Muslim western and a Hindu–Sikh eastern province. Since the ostensible reason for this proposal was that it might, if implemented, put an end to the violence in the Punjab, it did not include Bengal, but it was clear by implication that Congress would rather demand a similar partition of Bengal than let the whole province be drawn into Pakistan. The Punjab resolution was more of a threat to Jinnah than a clear acceptance on the part of Congress of the inevitability of India's division. For, despite the fact that Congress felt threatened by continual League harassment, and Nehru had come to realise that there was no prospect of an agreement with the League and that the only alternative to the Cabinet Mission Plan (which he thought was the best solution of the Indian problem if it could be carried through) was the partition of the Punjab and Bengal,[63] the Congress leadership still believed that the Muslim League would never accept the partition of Bengal and the Punjab; and, further, that if Jinnah was faced with the option of having only a truncated Pakistan he might shake off his dream and fall into line with an Indian union. However, whether a mere threat or an endorsement of the principle of partition, the Punjab resolution of Congress was generally accepted as laying down the conditions under which Congress would accept the creation of a sovereign Pakistan. Gandhi bitterly resented it, but Mountbatten welcomed it as the only alternative to fall back on if he failed, as he did, in his last-minute efforts to preserve the unity of India.

The period between 2 September 1946 (when the interim government was first constituted) and 22 March 1947 (when Mountbatten took charge of the viceroyalty) was significant in two ways: during this period the country moved to the verge of partition, and Nehru, while becoming increasingly frustrated as a nationalist, found solace and inspiration in laying down the basic structure of an independent India. He regarded this interim period as of great importance, for he believed that out of it would arise the structure of the future India. On 13 December 1946 he moved a resolution in the Constituent Assembly laying down the form and principles of the Indian constitution, which was to be inaugurated on 26 January 1950. This resolution guaranteed to the people of India a secular, democratic republican constitution and the fundamental rights – social, economic and political justice; equality of status and of opportunity; freedom of thought, association and action.[64] It was for Nehru a moment of personal triumph; his dream that India might have a modern constitution framed by her own people had come true.

It was also during this period that Nehru launched his foreign policy, the basis of which was friendliness towards all nations – particularly America, the Soviet Union and China – and non-alignment with either of the two main groups – the American and Russian – into which, as it seemed to him, the world was then divided. He believed that destiny had given America a major role to play in international affairs, but on the whole he found more reason on the side of Russia. To offend neither power while at the same time speaking frankly and freely on world problems was the core as well as the problem of Nehru's foreign policy. While addressing the Indian delegates (Mrs Pandit, Krishna Menon, K. P. S. Menon) to the United Nations General Assembly he emphasised the problem implicit in his non-alignment policy:

> If Russia helps us and speaks for us, it is right for us to express our gratitude and our friendliness. Not to do so for fear of offending America or England or of losing some votes would be to become totally ineffective and untrue to our-

> selves. Only those are respected, as individuals or as nations, who have the strength to speak frankly whatever they have in their minds and not be afraid all the time of the results of frankness. Yet obviously too much frankness may break up the best of friendships and one has to draw the line somewhere.[65]

The object of his foreign policy was to secure the re-entry of Asia into world politics and to turn India into a natural focal point. This aspect of Nehru's policy found expression at the first Asian Relations Conference held on 23 March 1947. In his inaugural speech he referred to the glory of Asia, where civilisation first began and 'the mind of man searched unceasingly for truth and the spirit of man shone out like a beacon which lighted up the whole world'.[66] It was fitting, he maintained, that the Conference was held in India, for India had for centuries been the meeting-point for all Asia.

On the domestic front Nehru had to face a new problem arising out of Congress entry into the interim government. The problem concerned the relationship between Congress Party and Government, and more specifically between the Working Committee and the Cabinet and between the Congress President and the Prime Minister. The problem would not have emerged so soon but for J. B. Kripalani, who, having been Congress General-Secretary since 1934, was elevated to its presidency in 1946 when Nehru resigned from the post in September. With an unattractive personality and with no political power-base, Kripalani suffered from an inferiority complex. While serving as the General-Secretary he had often complained of being treated as a doormat by the Congress presidents S. C. Bose and A. K. Azad. On becoming President in 1946 he asserted the power of his office and of his Working Committee over the Congress Cabinet, and felt humiliated not only at being ignored but also because he was not even informed about the important decisions Nehru made on national and international issues.[67] Confrontation with Nehru became for Kripalani a matter of personal prestige. Nehru was too occupied to take the challenge seriously but he did make it clear that on the grounds of secrecy alone the government could not seek guidance from the Working Committee before making decisions on specific issues. He asserted that the government must have freedom to shape policies and act up to them 'within the larger ambit of the general policy laid down in Congress resolutions'.[68] The problem was not resolved until after independence, when Kripalani resigned and Prasad stepped into the post.

Technically the interim period lasted until 15 August when Vice-President Nehru became Prime Minister of an independent India. But in reality it was interrupted by the commencement of Mountbatten's viceroyalty on 22 March: from then till the middle of August all parties and all governments were involved in the division of India and the integration of the Indian states. The last six months of British rule in India were, in a way, not as significant as they are believed to have been. The course of Indian history had already taken an inevitable turn before Mountbatten arrived on the scene. There was little or no room left for the leaders to make or unmake history. Mountbatten was not aware of this when he arrived in India armed with extraordinary powers and charged with a sense of mission. In persuading Attlee to put a time-limit (June 1948) on the continuation of the 182-year-old British Raj, Mountbatten had hoped that this would convince the Indian political parties, particularly Congress, of the *bona fides* of British intentions and encourage them, and especially the Muslim League, to accept the Cabinet Mission Plan. Attlee's announcement of 20 February was thus intended to deliver from British rule, within a specified period, a united and free India. That the setting of a precise time-limit might produce results contrary to those intended did cross Attlee's mind but not Mountbatten's. Mountbatten further believed that such a declaration would make his viceroyalty popular and considerably strengthen his position in India. Indeed he had wished to take the post on the open invitation of the Indian parties but Attlee had thought this unfeasible. Mountbatten's viceroyalty was further distinguished by the plenipotentiary powers he obtained from the Prime Minister to act freely without much interference from London. In asking for such wide powers he had his predecessor's handicap in mind; Wavell could not even meet Gandhi without first obtaining the permission of the Prime Minister.

Characteristically, Mountbatten felt secure, effective, and

even inspired to act humbly provided he was well equipped with abundance of power. Eager to liquidate the British Raj at the earliest moment, Attlee was prepared to concede all manner of privileges and powers to the man he had chosen as best qualified to fulfil the task. He allowed Mountbatten to choose his own staff, gave him an assurance that his naval career would be secured, and even allowed the Viceroy-designate to write his own terms of appointment and confidential directives. Mountbatten's openness, his temperamental yet personal approach, his ability to understand and appreciate diverse characters and points of view without judging by a set standard, and his desire to be popular were more endearing to Nehru than to Jinnah. Jinnah's personality was concealed, and he worked most effectively in formal and calculated dealings. When faced with the warm, impulsive and open-handed approach of Nehru and Mountbatten he felt embarrassed, almost denuded, and tended to withdraw. He and Mountbatten did not like each other, which was a matter of frustration and injured pride to the latter, but only of relief to Jinnah.

Edwina Mountbatten helped to consolidate her husband's position. She was naturally drawn towards the have-nots, and found personal fulfilment in social and relief work, opportunities for which were abundant in the India of the late forties. In less than six months, when the face of India was to become swollen with millions of starving and sick refugees, she applied what Nehru called her healer's touch, and wherever she went brought solace, hope and encouragement. 'Is it surprising', Nehru said to her in June 1948, 'that the people of India should love you?' He was speaking for himself as much as for the people.

It took less than a month for Mountbatten to realise the inevitability of partition. On 31 March he began his interviews with the Indian leaders with a view first to reviving the Cabinet Mission Plan. By 25 April he was convinced that it was impossible to preserve the unity of India on the basis of the Cabinet Mission Plan. Jinnah was set against the revival of the Plan and asked for a sovereign Pakistan consisting of the six provinces. When told he could get only a truncated Pakistan, he threatened to ask for the partition of Assam and felt nonplussed when told by Mountbatten that it would be done as a matter of course once the principle of partition was accepted. The Congress leaders offered their acceptance of the Cabinet Mission Plan – provided that Punjab and Bengal were partitioned, that the Hindu-majority areas were not included in Sections B and C, and that parity between the League and Congress was not maintained in the central government. The Sikhs and Hindus did not want to stay in a united Punjab which would be ruled by the Muslim League. Likewise the Hindus were fearful of being left in a Muslim League-dominated, united Bengal. Thus Congress also stood for partition, though its leadership still cherished the hope of some form of Indian unity, if it were feasible. So did Mountbatten. Having abandoned the idea of reviving the Cabinet Mission Plan, he still hoped to preserve some form of central authority, to deal at least with defence, for he was at this stage very much opposed to dividing the armed forces of India on communal lines. He believed the Indo-Pakistan defence authority (or the Joint Defence Council) could function for at least a year under his continuing governor-generalship of both the dominions. His plan, however, was eventually foiled by Jinnah, who not only insisted on having a separate army for Pakistan but also on himself being its first governor-general.

However, Mountbatten's first partition plan – which Lord Ismay, Chief of Staff, took to London on 2 May – contained provision for the creation of a Supreme Defence Council. According to this plan the people in the Pakistan-claimed territories were to decide through their existing legislatures whether they intended to stay with India or opt for a sovereign Pakistan. The non-Muslim-majority areas in Bengal and the Punjab were to exercise the option of joining the Indian union. Though this plan overtly offered only two options for the provinces or parts of provinces involved, it did vaguely suggest the third option of independence, particularly for Bengal where Hindu and Muslim opinion appeared to be against the partition of the province and in favour of preserving its unity as an independent state. Mountbatten himself had come to believe that the 'independence option' might succeed in destroying Jinnah's mad dream of Pakistan, for in all probability the Muslim area of the North-West Frontier Province would decide to constitute itself into an independent state for the Pathans, and there might occur a similar movement in the Punjab. What he did not realise was that this option might also cause further disintegration of the Indian union, for not only would India lose Hindu West Bengal and Hindu–Sikh East Punjab, but it might well lose the large Indian states, which would assuredly be encouraged to exercise this option for themselves the moment British paramountcy lapsed.

The London authorities made no substantial changes in the plan, though it seems they put the vaguely worded third option in rather bolder relief. On 20 May, in Simla, Mountbatten had his original plan returned to him, slightly amended. On the previous day Nehru had arrived with Krishna Menon to stay with Mountbatten as his private guest. Mountbatten had a hunch that the way his plan had been re-drafted in London would not commend itself to Nehru.[69] The same day after dinner, when Krishna Menon had retired to bed, Mountbatten showed the plan to Nehru. Nehru read the plan in his apartment, and furiously showed it to Krishna Menon. The latter worked from midnight until 4 a.m. to calm Nehru down and convince him that Mountbatten, in letting him have a look at the plan, had acted in good faith.[70] In all his utterances made during the night and in the morning at breakfast with Mountbatten, Nehru was at least consistent in maintaining that the plan would lead to the balkanisation of India.

But why, historians have asked, did Nehru rage at sight of the revised plan when it was not very different from the original plan which had been shown to him before being taken to London? The fact is that Nehru had never been shown the original plan. Writing to Mountbatten a day before Ismay took the plan to London, Nehru maintained:

> Neither I nor my colleagues of the Interim Government, who were present at our meeting, know the full extent of the proposals that Lord Ismay is taking with him to London. But you have been good enough to keep me informed of the broad outlines of these proposals and I placed these before the Committee.[71]

In the same letter he further stated:

> In regard to the proposals which, I presume, Lord Ismay is carrying with him to London, our Committee are prepared to accept the principle of partition based on self-determination as applied to definitely ascertained areas. This involves the partition of Bengal and Punjab. As you know, we are passionately attached to the idea of a United India, but we have accepted the partition of India in order to avoid conflict and compulsion.[72]

It was the partition of the Punjab and Bengal between India and Pakistan and not the independence of these two provinces which Nehru had in mind. The plan caused him special anxiety about the Indian states. He had been using threats and persuasion in his negotiations with the Indian states; and some, like Baroda, had already agreed to join the Constituent Assembly.[73] A plan which gave the option of independence to any of the British Indian provinces was most likely to be used by the larger Indian states, and could ruin his own hopes. But with 565 states in their basket Patel and Nehru were prepared to bear the loss of Sind, West Punjab, East Bengal and even the whole of North-West Frontier Province. Nehru's reaction to the plan was very natural in the circumstances, and also fruitful, for within hours Mountbatten scrapped the plan and summoned V. P. Menon, his constitutional adviser, to draft a new one.

On 11 May, V. P. Menon drafted in less than four hours the plan for the end of the British Empire in India. It was acceptable to Nehru, and Patel signified his approval on the telephone. It was this third and final plan of partition which on 14 May Mountbatten himself took to London for cabinet approval. This was promptly given. He returned to India on 30 May, and on 2 June placed the plan before the Indian leaders – Nehru, Patel, Kripalani, Jinnah, Liaquat Ali Khan, Abdur Rab Nishtar and Baldeo Singh. The plan was accepted by all and formally announced in London on 3 June. The novel feature of the plan – that transfer of power was to take place on a dominion-status basis – was V. P. Menon's idea, endorsed by Patel and Nehru. The previous plans had envisaged the creation of two sovereign states, which implied that power could not be transferred until the two states were able to finalise their constitutions. The acceptance of dominion status by India and Pakistan for a short period while their constitutions were being framed meant that power could be transferred almost immediately by amending, not replacing, the existing Act of 1935. The plan did not contain the 'independence option'. The legislators of the non-Muslim areas in Bengal and the Punjab were given the option of demanding the partition of those provinces and joining the Constituent Assembly of their choice, which of course meant joining the Indian union. The electorates in Sylhet (the Muslim-majority area in Assam) and in North-West Frontier Province were to decide through a referendum which of the two dominions they wished to join. The legislators of Sind and the representatives of the people of British Baluchistan, which then had no regular legislature of its own, were likewise to decide the future of their respective provinces.

Nehru and Jinnah commended the plan to their respective peoples in their different styles. Admitting his defeat, but without any malice or regret, Nehru pinned his hopes on the future and asked his people to bury their past in so far as it was bad and to forget all bitterness and recriminations:

> For generations we have dreamed and struggled for a free, independent and united India. The proposal to allow certain parts to secede if they so will is painful for any of us to contemplate. Nevertheless, I am convinced that our present decision is the right one even from the larger viewpoint. . . . It may be that in this way we shall reach that United India sooner than otherwise and then she will have a stronger and more secure foundation.[74]

His hope for a united India had not yet died: partition might lead to reunion. Apart from doubting the viability of Pakistan – which was then questioned, among others, by Mountbatten himself, who believed that East Pakistan, having nothing in common with West Pakistan except a religion which was not enough to hold them together for long, might veer towards a reunion with India – Nehru was inclined to believe that the communal antagonism, which had been whipped up in the creation of Pakistan, might subside, leaving the path clear for a possible reunion.[75]

Jinnah in his broadcast message concentrated on North-

West Frontier Province (where the referendum was to be held) and referred to the sacrifices his people had made there for the Pakistan cause. It was a well-guarded statement but with subtle overtones of propaganda, showing that for a vigilant strategist like Jinnah the war was not over until the province was recaptured from the Congress hold. Nehru, having failed to secure an 'independence option' for North-West Frontier Province, abandoned it to its inevitable fate. The Khan brothers boycotted the referendum, which was held from 6 to 17 July. Of the fifty per cent of the electorate of North-West Frontier Province that voted, 289,244 voted for Pakistan and only 2874 for India. By 17 July voting had taken place in the other Pakistan provinces: by majority votes, Sind, West Punjab, East Bengal and Sylhet had opted for Pakistan, and East Punjab and West Bengal for India. Jinnah's truncated Pakistan had come into existence. It was to survive the remainder of Nehru's life and endure until 1972, when East Pakistan seceded from Pakistan and constituted itself into an independent state of Bangladesh. On that occasion the leader of Pakistan (Z. A. Bhutto) expressed hopes, similar to Nehru's, that the secession might one day lead to a reunion between the two Pakistans.

Soon after the acceptance of the plan on 3 June, Mountbatten set the partition machinery in motion. He fixed 15 August – the second anniversary of the Japanese surrender – as a propitious date for the transfer of power. As that day was pronounced by the astrologers to be an inauspicious date, the difficulty was to be overcome by summoning the Indian Constituent Assembly late on the evening of the fourteenth, and having it take over precisely as midnight struck – that being still an auspicious hour. Parliament succeeded in passing the Indian Independence Act on 18 July, well in advance of the date fixed for the transfer of power. An Armed Forces Reconstitution Committee was set up to divide the Army, Navy and Air Force, more or less on communal lines, and to establish in each of the dominions a separate operational command; administrative control over the forces of both the dominions was to rest, for some time after 15 August, with Field-Marshal Auchinleck who, as Supreme Commander, was to be answerable to a Joint Defence Council comprising, besides himself, the governor-generals of the two dominions and their defence ministers. This task was performed by the appointed date. A Partition Council under Mountbatten, an Arbitral Tribunal under Sir Patrick Spens and a Steering Committee consisting of one Pakistani and one Indian official and working through ten expert sub-committees were set up to divide all the assets of India (administrative, economic, financial) by the appointed date. Most important of all were the two boundary commissions established under the chairmanship of Sir Cyril (now Lord) Radcliffe – one to demarcate the boundaries of East and West Bengal and the other to separate East from West Punjab. Each commission, consisting of two Hindu and two Muslim judges, having failed to arrive at an agreed solution, Radcliffe took it upon himself to make the final award. This was submitted to Mountbatten on 13 August, but he let it lie unopened till the independence celebrations were over, for he knew that it would cause disappointment and uproar among the parties involved. The award, when made public on 16 August, was bitterly criticised by Congress, Muslim and Sikh leaders – a fact which made them wonder, after the heat of the moment, whether there might not be some merit in an award where all parties were equally critical.

At the same time as India was being dissected, the Indian states were being integrated. Here the odds seemed at first to lie against Congress, which had a bigger stake than the Muslim League in the future of the states. When it became clear that paramountcy would lapse on 15 August, the Political Department of the Government of India (which virtually exercised control over the states and was directly responsible only to the Viceroy) began not only to burn its files and dispose of its properties in the states but also to encourage the states to assert their sovereignty against India, at least for bargaining purposes. Sir Conrad Corefield – the Viceroy's political adviser, who was suspected of being generally hostile to Congress – was instrumental in setting this role for the Political Department during the last days of the British Raj. Nehru was alarmed. On 9 June he complained to the Viceroy: 'It seems to us extraordinary and highly improper for the Political Department to continue to take various steps to liquidate all our relations with the States without reference to us.'[76] Later in the same month he further expressed his concern to Lord Ismay:

> It is bad enough that India has to be partitioned. It would be disastrous if this process went further and resulted in the 'balkanization' of the country. . . . All this has little to do with paramountcy in the limited sense of the word. That paramountcy is not being transferred by the British government to an Indian government but the fact of geography cannot be ignored and the dominant power in India will necessarily exercise certain control over any State which does not choose to come into the Union.[77]

The other hazard for Congress was set by Jinnah, who rejected his two-nation theory and invited the Hindu rulers to join Pakistan on their own terms. This option seemed less risky to some rulers than opting for Nehru's socialist India, and the Hindu ruler of Jodhpur – a state abutting on Pakistan – would have fallen into Jinnah's net but for the timely intervention of Patel, V. P. Menon and, unobtrusively, Mountbatten.

Had it not been for the crisis created by the activities of the Political Department and Jinnah's manœuvres, Patel might have let things lie until after the transfer of power, for he believed that as soon as India became free the states' peoples would depose their rulers and join the Indian union. As it was, he was forced to take action, and on 27 June he set up two states departments, one each for India and Pakistan. Patel took charge of the Indian side and he appointed V. P. Menon as Secretary. Menon lost no time in evolving his master-plan for the accession of the states. The central authorities of India/Pakistan would be responsible for external affairs, defence and communications only – matters over which state rulers had not previously had control. In acceding to the Indian union on these terms they would thus virtually preserve their original autonomy. When showing his plan to Patel and Nehru, Menon emphasised that once the states had acceded it would be up to the Indian Constituent Assembly to devise in due course, after India's independence, a constitutional plan for the fuller merger of the states into the Indian union. He also pointed out to Mountbatten that the

Viceroy's assistance in the achievement of the basic unity of India would in effect heal the wounds of partition and earn for him the gratitude of generations of Indians.[78]

On 25 July, in full regalia, Mountbatten addressed the Chamber of Princes and advised the rulers most persuasively to accede to one or other dominion before 15 August. Though in theory the states were free to link their future with either dominion, Mountbatten pointed out that there were certain geographical factors which could not be ignored. Of the 565 states, the vast majority were irretrievably linked geographically with India and it was to India that they were advised to turn. During negotiations, Patel and V. P. Menon acted as cajolers and Nehru played the intimidator. The latter's frequent threats that those states which did not join the Indian union would be treated as hostile had their effect on those rulers who were less responsive to Patel's gentle persuasion. The draft of the Instrument of Accession was finalised by 31 July, and within a fortnight, by 15 August, it was signed by all the states except Junagadh, Hyderabad and Kashmir. These three states were to cause further tension and hostility between India and Pakistan soon after their independence.

During July and August, Nehru carried more responsibility than perhaps any other man in India. The imminent birth of the free nation of India required detailed planning at all levels. Nehru attended to all questions, great and small. What should be the nature of the Indian Republic? What role should India play in Asian affairs? Should the Union Jack be allowed to fly along with the Indian flag on Independence Day? What should be the design and colour of the Indian flag? What song should be adopted as the national anthem?

Two crises arose during these months – one on the international and the other on the domestic front. The outbreak of armed conflict between Dutch and Indonesian national forces prompted Nehru forcefully to indicate India's stand on the matter. He promised to support Indonesia against Dutch imperialism, banned Dutch Air Force flights over Indian territory, and laid pressure on the United Nations to intervene in the crisis. If the United Nations did not intervene, he warned, then it might meet the same fate as the League of Nations, which made no attempt to prevent aggressive action in Corfu, Manchuria, Abyssinia and Spain.[79] The United Nations did intervene, and in the first week of August a ceasefire was established in Indonesia. On 9 August, Nehru called for the adoption of a 'Monroe doctrine' for Asia, and declared that India would not tolerate any European or American forces on Asian soil.[80]

The domestic crisis was caused by the revival of Hindu communalism. India's fate of partition had weakened the hold of secularism on the Hindu mind, and Hindu militants demanded that the Indian constitution should have a Hindu religious bias. It was argued that Hinduism might succeed in uniting India where Congress secularism had failed. The Hindu revival first expressed itself in the cow-protection movement, which was financed by Hindu industrialists like Dalmia. Pressure was put on the Indian Constituent Assembly to ban cow slaughter by law. Nehru stood firm against the Hindu-isation of the Indian state. He asked his colleagues to look at the political implications of the cow-protection movement:

> India in spite of its overwhelming Hindu population is a composite country from the religious and other points of view. It is a vital problem for us to solve as to whether we are to function fundamentally in regard to our general policy as such a composite country or to function as a Hindu country, rather ignoring the viewpoints of other groups.[81]

Nehru set himself against the tide of Hindu revivalism and it was mainly owing to him that India emerged as a secular state.

The foundations of India's political structure and of her foreign policy had thus been laid before independence. India was indeed fortunate in being endowed with the Congress leadership, which provided integrity, continuity and stability to her provincial and central governments. In these respects Pakistan was at a disadvantage. The Muslim League had no democratic traditions: it depended entirely on Jinnah. The Pakistan Constituent Assembly of sixty-nine members, which met for the first time only on 10 August in Karachi, lacked vision. In seven years of office it was never to succeed in framing a firm constitution for Pakistan.

On 14 August 1947 the two countries began their independent lives. Pakistan adopted a dictatorial style. On 14 August, Jinnah became Pakistan's Governor-General and the President of the Constituent Assembly as well as of the Muslim League. He also kept certain ministries under his direct control. Jinnah was without doubt an outstanding leader and might have achieved great things for Pakistan. But he was already in the grip of a mortal disease which would take its toll on 11 September 1948.

At one minute to midnight on 14 August the Indian Constituent Assembly took over the sovereign powers of India; and India's first prime minister, Nehru, acclaiming himself as the first servant of the Indian people, paid a fitting tribute to the historic occasion:

> Long years ago we made a tryst with destiny, and now the time comes when we shall redeem our pledge, not wholly or in full measure, but very substantially. At the stroke of the midnight hour, when the world sleeps, India will awake to life and freedom. A moment comes, which comes but rarely in history, when we step out from the old to the new, when an age ends, and when the soul of a nation, long suppressed, finds utterance. It is fitting that at this solemn moment we take the pledge of dedication to the service of India and her people and to the still larger cause of humanity.[82]

Immediately after the brief ceremony in the council chamber, Nehru and Prasad (President of the Constituent Assembly) called on Mountbatten at the Viceroy's House (now Government House) to extend to him a formal invitation to become the first head of state of free India. From midnight festivities began all over India, but it was Delhi which on 15 August witnessed one of the greatest political spectacles of the twentieth century. A crowd of over half a million lined the routes and jostled on every rooftop and from every vantage point to watch the processions. With cries of 'Jai Hind' and 'Pandit Nehru ki jai' were heard 'Pandit Mountbatten ki jai' and 'Lady Mountbatten ki jai'. It was a great day for everybody. It was for Mountbatten a greater day even than the one in 1945 when he took the surrender of 750,000 Japanese sailors, soldiers and airmen in Singapore. He was overwhelmed with the sense of being the instrument of conveying power and freedom to one-fifth of humanity. Such a transfer of power had never before taken place in world history. But perhaps the most unique feature of this great show was the sudden disappearance from the mind of the nationalist Indians and their leaders of any feeling of animosity towards the British. A few years later when Churchill met Nehru for the first time he was overwhelmed with emotion to realise that the man whom the British had put in jail for several years bore no malice whatsoever towards them. On 15 August, having rid himself of the burden of the past, Nehru was convinced that a healthier relationship would begin between India and Britain. The long career of a nationalist came to an end, leaving its marks and constraints on the role and style which Nehru, now fifty-eight, adopted and was to pursue for the seventeen years of his prime ministership. At the start of his new career he looked at the world with clear and friendly eyes and at the future with faith and confidence.

INDIA
1947
at the time of partition
Boundaries
International
State
Undemarcated
Headquarters town
Nagpur
Foreign territories
Diu
Miles
AFGHANISTAN
TIBET
BURMA
N.W. FRONTIER PROV.
GILGIT AGENCY
Gilgit
Undefined
JAMMU AND KASHMIR
Srinagar
Jammu
Peshawar
Lahore
Jullundur
Simla
Chandigarh
PUNJAB
PUNJAB STATES
BALUCHISTAN
Quetta
DELHI
UNITED PROVINCES
Lucknow
NEPAL
Katmandu
SIKKIM
Gangtok
BHUTAN
Punakha
ASSAM
Shillong
Imphal
RAJPUTANA
Jaipur
Ajmer
Lashkar
GWALIOR
SIND
Karachi
Mt. Abu
Tropic of Cancer
STATES OF WESTERN INDIA
Bhuj
Rajkot
Baroda
CENTRAL INDIA
Allahabad
Benares
Patna
Rewa
BIHAR
Bhopal
Indore
BENGAL
Agartala
Dacca
EASTERN STATES
Calcutta
Chandernagore
(Fr.)
CENTRAL PROVS.
Nagpur
BERAR
ORISSA
Cuttack
Diu (Port.)
Daman
(Port.)
BOMBAY
Bombay
HYDERABAD
Hyderabad
Kolhapuro
DECCAN STATES
Panjim
GOA
(Port.)
Yanam
(Fr.)
MADRAS
MYSORE
Bangaloreo
Madras
Pondicherry
(Fr.)
Karikal
(Fr.)
Mahe
(Fr.)
MADRAS STATES
Trivandrum
R W FORD

CHAPTER TEN

The Years of Statesmanship, 1947–51

We have faced, and are facing, the gravest crisis that any government can have to face, more especially a new government. The consequences of each step that we might take are bound to be far-reaching. The world is watching us also and the world opinion counts. But above all we are watching ourselves and if we fall in our own estimation, who will rescue us?

Jawaharlal Nehru, September 1947

NEHRU'S government inherited its ethics and morality from the national movement; its structure, style and appearance of infallibility from the British Raj. The Gandhian legacy of non-violence caused Nehru immediate embarrassment when, compelled by the force of circumstance and much against his will, he was obliged to resort to military action in Kashmir and Hyderabad.[1] He was fully aware of an inconsistency between what India preached and the way in which she acted, and he asked his sister Mrs Pandit, then ambassador to the United States, 'not to talk too much about our high ideals', as she had been doing during her tour of the West Coast, for 'our immediate past and present is not in consonance with these high ideals and we may lay ourselves open to a courteous retort'.[2] He did, however, consult Gandhi throughout the course of the war with Pakistan over Kashmir, and the Mahatma had conceded that a government might be compelled to take up arms in certain circumstances. Nehru soon realised that idealism and ethics could not be rigorously applied to solving practical problems of government. A certain amount of hypocrisy was inevitable, although he still firmly held that in the great things of life truth was all-important. In defence of the politician, he said:

Then a politician or a statesman, or call him what you will, has to deal not only with the truth, but with men's receptivity to that truth, because if there is not sufficient response to it from the politician's or statesman's point of view that

> truth is banished into the wilderness till minds are ripe for it. . . . So unfortunately, but inevitably, compromises have to take place from time to time. You cannot do without compromises, but a compromise is a bad compromise if it is opportunist in the sense that it is not always aiming at the truth. It may be a good compromise if it is always looking at that truth and trying to take you there.[3]

Thus Gandhism was placed on a pedestal from whence it could inspire, but not interfere with, the affairs of state.

Nehru accepted for his government the style of the British Raj, and until the end of his life he remained a great defender of its appearance of infallibility, never once admitting publicly a single error likely to have been committed by himself or his colleagues in the Union Cabinet. He saw in the splendour and impregnability of the Government the surest safeguard against India ever disintegrating into chaos. He strove continuously to give the impression that the Government made no decision under pressure exercised by any group – even his own political party. The National Government had evolved out of the British Raj; it was not formed *ab initio*. The same bureaucracy which had loyally served the imperial order now served the National Government, having undergone no change in its manner or attitude. The bureaucrats remained the servants of the Government, not the people. They went by the old rules, making it their prime concern to preserve the dignity of their new masters and to protect them from public scrutiny. A member of the public was suspect until he proved himself otherwise. A national government surrounded by an ever-thickening wall of bureaucracy thus sought strength from its own remoteness.

In the beginning Nehru looked only at the bright side of the British legacy. It was, as he saw it, useful to have inherited a working machine and a body of outstanding Indian bureaucrats without whose assistance it would have been difficult for the Government to cope with the enormous upheavals that soon followed in the wake of India's independence. But Indian complacency was shaken, though temporarily, when in 1950 the new administrative experiments launched by communist China came to light. We were wrong, Nehru was told by a close colleague, to adopt all the instruments of the old government. As a revolutionary body Congress should have followed the example of Russia and China and brushed aside the debris of the old structure. Not only had Congress failed to do this, Nehru was reminded, but the Congress Government kept Congress workers at arm's length, permitting little infiltration into the field of administration. As a result the Government could not deal summarily with situations which demanded instant and exemplary action. 'We have adopted the trappings of democracy', Sampurnanand, the Congress minister in the United Provinces Government, warned Nehru, 'without preparing the country for democracy.'[4]

Nehru, as usual, put the matter into historical perspective. While admitting that it was a mistake to allow the old structure of government to continue almost unchanged, he pointed out that the mistake was almost inevitable in the circumstances:

> It seems to me that the very ease with which we succeeded had its own drawbacks and we cannot get over them. We have called ourselves a revolutionary body and undoubtedly we were so. But we functioned only partly in the revolutionary sense. Gandhiji, with his genius, found a method of action or inaction, which was peculiarly suited to the passivity of India's mind and habits. We succeeded, but that passivity itself came in our way and now again obstructs us. In the ultimate analysis, our failings are not of this method or that, but are inherent in us as a people. We are changing of course, but much too slowly. Our social background and structure are conservative, unchanging and static, apart from lacking unity.[5]

Congress had not trained and disciplined its cadres, Nehru argued, in the same way as had the communists in China and Russia. The Congress workers were thus of low quality and would be but poor substitutes for the Indian bureaucrats. India was, in Nehru's thinking, given to evolution through persuasion and not to revolution through coercion.

He believed that the Indian genius was well suited to speculative and imaginative thinking, to planning and mediation, and to a universal, as opposed to a narrow nationalistic, view of life. In 1950 he was pleasantly surprised to observe the impact India had already made on the international plane. On the domestic side, even while the country seemed to be disintegrating in the heat and passion of communal frenzy, it had been nonetheless firmly set on the secular path. By 1950 the country had given itself a constitution and was territorially integrated. Congress leadership had given the local and central governments a stability unmatched by those of any other newly independent country in Asia. Though suffering from food shortages, and with its resources over-stretched to provide food and shelter for nearly five million refugees displaced from their ancestral homes in Pakistan, India had by the beginning of 1950 committed itself to planned development, and taken to the middle path that lay between the rival systems of capitalism and communism. In all these spheres – external and internal, political, social and economic – Nehru played the role of statesman. He made rapid decisions, as he had never done before, with courage and confidence. He derived his strength mainly from his global outlook, and excelled in putting even a minor domestic issue into an international context. He made his impact on almost all aspects of the country's life. His success was mainly due to the fact that his perception of international affairs and his diagnosis of national problems, and of the inner urges to which Indians were the most responsive, turned out to be accurate and real.

In turning to the various spheres of Nehru's activities, the domestic front must come first, for it was here that the country was faced with unprecedented problems in the handling of which Nehru showed marks of great statesmanship. The greatest threat to India's dignity and to her survival as a composite state was posed by the Hindu communal fury. India was born in the midst of a communal civil war which, in the Hindu mind, was inflicted on the sub-continent by the treacherous Muslim League gang whose leader seemed to have abandoned his long-cherished two-nation theory soon after he had succeeded in obtaining Pakistan. The first cry of the infant Indian nation was for revenge andfor the foundation in India of a Hindu Raj. Congress's secularism was put under severe attack: it had failed to prevent the partition of India; it must, therefore, be abandoned and Hindus, having no theocratic state of their own apart from the small country of Nepal, must be allowed to assert their identity in India. Over thirty-five million Muslims who were left behind in India must be asked to leave for Pakistan. This initial Hindu feeling of outrage continued with mounting intensity through successive outbreaks of hostility and tension between Pakistan and India. The adoption by Pakistan of the name and style of an Islamic state, in which the highest office was to be held only by a Muslim; Jinnah's interference in the affairs of Hyderabad; the invasion of Kashmir by Pakistani forces; the outbreak in 1949–50 of fresh violence against Hindus in East Pakistan and the arrival of a new wave of Hindu refugees in West Bengal – all these agitated the Hindus to a point where they began to call for open war against Pakistan.

This Hindu revivalism of the post-independence period was much more than the spontaneous, short-lived, communal rage of the pre-independence period. It was more formidable, and sucked into its whirlwind the Hindu élite who had never before subscribed to communal thinking. In 1948 the movement had the sympathy, if not the open support, of the entire right wing of the Congress leadership and of almost half of Nehru's sixteen-member Cabinet; the other half included two Muslims and a Christian. Nehru alone fought against what he called the deadliest enemy of the nation. He derived his strength from the assurance of his own conscience, and based his hopes on the tolerance and flexibility of the Hindu people.[6] He was convinced that the Indian genius would reassert itself. In his role of crusader he fought Hindu communalism inside his government, in Parliament, and outside – in the streets, market-places, towns and cities – through legislation and speeches. His exhortations were numerous and varied – sometimes threatening, at times persuasive, and always appealing to the essential nobility of the Hindu heart.

Nehru overcame several successive obstacles. His own colleagues in the Government and in the Congress High Command presented to him a dismal view of the situation. They argued that the root cause of the communal crisis lay in Pakistan and until Pakistan stopped denuding its cities and towns of all Hindus and Sikhs it would be impossible to establish normal conditions in Delhi and other parts of northern India.[7] Admitting that the Pakistani leadership was treacherous and irresponsible, Nehru pleaded that its misdeeds must not be allowed to destroy the ideals which they in India had cherished for so long.[8] No matter where the root cause lay, he would not tolerate Hindu gangs hunting Muslims as in Delhi and searching the houses of foreign ambassadors for their prey. Some of his colleagues submitted to his way of thinking, but his Deputy Prime Minister remained obdurate. Relations between the two became strained when Nehru reprimanded Patel for a speech in which the latter, being generally hostile to the Indian Muslims for the part they had played in the creation of Pakistan, censored the community and told them that until they proclaimed their loyalty to India they would not be trusted and treated on a par with Hindu Indians. Nehru firmly declared that Muslims were on no account to be treated as second-class citizens and that he was determined to protect them in their enjoyment of equal rights. In Parliament he launched tirades against the communally biased members, and in supporting a private member's bill which banned those political parties who admitted or excluded from their membership persons on grounds of religion, race and caste he exhorted:

> In any event now there is no alternative; and we must have it clearly in our minds and in the mind of the country that the alliance of religion and politics in the shape of communalism is a most dangerous alliance, and it yields the most abnormal kind of illegitimate blood.[9]

Two years later, in August 1950, when Hindu fury was once again revived over the question of Hindu refugees from East Pakistan, and S. P. Mookerjee (who had resigned in April from Nehru's Cabinet on this issue) was talking in terms of war with Pakistan and a compulsory exchange of populations, Nehru again raised the battle standard of secularism in Parliament and, in language oddly reminiscent of a famous Churchillian passage, declared:

> They put us in a position in which we have to say to people who are our fellow-citizens, ' we must push you out, because you belong to a faith different from ours'. This is a proposition

> which, if it is followed, will mean the ruin of India and the annihilation of all that we stand for and have stood for. I repeat that we will resist such a proposition with all our strength, we will fight it in houses, in fields and in market places. It will be fought in the council chambers and the streets, for we shall not let India be slaughtered at the altar of bigotry.[10]

With equal vehemence Nehru carried his campaign into the towns and cities of communally affected areas; on 30 September 1947 he told an agitated audience in New Delhi that as long as he was at the helm he would not let India become a Hindu state.[11] The very idea of a theocratic state, he contended, was medieval and stupid. How, Nehru argued, could India fight racialism in other parts of the world – in South Africa, for example, where Indians were banned from entering certain areas; the Indian Government had complained to the United Nations about such segregation that same year – if Indians were bent on ejecting all Muslims from their own country?[12] On 29 January 1948 in Amritsar, the day before Gandhi's assassination, Nehru faced an agitated crowd of Punjabis who earlier in the month had demonstrated hostility to India's secular policy by trampling upon India's national flag. Trembling with anger, he denounced them as traitors and challenged the communalists, be they members of the R.S.S. (Rashtriya Swayamsevak Sangh) or of the Hindu Mahasabha, to come into the open and test their strength in a straight fight with Congress government.[13] The crowd responded to his challenge with silent repentance. From August 1947 until the first general election of 1951–2, Nehru waged incessant war against communalism. On the eve of the election he declared that the communalists were his personal enemies and that he would overpower them with all his strength.[14]

In those four and a half years he hunted communalists in all corners, not even sparing the right wing of his own Congress Party. In fact the last of his series of battles against communalism was fought on the Congress platform when, in August 1950, the seventy-year-old Hindu communalist P. D. Tandon, a United Provinces Congressman of long standing, was elected President of Congress. Tandon believed in the restoration of the Hindu Raj and the glorification of all Hindu customs, and was an ardent supporter of a belligerent policy towards Pakistan. He was also opposed to industrialisation. Above all, he believed that the Cabinet should function under the supervisory control of the Congress High Command. Tandon was a super-faddist, living on raw vegetables, uncooked rice, goat's milk and fruits, never using soap, shoes or razor. He was a threat to all Nehru stood for. He was supported by Patel, and by the Congressmen from United Provinces (including the Chief Minister, G. B. Pant) – the province which controlled most votes in the presidential election. Nehru was distressed at Tandon's nomination. He was fond of Tandon, but he was certain that 'his election would be definitely harmful' to the country.[15] The Congress presidency still carried a high status, and the conflict for supremacy between the President and the Prime Minister, between the Congress High Command and the Cabinet, which had been started by Kripalani in 1946, was not yet resolved. Kripalani was forced to resign in 1947, and his successor Rajendra Prasad, though outwardly complacent, resented the dominance of the Government over the Party and asked Patel for an early resolution of this continuing conflict.[16] Nehru feared that Tandon's election to the presidency would not only put renewed life into communalism but would also revive the conflict between the President and the Prime Minister. Yet Nehru did not openly oppose Tandon's election, nor did he wholly support the next main contender for the Congress presidency, Kripalani. He privately tried to influence friends and colleagues, as a result of which Kripalani secured more votes than expected – 1092 against Tandon's 1306.

Tandon's election to the presidency by no means symbolised, as has been made out by some observers, a struggle for supremacy between Patel and Nehru. Patel was dying and had no ambitions to become Prime Minister. Like all Congressmen he knew that Nehru was indispensable. But he maintained his role of being a check on Nehru, and a dent made in the monolithic power-image which Nehru carried gave the Sardar some gratification. It also gave him some consolation, for Nehru had injured his pride on a number of occasions since independence. Indeed on one occasion – in December 1947 when he was reprimanded by Nehru for his undue interference in Kashmir affairs – Patel had tendered his resignation. It was not, of course, accepted.[17] Tandon's election caused some jubilation in Patel's camp, however, and Nehru, who was under considerable strain, even suspected that there was a sinister scheme to oust him from power. In such moments of uncertainty he confided in his sister, and warned her of 'possible political developments here, which might well affect my own future work intimately'.[18]

Though Nehru's position was not really threatened, in September 1950 the Indian political situation appeared, on the surface, to have come under the dominance of the right wing. Patel–Tandon domination of Congress posed threats to the leftists, who suspected that Congress would now veer towards the Anglo-American bloc and would lay pressure on Nehru's government to abandon the policy of friendship towards Russia and China. Some leftists – Kripalani, A. P. Jain, R. A. Kidwai (the last two being at that time ministers in Nehru's Cabinet) – even began to think of deserting the sinking ship. It was at this time that the Nepalese Rana régime, generally understood to be an ally of Britain and America, was fighting for its survival against the United Nepali Congress. In 1949 the Tibetan Government, fearing an invasion from communist China, had sent missions to Nepal and India to request help, and had also begun extensive military preparations. Red China's foreign policy was at this time based on suspicion, speculation and self-confidence. It was inconceivable to Chou En-lai that the British Empire had really withdrawn from India and had no influence whatsoever on Indian policy. In December 1949 the New China News Agency described the Indian Government as a puppet régime set up and controlled by the imperialists for use against the national liberation movement of the Asian people.[19] The communist leaders suspected that forces hostile to China were operating in the Tibetan sector. In July 1950, Chou En-lai, while assuring the Indian ambassador in Peking that the liberation of Tibet was China's sacred duty, enquired of K. M. Panikkar whether it was true that the Nepal Government had offered to send troops to help Tibetans. 'That was the state of Chinese knowledge about the conditions on the Himalayan border,' noted the Indian ambassador in his memoirs.[20] On 7 October 1950, China invaded eastern Tibet. It is unlikely that Tandon's election to the Congress presidency had any relation to the timing of the Chinese invasion, but it certainly clouded Nehru's policies and style for a while.

The alarm raised over Tandon's election soon subsided, however. Those who had supported Tandon now began to do their utmost to please Nehru, and almost all the resolutions sponsored by him were passed at party meetings. But Nehru still regarded Tandon as an unnecessary liability since he jealously guarded the party machinery. He thus resolved to establish his control over the Congress Working Committee, and over the Party's Central Election Committee which, having the power to select candidates for the coming election, had come to acquire great importance. The tussle between the President and the Prime Minister passed through many phases before being finally resolved in September 1951 when Nehru resigned from Tandon's Working Committee. His example was followed by the other committee members. Tandon was forced to tender his resignation, and Nehru took over the presidency. The offices of President and Prime Minister were combined, Nehru remaining Congress President until 1954 when he selected his own successor – U. N. Dhebar.

By the autumn of 1951, Nehru's triumph over Hindu communalism was complete. His victory was achieved in three ways – through the framing of a secular constitution for India, the Nehru–Liaquat Pact of 1950 which neutralised the possibility of an open war with Pakistan, and through the results of India's first general election of 1951–2.

The Indian Constitution – which had been in the making since December 1946, was finally completed on 26 November 1949, and at Nehru's suggestion inaugurated on 26 January 1950 – is perhaps the longest constitutional document in the world. It proclaimed India to be a secular, democratic republic, an achievement which must be largely credited to Nehru. That a country like India – which is so deeply steeped in religious prejudice and had recently passed through the pangs of a partition which had been carried through solely on religious grounds – should produce the most secular constitution in the world is not as paradoxical as it seems, given the essential Hindu character which Nehru upheld and understood so well. Without a Hindu majority (as Dr K. N. Katju, a distinguished jurist and a cabinet minister, remarked in 1953), India could not have adopted a secular constitution. Nehru was confident that Hindu India, barring the orthodox militants, would find its real image in a secular constitution. The secularity of the Constitution lay first in its total separation of state from religion: there was to be no official state religion, no provision for religious instruction in state schools and no taxes to support any religion. Nehru was even opposed to inserting in the Constitution any religious symbol or the name of a Hindu god, which the orthodox Hindus demanded as consolation. Secondly, the Constitution laid down that the State should not discriminate against any citizen on the grounds of religion, race, caste, sex or place of birth. Any citizen in the Indian union could aspire to the highest office of the State. Finally, the Indian Constitution guaranteed religious liberty to individuals as well as to associations. Nehru considered the Constitution 'a monument of labour and industry', though in private he mentioned that it was not 'a very satisfactory document' and he thought that the 'lawyers might well profit by it later'.[21]

The Nehru–Liaquat Pact of 1950 was the culmination of Nehru's attempts to ensure against total war with Pakistan. Hindu communalism was in part nourished by the fear of such a war. In January 1950, Nehru renewed his proposal to the Pakistani Prime Minister, Liaquat Ali Khan, for a 'no-war declaration' by the two countries, hoping that such a declaration might further weaken Hindu communalism. But for various reasons, mostly connected with the continuing tension between the two countries over the question of Kashmir, Liaquat Ali Khan declined to enter into a 'no-war' agreement. Early in 1950 the Hindu minority in East Pakistan was subjected to discrimination and persecution and their exodus to India began. S. P. Mookerjee then raised the tone of Hindu militancy by proposing to Nehru that either the partition of Bengal be annulled or Pakistan be asked to cede some territory where the Hindu minorities of East Pakistan could be settled. It was against this background that Nehru met Liaquat Ali Khan on 2 April 1950 in New Delhi and an agreement was reached between the two prime ministers. The Pact contained a pledge to maintain equal rights for minorities in each country. The refugees were given the right to carry with them all movable property, to dispose of all other property and to carry the proceeds along with them. If they chose they could return to their place of origin without any hindrance. Nehru thought the agreement was 'really good and might mean a real turn for the better', but he suspected that the Bengalis would not like it.[22]

The day the agreement was announced S. P. Mookerjee and K. C. Neogy resigned from Nehru's Cabinet in protest. Mookerjee's resignation, however, caused no upsets in Bengal. With the support of the R.S.S., he founded his own party in May 1951. This soon became a national party – the Bharatiya Jan Sangh.

The Indian general election (spread over the period from October 1951 to May 1952, though the bulk of the polling for the House of the People and state legislative assemblies took place during December and January) was a colossal experiment for the world's biggest democracy with the largest electorate – 173,213,635 adult voters.[23] Political parties grew like mushrooms in the election year, and a total of 59 parties threw up over 17,000 candidates to contest more than 3800 seats in Parliament and the state legislatures. In addition, many thousands contested the election as Independents. Fourteen parties were recognised as national, though only four (Congress, the Praja-Socialist Party, the Communist Party of India and the Jan Sangh) retained that status after the election.

The large number of parties and Independents contesting the election represented a great variety of interests, some of which were anti-democratic and anti-national. This gave Nehru cause for worry: would democracy survive the election? The ban imposed on communal parties (the R.S.S. and Hindu Mahasabha) following the assassination of Gandhi had been lifted by mid-1949, and a few communal parties (the Jan Sangh, the Hindu Mahasabha, Rama Rajya Parishad) contested the election. Congress itself, at the state level, was rife with caste and factional politics, the worst case being that of

Bihar where caste played a dominant part in the selection of Congress candidates for the ensuing election.

The second main threat to democracy was posed by the communists. Toeing the Russian line, and in consequence being doctrinal and unrealistic in their condemnation of the Nehru Government, the Communist Party of India had adopted, since February 1948, a policy of waging a ceaseless campaign, open and underground, in preparation for an armed rising and a violent seizure of power. The communist challenge was taken up by Sardar Patel at the centre and by the state governments of Bengal, Bombay, Hyderabad, Travancore-Cochin, Madras and United Provinces. Government machinery was set in motion to suppress the danger. Communist terrorism proved ineffective, however, and except for Andhra, Telengana, Tripura and Manipur, where there were some hundreds of murders, its impact on the country was minimal. The communists even failed to bring the railwaymen out on strike – the single general strike they had so confidently planned for 9 March 1949. Early in 1950, Stalin's attitude towards Nehru's India became a little more conciliatory (a change brought about mainly by Nehru's policy of non-alignment); the Communist Party of India ceased openly to preach violence and began grooming itself to enter institutional politics and contest the coming election.

In fighting the communists as well as the communalists – both of whom he considered fascist and totalitarian – Nehru was reluctant to use the government machinery, preferring to rely on his own powers of oratory. He left it to Patel and the chief ministers, in the union and state governments respectively, to use coercive methods if they so wished. At times he even pleaded with his chief ministers to be gentle in their dealings with the young communists, for some were among the brightest young men and women in the country and might become embittered if subjected to harsh treatment.[24] Persuasion, not coercion, was his style and he believed that even the communists could be persuaded to realise the falsity of their position and to amend their objectives and methods. In ignoring Indian conditions, he maintained, the Indian communists had forgotten the fundamental principle of Marxism – that it must keep in step with the conditions of the country wherein it functioned. Lenin, even Stalin, had repeatedly said that one could not repeat in one country what had happened elsewhere.[25] Russian-style communism would hamper the progress of India by restricting the creative faculties of the common man, for in the Russian system, Nehru stressed, nobody could deviate towards the right or left in opposition to the policy framed by the ruling party.[26] When asked by a press correspondent which he regarded as a lesser evil – communism or communalism – Nehru retorted: 'An extraordinary question to ask, which do you prefer, death by drowning or falling from a precipice?'[27]

He could fight the communists and the communalists; but how, Nehru wondered, could he suddenly change the attitude of the common people and the way in which some reacted to democratic processes? In April 1951 he was shocked by an incident that took place in a United Provinces district during the official panchayat (local body) election.[28] Two groups contested five seats – one a Thakur caste group and the other a non-Thakur group. After a fiercely contested election, the non-Thakur group won and their five members were elected to the panchayat. The next day these five members were murdered. This might have been an extreme, even a unique case, but nonetheless it reflected darkly on the security situation as much as on the caste factions and feuds that prevailed in the Indian villages. That month Nehru informally created an inner circle – consisting of his close friends and colleagues and including R. A. Kidwai, G. B. Pant, Sampurnanand and Morarji Desai – to discuss ways and means of coming to grips with the deteriorating situation in the country.[29]

Such informal consultations might have given Nehru some insight into the situation prevailing in the different states and at various levels, but the real battle against the enemies of democracy had to be fought in public by him alone, for none of his colleagues had his popularity, his style and his zeal for the cause. Nehru was, in a way, the sole Congress campaigner during the election. He could not change the ways of his people, but nonetheless they were drawn to his side, almost with a religious fervour, for was he not, like the legendary King Rama, involved in a deadly battle against the demons? By putting the ballot in the 'Nehru box' many derived the same feeling of virtue and piety a pious Hindu acquired by bathing in the holy Ganges. Congress won the election. It secured an overwhelming majority of seats in Parliament (364 out of 499) and a working majority in 22 of the then existing 26 states of the Indian union, and in each of the remaining four it became the largest single party. In an election of such magnitude, infested with a multitude of caste, communal and factional issues, it was no mean achievement for Congress alone to secure 45 per cent of the total votes at the centre and 42 per cent of the total in the states.

Of even greater satisfaction to Nehru was the fact that the communalists and communists fared poorly at the polls. The Jan Sangh, the most formidable of the communal parties and the only one with a national stature, won only 3 seats in Parliament, although it had contested 93 seats. Having polled 3.06 per cent of the Parliament (Lok Sabha) vote, it succeeded by only a very narrow margin of ·06 in retaining the status of an all-India party. Of the total of 3283 state assembly seats, Jan Sangh won only 35. Compared to Jan Sangh, the Communist Party of India showed better results, winning 16 seats in Parliament and 106 in the state assemblies. The bulk of communist support came from the south; in the northern province of United Provinces the Communist Party put forward 42 candidates but failed to win a single seat.

Nehru's success in fighting communalism and in making India a secular state was in some measure aided by two events – the assassination of Gandhi and the accession of Kashmir to India. Having returned to Delhi from Bengal in September 1947, Gandhi spent the last five months of his life in attempting to humanise the metropolis which, at that time, was rife with hate and violence. Facing the vicious mood of Delhi and talking of forgiveness, tolerance, Hindu–Muslim unity and goodwill towards Pakistan was an act of courage in which only Gandhi and Nehru could excel. The seventy-eight-year-old Mahatma believed that, if Delhi were lost to sanity, India would soon collapse, taking with it the last hope of world peace. Gandhi prayed and preached and finally resorted to spiritual coercion by going on a fast from 13 January 1948 for an indeterminate period. The effect of his fast was first felt by the Government itself. Because of Pakistan's aggression in

Kashmir, and at the insistence of Sardar Patel, the Government of India had been withholding cash payments due to the Pakistan Government amounting to thirty-five crores of rupees. Gandhi insisted that the Government of India must discharge its obligation no matter how hostile its relations with Pakistan. On 15 January the Government decided to pay to Pakistan the cash balance. As a result the leaders of all communities – Hindus, Muslims and Sikhs – assembled in the presence of the fasting Mahatma and declared in favour of communal harmony.

Though Gandhi broke his fast on 18 January, some hearts were still fiercely turned against him. The Mahatma, fighting the demons, appeared in the eyes of some to be a demon himself, intent on destroying the Hindu race and its manhood by appeasing Pakistan and protecting the Muslims in India. The first attempt on Gandhi's life was made on 20 January by a Hindu refugee from West Pakistan – Madan Lal. A bomb exploded at his prayer meeting, but nobody was hurt. Madan Lal was arrested. Fanatical Hindus, now infesting Delhi, hailed Madan Lal as a hero and demanded his release. The cry was also raised to hang Nehru, Patel and Azad.[30] Gandhi refused all offers of protection: if he was to die by the bullet of a madman, he wished to die without anger and with God in his heart and on his lips.[31] It happened the way he had wished. On 30 January, at his evening prayer meeting, a madman – N. V. Godse, a Chitpawan Brahmin from Maharashtra – shot him at point-blank range, and he died instantly with God's name on his lips.

'The light has gone,' Nehru announced to the nation in a voice choked with emotion.[32] Gandhi was no more, but Gandhism, he declared, would live for ever. Nehru shared the sense of shame which seized the Government and the country, the shame that they had failed to protect their greatest treasure.[33] The lives of Indian Muslims hung in the balance as Nehru made his broadcast to the nation, for he did not name the 'madman'. Was he a Muslim? Patel revealed the truth in a broadcast which followed soon after that of Nehru. What kind of Hindu? the people asked. The assassin and members of his gang had been associated with the R.S.S. and Hindu Mahasabha, though it was never proved that these communal parties had any hand in organising the assassination. Nonetheless, when people came to know of Godse's past associations with these parties, they took instant action. The party offices were destroyed and their members chased through the streets. Many thousand leading members of both parties were arrested, and the parties disappeared from the political map of India for nearly a year. Gandhi's assassin succeeded in destroying the very cause of Hindu fanaticism which he had intended to serve.

While Gandhi's assassination served as a pointer to the disastrous consequences to which the communal fury led, Kashmir's accession to India came to signify a definite negation of Jinnah's two-nation theory, and highlighted India's gain in remaining a secular nation. Of the three Indian states – Junagadh, Hyderabad and Kashmir – which had not acceded to either of the dominions by 15 August 1947, Kashmir soon became an international problem. During the first few months of independence, India was faced with a problem jointly presented by these three states. The populations of Junagadh and Hyderabad were predominantly Hindu and of Kashmir Muslim. In September 1947 the Muslim ruler of Junagadh acceded to Pakistan. The Muslim Nizam of Hyderabad nourished the hope of independent sovereign status for his state. The Hindu Maharaja of Kashmir evaded the issue until October 1947 when the state was attacked by forces from Pakistan; on 26 October the Maharaja acceded to India. If India were to abide by their rulers' wishes it would lose Hyderabad and Junagadh and gain only Kashmir. If it were to abide by the people's wishes it would gain not only the two Hindu states but possibly Kashmir as well, for S. M. Abdullah, the leader of the Muslim populace, had always stood against the creation of Pakistan and now seemed firmly committed to India, Congress and Nehru. India thus followed the second course, and Nehru insisted that the people's verdict must prevail over the rulers' decision.

The results were most favourable for India. In the face of a popular uprising the ruler of Junagadh lost his nerve and fled to Pakistan. On 9 November 1947 the Indian authorities peacefully took over the administration of the state. In February 1948 a plebiscite was held in Junagadh and 190,779 voted for India and only 91 for Pakistan. The Nizam of Hyderabad, however, did not give in so easily. Deriving his inspiration from the size (32,000 square miles), population (16 million), revenue (26 crores) and history of his state – which together made it the premier state in the country – and having the support and sympathy of Jinnah and Churchill, the Nizam continued to prepare the state for independence. While secretly trying to secure arms from foreign countries, he adopted a façade of negotiating with the Indian Government for favourable terms of accession. Nehru made it clear that, situated as it was in the very heart of India, Hyderabad had no choice but to accede to India.[34] The negotiations were prolonged till June 1948 when they finally broke down. The stalemate lasted for nearly two months. But, when in late August the Nizam sent a delegation to the United Nations, Nehru's patience ran out. On 13 September the Indian Army marched into the state and on 17 September the Hyderabad Army surrendered. Nehru accorded a most liberal treatment to the Nizam and his advisers.

Left to himself, Sardar Patel would have ordered military action in Hyderabad long before September. But he was restrained by Nehru. During the nationalist phase of his life Nehru had come to regard the use of force as something inhuman, and his antipathy to any form of physical coercion affected his attitude and behaviour for the rest of his life. His conscience dictated that force must be used only as a last resort and in furtherance of an absolutely justified cause. He was also ever sensitive to world opinion, and was concerned as to how other nations would react to aggressive policies from a country which preached peace and universal brotherhood.

In the case of Hyderabad, India's deep military involvement in Kashmir from October 1947 to December 1948 formed an additional block to aggressive action elsewhere. By mid-1948, however, the Indian position in Kashmir had become stabilised, and growing criticism of Nehru's 'drift and delay' attitude to Hyderabad forced his hand.

The more reluctant Nehru was to meet force by force, the more aggressive he tended to sound. His ferocious barks often misled his enemies into believing that he was about to attack. When he threatened to invade Pakistan if the latter did not stop aggressive action in Kashmir,[35] nothing was further from his mind, but the emphatic manner in which he delivered the threat created war phobia among the Pakistani leaders.

Nehru's reluctance to use force was, however, minimal in the case of Kashmir. This was partly because there was not much time for reflection. On the evening of 24 October 1947, Nehru first received the information that a large-scale invasion of Kashmir by Pakistani tribesmen had begun. He had precisely one day in which to decide whether or not India should intervene to save Kashmir from being forcibly absorbed into Pakistan. He was convinced that the so-called 'tribesmen's incursion' into Kashmir was in fact a well-planned Pakistani Government scheme to capture the state.[36] He also believed that the people of Kashmir were not decisively in favour of opting for Pakistan; given the chance they might, under the leadership of S. M. Abdullah, either join India or opt for some kind of independence within the Indian sphere of influence. On 28 October, the day after Indian troops had been flown into Kashmir, Nehru confided to his sister: 'I do not mind if Kashmir becomes more or less independent, but it would have been a cruel blow if it had become just an exploited part of Pakistan.'[37] His attitude towards India's intervention in Kashmir was also influenced by his strong personal love for the valley of Kashmir and its people. Kashmir was to him like a crown on the head of India and the heart of Asia.[38]

The question which haunted Nehru for the two days of 25 and 26 October, when the Indian Government had to make up its mind, was in what capacity India should intervene in Kashmir. Valuing the wishes of the people, he feared that Indian intervention, following a formal accession of the state as offered by the Maharaja, might prejudice the people against India. It might also lead to further complications, for had not India disregarded the wishes of the rulers in the cases of Junagadh and Hyderabad? But Mountbatten, then Governor-General of India, advised that intervention should be legalised by a formal and temporary accession. Nehru was thus obliged to accept the Maharaja's accession to India on the condition that the will of the people of Kashmir would be ascertained by a plebiscite soon after the raiders had been driven out and law and order restored.

Fighting began with the airlift of Indian troops from Delhi to Srinagar on 27 October. On 1 January 1948, India referred the Kashmir issue to the Security Council of the United Nations, hoping that the Council would brand Pakistan as an aggressor and bring about a cessation of hostilities, to be soon followed by a plebiscite in Kashmir. The United Nations set up a five-member commission on Kashmir, which succeeded in effecting a ceasefire on 1 January 1949. The ceasefire left 32,000 square miles of Kashmir territory (comprising the western and northern regions) under Pakistani occupation, and the remaining 54,000 square miles (including the Srinagar Valley and Jammu) under Indian occupation. During 1949 the United Nations commission made several unsuccessful attempts to effect demilitarisation and establish conditions for holding a plebiscite in Kashmir under United Nations supervision. In 1950 the United Nations made a fresh attempt to resolve the deadlock by appointing an Australian judge, Sir Owen Dixon, as its representative in Kashmir, but Dixon's proposal for partition of the state based on partial plebiscite was rejected outright by Pakistan. In 1951 the United Nations appointed its next representative, the American Dr Frank Graham, who endeavoured in vain until February 1953 to strike an agreement between India and Pakistan on the procedure for demilitarisation and plebiscite. In October 1951 the Indian part of Kashmir formed its own constituent assembly, elected on adult franchise, and the assembly formally endorsed the accession of Kashmir to India in foreign affairs, defence and communication.

In his handling of the Kashmir issue over this period Nehru relied heavily on the United Nations and on Sheikh Abdullah neither of whom proved as supportive as he had hoped. In the last week of December 1947, when the decision to refer the matter to the Security Council was made, India's military position in Kashmir did not look bright, and Nehru feared that Pakistan's intransigence might lead either to total war or to the prolongation for an indefinite period of a local war. Dominated as it was in those years by the Anglo-American bloc, the United Nations adopted a strictly mediatory role, conceding to Pakistan the status of an equal party. The Anglo-American bloc felt reluctant to accept India's plea that it had the people's support in Kashmir. In due course, and on account of Nehru's non-alignment policy, his support for communist China and his opposition to the American role in the Korean War, the attitude of the United States towards India hardened. Besides, in comparison with India, Pakistan seemed the weaker party in the conflict. Thus, Anglo-American support for Pakistan increased. Nehru was disappointed to learn that the United Nations did not fully appreciate the implications of India's involvement in Kashmir. It did give him some kind of consolation to notice that the Anglo-American bloc was equally critical of India's involvement in Junagadh and Hyderabad. India's predicament was neatly summed up by Rajaji in a private letter to Nehru:

> We are in a sad pass. If the substance is in our favour, we are up against legalities, paramountcy, lapse and all that. If the law is in our favour, then morality is brought up against us. If both are right, then they say our non-violence is against us. Every way or some way we are wrong! We have put Bapu [Gandhi] aside – so the western democracies have taken him up. There is some compensation.[39]

Nehru's confidence in Abdullah proved more rewarding, at least at first. In spite of Patel's doubts about Abdullah's integrity, Nehru went all the way in installing the Sheikh in power. The Maharaja, Hari Singh, would have been content to join India with Jammu alone (the Hindu province of Kashmir), leaving the rest of Kashmir to its fate. But it was the Muslim valley of Kashmir, as Nehru impressed upon the Maharaja, and later upon Patel, which was most worth fighting for.[40] The only way of keeping Kashmir in the Indian union was by forming a popular government in the state. Abdullah must be the head of this government, for he was the only person who could muster mass support for Kashmir's accession to India. The Maharaja thus became constitutional head of state with Abdullah as his prime minister.

From January 1948 to the summer of 1949, Abdullah continuously supported Kashmir's accession to India. He condemned the two-nation theory and Pakistan, and declared that Kashmir would live and die with India.[41] During the same period he carried on his personal vendetta against the Maharaja, his old enemy, threatening to prosecute him for conspiracy and corruption unless he abdicated. But Abdullah was ambitious and began to resent India's dominance over the Kashmir Government. In April 1949, in an interview with the correspondent from the *Scotsman*, he betrayed his preference for an independent Kashmir,[42] and in May, perhaps for the first time, Nehru expressed a degree of disillusionment with Abdullah:

> The other headache about Kashmir is due to the activities of the Maharaja and Sheikh Abdullah in contrary directions. On the whole Sheikh Abdullah has been the more irresponsible of the two and has made some very foolish statements.[43]

The continuing feud between the Maharaja and Abdullah was resolved by Patel, who persuaded the former to abdicate in favour of his son – Karan Singh. In June, Karan Singh became the Regent of Kashmir. Abdullah continued to rule the state with almost dictatorial power until October 1951, when the Constituent Assembly of Kashmir came into existence. He resisted, with some success, the application to Kashmir of those provisions of the Indian Constitution which would have made the Government of Kashmir more democratic and liberal. Kashmir came to occupy a special place within the Indian union.

By July 1950, Nehru's policy towards Kashmir had changed. Patel had presented Nehru with some cogent reasons for abandoning the idea of plebiscite. He pointed out that it would create uneasiness among the non-Muslims in Jammu and Kashmir, who might start to emigrate to India. This would in turn revive communal tension in the sub-continent. But the most important consideration which Patel asked Nehru to take into account was the growing unpopularity of Sheikh Abdullah and his National Conference.[44] There was opposition to Sheikh Abdullah in his own party and he was losing his hold on the people. Patel also had grave doubts about Abdullah's loyalty to India, which Nehru now shared. In July 1950, Nehru confided to his sister:

> Meanwhile Sheikh Abdullah has been behaving very badly in Kashmir in regard to domestic affairs and he appears to be bent on seeking a conflict with us. He is gone to wrong hands there and is being misled. Poor Bakshi Ghulam Mohammad is very unhappy about it all, but does not know what to do.[45]

Bakshi Ghulam Mohammad was Abdullah's only rival, and he was loyal to India, but he could not be relied upon to win the plebiscite for India. The Indian Government thus encouraged Ghulam Mohammad to restrain the wild activities of Abdullah, who soon became aware of growing constraints on his power. The idea of an independent Kashmir came to have a greater appeal to him now than ever before, for not only would it mean more power for him but also a larger Kashmir. The division of Kashmir was beginning to appear permanent. Nehru himself was in favour of a formal division of Kashmir along the ceasefire line.[46] Thus in the context of the Indo-Pak conflict over Kashmir there existed no prospect for a united Kashmir. But Nehru, who initially might have accepted an independent status for Kashmir, was now opposed to it.

Accession of Kashmir to India had come to signify many things to Nehru. It disproved the reactionary two-nation theory and enabled Nehru to combat the revival of Hindu communalism. Kashmir, for Nehru, was the graveyard of the poisonous plant of separatism and hatred which Jinnah had sown years earlier. He believed that vital principles were involved in the Kashmir issue, and that India's involvement was 'a struggle of progress against reaction, of a secular nationalism against communalism and bigotry'.[47] The loss of Kashmir, Nehru feared, would create an upheaval in India and uproot millions of people.[48] Conscious as Nehru was that India's stake in Kashmir was high, convinced that India's cause was right and that the people of Kashmir would be happier in the Indian union, and apprehensive that if the bogy of Islamic brotherhood were let loose upon the people of the valley they might break their tie with secular India, Nehru pinned his hopes on Abdullah, who alone had provided the moral justification for India's involvement in Kashmir. Though Nehru had succeeded in establishing direct contact with the people and politicians of Kashmir and though pro-Indian feeling was strong, he was most reluctant to dispense with Abdullah, his long-time comrade. There was in his relationship with Abdullah much more than the expediency of a political partnership. From mid-1950 their relationship became severely strained and acquired something of the tragic nature of the relations between Henry II and Thomas à Becket. When the final act took place in August 1953 and Nehru had to sanction Abdullah's deposition, his eyes filled with tears.[49]

The accession of Kashmir to India strengthened the secular style which had begun to characterise the Hindu attitude since Gandhi's assassination. The militant Hindu communalists were subdued though not fully suppressed. In subsequent years they were to raise their heads again over the Kashmir issue and to demand fuller integration of the state into the Indian union. At the end of 1951, however, Nehru could sigh with relief at having broken the back of communalism and its twin sister, separatism, and having put the infant nation on a secular path.

In his economic policy Nehru, characteristically opposed both to expropriation and exploitation, focused on the middle path that lay between the capitalist and communist systems, and evolved a mixed economy in keeping with his thinking of the pre-independence years. The basic principles and prejudices underlying India's new economic structure were those of Nehru, and he believed they were suited not only to Indian conditions but also to the country's genius. When attacked by politicians and party spokesmen for going too far or not going far enough he appealed, rather mystically, to the silent masses who, in his opinion, represented the genius of the country.

In evolving or accepting ideas, Nehru would first react intuitively and then bring logic and morality to support his stand. He reacted intuitively in rejecting the American and Soviet models: the former defied his cultural and ethical values, the latter his faith in democracy and the individual. He was more firmly set against the Soviet model, for it was based on destruction and coercion which he could not stomach. The ruthless exploitation and limitless profiteering of the American model seemed to him coarse. He supported his rejection of these models with a variety of arguments, some of which were his own and some borrowed from experts like Dr Solomon Trone – an American engineer who had left China when the communists came to power and, on the recommendation of K. M. Panikkar, worked as Nehru's personal adviser until 1950. Nehru did not believe in the existence of a pure capitalistic or pure socialistic system. Modern capitalism as it existed in America was vastly different from that of forty years ago, and the brand of Marxism which was practised in the Soviet Union would have astonished Marx if he had seen it.[50] Each system was changing gradually with the changes in conditions in the country where it functioned. It would thus be meaningless to transplant either system root and branch on to Indian soil. India, with her own peculiar conditions and problems, needed to evolve a model of her own. Private enterprise in India, Nehru argued, lacked the capability to start the big projects – river-valley power-schemes, steel plants – which India needed. 'If private enterprise has full play,' he pointed out, 'one of the first casualties in this country will be private enterprise itself.'[51] On the other hand, it would be wasteful for the State to squander money in acquiring privately run industries. Nehru believed that, in view of the rapid progress of science and technology, most of the privately run industries in India would soon become obsolete.[52] It thus seemed wiser to concentrate on certain specific, vital, new industries than to nationalise many of the old ones.[53]

On 7 April 1948, India adopted what Nehru called a mixed economic system based on both public and private enterprise. Indian industry was divided into three categories: those which were to be exclusively owned and managed by the State, those which could be run by both state and private enterprise, and those which could be left in the hands of the private industrialists but subjected to some official controls. India had a tradition of both public and private enterprise. Before independence the Government of India had come to own and manage a number of industries, including railways, munition factories, salt and opium manufacture and a national broadcasting system. Private enterprise had distinguished itself in many fields and several industrial barons had emerged, some of whom had been pioneers in such industries as iron and steel, textiles and shipbuilding.

Left to itself, however, Nehru's mixed economic system would have had a haphazard and very slow growth. The system must be geared to a long-term planning programme. Nehru's interest in planned development had first been aroused by the Soviet Five-year Plan, but later in the 1930s he had come to reject the totalitarian basis of the Soviet Plan. A plan, he affirmed, must not only be formulated democratically but it must also be implemented with the full co-operation of the people. Thus in December 1938, when Congress formed a Planning Committee and an All-India Planning Commission with Nehru as its Chairman, he lost no time in impressing upon the members of the Commission, particularly upon its leading member K. T. Shah, that the Indian plan must avoid any suspicions of 'full-blooded socialism'.[54] He maintained that it was possible to have a planned economy without becoming socialist:

> If we start with the dictum that only under socialism there can be planning, we frighten people and irritate the ignorant. If, on the other hand, we think in terms of planning apart from socialism and thus inevitably arrive at some form of socialism, that is a logical process which will convert many who are weary of words and slogans.[55]

The war broke out, Congress lost its strong hold on the provinces, and the Planning Commission could not produce a plan. But Nehru's thoughts on the nature of planning remained intact. In 1944 the industrial barons of India signified their approval of a planned development for India by themselves producing a plan, called the Bombay Plan. Planning in those years was so much associated with the Soviet system that an American Congressman not only condemned the Bombay Plan as a communist document, but even went so far as to accuse J. R. D. Tata (Indian industrialist and a signatory to the Plan) of being a high-ranking leader in the communist movement.[56]

Nehru revived his thoughts on planning soon after he had directed India's economic structure along the middle path in August 1948. A six-member Planning Commission was created in March 1950 with the Prime Minister as Chairman. The draft outline of the First Five-year Plan, which appeared in July 1951, was scrutinised by the press, all political parties, labour and industry. The final draft appeared in December 1952 and, in commending it to Parliament, Nehru rightly claimed that the Plan was the result of a whole nation's efforts and not merely the work of six people in the Planning Commission. Nehru aimed to achieve two main objectives: as rapid an economic development as was possible democratically and by peaceful means, and emotional unity of the country:

> We often go off at a tangent on grounds of provincialism, communalism, religion or caste. We have no emotional awareness of the unity of the country. Planning will help us in having an emotional awareness of our problems as a whole.[57]

India's First Five-year Plan (1951–6) achieved Nehru's dual objective in great measure. It allowed for an estimated expenditure of about five billion dollars (nearly 2000 million pounds) over the plan period. Great stress was laid on agricultural production for, as Nehru pointed out:

> If our agricultural foundation is not strong then the industry we seek to build will not have a strong basis either. Apart from that, the situation in the country today is such that, if our food front cracks up, everything else will crack up too.[58]

All went well, and even the unpredictable Indian monsoon (on which 80 per cent of India's cultivated land depended for its water supply) was favourable during the First Plan period, though the rate of population growth was higher than the planners' estimate of 1·25 per cent per annum. Almost all targets were attained. Agricultural production increased by 10 per cent and industrial by 40 per cent. National income rose by 18 per cent. *Per capita* income increased by 10·5 per cent, 16 million acres of land were brought under irrigation, and electric power increased by 70 per cent. Investment in the public and private sectors of the economy came up to expectations. Of all its achievements, the steady increase in agricultural production seemed the most impressive. At the end of the Plan period India was self-sufficient in food, but that position was destroyed in subsequent years by repeated failures of monsoon and a steady increase in population. Of the three five-year plans which Nehru was to see formulated under his chairmanship, only the first was an unquestionable success.

In Nehru's economic planning there was much reliance on foreign aid and investment. At the time of India's independence the American emergency plans for the economic recovery of Europe, of Greece and Turkey were afloat. The Marshall

Plan and the Greek–Turkish programme expressed America's concern to insulate the 'free world' from any further communist contamination. Nehru disregarded the principle that underlay the American aid programme, and took it for granted that the developed nations should help under-developed and developing countries without any strings attached. He reasoned that it was in the interests of the rich to help the poor: 'Poverty anywhere was a danger to prosperity everywhere, just as some infectious disease somewhere might be a danger to healthy conditions elsewhere.'[59]

During this period, though India's relations with the United States were strained and on several occasions Nehru's patience was heavily taxed by what he considered the immaturity of American foreign policy, he never refused American aid if it was given unconditionally. With an acute food shortage in India and with no prospect of aid from the Soviet Union, Nehru had virtually no option but to rely on American 'good sense'. Yet his general disappointment with American foreign policy and his personal pride inhibited him not only from openly asking for American aid but also from publicly acknowledging such aid. In February 1950, when the American Congress was about to sanction its first gift of one million tons of food for India, Nehru fell into a dilemma. As the country badly needed the food, he thought it would be 'rather silly for us to refuse this in a huff'.[60] On the other hand he did not want his foreign policy and general approach to become affected by such a gift. Characteristically he made a declaration of India's policy but did not refer to the gift. At the same time he felt under an obligation: 'Whatever we may feel like doing,' he confided in his sister, 'there is no doubt that a gift of this kind does create some obligation.'[61] He thought that the Americans, not being as subtle as the British, were apt to talk about that obligation and even insist on some kind of repayment.

President Truman's administration was equally sceptical about Nehru's foreign policy, and American aid to India was not specifically aimed at winning Nehru over. It in fact formed a part of the 'Point Four Programme' to assist the developing countries of Asia, Africa and Latin America with technical staff, capital and food – the last of the four programmes which Truman laid out in his Inauguration Day speech on 20 January

1949. By the end of 1951 the Point Four extended to 33 countries, and India alone by then had received $54 million. In Truman's own words the Point Four was realistic as well as idealistic: 'Common sense told me that the development of these countries would keep our own industrial plant in business for untold generations.'[62] Then there was his concern to keep the free world free, and beneath all this his awareness of how America herself was developed by the investment of foreign capital by the British, Dutch, Germans and the French.[63] American aid and investment, it was obvious, would be available to those countries which could guarantee security for American investment. Nothing was further from Nehru's mind than confiscation and forfeiture of foreign investment. In order therefore to allay any fears foreign investors might have as a result of the seemingly socialistic tone of his economic policy, Nehru declared, on 6 April 1949, that existing foreign interests would be free from any discriminatory restrictions, that the facilities for remittance of profits earned in India would be continued and that, if any foreign enterprise were compulsorily acquired, compensation would be paid on a fair and equitable basis.[64]

Nehru's regard for equitable compensation pacified foreign investors, but at the same time it delayed the abolition of landlordism (the feudal zamindary system) in India – the one ancient agrarian institution he had long pledged himself to destroy. Land legislation fell under the jurisdiction of the states, and the Congress governments of the states differed in their estimates of what should constitute fair compensation.[65] As a result the Zamindary Bill was a dead letter in some states which could not afford to pay compensation. In some states like United Provinces and Bihar the validity of zamindary abolition Acts was challenged in the courts by the zamindars and the process of abolition delayed. Nehru had to intervene by recommending an amendment to the Constitution which put the zamindary abolition Acts beyond the purview of the courts. By 1956 the system was abolished in all states of the Indian union.

A country's economic policy, Nehru once maintained, determines its foreign policy.[66] This was only partially true in the case of Nehru's India. His model of a mixed economy and the middle path did indeed accord with his policy of non-alignment, but the latter was not really the product of the former. Both plans grew simultaneously in Nehru's mind. In fact Nehru had greater interest in international relations than in economic affairs and, even though he was conscious that a foreign policy unsupported by internal economic strength would fail to make an impact, he succeeded in enhancing India's and his own prestige in the family of world powers. Like a high-caste but poor Brahmin priest preaching the gospel of peace to the warring lords of old, India confidently entered the arena of world politics and delivered sermons to the super-powers on the efficacy of co-existence and world peace, on the self-destructiveness of mutual suspicion and fear, and on the immorality of the pursuit of power, influence and wealth. Like a priest, too, India was ultimately rewarded, and gifts and loans flooded in from many directions. But in the beginning, from 1947 to 1951, it was hard going for Nehru, and his non-alignment role aroused only suspicion and hostility among the powers. He resolutely pursued his foreign policy regardless.

In formulating his foreign policy, the broad principles of which he had conceived during the pre-independence period, Nehru was influenced chiefly by his belief that the foreign policies of the great Western powers had hitherto been a total failure and by his pride in India's greatness. In his view the foreign policies of the great powers had failed from every point of view, 'from the point of view of moving towards world peace or preventing world war', neither had they succeeded from the mere opportunist and individual point of view of the particular country.[67] A once mighty Europe was depressed as a result of its own avarice, and the two super-powers, having divided the world into two blocs, were arrayed against each other for a third world war. By 1948 the Soviet Union had pulled within its political orbit the seven East European countries of Albania, Bulgaria, Czechoslovakia, Hungary, Poland, Romania and Yugoslavia. The loss of Poland was most resented by the Western powers, and the mysterious death, in March 1948, of Jan Masaryk – the Foreign Minister of the Czechoslovakian Republic and the last active campaigner against communist dominance in Prague – was deeply regretted by Nehru, who felt it as a personal loss. The American bloc, supported by Cold War theorists like Winston Churchill and Dean Acheson, had by March 1949 armed itself with pacts and alliances – the Inter-American Treaty of Reciprocal Assistance of August 1947, the Brussels Pact of 17 March 1948 and the Atlantic Pact of March 1949 – all designed to cultivate solidarity among the countries of Western Europe, South and North America in their confrontation with the Soviet bloc.

The Cold War appeared alarmingly hot in June 1948, when the Soviets imposed a complete blockade on all forms of traffic into Berlin. In Nehru's view, what saved the Berlin blockade from sparking off a third world war was the military unpreparedness of the powers involved.[68] He feared that, should a political crisis synchronise with military preparedness, the results could be disastrous. Two years later, when the Korean crisis developed, Nehru for a while believed that the world was on the verge of a third war unless desperate measures were taken to prevent it. India's Korean policy was designed to prevent a local war developing into a global one.

Nehru's pride in India's greatness – its ancient traditions, its record of nationalist movements with high moral principles, its geographical situation and the size of its populace – made him eager to create for India an independent and active role in international relations. India, he declared, would never become a satellite of any major power.[69] India was to him the natural leader of the Afro-Asian world. Whereas the Chinese and the Arabs had so little in common, the Indians had much in common with both peoples. Besides, India had the advantage in that she was 'not fettered by the past, by old enmities or old ties, by historic claims or traditional rivalries'.[70] She could thus enter the family of nations without prejudice or enmity. India was truly in a position to combine idealism with national interest. The emotional basis of Nehru's foreign policy thus rested on his urge to place Asia, under India's leadership, on the world political map in bold relief. In 1948, a year before the emergence of Red China, Nehru was happy to notice that the Western world was beginning to consider India as a potential great power and especially as a dominant power in Asia, second only to the Soviet Union.[71] With the emergence of communist China in 1949 the struggle between the two giants for Asian leadership began. Whereas the Chinese leaders resorted to force in their bid for power, Nehru remained wedded to the Indian idea of achieving power by peaceful and upright means.

Nehru's policy of friendship towards all countries and of non-alignment with either of the two power blocs was by no means a policy of absolute neutrality and isolation. Nor was it exactly as he himself once described it to an American audience: 'Where freedom is menaced, or justice threatened, or where aggression takes place, we cannot be and shall not be neutral.'[72] Nehru did in fact impose certain broad thematical and territorial restrictions on the scope of India's involvement in international issues.

India was to be directly involved in opposing racial discrimination and colonial subjugation wherever it was practised:

> Our main stake in world affairs is peace and to see that there is racial equality and that people who are subjugated become free. For the rest we do not seek to interfere and we do not desire other people to interfere in our affairs.[73]

Nehru's emotional repugnance towards racialism and colonialism, dating from his nationalist days, now found a fuller vent in his foreign policy. South African racialism became his first target, and when the matter was, at India's insistence, debated in the United Nations from 1946 to 1949 it was the Soviet Union which alone unequivocally condemned racial discrimination in South Africa and supported India throughout. Nehru thus came to dissociate the Soviet Union from racialism and colonialism, and when this favourable image of Russia was joined with other factors – the criticism of India's stand in Kashmir by the Anglo-American bloc, and America's total disregard of Asian sentiments on the Korean issue – Nehru gradually became more favourably disposed towards the Soviet Union. Anti-colonialism was the driving force behind Nehru's involvement during this period in South-East Asia, particularly in the Indonesian struggle for independence.

Asia provided the territorial expanse of Nehru's involvement. Anything that happened in Asia, especially when it involved Western intervention, was of the utmost concern to India. This concern was sustained by the feeling of pan-Asianism which Nehru had nourished from his nationalist days. His convinced pan-Asianism became less strong after the Bandung Conference of 1955, but until then it enthused him with a sense of responsibility for the whole of Asia. He felt, for example, more concerned about the unification of South and North Korea than that of East and West Germany. India's enlightened national interests, however, always remained supreme in his mind and often counterbalanced his idealistic involvement in Asian and world affairs. For example, in 1948 Nehru was less ruthless in his condemnation of French imperialism in Indo-China than he was of Dutch imperialism in Indonesia. When asked by his colleague Rajendra Prasad why he differed in his treatment of the two colonial powers, Nehru replied: 'In the United Nations France has sided with us on important issues. In regard to French possessions in India also their attitude, though somewhat dilatory, is not unfriendly and we hope to arrive at some settlement before very long.'[74] Negotiations with France had begun soon after India's independence, and in May 1950 the French Indian possession of Chandernagar was peacefully transferred to India.

Nehru's concern for Asia brought him into conflict with America over her intervention in the Far East and over Anglo-American support for the partition of Palestine. His own suggestion that Palestine be constituted into a federal state with autonomous parts had been lost on the United Nations, and it was only when partition became imminent that it was realised by some powers that the Indian solution was probably the best for the preservation of peace in the Middle East.[75] The Far East became Nehru's major concern from 1949 to 1951. It was a period of crises and momentous decision-making for Nehru, including India's formally joining the British Commonwealth as a republic in April 1949, Nehru's first visit to America, American intervention in the Korean War, the Chinese invasion of Tibet, and the palace revolution in Nepal concluding with the restoration of the King to power through Indian intervention; and these events put Nehru's policy of non-alignment severely to the test.

The main targets of his foreign policy were to maintain friendly relations with America without falling into her fold, to let India's foreign policy appear independent in the eyes of the Soviet bloc, and to befriend and contain Red China with a view not only to preventing her from forming any closer alliance with the Soviet Union but also to minimising her impact on countries of South and South-East Asia. In the face of the political thinking that prevailed in the world at that time, Nehru's objectives seemed almost impossible to attain. The Americans discounted the possibility of non-alignment – all nations were either allies or enemies. Equally incomprehensible to the Soviet and Chinese minds was the idea of friendship between communist and non-communist states. A non-aligned nation was thus variously regarded as a myth, suspect, or an enemy. Nehru's achievement during this period lay in turning this myth into a reality.

The emergence of China was the major event during this period, and it raised many problems. Nehru's conscience was stricken when his old friend Madame Chiang Kai-shek sought his support for the tottering Kuomintang régime through Mrs Pandit, who was in 1949 Indian ambassador to the United States. Indian public opinion was decidedly against the Kuomintang, and Nehru saw no chance for the survival of Chiang Kai-shek's rule in China. 'With all my friendship for the Chiangs,' he told Mrs Pandit, 'I cannot, as Prime Minister or Foreign Minister, shut my eyes to facts and to my own convictions.'[76] He further pointed out:

> I am quite convinced that if we stood up for the bankrupt Government in China now, we would be condemned in India and this would give a fillip to communism in India, strange as that sounds. The way to fight communism is not by armies, but by. . . the adoption of progressive policies.[77]

All Nehru was prepared to offer the Chiangs in July 1949 was to delay recognition of communist China; indeed, his main consideration here was to assess the American reaction – an important factor in view of his impending visit to the United States in October 1949.

Nehru was apprehensive about his first visit to America. Indo-American relationships had already been strained over the Kashmir issue and the State Department had on occasions held out threats to India. In June 1949, while privately expressing his annoyance at American policy, Nehru wrote:

> I am afraid I cannot get over the feeling that U.S. diplomacy is immature or it is too sure of its physical might to care for the niceties of diplomatic behaviour. They have had a very bad set-back in China and they have not succeeded in many other places. And yet, they have not wholly learnt their lesson yet. We rely upon them inevitably for many things and we want to be friends with them. But there are some things we just cannot swallow.[78]

One of Nehru's chief reasons for joining the British Commonwealth was to avoid having to rely on America for capital goods and credit which, Nehru argued, would have been readily given by America, but on condition that India aligned its foreign policy with that of the United States:[79]

> It would have been dangerous for us to isolate ourselves and risky for us to slope too much towards the U.S. in the present context. That would have made it more difficult for us at any time to play the role of a friendly neutral to any of the parties concerned.[80]

Armed with Commonwealth membership in April 1949, Nehru acquired some freedom and strength in his dealings with the United States. Nevertheless, though he had met many Americans and read several books about America, he was not at all sure how he should approach the American public:

> I think often, whenever I have the time to think, of this coming American visit. In what mood shall I approach America? How should I address people etc? How should I deal with the Government there and businessmen and others? Which facet of myself should I put before the American public – the Indian or the European, for after all I have that European or English aspect also. I shall have to meet some difficult situations. I want to be friendly with the Americans but always making it clear what we stand for. I want to make no commitments which come in the way of our basic policy. I am inclined to thinkthat the best preparation for America is not to prepare and to trust to my native wit and the mood of the moment, the general approach being friendly and receptive.[81]

Beneath these doubts lay his firm resolution not to be swept away by the Americans. He was also anxious to economise on the dollars which were then so precious to India. He travelled by Air India to London and from London to the United States in a plane sent for him by President Truman, but he insisted on paying Indira's fare himself. He landed in America dressed in the Western style, but he spoke what he considered to be the language of India. In August, only two months before his American visit, he referred to this 'language of India' in a private note explaining his reason for appointing S. Radhakrishnan, the philosopher, as India's ambassador in Moscow:

> This sending of Radhakrishnan to Moscow is rather an interesting experiment. I am more and more coming to the opinion that we should speak a little more the language of India in foreign countries, that is to say the language of the Indian mind. It may sound odd to others but it should make them think a little and realise that India is not just a copy of the West.[82]

Caught in the grip of the Cold War and shaken by the rise of communist China, the Americans were in no mood to understand and appreciate Nehru's policy of non-alignment and his denunciation of the Anglo-American thesis that the best way of preserving world peace was to remain prepared for war. Even those Americans who had come to admire Nehru and uphold his importance in world politics did so for the wrong reasons. They argued that Nehru would ultimately recognise that there was no halfway position between communism and freedom and would then side with America in fighting her deadliest enemy.[83]

Though Nehru failed to convert the American mind, he believed that he had succeeded in impressing on the Russians and Chinese that India was not a lackey of the Anglo-American bloc. However, the recognition on the part of the Sino-Soviet bloc of India's independent foreign policy did not imply any liking for it. In the eyes of Mao Tse-tung, any foreign policy which was independent of the two blocs was not only irresolute but also undesirable. Nehru was determined to disprove Mao's thesis by showing that India, because of its non-aligned position, could gain for China world recognition and the entry into the United Nations which communist China then badly needed. By befriending Red China and substituting it for Chiang's Formosa-based China in the United Nations, Nehru wanted to achieve two objectives: first the containment of China in an international organisation and secondly the weakening of the communist movement in India. The success of this policy depended on Nehru's having influence in both blocs.

As Indo-American relations were delicate, Nehru used the British Commonwealth to sustain India's link with and influence on the Anglo-American bloc. On his way back to India from America, Nehru conferred in London with the members of the Labour Government and secured their support for the recognition of Red China. On 30 December 1949, India recognised communist China; Britain followed suit in January 1950. At the Colombo Conference of the Commonwealth foreign ministers in January, Ernest Bevin and Nehru stressed that their recognition of communist China would prevent Mao's closer drift to the Soviet Union.[84] Their expectations, however, were not realised, for in the following month, on 15 February, the foreign ministers of China and the Soviet Union signed a treaty of friendship and alliance in Moscow. Nehru nevertheless continued to plead, in the face of American opposition, for Red China's entry into the United Nations. Relations between the two countries became more strained early in 1950, and Nehru's resentment and disapproval of American diplomacy increased when, in May 1950, America accorded a reception to Liaquat Ali Khan similar to that which they had given Nehru during his visit: 'I must say that the Americans are either very naïve or singularly lacking in intelligence. They go through the identical routine, whether it is Nehru or the Shah of Iran, or Liaquat Ali.'[85] His national vanity was hurt and he became sceptical of the worth of the superlatives the Americans had first showered on him and were now heaping on the Pakistani Prime Minister. Nehru suspected that America was strongly opposed to his foreign policy and was deliberately building up Pakistan's strength against India. As his relations with President Truman's administration deteriorated, so Nehru relied more on Britain, and in September 1950 he thought he had succeeded in acquiring Labour Government support for Red China's entry into the United Nations.[86]

In June 1950, North Korea invaded South Korea. In October, United Nations forces under General Douglas MacArthur crossed the 38th Parallel into North Korea and were forced to retreat by the Chinese. The United Nations branded China as an aggressor, and President Truman threatened to use the atom bomb. These major events of the first six months of the Korean War demonstrated Red China's strength and convinced Nehru of the urgency of securing United Nations membership for Red China and of American insensitivity towards the Asian mind: a Red China not tied to the United Nations because of the American veto would turn wild and irresponsible, and the 'future will be dark'.[87] At first Nehru gave support to the United Nations forces but, when they entered North Korea and China intervened in her support, Nehru defended Red China. In the same month, October 1950, the Chinese invasion of Tibet began.

Nehru was taken by surprise. He had not evolved any definite policy towards Tibet, being divided between his feeling that India, apart from commercial and cultural links, had no territorial or political ambitions with regard to Tibet, and the belief that Tibet should maintain its age-old autonomy under traditional Chinese suzerainty.[88] From neither of these views could he derive sufficient strength to alter his policy towards China and forcefully to intervene in Tibet. Only a few weeks before the Chinese intervention in Tibet, Nehru had recorded with satisfaction:

> The change in relations between India and China during the past few weeks has been rather remarkable. I think this began slowly after my visit to America last year when they realised that I was not exactly anybody's stooge, as they had imagined. Our championing China's cause in the United Nations has gone a long way also.[89]

Was this positive achievement to be thrown away over a sentimental regard for Tibet's autonomy? Besides, he argued, India's effective intervention would mean war with China; and he dreaded war. The American ambassador in India, Loy Henderson, paid a quick visit to the Foreign Ministry and promised American help if India intervened. Nehru declined the offer: 'Nothing could be more damaging to us and our cause than asking for American help to deal with the Tibetan situation.'[90] He merely protested to the Chinese Government against the violent liberation of Tibet and pleaded for a peaceful settlement. The Chinese were quick to take offence, and alleged that forces hostile to China were pressuring India to intervene in Tibet, which was exclusively China's domestic concern. Personally, Nehru felt let down by China and thought that the Chinese had acted 'rather foolishly and done some injury to their cause'.[91] 'It is natural', he wrote to his sister, 'that our enthusiasm for supporting China wanes somewhat and we shall have to be careful about the steps we take', but 'our general policy', he affirmed, 'remains the same'.[92]

Nehru's affirmation of his policy towards China was not to the liking of the Congress rightists, headed by Patel and Tandon. Tandon publicly condemned Chinese intervention in Tibet and Korea. Patel wrote a long letter to Nehru advising the Prime Minister to regard China as an imperialist power and a potential threat to India's security on its northern and eastern frontiers.[93] Chinese occupation of Tibet, he argued, made certain zones on India's frontiers most vulnerable; Ladakh, Nepal, Bhutan, Sikkim, Darjeeling, and certain parts of Assam inhabited by the Nagas and other hill tribes – all these Himalayan regions would now be open to communist infiltration from the Tibetan side. China might disregard the McMahon Line, which defined the Indo-Tibetan border in the north-eastern region, and lay claim to the North-East Frontier area at present belonging to India. Patel further pointed out that the expansion of the Chinese in Tibet and their infiltration into Burma would pose problems of internal security, for the Indian communists would be in a position easily to secure arms from the Chinese, now perched on India's northern frontiers. He was convinced that it was only a matter of time before Chinese irredentism would impel China to lay hands on some tracts of India's Himalayan territories.

Though temporarily shaken by the Chinese intervention in Tibet, Nehru firmly adhered to the view that China must be befriended and contained non-violently; the only alternative was to confront China head-on, which would ruin India's foreign policy and damage its growing image in the world as a power for peace. However, Nehru now became more concerned about establishing India's control or influence over neighbouring states, particularly Nepal. India's sovereignty over Ladakh was reaffirmed, as was her protectorate over Sikkim and Bhutan. While keeping constant watch on Burma, Nehru tightened India's hold over Nepal. An opportunity offered itself in November 1950 when the King of Nepal, hitherto a captive of the Ranas who had ruled the country in his name, sought asylum in the Indian embassy at Khatmandu. India intervened, restored the King to power and brought to an end the Rana régime. Explaining India's intervention, Nehru maintained:

> We would like every other country to appreciate the intimate geographical and cultural relationship that exists between India and Nepal . . . . Our interest in the internal conditions of Nepal has become still more acute and personal, because of the developments across our borders, to be frank, especially those in China and Tibet.[94]

The heart of Nehru's policy, however, continued to lie in good relations with China. The role of India in the Korean War came to be recognised as that of an impartial mediator, and in 1953 it was under India's chairmanship of the Neutral Nations Repatriation Commission, and with an Indian custodian force, that the deadlock on the question of how prisoners of war were to be repatriated was finally resolved and peace restored in the area, though North and South Korea remained divided.

Nehru made a major policy-decision with regard to the Sino-Soviet bloc in August–September 1951. The terms of the Japanese Peace Treaty, as sponsored by the United States and opposed by the Soviet Union and China, created some division among Indian diplomats and policy-makers. G. S. Bajpai (Secretary-General of the External Affairs Ministry) and Mrs V. L. Pandit (Indian ambassador to the United States) were in favour of India signing the Treaty. But K. M. Panikkar, Radhakrishnan and Krishna Menon – then India's ambassadors respectively to China, the Soviet Union and Britain – were against India being a signatory to it. Nehru was most certainly opposed to the Treaty, and it was his view which ultimately prevailed. In the projected terms of the Treaty – which gave the United States not only military bases in Japan but also administrative control over the Japanese islands of

Ryukyu and Bonin – and in the various security pacts which the United States had separately signed with Australia, New Zealand and the Philippines, Nehru saw a display of American militarism which seemed to him to have marked fascist tendencies. He feared that America was weakening, consciously or unconsciously, the cause of democracy:

> There is still strong feeling in Europe and elsewhere against fascism and nazism. This is raised up by this pro-fascist policy and the communist countries take advantage of this. The U.S. looking at everything from a purely military point of view, misses, or deliberately ignores, this major psychological factor which ultimately affects the morale of nations and of armies .... The result of all this is that moderate tendencies and really democratic ways and policies find less scope and the fascists and the communists hold the field against each other, ultimately probably leading to war.[95]

This frantic quest for 'faithful allies', Nehru regretfully noted, had led the United States to strike an alliance with such a fascist régime as that of Franco in Spain. America was fighting communist forces in the wrong way. Red China should not be isolated – which was the aim of the Japanese Peace Treaty – but should be contained within the United Nations:

> To accept the Japanese Treaty as it is now is to put an end to our present policy and, in fact, turn a political somersault. It might mean almost, though not quite, a political break with China. We would have no logic left in any policy that we pursue.[96]

Thus, even at the risk of arousing greater ill-will in the United States, Nehru declined to sign the Treaty.

During this period, and subsequently, Nehru made basic policy-decisions almost single-handed, not only on matters of external relations but also on social, political and financial issues. He held many offices at one time: he was Prime Minister and Foreign Minister, in charge of Commonwealth and scientific affairs, Chairman of the Planning Commission, and President of Congress from 1951 to 1954. He made speeches almost every day, toured the country extensively, seldom declined an invitation to visit a foreign country (during 1947–51 he visited America, Canada, Indonesia, Burma, Europe, and Britain almost every year), and yet he always found time, even in the midst of a grave national crisis, to look after his daughter's and sister's families and attend even to such details as scrutinising his niece's engagement to a Punjabi boy and reporting at length to his sister, then in the United States, on the character and suitability of the boy. Through his fortnightly letters he tutored and briefed the chief ministers of the states on all public matters. He had time for every job, and offered his advice on every matter, public or private, that came to his notice. This may not seem so surprising if one looks at the working-hours he kept in those years. He worked regularly from 7 a.m. to 2 a.m. (with brief interruptions for yoga exercises and meals) either at his residence – the palatial Teen Murti House – or in his offices at the Ministry of External Affairs and in the Parliament building.

What may seem surprising is that he relied on so few committees and consultants in making policy-decisions on such a vast range of issues. There was indeed the Union Cabinet consisting of fourteen to sixteen ministers, and there were a few committees of the Cabinet, the most important being the Foreign Affairs Committee which, in 1962, became the Emergency Committee. Nehru's influence over the Cabinet and its committees was overpowering, though it met heated opposition so long as Patel lived.

As Deputy Prime Minister of India, Patel challenged on many occasions the powers of the Prime Minister. There had always existed between them not only temperamental differences but differences in their approach to economic and communal matters. Their differences and conflicts intensified after India's independence, and crisis-point was reached in January 1948 when each disputed the other's role in the Government. Referring the matter to Gandhi on 6 January, Nehru complained of Patel's hindrance in the exercising of his functions as Prime Minister, and claimed:

> As I conceive it, the Prime Minister's role is, and should be, an important role. He is not only a figurehead but a person who should be more responsible than any one else for the general trend of policy and for the co-ordination of the work of various Government departments. The final authority necessarily is the Cabinet itself. But in the type of democratic set-up

> we have adopted, the Prime Minister is supposed to play an outstanding role.[97]

Patel disputed Nehru's claims:

> I have found myself unable to agree with his conception of the Prime Minister's duties and functions. That conception, if accepted, would raise the Prime Minister to the position of a virtual dictator, for he claims 'full freedom to act when and how he chooses'. This in my opinion is wholly opposed to democratic and Cabinet system of government.[98]

Gandhi wanted both to remain in the Cabinet, but if they found it impossible to pull together, then it was Patel who must leave. Gandhi's fast and his assassination prevented a final rupture between the two, but Patel continued to function as a counterweight against Nehru's powers. Much against Nehru's wishes, he elevated Tandon to the Congress presidency and Rajendra Prasad to the presidency of the Indian union in 1950.

It was only after the death of Patel on 15 December 1950 that Nehru became the sole custodian of power. He functioned not as 'first among equals' but as 'first above equals'. Nehru wielded absolute power, not for love of it but for the fear of its being misused if shared with his colleagues. His fear arose from his continual awareness of the wide intellectual gap that persisted between him and his colleagues. His different cultural background, his attitudes and thoughts isolated him from his colleagues, particularly in those years when, with a view to strengthening his Cabinet in times of national crisis, Nehru included in it non-Congressmen whose basic political views clashed with his own, occasionally resulting in resignations. Most of the ministers who resigned from Nehru's Cabinet during this period were non-Congressmen – Chetty, Mathai, Mookerjee and Ambedkar. But even among his Congress colleagues Nehru found none who fully understood his policies and in whom he could place his entire confidence. Of the four cabinet ministers (Azad, Ayyangar, Pant and Kidwai) who came closest to him and on whose practical wisdom, loyalty and efficiency Nehru occasionally relied, R. A. Kidwai was the only leftist, and the only one to come near to becoming his friend, but he was erratic and Nehru found him (as in July 1951, when Kidwai offered to resign from Congress in protest against the policies of Congress's President, Tandon) 'a very unsafe' and embarrassing friend.[99]

Nehru, however, never harboured malice, though he was acutely sensitive to criticism and opposition. His sensitivity in part arose from his constant concern for his public image as a just, fair and far-sighted leader. Of the ministers who resigned from his Cabinet, two – Mathai and Ambedkar – made virulent attacks on his policies and style, and on each occasion he was badly hurt. There were also complaints occasionally made against him by his relations because he had done nothing to advance their material interests. Then there were his erstwhile socialist friends, especially R. M. Lohia, spitting fire at him in order, as Nehru often thought, to make their existence felt.[100] He felt more responsive to criticism than to praise, and this caused him momentary distress. He tried to regain his balance through assuring himself that nothing but his honesty and integrity and his loyal regard for the national interests lay at the root of his policies and actions. At the end of 1951, the sixty-two-year-old Nehru was confident of himself and about the policies he had laid down in various spheres of the nation's life. He believed that he had sown the seed of India's greatness and of world peace. Now it was time to look forward to the harvest.

CHAPTER ELEVEN

The Leader of the Third World, 1952–8

> Greatness comes from vision, the tolerance of the spirit, compassion and an even temper which is not ruffled by ill fortune or good fortune. It is not through hatred and violence or internal discord that we make real progress. As in the world today, so also in our country, the philosophy of force can no longer pay and our progress must be based on peaceful co-operation and tolerance of each other.
>
> *Jawaharlal Nehru, December 1952*

> I am greatly conscious of the delay that the democratic processes involve, but still I am convinced that for my country this system of parliamentary democracy is the best.
>
> *Jawaharlal Nehru, November 1954*

DURING this period Nehru was to enjoy the first fruits of the policies he had laid down between 1947 and 1951. Confidence, a sense of urgency and hope characterised his leadership from 1952 to 1958. On the international front Nehru succeeded in raising India's stature to that of a world power, and he himself came to occupy an honourable position in the gallery of world statesmen, being widely recognised as the leader of the non-aligned Third World. He was then in his mid-sixties, and was the eldest of those world statesmen (Dwight Eisenhower, Anthony Eden, Harold Macmillan, Nikita Khrushchev, Josip Tito, Gamal Abdul Nasser, Ahmed Sukarno, Mao Tse-tung and Chou En-lai) with whom he had to deal at that time. He was generally respected among them for his learning, his charm and sophistication, his forty-year-old political career and for the popular power he gently wielded over 400 million of his countrymen. His sense of his own superiority, his arrogance, his sense of his own rightness and his intellectualism, however, were silently resented by Asian and African leaders, some of whom, like Chou, Mao and Sukarno, vied with him for the Afro-Asian leadership.

The international scene was dominated by Asian politics – the end of the Korean War (1953), the Geneva Conference on Indo-China (1954), the South-East Asia Treaty Organisation (1954), the Baghdad Pact (1955), the Bandung Conference (1955), the Suez crisis (1956), the Syrian problem (1957) and the Iraqi revolt (1958). Nehru played an important role in these affairs but his sincere attempts to achieve peaceful settlements were not often openly acknowledged by the Anglo-American bloc. This sometimes hurt the sensitive Indian mind, and many believed that India's great role in world politics was deliberately played down by the jealous Britons and unimaginative Americans. Nehru himself seemed unperturbed by such remissness, however, for his confidence was strengthened by his achievements in befriending the Soviet Union and containing communist China.

These were also for Nehru the finest years on the domestic front. He derived satisfaction from further strengthening India's unity and her democratic structure. With much optimism, arising from the success of the First Five-year Plan, he launched the Second Five-year Plan which, he believed, was India's best alternative to the Chinese system. He became in these years firmly set against communism, and gradually renounced many of the Marxist concepts to which he had formerly subscribed. Having no convenient ideological system from which he could seek guidance, he resorted to Gandhism and spoke more of his master's language in these years than ever before. He even emulated Gandhi in rising above institutional power-politics, and threatened to relinquish his office on at least two occasions. Power often bored him and at times gave him a sense of confinement; indeed he sometimes yearned for the freedom of his nationalist days and even dreamed of the British prisons in which he had had the time to read and write. His paternalistic style of government made him perhaps the busiest head of government in the world, yet he remained a lonely man, seldom finding a truly intimate companion.

Turning first to India's domestic affairs, there were developments during these years that were not much to Nehru's liking. The movement for the linguistic reorganisation of the Indian states was one significant development to which Nehru gave way with much reluctance. He could have suppressed the movement in its infancy when it had no mass support and was sponsored mainly by those of the middle classes who aspired to economic and political power in a newly created state, but his resistance was weakened by his awareness of the pledge Congress had first given in 1920 and renewed frequently thereafter to rearrange the boundaries of the provinces on linguistic lines. This pledge, made initially in the context of the British Raj and with the prime objective of giving a mass basis to the national movement in the provinces, could now damage the very unity of India. In early 1948, when the question was first revived by some interested southern politicians, Nehru therefore resisted the temptation merely to browbeat its proponents, and referred the matter to Rajendra Prasad with the recommendation that if it should prove possible to create new linguistic provinces, then steps must be taken 'to demarcate the boundaries by the appointment of a boundary commission or otherwise'.[1] Prasad appointed an enquiry commission, and the matter soon began to acquire public notice. Nehru became alarmed, and in September of the same year he complained to Prasad:

> The Enquiry Commission which you appointed, to my surprise, is functioning in public and thereby encouraging an atmosphere of argument and passion. I had hoped that the Commission would not hold public sessions. Is it possible to do anything in this matter now?[2]

But it was too late to hush up the matter. Though the reports both of the official commission and of an unofficial Congress committee were unfavourable to the creation of linguistic states, the movement had, by the end of 1949, gathered momentum and its advocates, knowing well that Nehru would never oppose it as firmly as he was then opposing the communalist movement, began manœuvring for mass support. Between 1950 and November 1956 the movement passed through many phases and assumed various dimensions. Indian unity was assailed by demands for the creation of separate Telugu, Malayalam, Marathi and Punjabi states. There was even a demand for a Nepali-speaking state to be carved out of North Bengal. Nehru's initial attempts to ignore the movement were frustrated by a Telugu leader, Potti

Sriramulu, who in 1952 fasted to death for the Telugu-speaking state of Andhra. The central government bowed to the Andhra cause, and the new state was formally inaugurated in October 1953. At the end of the year the Government also appointed the States Reorganisation Commission to examine the whole question of linguistic boundaries. The Commission reported in October 1955, and in November of the following year the States Reorganisation Bill, based substantially on the report, was passed by the Indian Parliament.

These twelve months marked the apogee of the linguistic movement. The storm blew mainly over Bombay and the Punjab. Should Bombay be partitioned into two states (Bombay and Vidarbha) as the Commission had recommended, or into the three states (Bombay City, Gujarat, Maharashtra) that the central government had proposed, or should it remain bilingual – a status which was finally conceded to it by the States Reorganisation Act of 1956? Should Punjab be divided into two states – one Punjabi-speaking and the other Hindi-speaking? The Sikhs agitated for a division, and the Hindus for the continuation of its bilingual status which gave them a certain dominance over the Punjabi-speaking Sikhs. Here again the controversy was resolved in favour of retaining the Punjab as a bilingual state (as the Commission had proposed in its report), but its Hindu dominance was reduced by not joining it to the Hindu-majority state of Himachal Pradesh. However, these settlements of November 1956 turned out to be temporary. Linguistic controversies lingered in these areas, and in 1960 Bombay was partitioned into two states – the Marathi-speaking Maharashtra and the Gujarati-speaking Gujarat. In 1966, two years after Nehru's death, the Punjab also ceased to exist as a bilingual state. It was divided into two states, the Punjabi-speaking zone retaining the name of Punjab and the Hindi-speaking zone assuming the name of Haryana.

That the linguistic movement did not fully realise its goals in 1956 was due to Nehru. From October 1955 to November 1956 he concentrated his efforts on striking a compromise between linguistic regionalism and national unity. His public arguments against the linguistic movement became more persuasive and less militant. The idea of a unilingual state was a myth, he argued, for as long as the people of one state were not prevented from going to another there would always be bilingual areas.[3] Further, 'There is no exclusiveness about culture. The more inclusive you are, the more cultured you are. The more barriers you put up, the more uncultured you are.'[4] He then put forward economic arguments against the creation of new states. The Second Five-year Plan, tailored as it was down to the district level of an existing state, would be disrupted if the entire state structure were uprooted.[5] He would have preferred the division of India into four to six major groups regardless of language, but as this was no longer possible since a number of linguistic states had come into existence he mooted the idea of having advisory zonal councils, each consisting of four to five states. The councils, he hoped, would be able to contain regionalism within the national fold.

Though the creation of new states or units on linguistic, religious or ethnic grounds posed some overt threat to national solidarity, it was nonetheless the only device, as far as Nehru was aware, that could be used by the central government to out-manœuvre the secessionist movement. This device had been used in the case of Kashmir and was to be used to pacify the Sikhs of the Punjab and the Nagas of Assam. The division of the Punjab in the post-Nehru era and the creation of Nagaland, the foundations of which were laid in 1957 when Nehru agreed to form the Naga Hills into a separate unit under the central government, symbolised the Government's attempt to contain separatism within the national fold. Indian unity was still a delicate phenomenon and there was little consensus among the political parties and state leaders on the national interests which Nehru presented to the nation. Even his own colleagues in the Government and Congress High Command did not always subscribe to Nehru's ideas of top-priority matters.

The country seemed more divided on the question of an official language for India than on the reorganisation of the states, and yet more so on the modernisation of Hindu law. Though in some ways Nehru was more of a Hindu – more tolerant, more non-violent and much more dedicated to the consensual mode of life – even than Gandhi, he was always conscious of his own separation from the traditional and ritualistic mode of life, considering himself an outsider in religious, social and cultural matters. He thus became inhibited when pleading, say, for the recognition of Hindi as an official language, or when attacking the adoption of a highly élitist and Sanskritised version of Hindi, or supporting the introduction of monogamy and divorce into the Hindu system of marriage. Yet, with all his limitations, Nehru played a significant role in the controversies which arose over the questions of an official language and the Hindu marriage issues. His was a conciliatory role – that of striking compromises between conflicting groups of interests and thereby pulling the entire body, not just one dominant group, towards the desired goal. Compromises were made on methods and time but seldom on the goal itself. Gradualness was thus the keynote of his style and he was not apologetic about it even when reminded of the rapid pace at which the Chinese were moving in all walks of life. Having committed himself and the country to a democratic mode of life he would rather suffer delays than force the pace by compulsion or 'the power of the stick'.[6]

There was no doubt in Nehru's mind that Hindi must become the exclusive, official language of India. The Constitution of 1950 guaranteed that position to Hindi after fifteen years, when English was to cease to be the joint official language of India. Whether Hindi would be able to replace English in 1965 was a question on which Nehru kept an open mind. If Hindi was not found to have enriched itself sufficiently by 1965 to become the exclusive official language, he was prepared to grant English a longer life than that envisaged by the Constitution. But the controversy which arose soon after the appointment of the Official Language Commission in 1955 was not confined to English versus Hindi. It raised once again the basic question of whether Hindi should ever be allowed to become the official language of India. South India rose against what it called the Hindi imperialism of the north, and Rajaji, the elder statesman of Madras, threatened to withdraw his state from the Indian union if Hindi was imposed on the south. At the root of the southern opposition to Hindi lay the fear of losing employment prospects in the central government services, which until then employed a fair percentage of south Indians. Nehru dispelled this apprehension straightaway by guaranteeing that the initial test for entry into the central services would be conducted 'in Hindi or in English or in the regional language of the candidate'.[7] Only after the candidate had passed his examination would he have to learn Hindi. He further allayed the fear of the southerners by lashing out at the extremism of the Hindi fanatics and by indicating that the changeover to Hindi as an all-India official language had to be gradual and with the consent and support of the non-Hindi-speaking people. Furthermore, he assured the south Indians that English would persist as a joint language for some time after 1965. All parties were mollified by the compromise solution which was thrashed out by Nehru at the Congress annual session held in Gauhati in 1958.

In dealing with the reorganisation of states and the official language, Nehru had the substantial backing of his Cabinet (he lost only one cabinet minister – C. D. Deshmukh, who resigned during the persistent conflict over the linguistic reorganisation of Bombay state) and Congress High Command. But this was not the case when he came to sponsor the modernisation of Hindu law. Here he faced fierce opposition from the rightists within his party and the Cabinet. Nothing distinguished a rightist from a leftist more than the former's belief in the efficacy of Hindu tradition. This belief was tactical in the case of some politicians, such as Sardar Patel, who, though not enamoured of the ritualistic aspect of Hinduism, would defend it nonetheless to maintain intact his power-base among his conservative constituents. But it was different with Rajendra Prasad, who genuinely believed in all the manifestations and paraphernalia of Hindu tradition. He was, during this period, President of the Indian Republic and therefore unable to offer any effective opposition to the modernisation of the Hindu social system. But, prior to becoming President of India, he had opposed and contrived to delay the codification of Hindu law.

The proposal to codify and make uniform the various personal laws of the Hindus (laws relating to marriage, succession, inheritance, adoption, the joint family), which was first mooted in 1941, received an impetus from the directive principle of the Indian Constitution of 1950 which enjoined upon the State the duty to endeavour to secure for the citizens of India (Hindus, Muslims, Christians, Parsis and others) a uniform civil code. The modernisation and codification of Hindu laws was considered the first step towards the modernisation of other personal laws, including Christian and Muslim. The draft Hindu Code Bill, prepared in 1947, was discussed in the Constituent Assembly in 1948. Nehru was in favour of the general principles embodied in the Bill. He implored Rajendra Prasad to give his support to the Bill lest the people of India brand Congress as a socially reactionary body.[8] Prasad would not comply; instead he vehemently opposed the proposed measure. He pointed out to Nehru that Congress had never discussed the Bill, that the Constituent Assembly was not empowered to deal with such a measure, and further maintained:

> I know that there are some people who want it but if you were to take the people at large, I am afraid a vast majority would not go for it. So it is not so much giving up something which you consider right because some people object to it, but forcing something on the people at large because some people consider it to be right and want it. Apart from these considerations, I might mention that it is bound to rouse bitter feelings and will have repercussions which may affect the chances of the Congress at the next election.[9]

Nehru gave in, temporarily, and in September 1951, on the eve of the general election, the Bill was dropped. But shortly after the election the main parts of the Bill were introduced in the new parliament as separate Bills, and these were finally passed: in 1955 the Hindu Marriage Act, and in 1956 the Hindu Succession Act, the Hindu Minority and Guardianship Act and the Hindu Adoptions and Maintenance Act.

Nehru put all his weight behind this legislation and from 1952 to 1956 he tutored the Members of Parliament and the general public in the principles underlying the bills. Political and economic change must go hand in hand with social change, and the Bills, he claimed, strove to bring in a long-overdue social change in India – the emancipation of women.[10] By rendering Hindu marriage monogamous, by giving the daughter an equal share, along with son and widow, in the intestate succession to a father's estate, and by making provisions for the dissolution of marriage in certain cases, the proposed legislation was intended to restore to women their dignity and rights as human beings. Hindu orthodoxy found the introduction of divorce into Hindu marriage a particularly bitter pill to swallow. But Nehru insisted that by providing for divorce they were making for happier marriages:

> I would particularly beg the House to take the view that this clause about divorce by mutual consent, subject to time, subject to reconciliation, subject to all such approaches, so that nothing may be done in a hurry, is a right and proper clause. It will produce a happier adjustment and a better relationship between the parties than would be produced if one party thinks that he can misbehave as much as he likes and nothing would happen.[11]

He pointed out to the Members of Parliament that in just one state of India, the state of Saurashtra, 'there is on an average one suicide a day among women because of maladjustments in human relationships'.[12] Though not all Members of Parliament were genuinely converted to the idea, they did not want to be branded as reactionaries. Besides, Nehru's personality had come to assume a force which none in his party could think of openly defying. The Bills were passed with a considerable majority.

'Change with continuity' was Nehru's motto in dealing with other domestic matters. The motto suited not only his style and temperament but also the system of parliamentary democracy to which he was dedicated. He maintained:

> If there is no change and only continuity, there is stagnation and decay. If there is change only and no continuity, that means uprooting, and no country and no people can survive for long if they are uprooted from the soil which has given them birth and nurtured them.[13]

The system of parliamentary democracy, he emphasised, embodied these principles and throve on them. He told his Members of Parliament that it was up to them to make the pace of change as fast as they liked but subject to the principle of continuity. Once continuity was broken the whole system would collapse. In balancing these two processes he gave, sometimes against his wish, more room to continuity than to change.

The principle of continuity determined the formation of his own Cabinet. Old colleagues and nationalists, irrespective of age and merit, were drawn into and retained in the Cabinet. He also retained, as far as possible, the practice of having territorial and communal representation in the Cabinet. These considerations obliged him at times to draw into his Cabinet persons whom he positively disliked, like K. M. Munshi. 'But all kinds of considerations', he believed, 'have to be borne in mind in making a Cabinet.'[14] His Cabinet was thus not a homogeneous body; many of his ministers either did not understand or did not believe in his policies. But there was always among the Congress ministers unanimous support for Nehru because they were overpowered by his personality. They silently resented being treated as pygmies but none could stand up to him. Instead, they vented their suppressed emotions among themselves and there were often, as Nehru noticed, personal conflicts among his ministers:

> It seems to me, whether in Delhi or elsewhere, that far the best part of my time is taken up in reconciling people or in soothing them when they get ruffled with each other. It is extraordinary how little our capacity is for friendly co-operation. I have to deal with this matter on the governmental level, right from the top downwards, and at the Congress level.[15]

For his own part, Nehru often resented his helplessness in having to put up with people cast in different moulds, and this made him impatient and overbearing in his dealings with them. There was hardly anybody in his Cabinet, except Krishna Menon (who joined the Cabinet in February 1956), with whom Nehru could converse openly and fruitfully. But, even Krishna Menon, who shared most of Nehru's opinions, was a psychological misfit. Nehru had a fairly clear appreciation of Menon's abilities, virtues and failings, all of which were considerable. In 1957 he wrote to his sister:

> Krishna has often embarrassed me and put me in considerable difficulties. If I speak to him, he has an emotional breakdown. He is always on the verge of some such nervous collapse.

> The only thing that keeps him going is hard work. There is hardly a person of any importance against whom he has not complained to me some time or other. Later he has found out that his opinion was wrong and he has changed it.[16]

He never allowed his affection for Menon overly to influence him, however, and even though he wanted to bring him into the Cabinet in 1953 he waited until 1956, by which time Menon had acquired an international standing and the right-wing opposition to his inclusion in the Cabinet had somewhat subsided.

Motivated more by consideration for stability than for reform in 1953, Nehru pressed two chief ministers – G. B. Pant of Uttar Pradesh and Morarji Desai of Bombay – both right-wingers, to join the Union Cabinet. Both were at first reluctant to be uprooted from positions of absolute power in their respective provinces.[17] Desai argued that if he left the province his successor was bound to be B. S. Hiray, an undesirable choice for himself and Nehru.[18] At the same time he bargained for either the Home or Defence portfolio. Pant pleaded his incompetence to run the Finance Ministry which Nehru offered him. But Nehru continued to press them until he succeeded in persuading Pant to join his Cabinet in 1955 and Desai in 1957.

As a result of Nehru's preference for continuity and stability in the Government, the face of his Cabinet remained almost unaltered throughout his prime ministership. In his third Cabinet of thirteen ministers, reconstituted on 17 April 1957 after the second general election, there were only two new entrants, Desai and S. K. Patil, both Congressmen of long standing. Other changes from his Cabinet of 1948 were due to such causes as death (Patel, Ayyangar, Kidwai), resignation (Chetty, Mookerjee, Neogy, Ambedkar, Mathai and Deshmukh), or transfer, as in the case of K. N. Katju who in 1957 relinquished the Defence portfolio to become the Chief Minister of Madhya Pradesh. Nehru rarely dismissed a minister, and all those who resigned owing to differences with Nehru were non-Congressmen.

The principle of continuity dominated the structure of the state cabinets as well. All chief ministers were Congress nationalists of some political standing and in almost every case they stayed in office throughout this period: the chief minister who remained in office longest (sixteen years) was B. C. Roy of Bengal. Though there was sometimes a struggle within the state congress for the leadership of the state government Nehru, as chief arbiter, often supported the functioning old guard, as is evident from his continuing support for Sampurnanand (the Chief Minister of Uttar Pradesh from 1955 to 1961) throughout 1958 when his leadership was challenged by a faction in the state congress; it was in fact one of the rare occasions when Nehru went so far as to ask the opponents to resign from the state cabinet.[19] The state cabinets, like the Union Cabinet, were almost entirely manned by rightists – men of the upper castes (of the sixteen chief ministers between 1947 and 1964, nine were Brahmins) who had vested interests in the preservation of the *status quo*; so much so, indeed, that they succeeded in delaying or staving off certain proposals for agrarian reforms which Nehru himself supported.

Nehru's parleys, between 1952 and 1953, with the leaders of the Praja-Socialist Party (Jayaprakash Narayan, J. B. Kripalani, Narendra Deo) for coalition government at all levels were yet another manifestation of his desire to have his old comrades with him, in the hope, no doubt, that their co-operation would further strengthen the stability of the Government and advance the cause of national integration. Nehru advanced two main reasons for seeking the co-operation of the Praja-Socialist Party.[20] It was the only opposition party ideologically at all similar to Congress, the other two – the Communist Party and Jan Sangh – being reactionary and alien to the Indian setting. In addition, the Praja-Socialist Party contained several old friends and colleagues who were tried soldiers of the national movement. The second reason was the more important to Nehru. Negotiations broke down in March 1953, as the conditions for co-operation demanded by the socialist leaders were unacceptable to Congress. The Praja-Socialist Party was weakened in subsequent years owing to conflicts of leadership within its ranks and also because Congress adopted in 1954, at Nehru's instance, a socialist programme. The Praja-Socialist Party became split, with R. M. Lohia as leader of the breakaway faction. The more the Party disintegrated the more fierce its leaders became in their criticism of the Congress Government.

Nehru never attacked the socialists as severely as he attacked the communalists and communists, however. He sympathised with the socialists' extreme frustration and anger with a world that would not listen to them.[21] He retained his regard for some of them despite all political differences. Even when Narayan became a Gandhian constructive worker, joined Vinoba Bhave's movement and increased the anti-Congress orientation of the constructive workers, and the tension between what Nehru called 'the so called successors of Gandhi' and the Congress Government mounted, as in 1958, Nehru did not bear down on him; he merely wrote to him privately, mildly protesting against his woolly ideas.[22]

The same considerations which urged Nehru to seek co-operation from his socialist friends strengthened him in waging war against the communists and communalists. He considered both ideologies as reactionary and alien to India. Both were threats to the continuity and stability of parliamentary democracy in India. As for the communalists, 'They are neither in the past nor in the present and they are hung in mid-air. India tolerates everybody and everything including madmen, and they also exist and carry on.'[23]

He concentrated his attack during this period on the communists, who had gained some ground in the first general election of 1951–2 and since then appeared to be steadily gaining strength in some parts of south India – Travancore-Cochin and Andhra. Travancore (which in 1957 was reconstituted into the state of Kerala under the States Reorganisation Scheme) had the highest literacy rate in India and also a large army of educated unemployed. It was the most fertile state in which communism could breed. The Congress organisation in the state was of recent growth (because the area formed a part of princely India until 1947) and it was weak and corrupt. Thus, when a Congress government fell out following a vote of no confidence and fresh elections were held in 1954, Congress, in spite of Nehru's five-day election campaign in the state, received a setback and the communists gained. From then on Nehru became more vigorous in his attack on the communists. He ignored the élites and directly appealed to the masses: communism, he pointed out, was based on violence, and even Russia, which had paid an enormous price in violence, might, if given a chance, refrain from choosing such a course again. The so-called revolution of the Indian communists, he argued, consisted not in an application of intelligence but in trying to find out what was happening in Russia and China, and trying to copy it, whether it fitted the present state of India or not.[24] The communists, he declared, were as rigid as the old religious bigots, and since he had always refused to bow to bigotry he refused to bow to the bigotry of this new religion. Communism was out of date.[25]

The next occasion (after Congress reverses in the Travancore election) for a trial of strength between Nehru and the communists arose in 1955, during the state election in Andhra Pradesh. The communists seemed to be strongest in Andhra since the creation of that state in 1953; they held forty-one seats in the state legislature against Congress's forty. With the co-operation of the Praja-Socialist Party a Congress government functioned precariously for over a year and was then brought down. Fresh elections were held in February 1955. Most Indians predicted a communist victory and the emergence for the first time of a communist government in an Indian state. As if to make matters worse, a distinguished London journalist Kingsley Martin, while touring India at this time, made a speech in which he supported the communists of Andhra and criticised Congress for having done nothing for the poor peasants of the state. His speech was fully publicised by a communist newspaper in Andhra. Nehru was annoyed and conveyed his mild protestations to Martin through the Indian High Commissioner in London.[26] Nehru would not normally have taken much notice of an event of this kind but he did so on this occasion because he believed (and his belief was strongly shared by Anthony Eden, who visited India in March 1955 as Britain's Foreign Secretary) that the Andhra election 'was an event of greater world importance than anything else that had happened recently'.[27] The results of the election were calculated to have a powerful effect not only on the future of the Communist Party in India but in other countries also, notably the

United States. With the stakes being so high, Congress poured money and men into its election campaign. The result was a spectacular Congress victory; it won 119 of the 196 seats, the communists securing only 15 seats. Nehru rejoiced in the victory:

> There could be no more smashing defeat for the communists in an area which they had nursed for years and where their organization was far the best. They had hoped to get a majority there to form a Government. The Congress organization, on the other hand, was almost non-existent. The voters nevertheless voted solidly for the Congress and even more so voted solidly against the communists. In fact the feeling against the communists was stronger than the positive feeling for the Congress.[28]

The confidence Nehru gathered against the communists at the Andhra elections was by no means dented by the result of India's second general election, held between 25 February and 14 March 1957. The communists gained Kerala, raised their strength in the Bengal legislature, increased their number in Parliament from 16 to 29, and gained 9.8 per cent of the total votes cast – nearly double what they had secured at the first general election. To an election analyst these figures might mean a slow but steady advance of the communist force in India but to Nehru they meant no such thing. Congress gains at the election were so resounding as to make its losses fractional. Congress raised its share of the total votes from 42 to 46.5 per cent; it secured 365 of the total 500 seats in Parliament; it retained power in all the states of the Indian union except Kerala. Furthermore, the additional gains made by the communists did not seem so alarming to Nehru when they were set against the total of 193 million electors – an increase of 20 million over the 1951 electoral roll of 173 million. As for the communists coming into power in Kerala (a novelty for them to be put in power through democratic elections), Nehru maintained that it was not the Communist Party that won the election in that state but rather the Congress Party that lost it.[29] He believed that the voters had reacted against the weakness and corruption of the Congress organisation in Kerala in voting for the communists. As far as he was concerned the communists had made no advance and they occupied the same position in 1957 as they did in 1952. He disputed, perhaps rightly, that the visit of the Russian leaders in the winter of 1955 might have in some measure popularised the communist movement in India. This visit, in his calculations, should have had an adverse effect on the communist movement in India, for did not the Russian leaders admire and approve of almost everything he and the Indian Government stood for?

Nehru was also gratified to notice that the election did not boost the communalists either. The Jan Sangh (whose leader S. P. Mookerjee had died in the summer of 1953 while agitating for the fuller integration of Jammu and Kashmir in the Indian union) increased its strength in Parliament from three (reduced to two after Mookerjee's death) to four, and in the state assemblies from 35 to 46. His old socialist comrades in the Praja-Socialist Party lost all along the line. It was the only national party whose share of the national poll declined, from 16.4 per cent (1952) to 10 per cent.

Just before the election Narayan had asked Nehru to build up a strong opposition – a curious request, somewhat reminiscent of an episode in the Mahabharata epic in which an indestructible, but honest, warrior is asked by his enemies how he could be destroyed. But in view of Nehru's national stature – which had by 1957 become as overshadowing as a banyan tree, so that nothing underneath, not even a sapling of opposition, could grow – Narayan's request was not curious. Nehru had come to be regarded as standing above party politics. He was identified with the national interest. Narayan merely pleaded that it was in the national interest, in the interest of parliamentary democracy, that a strong opposition party capable of forming an alternative government should be built up in India. In the absence of a strong opposition, and in the event of Nehru's death, it was feared that the Indian system might collapse. Nehru's reply was also based on the national interest: too many opposition parties, he argued, would make the Government unstable:

> Suppose in Parliament, instead of the strong Congress Party, we had a dozen or twenty small groups with nobody in a majority. What would happen? There would be no stable

> government, and each little group would intrigue with the other. There would be offers of ministerships for people who gave up a party to join another.[30]

And, even if he wanted to, how could he unite all the opposition groups into a single party? Besides, how many of the opposition leaders thought of 'such a thing as India and the good of India'?[31] The dialogue ended. The unanswered questions – what after Nehru? who after Nehru? – began to haunt many minds. Even Nehru, though publicly denouncing such questions as meaningless, began privately to brood over them sometimes guiltily and in the same manner as Gandhi formerly contemplated his indispensability and the usefulness of his withdrawal from institutional politics.

Nehru had first talked of resigning in 1954, then again in 1956 and once again in 1957, but his last 'resignation speech', delivered to the nation on 29 April 1958, was rather more serious and sincere, designed to seek assurance from the people at large that he was not clinging to power. It was by no means a desperate attempt on his part to relieve himself of responsibility; he sought only popular justification for his remaining in power. Above all he wanted to prove to himself that it was not he who, by acquiring more and more power, had made himself indispensable to the nation. He wanted also to dispel any false image of himself which might have found currency in the international market and according to which he, like other statesmen, had lustfully entrenched himself in the citadel of power. He believed he was different from his counterparts elsewhere. Indeed only he could confidently indulge in this exercise of self-renunciation, for he knew very well that his people and his party would never let him renounce office; his was a unique case, for even most of his opponents from the opposition parties of India wanted him to remain in office as India's custodian of power, as indeed he virtually was.

On each occasion Nehru's talk of resignation led to national confirmation of his leadership. What made him seek this assurance from time to time? Rather than accepting Nehru's own reasons, which tended to be non-specific and repetitive, it might be helpful to consider the circumstances in which his statements were made. On 11 October 1954, Nehru suggested resigning in a letter to all chief ministers and presidents of state congresses – just eight days before he was to visit communist China. In this statement he said that he felt stale and wanted to opt out temporarily and devote his time to reading and thinking.[32] He said also that his temporary retirement might resolve the question – who after Nehru? He did not make a positive offer to resign from the prime ministership but expressed his ardent desire to lay down the Congress presidency. It is most unlikely that China did not figure in his mind when he was, as he put it, just thinking aloud about relinquishing his office. The other circumstance which might have had some significance in relation to the timing of his statement was the grant of American military aid to Pakistan, which had been announced in February. President Eisenhower's offer to give similar aid to India had, of course, been rejected by Nehru. At the same time Nehru remained firm against internal pressure to increase the strength of India's defence forces. He thus seemed to stand alone, perhaps, as the Chinese and Americans might have conjectured, against the wishes of his own people and party. Nehru would particularly have wished the Chinese leaders to realise that he was not just a bourgeois right-wing leader, as they had earlier taken him to be, but that he had the whole nation of peasants and workers firmly behind him.

These considerations, together with the fact that in October he was physically ill and mentally depressed (a circumstance to which he did not admit in his statement of 11 October), might have urged him to seek national affirmation of his leadership. While he was in China (18–30 October) the Indian newspapers expressed general apprehension of the national tragedy that would follow if Nehru retired. On 8 November 1954 the Congress Working Committee unanimously appealed to Nehru (who had by now returned from China) not to resign from the prime ministership. He was, however, allowed to relinquish the Congress presidency, which was offered to U. N. Dhebar, then the Chief Minister of Saurashtra.

Precisely two years afterwards, on 18 October 1956, while addressing a conference in Uttar Pradesh, Nehru again expressed his wish to retire, but this was a casual remark which made little stir. Again in 1957, soon after the election, he impulsively threatened to resign when manœuvred by the rightists, much against his wish, into letting Rajendra Prasad continue for a second term as President of India. He wanted S. Radhakrishnan, the Vice-President since 1952, to succeed Prasad. But his last gesture of 29 April 1958 was the result of much real heart-searching, inner conflict, and the consciousness of a general malaise.

The gesture stemmed mainly from a sense of loneliness and a feeling that he was fast ceasing to be dynamic and useful. In 1958 he was in the seventieth year of his life. He had been in the Government for eleven and a half years. The longer the life at the top, the lonelier it became. He felt this more in 1958 because it was a relatively complacent year for himself and for the country. Much had been achieved in the preceding years. The year 1958 offered no challenge, on either the national or the international level; life seemed placid and dull. Nehru had plenty of time to think, and felt a growing contempt for the vulgarity, jobbery and pettiness which surrounded him.[33] The power of office lost its fascination for him; he longed for the kind of glory Gandhi had achieved in his lifetime, but saw no clear path towards this end. In his statement of 29 April he rather vaguely suggested that if relieved from office he could do constructive work in restoring world peace. But this was wishful thinking. Neither Congress nor the country would let him retire. He was told he was indispensable. The nation, in rejecting his request, restored in him a sense of purpose and of his own selflessness. On 3 May he bowed to his people's wishes, and three days later he wrote to a colleague challenging the claim occasionally made by the constructive workers, including J. P. Narayan, that they were the only true disciples of Gandhi.[34] He then went on holiday to Manali, a hill resort in the Kulu Valley, where he read books and articles on the economics of underdeveloped countries (including some articles by Gunnar Myrdal and D. R. Gadgil). From these readings he found support for some of his own views, one of them being: 'India's 1st and 2nd Five Year Plans – truly a pioneering effort – are an attempt to do a totally new thing in history.'[35]

Though Nehru's faith in India's planned economy was

never seriously shaken, the cumulative effect on the country of natural calamities (floods, drought, hailstorms) which had occurred during 1956–7 and the explosive growth in population (from about 361 million in 1951 to 438 million in 1961) had temporarily depressed him in the early months of 1958, and he became deeply concerned about India's rate of progress and the question of whether the steadily increasing gap between the richer and poorer countries of the world would ever be bridged.[36] This question led to another: would India's mixed economic system ever deliver the goods? It was a subject of constant unofficial debate among the economists and politicians of India. In times of distress, as in 1958, many eyes would turn hopefully to China and the Soviet Union and the idea of total planning. Partial planning appeared to be full of contradictions; based as it was on consent, incentives, disincentives (taxation) and controls (licences), it gave full operational scope neither to private nor to public enterprise. Such an economy, some argued, was bound to move at a snail's pace, and would move more slowly in India than elsewhere because of the country's peculiar conditions. Some felt that only Chinese totalitarianism, based on coercion, could save India from the malaise of poverty. This view did not, however, gain any marked ascendancy during this period; nor did the opposite view that India should completely discard planning because it was inconsistent with democracy.

During 1952–8 this central issue – whether to adopt total planning or unrestricted free enterprise – was never publicly raised. Nehru, however, frequently referred to the subject in order to ensure that public confidence in the mixed economy which India had so enthusiastically adopted was not damaged in any way. Time and again he condemned economic totalitarianism as inevitably leading towards political absolutism. India had accepted the democratic process because she attached great value to individual freedom:

> We do want high standards of living, but not at the cost of man's creative spirit, his creative energy, his spirit of adventure; not at the cost of all those fine things of life which have ennobled man throughout the ages. Democracy is not merely a question of elections.[37]

Besides, a revolution of the Chinese type would not bring instant prosperity. It had taken the Soviet Union over thirty-five years, and would take China over twenty years (as he was told by Mao himself), to achieve some kind of socialism.[38] As to the communist argument that a mixed economy was full of contradictions, he argued that the communist system itself was no exception. The communist system, for example, encouraged education on the one hand, and suppressed freedom on the other, yet the spread of education was itself a tremendous liberating force which ultimately would not tolerate that suppression of freedom.[39] Communism had become associated with violence, and violence, by encouraging the evil tendency in human beings, had tainted the very idea for which communism stood – a clear example of how means distorted ends.[40] How to attain an adequate rate of economic development without sacrificing democracy was India's major problem. And this problem, Nehru emphasised, could only be resolved by planning. Planning alone would bridge the gap between India and the developed countries. Indian planning, he maintained, was consistent with democracy. India's Second Five-year Plan, he proudly pointed out, was the most balanced effort in planning, and India's Community Development Programme was a novel experiment in world history.

Nehru genuinely believed in his public statements. The Chinese challenge had to be met in traditional Indian style. In ancient India, when Buddhism challenged Hinduism, the latter met the challenge by adopting many of the Buddhist tenets and even Buddha as one of the Hindu gods. Perhaps in the same manner Nehru reacted to the ideological challenge China posed. He adopted for India a socialist pattern of society; Congress endorsed it officially in Avadi in January 1955 during its annual session. The image thus created was that India was heading towards the same goal as China but not necessarily in the same manner. Though there was to be in India growing public control over means of production and distribution, private enterprise was not to be entirely banished nor would destruction, coercion and confiscation play any role in the mobilisation of natural resources. India was to apply its own peaceful methods and to have its own brand of revolution – revolution by consent. But this was not enough. For further protection against the Chinese challenge the Indian system must produce results.

Though conscious of the fact that the Indian system, based as it was on reconciliation and not on total mobilisation, would not match the Chinese in speed, Nehru was nonetheless anxious to set as fast a pace for the Indian model as was possible. A year of careful groundwork, beginning on 17 March 1955, when the Plan-Frame was prepared by Nehru's economic adviser P. C. Mahalanobis, resulted in the final draft of the Second Five-year Plan in March 1956. The Plan estimated a government expenditure of £3600 million (Rs. 4800 crores or more than $10 billion), and private investment of nearly half that amount. With this enormous outlay, nearly double that of the First Five-year Plan, the planners intended to achieve by 1961 a twenty-five-percent increase in national income; rapid industrialisation, with particular emphasis on the development of basic and heavy industries; a large expansion of employment opportunities (ten million new non-agricultural employment opportunities were to be created in commerce and industry); and reduction of inequalities in income and wealth and a more even distribution of economic power. The main emphasis of the Second Plan was on industrialisation and the expansion of state enterprise. Though the three categories of industry, as originally defined by the Industrial Policy Resolution of 1948 (see page 317), were retained under the second Industrial Policy Resolution of April 1956, eleven more heavy industries were included in the public sector. In addition, state enterprise was given priority over private enterprise in the mixed sector and was also granted the option to build and run industries even in the private sector, thus invading what till then had remained the exclusive domain of private enterprise. Nehru's sense of urgency was satisfied. He believed that the further expansion of state ownership, which the Plan envisaged, would lead to rapid industrialisation and keep India industrially ahead of China.[41]

To orthodox Gandhians, who frowned at this craze for industrialisation, Nehru argued that 'without the big factory' and all that it represented India could not even maintain her independence.[42] Besides, there was plenty of room in the Second Plan for the cottage industries which were to produce cheap consumer goods during the plan period. To private industrialists and right-wingers, who were slightly alarmed by what seemed to be India's sudden turn towards socialism, Nehru gave the assurance that private enterprise would play a full, though regulated, role in the economy of the country. As it turned out, the measure of nationalisation which the Government carried out during the Plan period hardly touched the industries in the private sector. The nationalisation of the Imperial Bank of India in 1955, of the life insurance companies in 1956, of the civil airlines (which had been acquired by the State in 1953) and of the Kolar goldfields in no way ruffled the private industrialists, who continued to run the bulk of Indian industry. Besides, all land, upon which over seventy-five per cent of the Indian people depended for a livelihood, remained privately owned.

Nehru's optimism derived additional support from the Community Development Programme which had been operating since 2 October 1952. Indeed he considered this programme the most effective weapon in his armoury with which to confront the communist challenge. If India should be the chief testing-ground for democracy and if she were to succeed in demonstrating to Asia and to the world that men could have bread and freedom too, then the programme, he declared, was India's main hope. Paradoxically, the programme had a Chinese connection: it was first suggested to Nehru in 1952 by Chester Bowles (the American ambassador to India), who had himself borrowed the idea from one James Y. C. Yen who, in turn, had successfully experimented with it in Chiang Kai-shek's China.[43] It was a programme to rejuvenate the long-dormant peasantry of India, who constituted eighty-two per cent of the population and lived in India's 600,000 villages; to teach them self-help; and to mobilise their energy in changing the centuries-old face of rural India. This was to be achieved by persuasion. Village India was to be organised in blocks, each block consisting of a hundred villages. Government officers and agrarian specialists were made available at all levels within each block to guide and coach the villagers in the formulation of their needs (health clinics, schools, new roads, new methods of cultivation, new seeds) and in pooling their efforts and resources in co-operatives. About four per cent of the total outlay in the first and second plans was set aside for the programme. By the end of the Second Plan period the programme was to cover the whole of rural India; this target, like the others, was not fully achieved by the end of 1961, mainly because of lack of money.

The success of India's 'revolution by consent' depended on foreign aid; on the efficiency of the Indian bureaucracy; and on the co-operation of politicians at all levels. The Second Five-year Plan depended upon much larger imports of capital goods and equipment from abroad than previously. Thus foreign currencies were required for purchases abroad. India's foreign-exchange reserves bore the burden for the first year and then began to sink. In the ensuing exchange crisis India made severe cuts in imports of consumer goods and facilities for travel abroad. But the savings arising out of these cuts were not enough to keep the Plan going. She thus appealed for foreign assistance. Foreign aid began pouring in from all directions, from the World Bank and its Aid India Consortium, from America, Russia, Britain, Canada, Australia, New Zealand, West Germany and Japan. In spite of Nehru's independent foreign policy, which ruffled the Americans throughout this period, the United States became the largest individual donor. Even this aid could not fully bridge India's foreign-exchange gap, and the Plan had to be pruned in the latter part of 1958.

The nature and style of Indian bureaucracy were held responsible for delays in the implementation of the Plan and the Community Development Programme. Nehru was amused to notice that both the Russians and Americans spoke with one voice in their criticism of Indian bureaucracy. Being based on checks and counterchecks and miserably lacking in initiative and imagination, the administrative machinery seemed to them outrageously slow. This was so, Dr Paul Appleby of New York State explained, because its framework was inherited from the British. It needed an over-all change. Besides, the Indian bureaucracy was corrupt from the bottom upwards. Nehru was aware of this: 'The biggest factor that leads to corruption is delay. The moment you give an officer a chance to delay matters, he can extort money in order to do something. Therefore, a method should be evolved which makes delay impossible.'[44] But no effective method was evolved. Nehru's general theme that the more public servants worked in the open the less the chances of corruption did not find a practical form. Nehru had no stomach for drastic changes; he was afraid of breaking the link of continuity. A certain measure of decentralisation which he carried out at top level did not have any impact on the character of the bureaucracy.[45]

The responsibility for the delay in land reforms might be laid generally at the feet of the politicians and particularly the chief ministers of states. The chief ministers had come to play an important role in national planning and its implementation. Together with the Prime Minister and members of the Planning Commission, they formed the National Development Council which had been established in August 1952. It was this Council which supervised the making of the Plan and its implementation. The majority of chief ministers and the majority of ministers in the state cabinets were right-wingers. They went along slowly, cautiously, sometimes obstructively, with land reforms. Although by 1961 India had succeeded in reforming land tenures, reducing state rents and imposing a ceiling on land holdings, it had failed to introduce one vital reform – the consolidation of land and the introduction of co-operative farming – without which there could be no appreciable increase in agricultural production. Fragmentation of individual land holdings was India's worst agrarian feature, for it made inapplicable the improved means of production. The peasants were generally opposed to consolidation and collectivisation, but they would have yielded had not their cause been taken up by right-wing politicians in cabinets and party meetings. Nehru's dream of securing the participation of the whole nation in the Plan and Programme was not fully realised, but he was not disheartened. He realised that progress via democratic planning was a long process and required a considerable amount of training and persuasion. For his own part, he continued coaching his chief ministers, through his fortnightly letters, and often referred them to a recently published book or article, few of which they ever read![46]

In spite of various setbacks the Second Five-year Plan reached a great number of its targets. There was increased production on all fronts, but perhaps the most impressive results were recorded in the industrial sector, where by the end of the plan period the output of steel ingots and pig iron had increased nearly three times, and work on three steel works – built with British, Russian and West German collaboration at Durgapur, Bhilai and Rourkela – had been greatly accelerated.

Nehru sincerely believed that the success of the Indian experiment – in planned development and in parliamentary democracy – depended on world peace. Peace was for him not just a fervent hope but a necessity. His foreign policy was thus geared towards the preservation of peace. How could war be avoided? His answer was simple:

> There are only two ways of approaching the problem of international relations. One is the conviction that, even though we try to avoid it, war is bound to come. Therefore, we should prepare for it and when it comes, join this party or that. The other way starts with the feeling that war can be avoided.[47]

The psychological approach to the problem was for him most essential, but he realised that he could not easily persuade the Russians and Americans to share his conviction, for they were presently consumed with mutual hatred and fear and their minds were clogged.[48] He had no shadow of doubt that the more they came to know each other the more tolerant they would become towards each other. His policy was thus to continue on the one hand to bring the power blocs closer to each other and on the other to keep on widening the area of peace.

The first object he tried to achieve by acting as mediator between the super-powers and by explaining one to the other. The second he, in some measure, succeeded in achieving by enlarging the group of non-aligned nations. As a result this period witnessed the emergence of a 'third world' or 'third force'. Nehru preferred to call it a 'third area', an area which did not want war, worked for peace and believed in co-operation.[49] He tried to avoid the role of sponsor or leader of this 'third world', for he feared this might not only antagonise the Western world but would also create rivalries for leadership among the non-aligned nations. This was at the back of his mind when in 1953 he rejected the Iraqi Prime Minister's proposal that India should convene at New Delhi an Afro-Asian conference. He argued that the conference would lose all significance if India were to convene it.

> India at present is not *persona grata* with either the European Western Powers or America who accuse India of far-reaching designs. If we convene a conference, it will mean to them that we are merely trying to extend our influence.[50]

Nonetheless, he remained convinced that the Indian example was the best for the Afro-Asian nations to follow and that India was well qualified to be the leader of the Third World. As he increased in stature during this period, Nehru came to be acclaimed as the most distinguished statesman in the world, the leader of the Third Force – or simply the leader of Asia, as the Syrians called him when he visited Damascus in June 1957.[51]

Peace in Asia was of immediate relevance to India, and it was the Asian peace which was most threatened during this period by the rise of internal communist forces in many Asian countries – a phenomenon which in turn drew the Americans and then the Russians on to the Asian stage. In this Asian drama Nehru played many roles, but principally those of mitigator of fear of communism among the Asian nations, a peace-maker between the two power blocs, and a proud and sensitive nationalist. He maintained a unique ideological consistency between his different roles but when there arose a conflict he chose, sometimes reluctantly, to act in India's national interest.

In assuaging the fear of communist expansion, which tormented the minds of the newly independent nations of Asia, Nehru played a complex and difficult role. The source of fear was communist China, and at the beginning of this period all speculations about China's future designs were shrouded in uncertainty. China – being Asia's first and the world's second most powerful communist power, and being committed as she was to the international spread of communism – aroused many apprehensions in the minds of Asian nationalists. Those countries bordering on China feared direct Chinese expansion and infiltration, and others feared that China might use the Chinese residents or the local communists to overthrow their so-called bourgeois nationalist governments. By 1952, Nehru's policy of befriending and containing China seemed not to have yielded any practical results. The Chinese invasion of Tibet in 1950 had, in fact, intensified fear of China among the countries of South and South-East Asia. Nehru himself was apprehensive of China in the early 1950s. In March 1952, while briefing Indian intelligence officers, Nehru pointed out that China considered India as the biggest obstacle in her struggle for supremacy in Asia.[52] By proving her superiority over India in the political and economic fields China would attempt to establish her influence over the whole of Asia.

Nehru in fact never dispelled from his mind the fear of China. Even after having inaugurated, jointly with Chou En-lai, the era of Indo-Chinese brotherhood in the summer of 1954, Nehru advised his colleagues to avoid complacency because in international affairs 'one can never be dead certain and the friends of today might be enemies of tomorrow'.[53] This lingering suspicion of China, however, never lessened his conviction that a confrontation or war with China could be avoided. Besides, an abandonment of the policy of what he called collective peace (as opposed to Foster Dulles's policy of collective security), which Nehru had been vigorously pursuing since 1949, would have brought him into conflict with his role as the world's most avowed peace-maker, demolished the ideological base of his foreign policy and demoralised him. He was essentially a man of peace and there was no pressing need for him to change his style, especially when his policy of containing communism by befriending China and Russia had come, in the years 1954–5, to yield practical results for the whole of Asia.

Nehru's policy yielded its first dividend in 1954 when the Sino-Indian Trade Agreement was signed in Peking on 29 April and was followed by the Chou–Nehru joint statement on co-existence, made in New Delhi on 28 June. The immediate background to this Sino-Indian agreement was the Geneva Conference (16 June–21 July 1954) of nine powers assembled to resolve the problem of Indo-China and to bring to an end the nine years' war in that region. France's persistent efforts to maintain her colonial stronghold over Indo-China (Laos, Cambodia and Vietnam) had been finally frustrated on 7 May 1954, when Ho Chi Minh's Viet Minh forces inflicted a disastrous defeat on the French at Dien Bien Phu. At the Geneva Conference, France was therefore reconciled to the inevitability of withdrawal from Indo-China. But French withdrawal meant leaving North Vietnam under Ho's Communist Democratic Republic – a proposition which was most distasteful to America's Secretary of State, Dulles, and Vice-President Nixon. While the partition of Vietnam seemed imminent, America's efforts were thus concentrated on thrashing out a collective-security plan for South-East Asia – a plan which could effectively stop any further expansion of communism in Asia, particularly in Vietnam from the north to the south. Nehru's main objective was also to contain communism. But he wanted to insulate the whole of Indo-China against any intervention either from America or China and thereby to include the whole region in the area of peace. Nehru feared that American intervention in Indo-China would draw the Chinese into the arena and that the Korean story would repeat itself in yet another part of Asia. He was prepared to accept communist rule in North Vietnam in preference to the possibility of a super-power confrontation in the region. In fact he was more anxious to see that the French withdrew from, and the Americans did not intervene in, Indo-China than to estimate the consequences of such events.

On 20 April, in Washington, Dulles met the ambassadors of Great Britain, Australia, New Zealand, France, the Philippines, Thailand, South Vietnam, Laos and Cambodia to study the collective defence of South-East Asia. On 28 April, at Colombo, Nehru met the prime ministers of Indonesia, Ceylon, Burma and Pakistan (who, together with India, formed the Colombo Plan Powers) and put forth his six-point plan for the solution of the Indo-Chinese problem. The plan included a call for a ceasefire, for the complete independence of Indo-China, and for an agreement between Russia, America, China and Britain that none of them would intervene in Indo-China. The Colombo Powers endorsed Nehru's six-point proposal. Nehru's plan and the work of his emissary Krishna Menon (who lobbied every party involved in the conference) had an important influence on the agreement finally reached at Geneva. The Geneva settlement recognised the independence of Laos, Cambodia and Vietnam. Vietnam was to remain temporarily divided: the region north of the 17th Parallel was to remain under Ho Chi Minh's Democratic Republic and the southern area would come under Bao Dai's administration. The principle of Vietnamese unity was recognised, and provisions were laid down for a free and secret election to be held in both regions after two years. To supervise the ceasefire, the exchange of prisoners and other related matters, an International Control Commission, consisting of India, Canada and Poland, with India presiding, was established.

The Geneva settlement was regarded by Nehru as a memorable event in history, one in which he saw united Asian opinion tipping the scales in favour of peace.[54] But, most important, the Geneva Conference brought India and China closer together, and Nehru took this opportunity to lessen the fear of Red China that had been haunting the minds of Asian leaders. While Nehru was in Colombo and Chou En-lai in Geneva, the representatives of India and China signed in Peking an agreement on trade and intercourse between the Tibet region of China and India. Apart from providing for trade, travel and pilgrimage facilities between India and Tibet, the agreement laid down the five principles (which later came to be called the Panch Sheel) which were to govern the relationship of the two countries. These were:

1. mutual respect for each other's territorial integrity and sovereignty,
2. mutual non-aggression,
3. mutual non-interference in each other's internal affairs,
4. equality and mutual benefit, and
5. peaceful co-existence.

This agreement gave great satisfaction to Nehru, for he saw in it not only the preservation of the old Indo-Tibetan trade-link but also an unequivocal assurance on the part of China not to interfere in any manner in the internal affairs of India.

Both prime ministers congratulated each other, and Nehru invited Chou to visit India. Chou arrived in Delhi on 25 June in an Indian aircraft which Nehru had sent to Geneva to fetch the Chinese Prime Minister and his party. It was Chou's first visit to India and his first meeting with Nehru. Both had certain features in common: an aristocratic family background (though Chou preferred to call his a bankrupt mandarin family) and great personal charm. But there were differences in their age, educational background and outlook. Chou was ten years younger than Nehru; he had spent some of his most formative years in France. Unlike Nehru, Chou had no personal fondness for continuity; he was cool, logical and calculating, and could be much more ruthless than Nehru. Strangely enough Chou's qualities were shared more by Nehru's daughter Mrs Indira Gandhi, who also had more French than English influence in her educational and cultural upbringing.

However, in the summer of 1954 Chou En-lai was equally anxious to strike a non-aggression pact with India. He had as good reason to be apprehensive of Indian aggression in Tibet as Nehru of Chinese intervention in South and South-East Asia. China's hold on Tibet was still not secure. Roads were being constructed to gain access to the heartland of Tibet from all directions – from the north-east, east and west; but until these roads were completed China was virtually dependent on India for transporting military supplies into Tibet through the port of Calcutta. The Chinese had begun work on the motor highway from Yarkand (in Sinkiang) to Gartok (in western Tibet) but this was not to be completed until the end of 1956. Then there was the fear of American aggression against China. John Foster Dulles was busy formulating his plan for the collective security of South and South-East Asia. Nehru alone stood against American intervention in Asia, and it would have taken very little imagination on Chou's part to realise that in Nehru's plan of collective peace lay China's immediate security. Asian nationalism and Sino-Chinese joint leadership of Asia figured prominently in the historic Nehru–Chou meeting.

While the peace of Asia was still threatened, Chou declared in one of his public speeches, the friendship of 960 million people of India and China constituted a mighty force for maintaining peace in Asia and the world.[55] Nehru thus had no difficulty in persuading Chou to abide by the five principles in China's relations with the other countries of Asia. In their joint statement of 28 June the prime ministers declared that those principles should be applied in their relations with other countries in Asia as well as in other parts of the world. Thus, the Nehru–Chou statement marked the beginning of an era of peaceful co-existence. After the conclusion of his three-day visit to India, and on his way back to Peking, Chou En-lai visited Burma. Like India, Burma too had undefined borders with China. It was thus a great relief to U Nu, Prime Minister of Burma when, on 29 June, the Chinese Prime Minister affirmed that the relationship between the two countries was to be governed by the five principles. Furthermore, Chou En-lai persuaded Ho Chi Minh to withdraw his forces from Laos and Cambodia by pointing out that Indian and Asian opinion would be adverse to the Viet Minh's aggressive infiltration into those territories.

Containment of China, the resurgence of Asia, solidarity of Afrasia (a term coined by an Egyptian) and the enlargement of the area of collective peace in the world – these were Nehru's main concerns in the years 1954–5.[56] Did he, as a consequence of his preoccupation with these ideals, pay less attention than he ought to India's national interest, particularly to India's border problem with China, which Patel had emphasised just before his death in 1950? It was certainly characteristic of Nehru to avoid talking about and publicly taking notice of the problem which bothered him most. But his reason for not discussing the border problem with Chou in the summer of 1954 was quite simply that he did not consider there was any problem. During the negotiations carried on between Indian and Chinese representatives in Peking and concluded by the Sino-Indian Agreement of 29 April 1954, the Indian delegation had insisted time and again that all questions pending between the two countries (by which was implied the border question) should be settled then and there. The Chinese delegation, by declining to discuss any issue which was not ripe for settlement – thus implying that there were no questions pending between the two countries – led the Indians to conclude that there was no border problem. By remaining vaguely noncommittal, the Chinese were on the one hand trying to preserve their interest by keeping the question open and on the other avoiding provoking India at a time when their position in Tibet was precarious.

Nehru thus had no doubt that India's border with China, particularly the McMahon Line, was a settled fact. In July 1954, soon after Chou En-lai's departure from India, he directed the officials of the Defence and External Affairs ministries to consider India's northern frontier as a definite fact which was not open to discussion.[57] Between July and October 1954, however, his complacency was slightly disturbed when his attention was drawn to maps recently published in China which gave 'a wrong borderline between the two countries'. But when Nehru mentioned the maps to Chou during his visit to China (18–30 October 1954) Chou assured him that they were reproductions of old maps which had not yet been revised.[58] Chou also assured Nehru that the boundaries between the two countries were quite clear and were not a matter for argument.

In November–December 1956, while visiting India, Chou, on his own initiative, referred to the Sino-Indian border, indicating that, much as he disliked the border being called the McMahon Line, he was quite prepared to recognise this line as demarcating the border not only between India and China but also between China and Burma.[59] Chou's timing in raising the border question again coincided with the near-completion of the Sinkiang–Tibet highway, which ran across the Aksai Chin region of Ladakh and which India claimed as falling within its border with China in the western sector.[60] From this and subsequent evidence it can be reasonably inferred that China was prepared to accept the McMahon Line in the eastern sector in return for the Aksai Chin region in the western sector. However, Chou did not formally reopen the border issue at this time. Nehru considered the matter closed, and had no reason to suspect that for the Chinese the matter was not settled. Thus, when in July 1958 the old Chinese map again appeared, this time in the *China Pictorial*, Nehru was puzzled. How was it possible, he enquired of Chou En-lai in December 1958, that the Chinese Republic, having now been in existence for nine years, had not found time to revise the incorrect maps? The autumn of 1958 marked the end of Sino-Indian brotherhood. A new phase was to begin in January 1959 when Chou formally reopened the entire Sino-Indian boundary question.

Nehru was thus not oblivious to India's national interests while he was playing a major role in international politics. Furthermore, though during this period he derived a fuller sense of security for India from his diplomatic manœuvres, he did not in any way discourage military vigilance on the country's frontiers. In February 1951, soon after Patel's warning, a Committee of North and North-East Border Defence had been appointed to study the problems created by Chinese aggression in Tibet. On the recommendation of this Committee the Indian Government tightened its security in the eastern sector of its border with Tibet (the North-East Frontier Agency area along the McMahon Line),[61] and the Indian protectorates Bhutan and Sikkim were brought under stricter surveillance. Nehru himself paid a visit to these states in September 1958 – two months after the reappearance of the Chinese map which, among other things, showed a considerable region of Bhutan as belonging to China – to assert India's overlordship. The route from Sikkim to Bhutan lay over China's Tibetan territory, and gave Nehru his first glimpse of Tibet. He noticed that the Tibetans were anxious to welcome him but restrained themselves for fear of Chinese reprisals.[62] He also noticed that the Chinese in Tibet kept Peking time, which struck him 'as being rather significant in many ways':[63] he was amused, when at Yatung, to be given an unusually early dinner by his host, a Chinese general – for though it was only 5.30 p.m. local time it was 8 p.m., dinner time, in Peking.

Closer surveillance was also kept on Nepal, though it was an independent country. Sandwiched between India and

Tibet, Nepal was of great strategic significance to both Nehru and Chou En-lai: for Nehru it was a possible source of Chinese infiltration; for Chou it provided a useful base for an American onslaught on China. Nehru's aim was to bring Nepal within the Indian sphere of influence and to keep both the Americans and Chinese out of it. When visiting China in October 1954, Nehru secured Chou's recognition of India's special position with regard to Nepal.[64] India's involvement steadily deepened and Indian troops, money and skill began to pour into Nepal. Chinese links, however, could not be totally excluded. China wanted to keep an eye on Nepal, and there were strong trade links between Nepal and Tibet which must now be put on a new footing. With this in view, China established diplomatic relations with Nepal in 1955, and in September 1956 a Sino-Nepalese agreement on trade and friendship (similar to the Sino-Indian trade agreement of April 1954) was signed. Nehru could not object to these arrangements but his eyebrows were raised when on 7 October 1956 China agreed to give Nepal aid worth sixty million Indian rupees.[65] Even though China did not attach any conditions, and agreed to despatch no technical personnel to Nepal, Indian suspicions were aroused and India's President, Dr Rajendra Prasad, was hurriedly sent to Nepal in the same month to assert his country's special position and to declare that any threat to the peace and security of Nepal was a threat to the peace and security of India. In December of the same year Nehru, while welcoming the Prime Minister of Nepal in New Delhi, repeated that the two countries had an unbreakable bond of history, geography and culture.[66] Obviously these assertions were made to warn off China, a fact which the latter could not have failed to notice, with perhaps a certain amount of annoyance.

In addition to a lingering mutual suspicion and fear – which occasionally erupted, as in the autumn of 1956, and disturbed the face of Sino-Indian brotherhood – the relationship between the two countries was also characterised by a mutual competitiveness. This came to the surface perhaps for the first time at the Afro-Asian conference of twenty-nine nations held at Bandung in Indonesia from 18 to 24 April 1955. The Bandung Conference – proposed by the Indonesian

Prime Minister and sponsored by the five Colombo Powers – was unique in the sense that for the first time in modern history a group of former colonial nations met to discuss their problems and to promote goodwill and solidarity among themselves. Nearly all of Asia, except for the Soviet Union, the two Koreas, New Zealand, Australia, Formosa and Israel, was represented. Most of independent Africa was also represented: Egypt, Ethiopia, the Gold Coast (subsequently Ghana), Liberia, Libya and the Sudan. The holding of the Conference was in itself a grand enterprise (the Colombo Powers were in fact surprised at the enthusiastic response they encountered), and although the Conference did not foster much Afrasian solidarity it did succeed in boosting the reputation of non-aligned nations and in driving out from the Asian mind the fear of communist China.

Nehru expected these results to follow from the Conference. He also hoped that, as a result, Washington and London would realise that the world's affairs, and especially Asian affairs, could no longer 'be disposed of in western parlours, ignoring Asia'.[67] Nehru's mistrust of America had increased since the coming into being on 8 September 1954 of the South-East Asia Collective Defence Treaty (SEATO). This defence pact – concluded at Manila between Britain, America, France, Australia, New Zealand, the Philippines, Pakistan and Thailand – was John Foster Dulles's device to stop any further expansion of communist power in South, South-East and Far-East Asia. This plan for collective security ran counter to Nehru's idea of collective peace. But what annoyed Nehru most was that Dulles had deliberately ignored India in devising this scheme. The Bandung Conference was thus Nehru's rejoinder to America. He hoped that America would realise 'that Thailand and the Philippines', the two South-East Asian members of SEATO, were 'not exactly the standard-bearers of Asia'.[68] The Bandung spirit, Nehru hoped, would not only cast SEATO into limbo but would also show up the hollowness of Anglo-American policy in the Middle East. He was in fact very critical of America's so-called 'northern tier policy', aimed at preventing Russian expansion in the Middle Eastern area.

At the time of the Bandung Conference, the Baghdad Pact

had just come into being. Its beginning was marked by the signing in February 1955 of the Turco-Iraqi Pact and its growth by Britain's accession to it in the first week of April 1955. Its emergence as a five-power security barrier against Soviet expansion in the Middle East was signalled in September–October of the same year when Pakistan and Iran joined it. Linking with NATO in the west and SEATO in the east, the Baghdad Pact was, for Eisenhower's administration, a great achievement. For a variety of reasons America did not join it, but it was America's creation and was blessed from its inception with American money and arms. Not all members of the Pact were, however, beset with fear of Russia. Through membership of the Pact, Britain hoped to protect her oil interests in the Persian Gulf area. Having concluded treaties with Egypt to evacuate the Sudan and the Suez Canal zone (in February 1953 and October 1954 respectively), Britain needed some link with Iraq and Iran to preserve a footing in the Middle East. Pakistan was equally indifferent regarding Russian expansion: she needed American dollars and arms to strengthen her stand against India. Though historically Iran had always been suspicious of Russia, she had customarily sought security in neutrality. But after the fall, in August 1953, of her nationalist prime minister, Dr Muhammad Musaddiq, the Shah had become Western-oriented; seeing how Turkey had immensely benefited from American dollars and arms, he thus opted for the Baghdad Pact.[69] Iraq had a similar motive, though her prime minister, General Nuri al-Said, played at the time on the Russian danger in order to overcome domestic opposition to the country's joining the Baghdad Pact.

Iraq's entry into America's northern-tier alignment disrupted Arab unity against Israel and instantly brought into the Middle Eastern arena a confrontation between Egypt and Syria on the one hand and Iraq, Iran and Turkey on the other, with Jordan and Saudi Arabia as bystanders. Since September 1953, when he came into power, Nasser had been solicited by the Anglo-American bloc to join the Middle East defence system, but he had resisted, in spite of his equally great need for American aid. Nasser became America's problem and Nehru's hope in the Middle East.

The two leaders met in New Delhi, in April 1955, and together went to Bandung. The Baghdad Pact had driven Nasser into Nehru's non-aligned world.

Nehru's opposition to the Baghdad Pact was on both ideological and practical grounds. Military pacts were in no way conducive to peace. Besides, Nehru argued, the very thing the Baghdad Pact was intended to prevent was bound to come about.[70] He also rightly indicated that the Pact had already created disunity and tension in the Arab world. While deploring America's unimaginative and inhibited approach to the security of the free world, he cited the example of Pakistan's involvement in both SEATO and the Baghdad Pact. No sensible person could imagine, he said, that the Pakistan Government entered into these pacts because it expected some imminent or distant invasion from Russia or China. At the same time he was convinced that the American leaders, in providing military aid to Pakistan intended no ill to India: 'They probably did not even think of India in this connection. Their minds were elsewhere, on the northern, western and middle tiers of defence.'[71] Those Asian nations which were allying with the United States, Nehru believed, were doing so solely for economic reasons. Indeed, many Afrasian leaders who visited India assured Nehru that they entirely agreed with India's policies and would like to associate themselves with him, but because of their bad economic situations they had to fall in line with the United States in order to obtain American aid.[72] If India could help them they would gladly change their allegiance.[73]

SEATO and the Baghdad Pact loomed large in the minds of the leaders of the non-aligned world when they met at Bandung. The Afro-Asian conference itself, together with Nehru's vigorous leadership of the non-aligned world and his containment of China (and of the Soviet Union later in the year), could be held responsible in great measure for putting into disuse these military pacts. SEATO was still-born, and the Baghdad Pact collapsed in 1958 when Iraq withdrew from it. In the long run it was Nehru's plan of collective peace and not Dulles's collective security which succeeded in restoring some measure of peace in Asia. But this is not to say that the Anglo-American preparation to resist communist expansion by force might not have made easier Nehru's task of winning China and the Soviet Union over to the cause of peaceful co-existence. But the most important factor, which ushered in a new era in international politics and carried weight first with the Soviet and later with the American bloc, was the resurgence of Afrasia and its new influence in shaping world public opinion. The Bandung Conference marked the beginning of this new era. For Nehru it was the realisation of a long-cherished dream. He saw at Bandung that 'we are the future, in Asia and Africa'.[74] In asserting at the Conference the importance of this new force in the world he maintained: 'We are not copies of Europeans or Americans or Russians. We are Asians and Africans. It would not be creditable for our dignity and new freedom if we were camp-followers of America or Russia or any other country of Europe.'[75]

Bandung thus provided a new experience and belief, shared and cherished by all the participants irrespective of their different creeds, ideologies and alliances. Among the concrete achievements of the Conference, however, was the assurance which Chou En-lai gave, charmingly and convincingly, to the leaders of Asia that China would not intervene in the affairs of any country and would not participate in any subversive activities. He declared that China would strictly adhere to the five principles in her relationship with the countries of Asia, Africa and with all the other countries in the world.[76] Chou virtually dominated the proceedings. His reconciliatory and understanding attitude, which he displayed more often than Nehru in dealing with the delegates of such nations as Pakistan, succeeded in creating, among the Afro-Asian states, a new image of China as a reasonable and peaceful neighbour.

Indeed, India and China represented the two giants of Asia at the Conference. A certain rivalry between the two for the leadership of Afrasia was inevitable. Nehru had on many occasions conceded to China the status of the third great power, after the United States and the Soviet Union, and hoped that India might emerge as the world's fourth great power.[77] But he believed that India was better qualified than China or any other Afrasian power to lead the non-aligned world. The leadership of India meant the leadership of Nehru: at Bandung, Nehru was regarded as the champion of non-alignment and an elder statesman of international distinction. He played this role well but rather patronisingly – a characteristic especially obvious in his dealings with Afrasian leaders. He was admonitory towards the delegates of aligned and Western-oriented countries – Pakistan, Iraq, Turkey, Iran, the Philippines, Thailand and South Vietnam. And, even though he was excessively benevolent and enthusiastic in espousing China's cause, in introducing Chou to the Conference, and in making him acceptable to Nasser and other delegates, and painstakingly concerned that no insult or criticism should be suffered by the Chinese leader at the hands of the delegates of Western-oriented countries, his patronising manner caused some inner resentment even to Chou, who himself wanted to play the role of Big Brother and did not wish to appear dependent on Nehru. Chou read in Nehru's kindness an implication of superiority, and ten years later he was to remark to some visiting politicians that he had never met a more arrogant man than Nehru.[78]

Nehru, however, did not receive any open rebuff from Chou or from any of the delegates of the aligned nations. He received it, rather unexpectedly, from the Ceylonese Prime Minister, Sir John Kotelawala, who interrupted the Bandung chorus of anti-colonialism by launching an attack on another form of colonialism – Russian domination in central and eastern Europe. Chou and Nehru were both agitated, but when Nehru asked John Kotelawala, 'Why did you do that, Sir John? Why did you not show me your speech before you made it?' the Ceylonese Prime Minister rebuffed him with 'Why should I? Do you show me yours before you make it?'[79] Kotelawala's speech created a split at Bandung when the Western-oriented nations (Turkey, Iran, Iraq, Japan, Lebanon, Pakistan, Libya, Liberia, the Sudan and the Philippines) rallied to his side in condemnation of Russian colonialism. Nehru saw in this division a threat to Afrasian solidarity and to the non-aligned world, and in opposing this disruptive trend he made a positive statement to the effect that he regarded the states of central and eastern Europe as independent nations and not as the colonies of the Soviet Union. This must have gratified the Russian leaders – Khrushchev and Bulganin.

Nehru's role at the Bandung Conference was adversely interpreted in Iran, Iraq, Turkey and Pakistan; as reported by the Indian ambassador in Tehran, the Iranian press rejoiced in what it considered to have been the defeat of Nehru at Bandung.[80] Nehru returned to India with no sense of defeat, however, but with an awareness of the challenge which Cold War affiliations presented to the area of peace.[81] In his confidential note on the Conference, which was sent to the chief ministers, he remarked that Turkey, Pakistan, Iran, Lebanon and Iraq were aggressive, but that it was not necessary for India to play an aggressive role or indeed 'to seek the limelight', for the fact remained that the 'two most important countries present at the Bandung Conference were China and India'.[82] This same note, however, also revealed his scarce-concealed anxiety over a possible Chinese challenge to India's leadership, though he did not fail to point out to his chief ministers and ambassadors that Chou En-lai had personally assured him that China had no intention of introducing communism in Tibet, because the latter was an autonomous state.[83]

Nehru's role at the Bandung Conference also strengthened Russia's friendliness towards India which had been growing steadily since the death of Stalin in 1953 and the appointment of Khrushchev as First Secretary of the Communist Party. Finding in Nehru an avowed opponent of the collective defence system, Khrushchev became more confirmed in his view that Russian security lay in befriending the non-aligned nations and in supporting the principle of peaceful co-existence. This new outlook might in some measure have arisen from Khrushchev's realisation that the communist world itself lacked unity. He suspected that Mao, whom Stalin called a 'margarine Marxist', was a staunch nationalist at heart and that he would never accept the Russian lead. On his return to Moscow from a visit to China in 1954, Khrushchev confided in his colleagues that a conflict with China was inevitable.[84] He would rather reconcile a breakaway Tito and befriend a non-aligned Nehru than blindly rely on Comrade Mao, whom the Chinese, to Khrushchev's disgust, had come to regard as a god. The Russian leaders invited Nehru to visit Moscow on his return from China in October 1954, but Nehru preferred to make a separate visit to the Soviet Union. The invitation was renewed and accepted soon after Tito's eighteen-day visit to India in December 1954. Nehru's visit to Russia was thus arranged before the commencement of the Bandung Conference.

By the time Nehru visited the Soviet Union in June 1955 the Russian leaders had already displayed a spirit of co-existence in signing an Austrian Peace Treaty, in agreeing to meet the Western leaders at a summit conference, and in reconciling Yugoslavia. Nehru's visit was a unique event. Never before had the head of a non-communist nation been permitted to address audiences in the Soviet Union, and perhaps never before had an estimated 80–100,000 people assembled in Moscow's Dynamo Stadium to listen to the leader of a foreign country.[85] Every country viewed Nehru's visit to Russia with curiosity, though speculations about the results of his visit varied. It seemed that Nehru's visit might have lifted the Iron Curtain from over Moscow and that a new era was about to begin. Nehru was overwhelmed; though not carried away, as the Americans feared, by his unprecedented reception. The joint communiqué which was issued by the Indian and Soviet leaders was Indian in style and substance. The Soviet leaders agreed with Nehru that states with different social structures could exist side by side in peace and work for the common good, and gave their unflinching support to the principles of co-existence. Nehru boldly maintained that military pacts were not conducive to peace and that he disliked the Cominform as much as he disliked NATO, the Baghdad Pact and SEATO.

Nehru's visit to the Soviet Union marked the beginning of Indo-Soviet brotherhood. But perhaps more important from India's point of view was the visit of the Soviet leaders to India in November–December 1955. Khrushchev and Prime Minister Bulganin visited India for three weeks. They also paid a short visit to Burma, and to Afghanistan on their return journey; Afghanistan was included in their itinerary because Khrushchev wanted to keep it outside the sphere of American influence and had reasons to believe that the

Americans were busy entrenching themselves there.[86] It was, however, the success of their Indian visit which aroused the concern, resentment and even the jealousy of the Anglo-American bloc. The main object of the Soviet leaders was to befriend India and the other non-aligned nations and to use India as a forum for launching their attack on the Baghdad Pact, which was by then completed; Britain, Pakistan and Iran had joined it during the period from April to October 1955. Khrushchev's speeches and statements (often directed against Britain and America, and made to the multitude of the Indian people who at some places, as in Calcutta, gathered in numbers of nearly three million to listen to the Soviet leaders) annoyed the British and the Americans and sometimes caused embarrassment to Nehru. Though Nehru was inclined to believe that Khrushchev had spoken thus more through habit than with any deliberate intention of making propaganda, he did try to restrain the Soviet leaders whenever he found that their speeches had overstepped the mark. But much as he wanted to prevent any misunderstanding developing between India and Britain he could not help noticing that, whereas the Russians treated Indians as equals, the British and American officials and press were scathing and patronising in their interpretation of this historic event. He confided in his sister, who was then Indian High Commissioner in London:

> The visit of Bulganin and Khrushchev has of course been a significant event of some world importance. It is good that other countries are somewhat shaken up by it. People in England and America are very courteous to us and friendly but, in the final analysis, they treat India as a country to be humoured but not as an equal. Indeed the United States hardly treats any other country as an equal. The British Foreign Office of course cannot get out of its old traditions. The world goes on changing and the U.K. and the U.S.A. somehow cannot catch up to it and then blame others.[87]

It was, however, during the second part of their visit that the Soviet leaders made statements which turned out to be of special significance to India and to Indo-Soviet relationships. Kashmir was not included in the original itinerary of the Soviet leaders. It was at the personal invitation of Karan

Singh (the head of the state) that they unexpectedly visited Kashmir, ignoring Pakistan's protestations. And it was in Kashmir, on 9 December, that Khrushchev emphatically declared that the Soviet Union regarded Kashmir as a part of India. It was the first time that any foreign country had openly expressed support for India's hold on Kashmir. It came as a pleasant surprise to Nehru: 'That was none of our seeking but the fact remains that the Soviet Union has gained the goodwill of vast numbers of people in India by saying that, and has put the U.K. and the U.S.A. and Pakistan in a very embarrassing position.'[88]

Khrushchev's statement on Kashmir certainly succeeded in provoking the British and, when Lord Home went so far as to ask India to make a gesture of goodwill in regard to Kashmir, Nehru called the request 'sheer impertinence'.[89] Yet Nehru was all the time anxious not to let India's relationship with Britain and America be in any way damaged by the visit of the Russian leaders. He was amazed at the panic this visit had caused in the British quarter:

> As a person who has all along been rather friendly to England and the British, and who has a great deal of the British background in him, I feel distressed at the way the British people are rapidly going to pieces. I thought they had some restraint in them.[90]

Earlier on in his visit Khrushchev asserted that Goa (the Portuguese possession in India) belonged to India and that 400 years of Portuguese occupation did not make it Portuguese. Portuguese possessions on the western coast of India (Goa, Daman and Diu) were the only surviving remnants of colonial days. Nehru had hoped that Portugal, like Britain and France, would be ultimately prevailed upon to transfer these settlements peacefully to India. But Portugal regarded her Indian holdings as part of her territory and argued that the culture and religion of 200,000 Catholics who lived in these territories would be put in jeopardy if they went to India – an argument which carried no weight with secular India, the population of which already included nearly five million Catholics. Being ever anxious to preserve the image of India as an unaggressive and peace-loving power, Nehru had consistently resisted internal pressure to take military action against the Portuguese in Goa. The Goa issue, however, became dominant in August 1955 when the opposition parties of India (Jan Sangh, the Praja-Socialist and the Communist parties) joined together in launching a Goa satyagraha. Nehru believed that their real intention was to embarrass Congress and the Government by forcing the Government to send military support into Goa.[91]

The satyagrahis were fired upon by the Portuguese while entering Goa, and over twenty Indians died. Nehru intervened and ordered the cessation of the satyagraha. He also ordered an economic blockade of Goa and the closing of land and rail communications between India and the Portuguese possessions. But he continued to resist public pressure to use military force in Goa: 'From the very outset our policy, both at home and abroad, has been to solve all problems peacefully. If we ourselves act against that policy we would be regarded as deceitful hypocrites.'[92]

Goa was thus very much on the Indian mind when the Russian leaders visited India. Khrushchev's statement on Goa soothed Indian feelings but at the same time provoked John Foster Dulles into making a joint statement with Portugal's Foreign Minister, Dr Paulo Cunha, on 2 December 1955 in Washington, condemning Khrushchev's statement as an attempt to foment hatred between East and West. Dulles added that he considered Goa to be a province of Portugal. Dulles's statement not only disillusioned Nehru, who had hoped to get the Goan problem settled through the good offices of America and Britain, but it also aroused anti-American feelings among Indians which Nehru personally would have very much liked to have prevented. Nehru remarked to his sister: 'Dulles's statement on Goa was, of course just astounding stupidity and has done more harm to the U.S. in India and other countries than almost anything that has happened in the course of some years'.[93]

If 1954 marked the beginning of Sino-Indian brotherhood, 1955 inaugurated the era of Indo-Soviet brotherhood, and the latter in some measure came to diminish the former. The Indian gain from the Indo-Soviet *rapport* was Russian support for India's claim on Kashmir, a support which from now on was to be continuously displayed at the United Nations. Nehru's status increased, and with it rose India's credit in the world market. Indo-Soviet *rapport* gave further strength to the principles of co-existence, and emboldened the non-aligned nations (particularly Egypt, who was hitherto only marginally inclined towards non-alignment) to remain un-aligned, while accepting at the same time money and skills from both the Soviet Union and America. What until recently might have been regarded as impossible in international relations was now made possible by India's example. The Soviet leaders' visit to India also opened up the prospect, as was intended by Nehru, for a *rapprochement* between the two super-power blocs. But this was going to take time, for the mutual suspicion and fear that subsisted between America and the Soviet Union constituted a powerful deterrent to any such *rapprochement*. Any reconciliatory move that was hedged with suspicion and caution was most likely to end up in a diplomatic imbroglio, as was shown by the events of 1956.

The events which marked the first part of 1956 were conducive to world peace – Khrushchev's denunciation of Stalinism at the Twentieth Congress of the Communist Party of the Soviet Union, which met in Moscow from 14 to 25 February, and the visit of Khrushchev and Bulganin to Britain in April. The events of the second half of 1956 (the Anglo-French invasion of Egypt on 31 October, and the Russian suppression of the Hungarian Revolution in November) put the clock back. It was thus for Nehru a year of hopes and disappointments, and of conflict between high principles and national interests. India, by championing the option of non-alignment, had made it difficult for the super-powers to gain allies, and introduced a new form of competitiveness into the winning of friends. Khrushchev took this new phenomenon into account, and at the Twentieth Congress of the Communist Party he thus outlawed war as a means of furthering the expansion of communism. There were only two paths: either peaceful co-existence, or the most devastating war in history. The principle of peaceful co-existence, he claimed, had already become the keystone of the foreign policies of China, Yugoslavia, India, Burma and other countries. He pointed out that there were various forms of transition, even parliamentary, to socialism. Civil war was thus no longer the only means of bringing about this transition.

Khrushchev's denunciation of Stalinism, of the personality cult and of revolutionary communism did not please the Chinese, but it certainly gladdened Nehru, who saw in this new development a greater prospect for world peace. Russia's new policy marked for Nehru the transition of Russia herself from an abnormal, revolutionary state to normalcy, for revolution was not a theory compatible with normalcy. In welcoming this change he said: 'This new line, both in political thinking and in practical policy, appears to be based upon a more realistic appreciation of the present world situation and represents a significant process of adaptation and adjustment'.[94] This turn in Russian policy was not taken seriously in the Western world, however. The visit of Bulganin and Khrushchev to Britain in April 1956 did not bring about any change in the British attitude towards the Russians. The Russian leaders were treated with suspicion; Anthony Eden judged and interpreted them by what their predecessors had done in the 1940s or even further back in the 1920s, in the days of the British Empire in India.[95] As soon as they left, Eden occupied himself in devising new means of resistance to any Soviet encroachment, particularly in the Middle East.

It was mainly Britain's failure to grasp the new spirit, and to recognise the strength of public opinion in world politics, that caused the Suez crisis. Here the old colonialism offered its last resistance to an aggressive nationalism. The struggle between Arab nationalism and the colonial powers was the main factor, but the crisis was also the outcome of two other separate power struggles in the Middle East: the struggle between Israel and her Arab neighbours and the cold war between the Soviet Union and the United States. Although in the early stages America put a good deal of pressure on Nasser, she abstained from joining Britain and France in the use of force, for, as Eisenhower explained, this would have permitted the Soviet Union to lead the struggle against the use of force in the Middle East and thereby to win the confidence of the newly independent nations of the world.

America's dislike of Nasser's receiving arms from the communist block was counterbalanced by her regard for the opinion of the non-aligned world. Although it was America's refusal to finance the Aswan Dam project – conveyed to the Egyptian ambassador by Dulles in Washington on 19 July when Nasser was on Brioni Island in Yugoslavia with Tito and Nehru – which led Nasser to nationalise the canal on 26 July, she would go no further in teaching lessons to Nasser.

In contrast, Britain's need to procure Nasser's downfall was urgent and practical. Nasser's nationalisation programme was a threat to Britain's oil supply, to British positions throughout the Middle East and Africa, and to the Baghdad Pact. Even though Nasser promised full compensation to canal-owners and laid no restriction on its use, Anthony Eden would not accept that a man with Nasser's record should have his thumb on Britain's windpipe.

Nasser's aggressiveness, aggravated by the overbearing behaviour of America, Britain and France, found support and sustenance from members of the non-aligned world, in particular from Nehru and Tito. Nehru had no stomach for conspiracies, however, and even though he now had a direct line to Moscow he would not, as a matter of principle, ask the Soviet leaders to intervene. He confined himself to giving diplomatic support to Nasser and raising public opinion in his favour. It was Tito who, when the crunch came and the Anglo-French attack commenced on 31 October, goaded Khrushchev into coming to Nasser's aid. Khrushchev's ultimatum of 5 November – to use force if Anglo-French aggression did not cease immediately – coupled with Eisenhower's threat to use economic sanctions against Britain and France, brought a ceasefire in Egypt. In the period between the nationalisation of the Suez Canal and the Anglo-French–Israeli attack on Egypt, Nehru played the role of moderator. He criticised the aggressive speeches of British and French politicians and the sabre-rattling that was going on in Anglo-French quarters,[96] but his protestations and warnings fell on deaf ears. He did, however, succeed in persuading Nasser to take a more reasonable line.[97] Nehru condemned the invasion when it took place, though in restrained language, pointing out that the very things which Britain and France intended to gain by aggressive action would be lost on account of it.[98] He proved to be right: the Suez Canal was blocked and Britain suffered a petrol scarcity; Arab nationalism was intensified, which on the one hand led to the collapse of the Baghdad Pact and on the other to the strengthening of the Algerian freedom movement; and the Soviet Union became more involved in the Middle East. The Suez invasion, Nehru maintained, had opened a door for the Russians, just as the Baghdad Pact, which was meant to protect the Middle East from the Soviet Union, resulted in the Soviet Union taking a far greater interest in that region than she had done previously.[99] However, accustomed as he was to seeing the brighter side of things, Nehru saw in the Suez crisis the end of an age when a great power could suppress a small nation.[100]

Disappointment and hope also figured in Nehru's attitude towards the Hungarian tragedy, which coincided with the Suez crisis. The Hungarian uprising of 27 October represented the people's demand for a higher standard of living, for a less rigidly centralised economic system, and for a greater degree of independence from the Soviet Union. The Soviet forces withdrew from Budapest on 30 October. On 4 November they re-entered the capital, and the revolt was suppressed by the fourteenth. About 20,000 Hungarians lost their lives in their fight against Soviet dominance. Though Russia had, earlier in the year, adopted a policy of peaceful co-existence, she lacked the confidence to allow her satellites to become neutral. Khrushchev also suspected a Western hand in the Hungarian uprising and was not prepared to take the risk involved in letting Hungary lead her own life.

Nehru's reaction was slow, partly because of the lack of first-hand information from Hungary and partly because of his greater occupation with the Suez crisis. Nonetheless he was worried from the very beginning, for Russian intervention in Hungary would constitute a repudiation of her policy of peaceful co-existence. His concern was conveyed to the Russian Government by the Indian ambassador on 5 November.[101] When the picture became clearer, Nehru's sympathy flowed out to the Hungarian people. 'The major fact stands out', he told his Members of Parliament, 'that the majority of the people of Hungary wanted a change, political, economic or whatever else, and demonstrated and actually rose in insurrection to achieve it but ultimately they were suppressed.'[102] He also affirmed: 'From the very beginning we made it clear that, in our opinion, the people of Hungary should be allowed to determine their future according to their own wishes and that foreign forces should be withdrawn.'[103] He made it clear that the Hungarian tragedy adversely affected the prestige of the Soviet Union among the non-aligned nations of the world: 'What happened in Hungary was not essentially a conflict between communism and anti-communism. It represented nationalism striving for freedom from foreign control'.[104] The struggle for freedom could not be suppressed for ever, and he believed that the Soviet system would ultimately give way to liberating forces. In the Hungarian tragedy he thus saw the germs of future developments which would lead to the liberalisation of the Soviet system itself, and consequently to a relaxation of control over her satellites.

Nehru was, however, more restrained in his criticism of Soviet oppression in Hungary than he was of the Anglo-French adventure in Egypt. His consideration for India's national interests tempered his condemnation of Soviet activities in Hungary, for he wished to avoid straining his recently gained friendship with the Soviet Union. But, most importantly, Nehru believed that the Western world was highlighting Hungary in order to hide what was happening in Egypt: 'The struggle in Hungary was represented as the basic thing so as somehow to cover up the misdeeds in Egypt.'[105]

By the end of 1956 Nehru had virtually come to acquire the role of mediator in world politics. He was at that time possibly the only major statesman who did not belong to any power bloc, who frequently exercised his freedom to criticise every bloc and who yet had access to and was respected and trusted in each bloc, sometimes for his ideas but always for his sincerity, integrity and moderation. He had been more critical of the Anglo-American bloc than of the Soviet, yet all along had felt he had stronger links with the former. India's democratic structure and the English language forged a strong bond with the Anglo-American bloc. In admitting this he said:

> I have no doubt that it is the English language more than anything else that ties us to the Anglo-American bloc and yet I have not heard it cited as a reason for our so-called subservience to the Anglo-American bloc. It brings us nearer to their thoughts, their activities, their books, newspapers, cultural standards and so on, whereas we are cut off from those parts of the world with which we have no linguistic ties.[106]

He believed that only in a world of peaceful co-existence lay the security of democracy and of the so-called free world.

Without committing herself to Nehru's ideology, America had by 1956 come to trust Nehru as an ardent defender of the democratic way of life. America's opposition to Anglo-French aggression in Egypt had pleased Nehru, and a prospect for a closer understanding between the two countries emerged. Nehru's visit to America in December 1956 fostered this mutual understanding. The American press was more appreciative than latterly: the *New York Times* acclaimed him 'as one of the great figures of our times – and it is a time of giants'.[107] Nehru, for his part, realised that American foreign policy was not as rigid as he had thought.

American fear of Russia, however, remained undiminished. In fact now that Britain and France had withdrawn from the Middle East the American administration felt more concerned than ever before about the collective security of the region. Her 'northern tier' policy now found additional support from the 'vacuum theory'. America moved in the Middle East, rather aggressively, to keep the region uncontaminated by the Nasserites and the communists. The years 1957 and 1958 turned into years of grave crises in the Middle East. A series of events took place each accompanied by sabre-rattling between America and the Soviet Union. America succeeded in establishing her influence in Jordan and the Lebanon, but failed to break the neutrality of Saudi Arabia and to overthrow the pro-Nasser and pro-Soviet Union régime in Syria. The alleged American plot raised a war scare over Syria. The first serious setback for American policy occurred in February 1958 when Egypt and Syria came together in the United Arab Republic. The Anglo-American security system in the Middle East finally collapsed in August 1958 with the military *coup* in Iraq and the coming to power of

Abdul Karim Kassim. Iraq, the pillar of the Baghdad Pact, now ceased to be a committed member of the Anglo-American bloc.

Personally, Nehru had no stomach for the military *coups*, self-seeking dictators and brutal violence in which the Middle East seemed to excel. He also looked with disfavour on the reactionary régimes of Shah, Sheikh and King. He had a particular dislike for rigid policies and fanatical attitudes. He had in fact no personal liking for, or understanding of, any ruler in the Middle East, excepting Nasser, and even Nasser's ways and methods were antipathetic to Nehru, who inwardly disapproved of the hysteria and fanaticism which coloured Arab nationalism. But Nasser had turned into a powerful nationalist, and hence, in Nehru's estimation, into a more effective bulwark against communist expansion in the Middle East than the American collective-security system. Besides, the Indo-Egyptian relationship had, for Nehru, a historical background: since the 1920s he had given sympathetic support to the Egyptian national movement. But, above all, continuing hostility with Pakistan dictated that India must have friends in the Islamic world. Nehru had no feeling of animosity towards Israel and would have hated to see the Jewish state wiped out of existence or even crippled by the Arab nationalists. The reason for his refusal to have diplomatic relations with Israel was tactical; it was his fear that India might lose the friendship of the Arab world. Nehru admitted that his policy towards Israel lacked high principle and was pursued because it served India's interest in the Middle East.[108]

Although Nehru was sceptical about certain features of Middle East politics he was not prepared to condone America's aggressive manœuvres in that region. At the root of the crisis he saw only mutual fear between America and Russia. The Soviet Union and the United States had each offered separate proposals to resolve the crisis, but Nehru was convinced that 'any proposals that were made in an atmosphere of suspicion and fear would not take one far, even when they were good proposals, because nobody accepted them as *bona fide* proposals'.[109] Arising out of this fear was America's 'vacuum theory' (the theory that America must fill in the vacuum created by the Anglo-French withdrawal from the Middle East) which distressed Nehru, for it had created a war scare in the Middle East.[110] Why did America not realise, he asked, that her Middle East policy had succeeded in bringing about the very things which it was intended to prevent?[111]

It seemed to Nehru that the only way towards world peace, the only way to lessen mutual suspicion between the super-powers, was for the giants of the world to meet each other at a summit conference. Also, the super-powers must agree to stop nuclear test explosions. In November 1957 Nehru directly appealed to America and the Soviet Union to stop all nuclear test explosions and to bring about effective disarmament:

> But it is not merely a physical change that is necessary, but an attempt to remove fear and reverse the perilous trend which threatens the continued existence of the human race. It is only by direct approaches and agreements through peaceful methods that these problems can be solved.[112]

The Soviet response to his appeal was quick and favourable. Bulganin's proposals for disarmament were circulated in January 1958. Nehru impressed upon Harold Macmillan, during the latter's visit to India in January 1958, that the Soviet Union had made the first move to bring about some kind of top-level meeting to consider the Cold War and disarmament, that the messages from Bulganin had been very moderate in tone, and that if Dulles were consistently to oppose any such move the Western powers would lose credit with their own people and certainly with Asia and elsewhere.[113] Macmillan himself pursued the summit idea consistently, visiting Moscow in 1958 to break the ice. Although, in the summer of 1958, Nehru was deeply distressed at the execution of Imre Nagy (the Hungarian nationalist leader, whom the Russians had arrested on 22 November 1956), and feared that this might dim the prospect of a summit meeting, he was nonetheless certain that the execution did not indicate a complete reversal in Soviet policy. He believed that the trend of liberalism which Khrushchev had introduced into the Soviet system would continue to grow.[114] However the idea of a summit meeting between the four powers (the

United States, the Soviet Union, France and Britain) took nearly two years to materialise.

At the end of 1958 Nehru had good reason to feel contented with the foreign policy he had pursued and the rewards he had gained. World peace was still precariously balanced and the Cold War persisted, but he had been instrumental in introducing certain new norms and trends which were to change the style of international relations. When asked by an interviewer what he regarded as the major trends in the twentieth century, he said, 'I think that people want to be themselves.'[115] He had, indeed, striven throughout this period to create an international atmosphere in which people and nations could lead their own lives, could be themselves.

CHAPTER TWELVE

Defeat into Victory, 1959–63

I hope that our nation, much less my humble self, will never be brutalised because that is a strange idea that one can only be strong by being brutal. I reject that idea completely. Our strength lies in other factors. Brutality is a thing which we have associated with certain movements which we have objected to or rejected. By becoming brutal and thinking in those brutal ways we lose our souls and that is a tremendous loss. I hope that India which is essentially a gentle and peace-loving country will retain that mind even though it may have to carry on war with all its consequences to the utmost.

Jawaharlal Nehru, 14 November 1962

ON the domestic front during this period the concern of India's ageing Prime Minister lay mainly in achieving national integration, in strengthening the roots of democracy and parliamentary government, in fighting corruption and disintegration within the ruling Congress Party, and in leading India further along the road to socialism. Though he remained wedded to ideals, he made reluctant compromises with reality. He suffered from a crisis of conscience when dismissing the communist government of Kerala (1959) and liberating the Portuguese colonies in India (1961) but he sought consolation in the fact that these decisions were dictated by the popular will (which was to him almost the will of God), and that they were not as inconsistent with his ideals as they outwardly appeared to be.

Turning defeat into victory also characterised his style on the international front. He was positively grateful to China for invading India, for the invasion, as he saw it, fostered a kind of unity in India which the country had never experienced before. China occupied much but not all of his mind. He welcomed the emergence of independent nations on the African continent and was guided by his anti-colonial and anti-racialist feelings in boycotting the white government of South Africa, in supporting the nationalists in Algeria and in condemning the secessionists in the Congo. He had, however, overcome the passion and intensity which had characterised his earlier attacks on colonialism and racialism. Among the leaders of the non-aligned world (Sukarno, Nasser, Nkrumah and Tito) Nehru was the only one to be intensely concerned about disarmament, a ban on nuclear tests, and *rapprochement* between America and the Soviet Union. He thus felt greatly rewarded when, in August 1963, a partial Nuclear Test Ban Treaty was signed in Moscow by Britain, America and the Soviet Union. In identifying new trends and fostering new norms in international relationships he had made his own contribution towards the ending of the Cold War. For him the Nuclear Test Ban Treaty marked the end of the era of Cold War.

In his own life (which as usual was more public than private) during these years, he became increasingly isolated from his colleagues, friends and relations. This was not because he distrusted people, but because he did not find anybody around him echoing his feelings, doubts, conflicts and aspirations. Nehru had, in fact, no intimate friend. Certainly he had difficulty in making friends, but the chief reason for this was his monolithic power which was a barrier between him and his colleagues and relatives. His colleagues put him on a pedestal and looked up to him. From that height he often looked down upon them, at some with derision. He had indeed respected and relied upon some of his old colleagues even though they were cast in moulds quite different from his. Patel, Azad and Pant fell into that category. But Patel was now long gone, Azad died in 1958 and Pant in 1961. Different considerations regulated his relationship with Morarji Desai, T. T. Krishnamachari, Krishna Menon and Lal Bahadur Shastri – the four cabinet ministers who came closer to sharing power with him during this period. Nehru was greatly impressed by Desai's efficiency and integrity which the latter had displayed as Bombay's Chief Minister from 1951 to 1957. Desai joined the Union Cabinet in 1957 as the Minister for Commerce and Industry; in 1958 he succeeded T. T. Krishnamachari as Finance Minister. He was a committed rightist, but it was not his political views which irritated Nehru most. Desai's puritanical streak and his inflexibility made Nehru uneasy and he was somewhat relieved when in 1963 Desai resigned his ministerial position under the Kamaraj Plan. But in 1964, a month or so before his death, when he was looking for someone to give continuity and stability to the Government, Nehru offered to take Desai back into the Cabinet provided the latter were willing to undertake that in any matter of controversy he would accept the Prime Minister's decision.[1] Desai has gone on record as saying that he did not accept the condition.

T. T. Krishnamachari, a Brahmin from Madras, was more of an intellectual than a professional politician. Though he had been active in politics for some time he had not succeeded in creating for himself a power-base in his own state. He had been Minister of Commerce and Industry for nearly five years when, in 1957, he succeeded Deshmukh as the Finance Minister. He was in Nehru's estimate 'a very good Finance Minister', and he was also very hard-working.[2] Besides, he was the only Tamil member of Nehru's Cabinet in 1958. He was almost indispensable to Nehru. But among his shortcomings, as Nehru saw them, were his quick temper, his indiscretion and his 'way of making enemies'. His enemies had their opportunity early in 1958 when Feroze Gandhi (Nehru's son-in-law and a Member of Parliament but no relation of Mahatma Gandhi) exposed in Parliament the fraudulent dealings of high officials employed in the Government-owned Life Insurance Corporation with a private businessman, Haridas Mundhra. The Life Insurance Corporation had purchased fifteen million rupees' worth of allegedly poor shares in corporations controlled by Mundhra. As the Life Insurance Corporation came under the Ministry of Finance, Krishnamachari was technically responsible for any collusive dealings between the officials and Mundhra. Nehru was forced to sanction an enquiry into the 'Mundhra scandal', though he was convinced that the Life Insurance Corporation had not suffered any material loss by this investment and that his Finance Minister was not personally guilty of any corrupt practices.[3] But Krishnamachari's enemies in Parliament demanded his head, and much to Nehru's regret the Finance Minister had to resign. Krishnamachari, however, did not remain in the wilderness for long. Nehru brought him back into the Cabinet in 1962, and Krishnamachari remained his trusted adviser and colleague during the last years of the Prime Minister's life. As Krishnamachari was never in the running for the succession to Nehru, he was able to offer advice more freely to the Prime Minister on all issues, including the question of the succession.

Like Krishnamachari, Krishna Menon, too, was never thought of as a possible successor to Nehru. Menon, however, had more enemies than Krishnamachari and his influence on Nehru was deeply resented by the Congress rightists. Some even suspected that Menon was blackmailing Nehru over escapades the two men might have enjoyed together in the 1930s.[4] Such speculations about the Menon–Nehru relationship were groundless. As explained earlier, Menon had been Nehru's only intellectual companion. And, although Nehru had always been aware that Menon lacked political stability, he had nonetheless relished Menon's tirades so frequently delivered against the Anglo-American style of diplomacy. Besides, Nehru never failed to be intrigued by the fact that Menon was different from any other member of the Indian ruling class and that nobody really liked him. In retaining and protecting Menon, Nehru thus felt himself to be championing the cause of an underdog. But, when protecting Menon became too risky and involved defiance of the public will, Nehru had to forsake him. Menon, who had been in Nehru's Cabinet since 1956, had to resign in November 1962, when politicians put the entire blame on him for the Indian reverses on the Himalayan frontiers. From then onwards Menon continued to see Nehru frequently late at night, but there was for him no return to the Cabinet.

Lal Bahadur Shastri, a little man from United Provinces, was a gifted organiser and a shrewd negotiator, and perhaps one of the very few Congress workers in the pre-independence days who was content to work behind the scenes. His outstanding political asset, in fact, was his humility. Whether he intended to or not he drew more attention, applause and power to himself by always being willing to renounce, to resign and to occupy a position at the bottom of the ladder. He had acquired his first mass popularity in the winter of 1956 by resigning his ministership of railways, merely because a terrible railway accident had occurred – an accident for which he was in no way responsible. Not only did he set a unique precedent but also, as Nehru noticed, he went up in people's estimation by his resignation.[5] Nehru was impressed and, although with great reluctance he accepted Shastri's resignation, he was determined to bring him back into the Cabinet at the earliest opportunity. Shastri resigned only a few months before the general election of 1957. He was back in Nehru's Cabinet after the election, with added prestige and a national political stature. He remained in the Cabinet until 1963, when once again he resigned under the Kamaraj Plan. But he was back in the Cabinet before long, as a minister without portfolio. From this many have inferred that Shastri was Nehru's favourite and that he had possibly accepted him as his successor. Nothing, however, was further from Nehru's mind than to choose his successor. As will be explained later, he left that to the nation. He did, however, consider Shastri as a potential candidate for the succession, and the thought, if one is to believe Krishnamachari, did not please Nehru.[6] Beneath Shastri's humility, Nehru suspected, lay a certain measure of meanness and cunning. And, much as he liked Shastri, Nehru's vanity inhibited him from acknowledging Shastri (or any other of his colleagues) as his ideal successor.

The four cabinet ministers, different as they were from each other, fulfilled different needs in Nehru. All were close to him but none close enough to become his right arm. There was none outside the Union Cabinet to claim Nehru's intimacy. In 1963 emerged what is popularly called the syndicate – a caucus of chief ministers and state congress bosses including K. Kamaraj Nadar (Chief Minister of Madras), Sanjiva Reddy (Chief Minister of Andhra Pradesh), S. Nijalingappa (Chief Minister of Mysore), S. K. Patil and Atulya Ghosh, the Congress bosses respectively of Bombay and Bengal. As no member of this caucus had any apparent prospect of becoming the Prime Minister of India, they all combined to assume the role of collective kingmakers. In October 1963, at the pilgrim town of Tirupathi in Andhra Pradesh, a vow of self-denial was religiously taken by the prominent members of the syndicate. The caucus as a body came to wield a major influence on Nehru during the last years of his life. It was this body which put Shastri back in the Cabinet in 1964 and after Nehru's death chose him as India's second prime minister.

During the preceding period Nehru had trusted and leaned heavily on his personal assistant M. O. Mathai, a man from Kerala who had joined Nehru's staff in 1946 and till 1958 controlled almost all access to the Prime Minister. That a man like Mathai, who had neither status in the Civil Service nor any intellectual standing, should become the most confidential assistant of Nehru was a puzzle to many, especially after it was found that Mathai had succumbed to temptation and amassed a little fortune of his own by selling secrets of which he knew more even than a cabinet minister. This came as a shock to Nehru, who was not given to suspecting people.

Towards the end his private life was well guarded by Mrs Indira Gandhi. With her two sons (Rajiv and Sanjay) Indira had been living with her father since he moved into the palatial Teen Murti House – the official residence of the Prime Minister. Her husband Feroze Gandhi shared the apartment with her until 1958 when he moved into an apartment of his own. Their marriage had been under strain for some time on account of Indira's constant work as her father's official hostess and his travelling companion on most of his tours abroad. Indira had given priority to her father's needs, perhaps hoping that when he was gone she would lead a normal married life with her husband. Feroze, however, was a sick man, and in 1960 at the age of forty-eight he died of a heart attack.

Apart from being the First Lady, Indira had also been pursuing her own political ambitions. In 1955 she was first elected to the Working Committee of Congress. In 1959 she became the Congress President. In both these adventures she was supported by U. N. Dhebar and Lal Bahadur Shastri. Her Congress presidency, however, turned out for Nehru as much a source of embarrassment as of pride. While in office, and particularly when bringing about the fall of the communist government in Kerala, she betrayed a strong vein of ruthlessness and disregard for parliamentary traditions, and she was unscrupulously tenacious in pursuing her goals which were often narrowly conceived. These qualities, coupled with her childlike decisiveness, though they turned her into an effective political operator, were not so endearing to her father. He was often put off, even hurt, by her assertiveness which she displayed just to prove that she could stand on her own feet. Nehru had often thought, and now he believed, that Indira inherited her qualities mostly from her mother. She was, in a way, more different from him than a Shastri or even Desai. However, Nehru's consciousness of a personality conflict between him and his daughter was in no way responsible for his decision not to bring Indira into his Cabinet. His regard for his own public image and his fear of being accused of nepotism set him against bringing any of his close relations into the Cabinet. When it was once suggested by Krishnamachari that Indira or Mrs Pandit should be given the portfolio of External Affairs, Nehru said definitely not while he was Prime Minister.[7]

His paternal relationship with Indirat hrived unruffled by their political differences. In these years he derived much comfort from the company of his grandsons and a host of pets (dogs, pigeons, squirrels, deer, pandas, crocodile and tiger cubs) which he had assembled in his private zoo. In spite of his round-the-clock engagements and his failing health he took, when occasion arose, great delight in looking after his daughter (as during 1960 when Indira was very ill) and his sisters. He retained until the end his humanity and warmth. His trust in people never faded even when, in 1955 in Nagpur, an attempt was made on his life by a madman who tried to reach him in his moving car with a knife. There was no conspiracy behind this episode, but from then onwards he had to accept, much against his will, stricter security around him.[8]

On the domestic front Nehru faced, during the years from 1959 to 1962, a challenge, more serious than in the past, to Congress policy from both the conservative and radical forces in the country. Having so far steered a middle course, Congress had failed to satisfy either the rightists or the leftists. The growing tension between India and China, from the beginning of 1959, impelled Nehru as usual to try to make

India more competitive by pushing her further on to the socialist path. The 1959 Nagpur resolution of Congress, prescribing joint co-operative farming as a remedy for India's agrarian ills, was in a way intended to meet the Chinese challenge. But it produced an instant reaction among the conservative forces in the country. Congress's socialism, which in fact had so far been mostly confined to speeches and resolutions, now seemed, the rightists feared, to be heading towards 'collectivisation' of the Russian and Chinese type. Indeed Nehru made it clear that no coercion would be used to implement co-operative farming, but that gave no consolation to the conservative elements of Indian society who believed that India's salvation lay through free enterprise and private cultivation of large holdings. Conservative elements had already organised themselves in such groups as the Forum of Free Enterprise and the All-India Agriculturists' Federation. Now, after Congress had put before the nation its Nagpur resolution, they began thinking in terms of founding an all-India political party. Leaders were not hard to find. Eighty-year-old Rajaji, once a Congress leader, had long ceased to be enamoured of Nehru's mixed economy. It was under his leadership and with the active support of M. R. Masani and K. M. Munshi that, in August 1959, the new all-India party was founded, just a year and a half before India's third general election. It was called the Swatantra Party – the party, as its name suggested, for the real freedom of India.

While Congress had gone too far for the conservatives it had not gone far enough for the socialists, who wanted more nationalisation, and stricter ceilings on land holdings. Nehru explained his position to his sister:

> Our friend Jayaprakash Narayan says that I am a block on the road to socialism and should be removed if India is to progress. Rajaji says that enemy number one is the Congress (he used to say that enemy number one was communism previously) and he attacks me with a venom which is extraordinary. So, you will observe that I am having a fairly interesting time.[9]

The more the Chinese pressed on India's border the fiercer became the press and the opposition parties in their criticism of Nehru's policies. Nehru could not ignore the pressure that mounted daily. Hence, much against his wish and in contravention of some of his principles, he had to sanction certain measures to gratify the people's aspirations. For the Himalayan border (to which we turn later) he sanctioned a forward policy. On the domestic front he was led by his daughter to interfere in Kerala.

Perhaps Kerala provided the only instance in the world where the communists had come to power (in 1957) through a peaceful parliamentary election. Nehru was not particularly distressed by the communist victory. His main concern being the preservation of democracy, he had hoped that the communists, now realising that they could attain power through the ballot box, would become more tolerant of democratic political processes. But his daughter Indira, now the Congress President, saw no reason to be charitable in power politics, especially when she observed that the communists were consolidating their power in Kerala by announcing reforms in land ownership, filling state bureaucracies with their own supporters and ousting anti-communist elements from the state educational system. For Indira the end justified the means. Much to Nehru's embarrassment she ordered Congress to ally with the anti-communist forces in the state, which in essence meant striking an alliance with such sectarian groups as the Catholics and the Nayyars. The secular Congress was thus led to court communal factions in its fight against the communists. This combined movement against the communist government brought the state to the verge of anarchy. Indira pleaded with her father for central government intervention. Nehru had reservations about the legitimacy and merits of such an action, which would mean the dismissal of the communist government in Kerala. At this point Indira betrayed her political attitude by making a harsh statement to the effect that if the Indian Constitution had no remedy for the people of Kerala, then it should be amended.[10] The law and order situation in the state had worsened to such an extent that even the communists, as Nehru was ultimately led to believe, would have felt relieved if president's rule were established.[11] But what really forced Nehru's hand in the matter was the pro-Chinese bias of Kerala's Chief Minister,

E. M. S. Namboodiripad, who in one of his speeches had warned the opposition parties that if they persisted in their opposition to the communists, then the latter would divide the people into two camps and create disruption in the country, similar to the situation caused by the protracted civil war in China.[12] On 31 July 1959 the communist government of Kerala was dismissed by the President's proclamation and the state passed temporarily under central rule. Soon after the dismissal, Mrs Gandhi formed a united front in Kerala. This was, in fact, Congress's electoral alliance with the socialists on the one hand and the state Muslim League on the other. Congress alliance with the Muslim League was indeed unholy but the end justified the means, at least for Mrs Gandhi. At the general election in 1962 the communists were defeated in Kerala.

The conflict of style between father and daughter was further displayed in 1959 when Indira went all out for the partition of Bombay between Maharashtra and Gujarat. The conflict was between principles and political gains. Nehru was attached to the concept of a bilingual Bombay; Indira, to forestall enemies of Congress (who were exploiting the issue) and with her eyes on the coming general election, was more concerned with political gains than with the principle. Bombay was divided.

Though it was not much to his liking, the settlement of the Kerala crisis did not, for Nehru, introduce any anti-democratic trends in the Indian polity. His attachment to democracy was almost devotional. He was constantly on guard against trends towards militarism which might follow from the mounting tension on India's Himalayan frontier. On India's list of precedence the generals were given a position towards the bottom; Nehru was entirely responsible for allocating to the military a position inferior to the civil authorities. Thus, on 1 September 1959 when the Chief of the Army Staff, General K. S. Thimayya, resigned owing to his differences with the Defence Minister, Krishna Menon, Nehru seized the opportunity to declare unequivocally that the civil authority must always remain supreme in India, at the same time persuading the General to withdraw his resignation.[13] The presidency of India itself, though a civil institution, could, in adverse situations and under an ambitious holder of the post, be turned into a danger to parliamentary institutions. There was nothing further from the mind of Rajendra Prasad than to be dictator of India, but when in December 1960 he casually made a remark that the Constitution was not clear as to whether he was bound by the advice of the Council of Ministers, Nehru reacted forcefully in asserting that the President was a constitutional head always bound by the advice of his ministers.[14]

Nehru faced a much more erosive crisis of conscience when he was obliged to use force for the liberation of Goa. Four interconnected sets of circumstances forced his hand in this operation. There was, of course, never any doubt in his mind that the Portuguese possessions belonged to India; he had sincerely hoped that Portugal would ultimately make a peaceful transfer of her colonies to India. He had waited for nearly fifteen years and had on many occasions stood firm against the public demand for the use of force. He would have waited longer but for circumstances which made it impossible for him to postpone action any further.

The factor that weighed most heavily was public opinion. The overbearing presence of China on the Indian border had, since the beginning of 1959, been filling the people with humiliation and anger. The opposition parties, more with a view to embarrassing the Government than of vindicating the national honour, were directing the nation's aggressive mood towards China and Portugal. In this state, when the people were beginning to lose self-confidence, the divisive forces – communalism, caste-ism, regionalism and linguism – came to the surface. Corruption and factionalism, which already existed in the lower ranks of Congress organisation and in the state governments, now attracted the attention of the people and further disturbed their mood. National disintegration became a real possibility. A conference on national integration was held in September 1961. Perhaps it was the first attempt, though unsuccessful, to identify the national interests. To stop panic Nehru, when opening the conference, maintained that the country was not facing any immediate peril, that some of the grave difficulties which faced India were inherited from the past and others were the result of the very progress which the country was making.[15] He used the forum to attack the divisive forces which were raising their heads again.

The conference did not pacify the country's aggressive mood. In early December 1961, two months after the conference, Portuguese soldiers from Goa crossed the Indian border and fired at the people of a village. To Nehru it seemed as if the Portuguese were deliberately provoking India to take steps against them.[16] In the same month a minister of the Portuguese Government visited Goa and promised some kind of autonomy to the people. At the same time Pakistan, while mobilising its troops on the Indian frontier, loudly expressed its support for Portugal and China. To the Indians the recovery of Goa now became a test of manhood. But Nehru was still reluctant to take military action. He hoped that America and Britain would succeed in persuading Portugal, a fellow member of NATO, to withdraw peacefully from her Indian colonies.

The second factor which led Nehru into the Goan operation was African pressure. Portugal was treating the nationalists brutally in its African possessions, which included large territories like Angola and Mozambique. Nehru was particularly distressed at the manner in which the Portuguese were suppressing the anti-colonial movement in Angola. African leaders and nationalists looked up to Nehru. In October 1961 a seminar on Portuguese colonialism was held in Delhi. Many important leaders of African parties and groups attended. At the seminar Nehru realised that 'in the eyes of the African leaders, and especially of those struggling against Portuguese colonialism in Africa, Goa was playing an important part'.[17] They attached much importance to what India did in Goa. Liberation of Goa would lead to the liberation of Portuguese possessions in Africa. The Africans by 'tying up Goa with Angola' placed an obligation on Nehru to make the first move towards the liquidation of the Portuguese Empire.[18]

The third factor was the failure of America and Britain to offer any effective mediation in the matter. Till the last moment Nehru relied on America for a peaceful settlement of the Goan affair, and even though, in the last week of November 1961, he had reluctantly given the go-ahead to the military, he postponed the date of the invasion twice, first when some Latin

American countries made a vague proposal for peaceful settlement, and the second time when on 14 December the American Government undertook to take the initiative in the matter by suggesting to Portugal that it should quit Goa on the understanding that India would preserve and protect Portugal's economic and cultural institutions in Goa.[19] Nehru welcomed the American proposal, and postponed the operation which was in fact fixed for 15 December. But the same day he was informed by the American Government that Portugal had given a negative response to their initiative.

The fourth factor, then, was the obstinacy of Portugal itself. Portugal had blatantly defied the United Nations resolutions (of December 1960 and November 1961) which in essence urged Portugal to indicate when she intended to grant independence to her colonies in Africa and India. Portugal also ignored representations made to her by India in the first half of December 1961. Some of these representations were made against the alleged aggression of Portuguese soldiers on Indian territory; finally Portugal turned down the last proposal made by the American Government.

The operation was finally fixed for the night of 17–18 December 1961. President Kennedy, U Thant and Harold Macmillan had all urged him not to tarnish his image as the apostle of peace by taking military action in Goa. On the eve of the operation Nehru was undecided and unhappy, and was exploring the possibility of postponing the invasion for a third time. But Lieutenant-General B. M. Kaul, in charge of the operation, warned him that his people and the armed forces would lose faith in him if he failed to act.[20] Nehru reconciled himself to the situation. When the Indian Army was already on its way to Goa came the American request to Nehru to postpone action for six months during which period the American Government, in co-operation with Britain, would try to lay some pressure on Portugal.[21] It was a vague proposal and it came too late.

The operation was all over within a day with very few casualties. The Portuguese authorities surrendered without much resistance, Goa, Daman and Diu were liberated, and, in the eyes of Indians, India's independence now became complete. It was a day of rejoicing not only for India but also, in Nehru's estimate, for practically the whole of Africa and for nearly all the countries of Asia. But for China, India's rival for the leadership of the Third World, it might have been a day for deep reflection. Not only had India pulled down a pro-Chinese communist government in Kerala, but it had also, through its Goan operation, projected an image of being a great military power and the champion of anti-colonial movements in Africa. The Chinese leaders were convinced that India would be prepared to use force in her border dispute with China. Soon after the Goan operation the Indian leaders, including Nehru and Shastri, began assuring the people and press that India might be obliged to use force against China if the latter did not withdraw from the Indian territories she had illegally occupied. These statements were made on the eve of the general election, and they did not in any way betray the real mood and intention of Nehru's Government, but they might, nonetheless, have been taken by the Chinese at face value. The Goan operation, therefore, probably indicated to the Chinese that it was time to prepare for a show-down.

Whereas the liberation of Goa contributed in some measure to India's integration, even though it did make the national mood a little more aggressive and self-assured, the third general election further strengthened the roots of democracy in India. Facing this time a somewhat stiffer challenge from the left-wing and right-wing opposition parties Nehru himself did more campaigning during this election than in the previous one. At the age of seventy-two he created almost a world record by travelling in 31 days nearly 18,000 miles by air, car and rail, addressing over 90 meetings and talking to the electorate for a total of 76 hours.[22] The 1962 election for Parliament, and all state assemblies, except for Kerala and Orissa which had gone through a mid-term election, was held between 16 and 27 February. The electorate now consisted of 210 million, an increase of 17 million over the 1957 figure.

Once again the election results gave Congress an over-all victory. In the Lok Sabha, Congress secured 361 of the total 494 elective seats (only ten seats less than its 1957 achievement), and of the total 3297 state assembly seats it captured 1984. Perhaps the real achievement of Congress lay in containing the parties of the extreme left and extreme right: the Communist Party of India secured only 29 seats in the Lok Sabha, just two more than it had in 1957. And even though the Jan Sangh more than doubled its strength in Parliament by acquiring a total of 14 seats, in terms of total poll cast in its favour it secured only 113,690 more than its 1957 figure. The new Swatantra Party secured 18 seats in the Lok Sabha; the bulk of its votes was acquired in 4 states – Bihar, United Provinces, Rajasthan and Gujarat. The Praja-Socialist Party, however, lost all along the line.

The election brought no significant changes in the personnel of the Congress governments at the centre or in the states. The only major change was caused by the retirement of Rajendra Prasad and the election in May 1962 of seventy-four-year-old Dr Radhakrishnan as the President of India. Nehru's new cabinet, formed on 9 April, retained its old face. The old guard were retained and the Cabinet was increased from twelve to eighteen by promoting five ministers of state to cabinet rank and bringing in T. T. Krishnamachari, the old-timer who had been out of the Government for a few years on account of the Mundhra scandal. By and large the chief ministerial posts and the state governments remained as before. Nehru never liked change for its own sake; but the fact that all the Congress leaders of national and state stature were in government and only second-rank leaders were left to run the Congress Party seemed, to some, to have steadily weakened the hold of Congress on the people. But there was no alarm in 1962 especially when the election had put Congress securely in power. There were visible signs of Congress having lost some ground in certain states – Bengal, Madras, Kerala and Rajasthan, but the Congress mind was not unduly agitated over this during 1962.

The Indo-Chinese war of October–November 1962, however, destroyed India's complacency, and 1963 became for the country a year of stock-taking and self-analysis. Many plans for national regeneration were conceived, some in panic and confusion. One of these was the Kamaraj Plan, popularly named after Kamaraj, who sponsored it, though the idea had simultaneously crossed the mind of many others – including the Chief Minister of Orissa, B. Patnaik. The Plan was typically Indian in that it invoked the Indian tradition of renunciation and sacrifice and called upon senior Congressmen in government voluntarily to relinquish their ministerial posts and to offer themselves for full-time organisational work. The Plan aimed at putting younger men in charge of the Government and sending senior leaders to the country to secure the people's participation in the nation's democratic revolution. The Kamaraj Plan was based on a diagnosis of the national malady, which hinged on the belief that the only serious ailment the nation suffered from was the continuing apathy of its people. A host of reforms and three five-year plans (the third plan with an estimated total investment, in both public and private sectors, of Rs.11,370 crores had been launched in March 1960) had failed to stir the masses and enthuse them with the spirit of self-help and co-operative effort. India's revolution by consent, it seemed, had not yet gathered any momentum. Nehru's dream of securing full mass participation in India's planned growth remained unfulfilled. Though the five-year plans had succeeded in effecting a break with economic stagnation, in raising the national income per head and in strengthening the infrastructure of the economy and thereby creating some of the preconditions for self-sustaining economic growth, they had not produced any change in people's attitudes and in their lifestyles. The people took all government reforms and aids as gifts from above, and the Government itself, so it appeared, was dependent on foreign assistance for the success of its economic planning; America, the Soviet Union, West Germany and Britain, in that order, were India's biggest creditors.

The sponsors of the Kamaraj Plan hoped that a handful of leaders would be able to mobilise the people in the task of national regeneration. Nehru had his doubts about the Plan. Besides, if he himself left the Government at this stage, he feared it would look like desertion. But he was persuaded by the enthusiastic sponsors of the Plan to give it his blessing. The plan was approved by the All-India Congress Committee on 10 August 1963. Nehru offered to resign but he was told it would not be in the national interest for him to leave the Government. However six central cabinet ministers (M. Desai, J. Ram, L. B. Shastri, S. K. Patil, B. Gopala Reddi and K. L. Shrimali) and six chief ministers (Kamaraj of Madras, Patnaik of Orissa, Bakshi Ghulam Mohammad of Kashmir,

B. Jha of Bihar, C. B. Gupta of United Provinces and B. A. Mandloi of Madhya Pradesh) resigned. Thus was brought about a sudden change in the personnel of the Government at the centre, and in some states.

The Kamaraj Plan, however, failed to achieve any success. On the contrary, by removing some old stalwarts from the state governments it created a power vacuum which in turn led to the growth of factions, and of struggles for the post of chief minister. If, as has been argued, the Plan was intended to help Nehru in getting rid of some of his ministers and chief ministers, then it did succeed to an extent;[23] but this would seem to be a doubtful interpretation of the original motive for the Plan. Nehru was hardly likely to be party to such a stratagem, no matter how much encumbered he might have felt by some of his colleagues.

On the international front Nehru displayed more optimism during this period than ever before. The events that took place during this period seemingly contradicted his beliefs and interpretations, but he continually maintained that the new spirit and new norms were steadily gaining ground in international relationships, in spite of a few temporary setbacks here and there. He saw the international crises hindering but not deterring the world from moving towards the desired goal. The civil war in the Congo, the East–West tension over Berlin, the Cuban crisis, the Sino-Indian border war – each of these had a brighter side for Nehru, and none destroyed his vision for the world and for India. He had been aware that certain foreign countries resented India's 'holier than thou' attitude but he believed that this attitude was not an affectation on his country's part. Its traditions and its national movement had conditioned India to play the role it was playing.[24]

This period was characterised by the decolonisation of black Africa. In 1955 there were only five independent African states; by 1969 there were forty-one. Seventeen new states were admitted to the United Nations in 1960 alone. This 'wind of change' in Africa, as Harold Macmillan called it, began with the independence of Ghana (1957). Between 1958 and 1963 about twenty-six African states became independent including the Belgian Congo (June 1960), British Somaliland (July 1960), Nigeria (October 1960), Tanganyika (December 1961), Algeria

(July 1962) and Kenya (December 1963). This was for Nehru a most welcome development. Ghana, and its leader Dr Kwame Nkrumah, symbolised to Nehru the hope for the salvation of all Africa. Nkrumah visited Delhi in December 1958 and acquired Nehru's blessing for his plan to unite the whole of Africa into an African commonwealth. He was also admitted to the club of the non-aligned leaders.

However, most of the independent states of Africa were soon faced with internal disruption and dictatorship. A great tragedy was enacted in the Congo (and repeated later, in 1966, in Nigeria). Soon after its independence the unity of the Congo and the leadership of its nationalist prime minister, Patrice Lumumba, were challenged by the secessionist forces headed by Moise Tshombe (and Colonel Joseph Mobutu) and supported by the Belgians. In July 1960, Tshombe declared Katanga independent. Lumumba sought Soviet support in organising a direct attack on Katanga, and thereby antagonised the British and Americans, who from then on lent their support to Tshombe and brought about the fall of the Congolese prime minister. With the complicity of the Katanga government Lumumba was murdered in January 1961. With his removal from the scene the Anglo-American bloc now became concerned about preserving the unity of the country. In September 1961, the United Nations Secretary-General Dag Hammarskjöld was killed in a mysterious air-crash. The United Nations finally succeeded, in December 1962, in ending the secession of Katanga.

Nehru was greatly agitated over the Congo crisis. All his sympathies went to Lumumba, and he had no stomach for the brutalities committed by Mobutu and Tshombe. But he was more distressed by the behaviour of America, Britain and France:

> These countries and, of course, Belgium have behaved in a scandalous manner which has no justification in principle, in constitutional theory or even in any practical results. It is largely due to their attitudes and policies that the situation has deteriorated very rapidly.[25]

He believed that these countries had obstructed the work of the United Nations forces in the Congo (to which India had contributed an army brigade), and had all along encouraged Belgium. This black cloud over the Congo, however, had for Nehru a silver lining. It marked a new phase in the activities of the United Nations because for the first time this organisation had intervened with military force in an international crisis.[26] Nehru always saw the United Nations intervention in Korea as an American rather than a United Nations action.

Success stories of freedom movements in Africa (particularly of the Algerian struggle) came to Nehru 'as a tonic and a blessing'.[27] But the racialism of the South African Government continued to depress him. He was aware that there were racial conflicts elsewhere in the world, in America and even in India itself; but South Africa was a unique case, for there it was 'the acknowledged and loudly-proclaimed policy of the Government itself to maintain this segregation and racial discrimination'.[28] He was thus at times shocked to notice countries, which stood for democracy and human rights, expressing themselves so moderately about the South African racial policy, which to his mind was more dangerous for the future of the world than anything else. The presence of South Africa in the multi-national Commonwealth was becoming embarrassing, and Nehru had no desire to be its neighbour at a Commonwealth table. Pressure to expel South Africa from the Commonwealth came from African leaders, particularly from Julius K. Nyerere of Tanganyika (now Tanzania). Nehru was relieved when in May 1961 South Africa was made to withdraw from the British Commonwealth. This, however, Nehru knew, did not solve the problem. On the contrary, it meant its continuation, for it was obvious that South Africa would rather leave the Commonwealth than compromise with its avowed policy.

Gratified though he was with the decolonisation of Africa and agitated over the racialism of the South African Government, Nehru's mind, during this period, was mainly occupied with bringing about a *rapport* between the West and the East and stopping the armaments race which threatened the very existence of mankind. The years 1960–1 were ones of crises caused, as Nehru saw them, by persistent suspicion between the super-powers. The tension between the East and West had nearly subsided and the four powers were heading for a summit meeting in Paris (May 1960) when the American spy-plane U2 was shot down over Russian territory. The summit meeting failed and Khrushchev, with a view to carrying propaganda against the Americans among the non-aligned world, summoned the heads of the governments of the world to attend a United Nations meeting in October 1960. The year 1961 saw a further increase of tension between the West and the East. In April 1961 America attempted to overthrow the pro-Russian government of Fidel Castro in Cuba. In August 1961, Khrushchev, with a view to halting the continuous escape of East Germans into West Berlin, sealed off East Berlin with a wall. And in the following month Russia resumed nuclear tests.

Nehru's efforts were directed towards easing this tension. He was placed in a privileged position. While preserving his friendship with Russia he came, during this period, much closer to America and Britain. Indeed the mounting tension with China was an important factor in causing Nehru to soften his attitude towards China's only avowed major enemy, the United States. This closeness was displayed by Eisenhower's visit to India in December 1959. Their rising hostility towards China impelled the people to give a more enthusiastic welcome to the American President than they gave to Khrushchev when the latter revisited India in March 1960. Then there was the Queen's visit to India in January 1961, which further strengthened the Indo-British tie. At the time of Queen Elizabeth's visit to India, Indo-British relations became more cordial and, among other things, Britain lent its full support to India in resolving the Laotian crisis and in maintaining the neutrality of Laos. Nehru himself visited America twice during this period, first in October 1960, at Khrushchev's call, to attend the meeting of the United Nations General Assembly, and secondly in November 1961, at President Kennedy's invitation. Jacqueline Kennedy's visit to India, in March 1962, gave a personal touch to the Indo-American relationship. It pleased Nehru, who enjoyed the company of good-looking women. And, as the American ambassador noticed with a sense of diplomatic achievement, Nehru let a picture of Jacqueline Kennedy and himself, arm in arm, be included among the select few (Gandhi,

Motilal Nehru, Tagore, Edwina Mountbatten) which decorated the walls of his sitting-room.[29]

Nehru used his status of respectability, which he enjoyed in both blocs, to bring the super-powers together on a level of mutual understanding and trust. While attending the United Nations meeting in October 1960 he supported the resolution sponsored by the five non-aligned nations (India, Egypt, Yugoslavia, Indonesia and Ghana) which asked for a meeting between the President of the United States and the Prime Minister of the Soviet Union.[30] Throughout 1961 he led the non-aligned world in exercising pressure on the Soviet Union and the United States for a summit meeting and disarmament. In September 1961, when the Soviet Union resumed nuclear tests, twenty-five non-aligned nations were holding a summit conference in Belgrade. While most of the leaders were engrossed in their own immediate problems, and while Nasser, Tito and Sukarno played mostly on colonialism, racialism and the admission of China into the United Nations, Nehru alone laid stress on disarmament, and criticised the Soviet Union for endangering world peace by resuming nuclear tests.[31] Under Nehru's guidance the conference appealed to America and Russia to stop nuclear tests and meet in a summit conference. Two months after, in November 1961, while on an official visit to America, Nehru stressed the urgency as well as the feasibility of the Russo-American *rapprochement*:

> I have repeatedly been impressed during my visits to the Soviet Union and to the United States by the many things they have in common. I am thinking more about the people than about politics. The people in both countries are in some ways remarkably similar to each other. They are frank and hospitable and are exceedingly friendly. . . . It is because of this I think that once they get over the present-day political difficulties the people of the Soviet Union and the United States are likely to come nearer to each other than possibly other countries might.[32]

There was no doubt, he assured the Americans, that in the Soviet Union there had been a very marked and progressive change from the rigid authoritarianism of Stalin's time. The Russians wanted to be friends with the British and the Americans. Why were they, then, so suspicious of the Americans?

Because, as Khrushchev himself had explained to Nehru, the Russians had lived for the last thirty years or so in a state of siege with their enemies surrounding them and trying to crush them. This state of siege had conditioned them and they were suspicious of everybody, especially of those people who had participated in that siege.[33] Hence they retaliated, without thinking, at the slightest provocation.

Nehru was, then, fully aware that any *rapport* between the Soviet Union and America would be most distasteful to the Chinese. The growing conflict between the Soviet Union and China was built, as he maintained, 'on the basis of the Soviets wanting to pursue a course of co-existence and the Chinese being opposed to it.'[34] He was also not oblivious of the fact that any *rapprochement* between the super-powers would make India's mediatory role in world politics obsolete. Peaceful co-existence for Nehru, however, lay in the logic of history, and he would rather bring this about than let his country's prestige thrive any longer on the continuing competitiveness between the super-powers.

The Cuban crisis and Chinese aggression against India seemed to many severe blows to Nehru's optimism, but Nehru himself thought otherwise. In his estimate, these two major events of 1962 set the world more firmly in an era of peaceful co-existence.

He interpreted the Cuban crisis as showing that the nuclear powers were most reluctant to go to war[35] – a healthy sign, for it was bound to lead 'to further *rapprochement* on various matters' that were in conflict.[36] Throughout 1962, Nehru lent his full support to the movement for disarmament and anti-nuclear tests. In the summer of 1962 he held an Anti-Nuclear Arms Convention in Delhi which was attended by some eminent people from America, Russia and Britain. To live under the shadow of the mushroom cloud was to him a most uncivilised existence. He opposed any grouping of nations which was likely to add to the tension between the East and the West. This was one of the reasons for his opposing, in September 1962, Britain's proposed entry into the Common Market. He feared that this might add to the world's tension, lead to an extension of the NATO alliance and diminish the chances of disarmament.[37]

The super-powers were not unresponsive to the pressure put on them by the non-aligned world. Kennedy and Khrushchev had met in Vienna in June 1961, but the Berlin crisis of August 1961 had set them apart. They came closer together again in 1962 when starting the eighteen-nation Geneva Disarmament Conference. The Conference was to function for a number of years. But in the meantime, on 5 August 1963, Britain, America and the Soviet Union signed in Moscow a partial Nuclear Test Ban Treaty; partial because it excluded underground tests from the ban. The Treaty gladdened Nehru's heart. He welcomed it as a great landmark in history.[38] For him and other leaders of the non-aligned world the Treaty marked the accomplishment of their purpose in bringing the super-powers together on specific points. It also marked for them the end of the Cold War. China, however, condemned the Treaty as a 'dirty fraud to fool the people of the world'.[39] But China stood in 1963 isolated, on account of its war with India in the autumn of 1962.

The Sino-Indian border war (20 October–21 November 1962) was a unique armed conflict of the twentieth century. Unique were the circumstances which led to the war and the manner in which it was fought and concluded. Two questions – what led China to attack India on 20 October, and why did it suddenly, on 21 November, end the war by a unilateral ceasefire and withdrawal? – have since puzzled critics and chroniclers of the event and, perhaps owing to the inaccessibility of the Chinese material, even the most serious studies have been speculative in their analyses and findings. Many theories have been put forward but none holds the ground exclusively. It appears to have been a most humane war; no brutalities were committed by either side, and the total loss of lives on the Indian side was not more than 1383, and far less on the Chinese side. It was not a total war (air power was not used by either side), not even a declared war, and both countries maintained their diplomatic relations intact. Confined as it was within a belt 50–100 miles wide on each of India's two border fronts, it was essentially a local war. And yet, as far as India was concerned, it was more of a people's war than one contrived by the Government and the Army, for the last two were in fact forced into it by the first. The Chinese strategy, of separating the

Indian soldiers and people from Nehru's 'bourgeois' government and appealing to the former to lay down their arms, did not work.

Before turning to the theories of the war, some basic facts must be set out. After the occupation of Tibet by China in 1950, India came to have 2600 miles of border with China, stretching from the trijunction of India, Afghanistan and Sinkiang in the north-west to the trijunction of India, Burma and Tibet in the north-east. Along this border-line in the eastern sector lay three mountain kingdoms, the independent state of Nepal and the Indian protectorates of Sikkim and Bhutan. These three kingdoms almost adjoined each other. The entire border, east of Bhutan, was defined by the McMahon Line (drawn in 1914) and was called the eastern sector. The border lying west of Nepal and stretching up to Sinkiang ran along the frontiers of the Indian states of United Provinces, Himachal Pradesh and the Ladakh region of Kashmir. In Sino-Indian parlance the portion stretching from the west of Nepal to Ladakh was called the middle sector, and the entire Ladakh boundary with Tibet and Sinkiang was called the western sector. India had inherited this border from the British Raj. India also sincerely believed that this long border with China had been delimited at various times in the past and had now become customary and international. Indian control and occupation, however, did not extend to all parts of the territories which India claimed lay within its border with China. Many parts of the border lands were barren and some lay at an altitude of above 14,000 feet where nothing grew. One such area was the Aksai Chin region of Ladakh across which China had built its Sinkiang–Tibet highway. India did not know until the autumn of 1957 that this part of its border territory had been 'seized' by China. Furthermore, India did believe, certainly up to the end of 1957, that it had no border dispute with China. As mentioned earlier India's belief grew stronger after 1954 when the Chinese, by declining to discuss any border problem, gave the impression to the Indian officials that there was no such problem. But the Chinese maps kept on appearing, and for the first time Nehru appeared suspicious and worried when he wrote to Chou in December 1958 complaining about the Chinese maps. Chou En-lai's letter to Nehru of 23 January 1959 opened the Chinese case for the first time.[40] Chou now maintained that the Sino-Indian border had never been formally delimited, and that the Chinese felt as aggrieved at India's claiming areas of Chinese territory in the western sector as the Indians might have felt at the Chinese maps disputing Indian holdings in the eastern sector. It seemed apparent from Chou's letter that China was willing to concede Indian claims in the eastern sector in return for India's acknowledgement of Chinese rights in the western sector, particularly over the Aksai Chin. China did not raise this point before, Chou said, because the point was not ripe for discussion.

At this juncture Nehru suspected China of deceitfulness, and thus Chou's suggestion that the entire border question be opened to negotiation appeared to him to be a trap. The Tibetan revolt of March 1959 strengthened, on the one hand, Nehru's suspicion about China and on the other caused confusion and misunderstanding in Chinese thinking about India. Nehru recalled Chou's assurance given to him in 1954–5 that China would not interfere with Tibetan autonomy and would not impose socialism upon its people for another thirty or forty years. He was distressed not only because the Chinese were destroying Tibetan autonomy but also because they were falsely proclaiming to the world that the Tibetan revolt was organised by a handful of reactionaries, the serf-owners, and was aided and abetted by the Indian expansionists from their base at Kalimpong (in India). Nehru had good reasons to believe that the Tibetan revolt against the Chinese was not the work of a handful of feudal lords but that it had mass support. He also knew very well that his government and his people had in no way abetted the revolt. He would, however, have been much happier if the Dalai Lama had not escaped to India, as he did on 30 March. If Nehru had refused asylum to the Dalai Lama, he would have antagonised Indian public opinion and inflamed the feelings of India's Buddhist population. Since the Dalai Lama could not be turned away, Nehru saw to it that he was settled in a remote place, Mussoorie. He himself called upon the Lama in Mussoorie partly to gratify public opinion and partly to impress upon the local officials that they should 'avoid making too much of a fuss of the Dalai Lama's stay there'.[41] He resisted the pressure laid on him by the foreign press and governments to condemn the Chinese:

> People used to cold war do not seem to realise that our approach to questions is different and that it does little good to shout loudly and denounce and condemn. We expressed sympathies with the grieved party which normally indicates our own thinking. To denounce and condemn is to use the methods of the cold war.[42]

Nehru was cautious because he did not want to provoke the Chinese. This in turn implied that he believed that Chinese suspicions, though entirely groundless, were in some measure sincere. He feared that the Chinese, unused to the democratic system, might regard the hostile public criticism of their behaviour in Tibet as representing the policy of the Indian Government.

There was much scope for misunderstandings on China's part, and Nehru's restraint was of no avail. The Chinese were led to believe that in giving asylum to the Dalai Lama and 13,000 Tibetan refugees India had deliberately displayed hostility towards China. Chinese aggression on the border mounted, and on 25 August 1959 the Chinese fired at the Indians at Longju (in the eastern sector), a post which the Chinese claimed lay on their side of the McMahon Line. The Indians had to retreat. This was the first shooting affray of the boundary dispute and was followed in a month by another in the western sector where on 21 October nine Indian policemen were killed by the Chinese.

It was against this background that Chou En-lai in his letter of 8 September 1959 to Nehru put forward, in what Nehru called a most aggressive style, China's full case relating to the border. While affirming that China had never been a party to any agreement on the delimitation of the border, he accused India of having taken advantage of the Tibetan revolt to occupy certain posts in the eastern sector which lay on the Chinese side of the McMahon Line. But perhaps the most aggressive part of the letter, for Nehru anyway, was that which referred to Sikkim and Bhutan almost as independent states.

Nehru was puzzled and annoyed. Why had China assumed such a rigid attitude? Had something happened in China to compel a change in policy? Or was it because China was angered and soured by India's grant of asylum to the Dalai Lama? Or was it because China wanted to put India in her place? Nehru also wondered about the problem of communication:

> I often wonder if we, that is the Government of India and the Government of China, speak quite the same language, and if, using the same words or similar words, we mean the same thing. Secondly, and I know this from experience, it is a terrific problem to translate Chinese into any other language. I am quite sure that Marx must be different in Chinese from the original German or the translations in English and other languages.[43]

However, even though Nehru was disillusioned by Chou's letter, he was adamant against pursuing an openly hostile policy towards China:

> We may get excited about the sacredness of the Indian soil and the Chinese people may get excited about something they hold sacred, if they hold anything sacred. But nothing can be a more amazing folly than for two great countries like India and China to get into a major conflict and war for the possession of a few mountain peaks, however beautiful the mountain peaks might be, or some area which is more or less uninhabited.[44]

This was said in all honesty to calm down agitated Indian feelings. But he was aware that people's passions had been brought to a high level not because of a patch of territory but because they felt that they had been ill treated, bullied and almost cheated by the Chinese Government. As a democratic leader Nehru had to follow his people, to bow to their demand for the vindication of India's honour against China. He could not resist the people's demand because it was based on their conviction, which Nehru could not contradict, that China had not only turned into a disloyal friend but also had stealthily occupied Indian territory.

China's position on the border in November 1959 (with its occupation of Aksai Chin in the western sector) was the one it wished to be conceded and legitimised by India and, as it turned out, this was the position which China came to retain after the war in 1962. In what happened between November 1959 and September 1962 perhaps lay the causes of the outbreak of armed hostilities on the frontier. Three major developments took place during this period. First, as has been observed earlier, India moved closer to the Anglo-American bloc. Secondly, these three years saw a widening of the rift between Russia and China, and a steady increase in Soviet aid to India. Thirdly, India pursued during this period a 'forward policy' on her frontiers.

Tension between the two countries began to build up in 1958 when Russia expressed disapproval of the Chinese communes, collectivisation and peasant revolution. In the same year Mao refused to allow the Russians to build a radio station in China to keep in contact with their submarines in the Pacific Ocean. Behind the Chinese refusal Khrushchev saw nothing but Mao's aggressive nationalism.[45] Mao did not want the Russians to lord it over the Chinese in the same way as the British, French and Americans had done before. Mao was proud of China's manpower and of the Chinese language, which, he pointed out to Khrushchev, did not contain a single word from any European language. Khrushchev's endeavours towards easing international tension, his visit to America and his meeting with Eisenhower in September 1959, displeased the Chinese leaders. Khrushchev was given a sulky reception when he visited Peking soon after his visit to America. In the background of the Khrushchev–Mao meeting on 30 September lay the Russian criticism of the Chinese action in opening fire on Indians at Longju. In essence Russia had accepted the Indian version of the Longju event, which of course had gratified Nehru as being a 'dispassionate view of the situation',[46] but annoyed the Chinese who in this saw the first instance when a socialist country condemned another socialist country which was confronted by armed provocation. The ideological war between Russia and China was fought in June 1960 (at Bucharest where the Romanian Communist Party was holding its conference) and again in October 1961 at the twenty-second Communist Party Congress held in Moscow. Chou En-lai left the Congress prematurely as a protest against Khrushchev's further attack on Stalinism. The rift between the two became public in March 1962 when the Russians and Chinese held their congresses separately in Moscow and Peking.

In June 1962, Nehru disclosed that India was planning to purchase MIG aircraft from Russia.[47] In August, Russia agreed to provide India with twelve MIG-21s and also technical assistance in establishing production facilities for this model in India. This angered the Chinese leaders.[48] Russia now stood thoroughly discredited in their eyes. Not only had Russia been supporting India financially (India had received from 1954 to 1960, according to Russian statistics, 3.2 billion old roubles, the lion's share of the credit Russia had extended to developing countries during that period) but was now also making available 'war material', knowing that this might be used against China. In September 1962 the radical communists, like Lu Ting-yi and K'ang Sheng who represented the aggressive policy, were firmly in the saddle in the Chinese Communist Party. It was in September 1962, so some sources have confidently assumed, that the Chinese leaders approved the plan of attacking India in the Himalayas.[49] In his post-mortem on the Chinese invasion Nehru maintained that one of China's reasons for attacking India was to force India to change her policy of non-alignment. If China could succeed in that, he said, it could then prove to Russia that the policy of non-alignment was fictitious and therefore it was pointless to give help to non-aligned countries. China thus wanted to show that her ideological analysis of the world was correct and that Russia's was wrong.[50] If it was China's intention to divide the world into two camps, as Nehru believed, then it did not succeed in bringing this about through its invasion of the Indian borderlands.

Nehru, however, did not take into account the possible impact on the Chinese of India's pursuing, from 1959 to September 1962, what came to be called a forward policy on her borders, particularly in the western and eastern sectors. India's forward policy aimed at establishing control over disputed border areas which had hitherto been almost inaccessible, and in reclaiming Indian territories, which had been already occupied by the Chinese, without provoking war. It involved constructing new roads in the frontier regions (from early 1960 to the end of 1962 nearly 2000 miles of roads were constructed), and sending police and military patrols as far forward as possible towards the international border, in order to prevent the Chinese from advancing any further into Indian territory and to make India's presence felt in those remote parts of the frontier area. It further involved establishing new guard-posts. By the end of August 1962, India had established nearly forty such posts in the disputed areas of the western sector and about twenty in the eastern sector. Two of these posts came into the limelight; the Galwan post in Ladakh which the Indian soldiers occupied in July 1962 and retained till 20 October, when it was wiped out by the Chinese, and the Dhola post in the North-East Frontier Agency which was established by the Indians in June 1962 and overrun by the Chinese on 8 September. India had by 8 September 1962 apparently improved her position on the border. When on that day the Chinese attacked the Indian position a number of events followed in quick succession leading to the outbreak of the border war on 20 October.

The forward policy was Nehru's only way out of the *impasse* into which he had been led by the Chinese Government and Indian public opinion. Chou's letter of 8 September 1959 set Nehru against starting any negotiation with China. Chou had revived China's claims on the basis of the old map which claimed large areas of Indian territory – half of North-East Frontier Agency, one-third of Assam and one-third of Bhutan, apart from claiming the whole of the Aksai Chin region in the western sector. It seemed to him absurd and fantastic that the Chinese should have based their demand on what happened in past centuries. If the Chinese argument – that while China was weak large parts of its territory were seized by the British imperialists – was taken further back in history and applied against China itself, Nehru wondered, 'how much of the great Chinese State would survive this argument'?[51] Was this great state not itself the creation of Chinese imperialism? 'I have a feeling', Nehru told the Members of Parliament, 'that just as there is a certain paranoia in individuals, sometimes there is a paranoia in nations.'[52] He was disinclined to meet a paranoiac China at a conference table. Negotiation on the entire border, which Chou demanded, was therefore in principle unacceptable to Nehru. He was also aware that Indian public opinion would not accept such a negotiation. Nehru was, however, prepared to negotiate specific border adjustments, and even to lease the Aksai Chin region to China for a limited period, an agreement he almost made when Chou En-lai met him for the last time in Delhi, in April 1960. But by then public opinion had been aroused against any kind of negotiation with China, and the Home Minister, Pant, decisively put his weight against it.[53]

Even though the last Nehru–Chou meeting was a failure, it brought into focus the importance China attached to 'the line of actual control' exercised by each party on the border. Any future settlement of the border dispute was likely to be made on this principle. This probability emphasised for India the need to extend its actual control in all areas it claimed as falling within its border. This was thus another factor in the evolution of India's forward policy.

India continued to take offence at China's activities on the Indian frontier. China concluded boundary treaties with Burma in October 1960 and with Nepal in October 1961. In May 1962, Pakistan and China agreed to negotiate their boundary question; an agreement was concluded in March 1963. It seemed to Indians that China, by peacefully concluding boundary agreements with these countries, was trying to prove to the Afrasian world that it was Indian obduracy and aggressiveness which had prevented such an agreement being peacefully concluded between India and China. The sudden growth of Sino-Nepalese friendship was particularly alarming to India. Critics blamed Nehru for having strained the Indo-Nepalese relationship. On 15 December 1960, King Mahendra of Nepal dissolved the elected parliament and arrested the leaders of the Nepali Congress Party, including the Prime Minister, B. P. Koirala. Nehru's love for democracy impelled him to toss political expediency to the winds and publicly condemn the King's *coup*.[54] The King veered towards China.

Pakistan's relations with India had improved in the latter part of 1959, and President Ayub Khan offered to enter into a joint defence alliance with India against China. For Nehru such an alliance would mean the abandonment by India of all the principles for which it had stood.[55] Besides, it would have pulled India into SEATO and the Baghdad Pact which Nehru had so vehemently criticised in the past. He rejected the offer. Finding no effective support from America and Britain on the Kashmir issue, Pakistan, during the years 1960 and 1961, looked to China and the era of Sino-Pakistani friendship began.

Opposed as he was to opening negotiations with China and embarrassed by China's diplomatic manœuvres with Nepal, Burma and Pakistan, Nehru was left with a choice between preparing for a border war and maintaining border vigilance. He ruled out war. India and China could not enter into a war. If it began it would never end. It would be suicidal. Having ruled it out himself, he believed till the last moment that China would never declare war on India. Thus the only option left for India was a vigilant forward policy on its border. If India had followed this policy from the very beginning, Nehru now realised, it would have prevented China from occupying Indian territories in Ladakh.[56] All other possibilities (negotiation, war, or sitting tight and doing nothing) being rejected, India adopted the peculiarly Indian approach of making its presence felt in its border areas. In view of the fact that nobody, from the Prime Minister down to the poorly equipped soldiers who trod the inhospitable mountains, believed that the Chinese would ever be provoked into a war, India's forward policy seemed to rely for its success more on Chinese sense of fair play and forbearance than on its own inner strength. It had the mental if not the physical characteristics of a Gandhian non-violent civil disobedience movement.

On these three major developments of the years from 1959 to 1962 are based the various theories concerning the causes of the outbreak and the cessation of the armed conflict on the Sino-Indian border. But before considering these theories it is worth recapitulating the main events of the period between 8 September and 21 November 1962.

On 8 September, Chinese soldiers crossed Thag La ridge, in the eastern sector, and overran the Indian post at Dhola. India considered this to be a further intrusion by the Chinese into its territory. That very day Nehru had to leave India for the Commonwealth Prime Ministers' Conference in London. The Defence Minister and the army commanders decided that the Army should be given the task of driving out the Chinese from Indian territory in the eastern sector. The Indians did not believe that this action would lead to war; however, the army officers on the spot had doubts about the Indians' ability to perform the allotted task. The Chinese appeared to have all the strategic advantages on their side, and the portion of the Indian Army deployed in the eastern sector was ill prepared to undertake a major offensive. A few skirmishes proved the truth of this. On 2 October, Nehru returned from abroad. Lieutenant-General B. M. Kaul, Chief of General Staff, was chosen to take over the army command in the eastern sector, and the most aggressive phase of India's forward policy began when he arrived there on 4 October. Kaul, like Nehru, believed that the Chinese would not fight back. He was shaken when on 10 October the Chinese did fight back and destroyed the Indian position at Tsangley, a post the Indians had occupied the previous day. Kaul returned to Delhi and a full conference of ministers, generals and high officials was held at the Prime Minister's residence on 11 October. The question posed was whether the Indian forces should withdraw further or hold on to the positions they still occupied. It was decided that they should not retreat. With a view to pacifying agitated public opinion, Nehru, before leaving for Ceylon on 12 October, made a statement to the press at the airport to the effect that he had ordered the Army to turn out the Chinese from Indian territory. This was the kind of statement which the Indian people expected from him. In making it, Nehru was not worried about the implication it might carry for the Chinese; it was intended to calm the Indian public and as a purely verbal threat to the Chinese whom he was still convinced would not provoke war. The Chinese, however, took it at face value. On 14 October the *People's Daily* warned the Chinese people of the danger of an imminent massive invasion of Chinese territory by Indian troops. However, on the assumption that the Chinese had already mobilised their forces on the frontiers before Nehru made his statement of 12 October, one may argue that the statement might have served as an excuse rather than a cause for the Chinese showdown with India.

Except for the half-hearted decision to hold on to the front the Indian forces took no real measures during the period 12–20 October. On 20 October the Chinese attacked the Indian positions in both the eastern and the western sectors. The war had begun in earnest. Almost all the Indian forward positions in the western and eastern sectors were overrun within days. The army commanders in the eastern sector, having neither heart nor determination to fight, planned at one point to evacuate the whole of Assam, but this plan was subsequently modified. It was now obvious that the Indian troops were quite unprepared for fighting at such high altitude. It would, however, be different if the Chinese advanced down to the plains where the Indians might have the advantage; but this was not to happen.

On 20–1 November, China declared a ceasefire, unilaterally, at the height of its victory in the mountain warfare. Both sides, China declared, were to withdraw to positions twenty kilometres behind the line of actual control which existed between China and India on 7 November 1959. In the eastern sector this meant a Chinese withdrawal to twenty kilometres north of the McMahon Line. When the news of the Chinese ceasefire was conveyed to Nehru he is reported to have exclaimed:

> I knew this. This had to happen. This was bound to happen. How could the Chinese come any further? They had already come too far. Our army was unnecessarily alarmed. The Chinese, now that they are at the end of their supply routes, want to get a diplomatic victory over us. They may try to have their way but we will not give in to their demands.[57]

The Indian reverses had infuriated the Indian people and some army generals (including Kaul) and Krishna Menon, the Defence Minister, fell victims to this fury. They were forced to resign. Nehru was most reluctant to blame anybody, except himself, but he had to give way to the popular demand for the dismissal of Menon. Menon was replaced by Y. B. Chavan, the Chief Minister of Maharashtra.

The ceasefire was followed by a conference of non-aligned nations (Ceylon, Egypt, Cambodia, Ghana, Indonesia and Burma) on 10 December in Colombo to discuss the ceasefire terms for India and China. India's counter-proposal that the positions both parties occupied on the border on 8 September 1962 (and not those of 7 November 1959) be restored was supported by Nasser, and for this the Egyptian leader received Nehru's personal gratitude. The Colombo proposals gave India a position up to the McMahon Line in the eastern sector and left India's position in the western sector virtually as it was on the day of the ceasefire. The proposals were not intended to delimit the boundary; they merely set conditions for the ceasefire. They were accepted by India and China, with some reservations on each side, and the positions the two countries occupied on their borders in November 1959 were virtually restored to them. China and India never met to delimit the boundary.

Why did China attack? And why did she suddenly declare a ceasefire? The lack of Chinese material had made any probing into China's real motives a difficult task for historians. Perhaps because of this some historians have tended to accept China's case (as represented by Chou En-lai's letters to Nehru and by the Chinese press) at face value, and have held India responsible for provoking China into a war.[58] By comparison with other approaches this is relatively simple, and is sustainable to a point. But it does not solve the puzzle entirely. For example, it does not explain why it was the Chinese who took the offensive. Even the supporters of this pro-Chinese approach here find the Chinese explanation untenable. The Chinese maintained that it was India who attacked first. In his letter of 15 November 1962 to the leaders of Asian and African countries the Chinese Prime Minister affirmed:

> Finally, in the early hours of October 20, Indian troops, on Prime Minister Nehru's orders, launched massive attacks all along the line. It was only when they had been repeatedly subjected to frenzied attacks by the Indian troops and had suffered heavy casualties that the Chinese frontier guards, pressed beyond the limits of forbearance and left with no room for retreat, struck back in resolute self-defence.[59]

This was untrue. Nehru had given no such order nor did the Indian Army launch the alleged massive attack along the border. Why, then, did China attack? It was certainly not to secure any additional territorial gains, either on the border or in the interior of India, for within a month China had retreated of her own accord to the position she held before the attack. The evidence suggests that China had planned in advance not only the invasion but perhaps its duration as well. What, then, were China's aims? Here other theories must come into play. Did the Chinese wish to undermine India's leadership of the Third World? Or try to destroy India's non-aligned status? Or did they expect that the invasion would arouse the anti-Nehru forces in India and lead to a collapse of his government? Or did China want to upset India's planned development and thereby destroy her potential for competition? Or is it possible that China just wanted to teach a lesson to the 'arrogant' Indian leaders? Or, finally, was the showdown primarily intended to consolidate the Chinese position in Tibet, and to prove to the anti-Chinese forces that India was in no position ever to play the role of a liberator in that region?

Various interpretations have also been advanced, mostly by Indians, to explain the sudden declaration of the ceasefire by the Chinese. The Chinese, having realised that they could not long maintain their advanced position, decided to withdraw with a great show of magnanimity and thereby to humiliate India further, and to establish China's *bona fides* among the Afrasian nations as a peace-loving nation. It is also possible, the Indian analysts have suggested, that Russian disapproval of their aggression obliged the Chinese to withdraw. Krishna Menon had no doubt in his mind 'that one of the conducive factors behind the Chinese withdrawal was the Soviet unwillingness to give them support, not only militarily but in fuel and other things'.[60] It is also suggested that fear that America and Britain would come to India's support might have induced the Chinese to call a halt. America and Britain were the first to respond to Nehru's letter of 27 October 1962, addressed to all heads of government (excluding South Africa and Portugal), asking for support and sympathy in opposing Chinese aggression. Even though President Kennedy was not convinced by Nehru's insistence that non-alignment was as strong as ever,[61] the first squadron of American C-130 Hercules heavy transport planes arrived in New Delhi on 22 November. That very day there arrived in New Delhi the British mission headed by Sir Richard Hull, Chief of the

Imperial General Staff, and a large American mission headed by Averell Harriman. The Chinese, however, had already announced a ceasefire a day earlier.

Turning now to Nehru's reaction, he was at first shocked by the news; he had been convinced that China would never wage a war against India. At the most he had expected a few more border skirmishes, not a massive invasion by two or three divisions.[62] His initial shock lasted only a few days during which time he made some statements which revealed his frustration and disillusionment. On 25 October he said: 'We were living in an artificial atmosphere of our own creation and we have been shocked out of it, all of us, whether it is the Government or the people though some may be in less fear.'[63] For the first time in his life, he felt, he had received 'evil' in return for 'good':

> Perhaps there are not many instances in history where one country, that is India, has gone out of her way to be friendly and co-operative with the Chinese Government and people and to plead their cause in the Councils of the world, and then for the Chinese Government to return evil for good and even go to the extent of committing aggression and invade our sacred land.[64]

But when his initial shock had passed he began to analyse the possible motives behind the Chinese invasion. In doing so he gave no serious thought to the possibility that China too might have felt aggrieved, and might have lived under the constant fear of an Indian attack on Tibet. The main reason why Nehru did not pursue this line of enquiry seriously was that he knew very well that India had never nourished such designs on Tibet. Giving asylum to the Dalai Lama and letting him appeal to the United Nations to take action over Tibet (as the Lama did in September 1959) were for Nehru the normal acts of a democratic government and in no way did they constitute hostility by India towards China. He would have made some allowance for misunderstanding on China's part, but the latter's past conduct (in occupying stealthily 12,000 square miles of territory in Ladakh, knowing that India claimed it as its own, and at a time when the two countries were on the friendliest of terms) left Nehru with no scope to offer a charitable interpretation of the Chinese motive.[65] Hence, though he was aware of the Chinese apprehension in relation to Tibet, he considered it to be groundless, merely the outcome of the Chinese 'queer feat of imagination'.[66] Likewise, the Chinese protests against India's so-called forward policy were for Nehru equally unreal. As far as he was concerned India had only tried to recover the territories the Chinese had illegally occupied. For Nehru, therefore, the Chinese fear of India was not the real reason for their aggression on the border.

Nehru came to believe that China had various sinister motives for her organised attack on India. The first and foremost purpose of the Chinese aggression, in Nehru's analysis, was to destroy the non-aligned status of India. China not only wanted to keep the world divided between the so-called imperialists and communists but also to keep tension mounting between the two. In Chinese ideology therefore there was no room for the non-aligned, hence:

> It is logical to conclude that China's multiple campaign against India is an exercise in *realpolitik* on those lines. India is such an outstanding member of the non-aligned community that her defection, whether voluntary or enforced, cannot fail to bring grave and far-reaching consequences in its train.[67]

The Chinese challenge, Nehru maintained, was not only to India's foreign policy but also to India's domestic policy, to India's economic and political system, in essence to all Nehru stood for.[68]

Having so analysed the Chinese motive, Nehru forsook his mood of frustration, took up the Chinese challenge in all seriousness, and from October 1962 to December 1963 he worked to preserve and strengthen all he himself had built, and all he thought China was out to destroy. This was for him the real battle with China and this battle he was determined to win.

First he tried to wipe from the Indian mind the sense of defeat. India had been conditioned, he told his people, 'in a democratically peaceful manner', which was different from China's conditioning.[69] Indian reverses on the frontiers were therefore the result of Indian conditioning. Indeed, although he was now obliged to increase spending on defence, he was nonetheless adamant against letting India veer towards militarism and an authoritarian system. The democratic apparatus was for him the best 'even from the point of view of war', and he was determined to preserve it unshaken. Even at the height of the Chinese aggression he asked Indians not to hate the Chinese people because emotions such as hatred and vengeance might damage the democratic structure of India.

The foremost task was to preserve the unity of India in face of the Chinese challenge. This task he thought the Chinese themselves had unwittingly accomplished for him. Even the Communist Party of India had promised its full support to the Government against China. Realising that the people stood firmly united behind his government, he felt secure against the Chinese challenge, and even grateful to China.[70] Chinese propaganda, which aimed at separating the people from the Government, was, to Nehru's delight, utterly defeated. During these months of trial, Nehru was more concerned than any of his colleagues in mobilising the resources of the nation, in speeding up production, and in implementing the Third Five-year Plan, which he maintained was India's best defence against China.

Nehru derived great satisfaction from his success in retaining India's non-aligned status. India received open support, moral and material, from the Anglo-American bloc. Apart from America and Britain, France too agreed to supply arms to India on a priority basis. In their talks at Nassau in the Bahamas in December 1962, Kennedy and Macmillan agreed to continue Western military aid to India. No strings were attached, although some pressure was being put on India to settle its continuing conflict with Pakistan over Kashmir. The Anglo-American concern over Kashmir was aroused particularly because Pakistan seemed to be veering towards China, and a Sino-Pakistani boundary agreement was in the offing. However, the Anglo-American endeavours to achieve some settlement between India and Pakistan were frustrated when the latter signed the boundary agreement with China on 2 March 1963. In the Indian view, Pakistan surrendered to China, by this agreement, 13,000 square miles of its 'illegally' occupied Kashmir territory.

Receiving arms from the Anglo-American bloc, particularly in a time of emergency, did not, for Nehru, imply any compromise with India's non-aligned status. He was, however, put in a slightly embarrassing position when in July 1963 India signed an agreement with America for the purchase of a powerful transmitter for use in the All-India Radio External Services. As part of the arrangement India had agreed to let America broadcast from the Indian radio station the 'Voice of America' for certain hours on certain days. When Nehru realised that the agreement might give China a basis for propaganda against India, and it might also be construed in other quarters as compromising India's avowed non-aligned policy, he hastened to obtain amendments in the agreement more in keeping with India's status.

The friendly attitude which the Soviet Union maintained towards India throughout the war was to Nehru a great proof of India's non-aligned status.[71] He was much gratified when in September 1963 the Soviet Union repeated its support for India on the Kashmir issue.

Since the beginning of 1960 Nehru had consistently maintained that the greater the danger of Chinese aggression the greater the need for India to stick to the policy of non-alignment 'because it is now the testing time for my thinking, for India's thinking'.[72] When the danger came he asked his audience, 'are our hands to shiver, our feet to grow cold, and are we to seek shelter under somebody's umbrella'?[73] Six months after the Sino-Indian war, he confidently affirmed:

> Whatever temporary military success the Chinese may have gained by their aggression on India, I think it would be correct to say that they have failed thus far in their main endeavour. Not only have they converted a friendly country like India into one basically hostile to them and united and determined against them, but the policy of non-alignment has not broken down and stands confirmed. China has lost the goodwill of most of the non-aligned countries and even of many of her communist allies. She stands isolated today.[74]

Furthermore, he saw that the two super-powers were nearer to each other now than ever before. The Cuban crisis had opened a new era in international relations and the East–

West antagonism of the 1950s seemed to have come to an end.

At the end of 1963 Nehru could look back over the events of the preceding years with a sense of triumph. He had turned many a defeat into victory and in his own way he had won the battle against China. For the people of India he was, even at the age of seventy-four, indispensable and seemingly indestructible. He was still unwilling passively to accept the progress of events and sought an active role. As if to remind himself of the task that lay ahead he had lately been carrying about with him four lines of poetry he had copied from Robert Frost:

> The woods are lovely, dark and deep
> But I have promises to keep,
> And miles to go before I sleep,
> And miles to go before I sleep.

With 1964 began his last battle, the only one which he had to lose.

CHAPTER THIRTEEN

The Last Struggle, January–May 1964

The chief concern that fills my mind is how to find a synthesis between the old and the new, because I do not find it good enough entirely to discard the old and, obviously, I cannot discard the new.

Jawaharlal Nehru, January 1964

AT the start of 1964, Nehru was not unusually perturbed by any problem. Only the crisis in Kashmir, which had been caused by the disappearance, on 27 December 1963, from a shrine in Shrinagar, of a strand of hair believed to be of the Prophet Mohammad caused him real concern. This holy relic, so the tradition went, had been brought to India from Medina in the seventeenth century and, in due course, found its habitat in Kashmir. Its sudden disappearance infuriated the Muslim people of Kashmir, and politically interested parties directed their fury against the Government of Kashmir. Also, Pakistan, which according to the Indian intelligence officers had had a hand in arranging the theft of the holy relic, now exploited the situation by accusing the Government of India of having engineered the theft to humiliate the Muslims of the Kashmir valley.[1] Law and order almost collapsed, and a demand for the release of Sheikh Abdullah grew among the people of Kashmir. Nehru became concerned about the recovery of the holy relic; he was disappointed that the people of Kashmir could, in the heat of the moment, attack his government, forgetting all it had done for them over the past fifteen years. He thought that a new policy towards Kashmir was necessary. But behind his thinking lay his desire to set free, on some excuse or other, his old friend Abdullah. As a democrat he hated detention without trial, and it was at his insistence that Abdullah had been set free, though only temporarily, in 1958. But in 1964 the trial of Abdullah for conspiracy was imminent and the prosecution seemed confident that his conviction was certain.

The holy relic, however, was recovered on 4 January.

Nehru was relieved, but Abdullah remained on his conscience. The growing political instability in Kashmir, coupled with his own wish to come to some final settlement with Pakistan, impelled Nehru to seek a solution of the problem through Abdullah. He succeeded in securing the release of Abdullah about a month before his death. Many of Nehru's colleagues silently resented the decision, for Abdullah was in their eyes an uncertain factor. But for Nehru it was a matter of personal gratification to meet him and to have him stay in his house. With Nehru's blessings he went to Pakistan on 24 May to explore the possibility of an Indo-Pakistan agreement on Kashmir. The outcome of this was a meeting between President Ayub Khan and Nehru, arranged to be held on 27 May – as it turned out, the day of Nehru's death.

Nehru had been struggling for life since 7 January when, while attending the Congress session in Bhubaneswar in Orissa, he had suffered a serious stroke affecting his left side. This was his second major illness; the first had been in the spring of 1962 when a kidney affliction had left him with a slight stoop. He recovered from the stroke but his physical style was changed: he was slightly paralysed on one side, he walked slowly with a dragging gait, and there were breaks in his speech; he now often delivered his public speeches while sitting. His superb body was now broken and he came to be regarded as 'an old man'. He himself now appeared almost as he had described his dying father, thirty-three years before – 'an old lion mortally wounded and with his physical strength almost gone, but still very leonine and kingly'; the difference was that, whereas his father resigned himself to the inevitable before it happened, Nehru fought it resolutely for five months until at last he fell into a state of coma and the inevitable happened without his knowledge and without his consent.

He took his illness as a challenge. The habit he had formed in his youth, never to give way to illness, and which he had pursued throughout his life, came to be useful. In this last as in all the previous struggles of his life, he derived strength and confidence from the people, for whom he was ageless and indestructible. But those who moved around him knew that he could not last much longer, that it was the beginning of the end. He had been the leader of his people for thirty-five years, ruler of India for nearly seventeen. His death, the politicians and the press felt, would create a vacuum which nobody could adequately fill. Those who could aspire to succeed seemed lightweights by comparison. But Nehru could, so urban India thought, enhance the political stature of any of his colleagues by choosing that colleague to be his successor. In a way the nation was expressing its absolute confidence in him by asking him to choose his own successor.

Nehru, however, did not comply. The most important reason for this was that no one among his possible successors stood above the others. Each had as much claim to be the head of the Government as any other. Nehru had never had a recognised second-in-command since the death of Patel, although Pant, during his lifetime, came very near to that position. Nehru had always been reluctant to exercise his personal power to choose, but now was even more hesitant because he thought it would be grossly unfair on his part to indicate a preference for any candidate. Besides, although the nation might accept his choice, the frustrated aspirants might feel aggrieved and consequently irreconciled to his nominated successor. He did not want to hurt or disappoint anybody and this was the main consideration, which on the one hand prevented him from interfering in the matter of succession and on the other led him into determining that the issue, as and when it arose, must be decided democratically by the nation. The democratic process suited his principles as well as the peculiarity of the situation.

Why did he not step down and let the nation choose his successor? This question was asked by some journalists and politicians who suspected that on account of his illness Nehru was unable to rule effectively, and that the Government was overcome by the crippling malaise of inertia. Indeed the Prime Minister's functions were in some measure discharged jointly by G. L. Nanda (the Home Minister), T. T. Krishnamachari (the Finance Minister) and Lal Bahadur Shastri. The last had been called back into the Cabinet in February as minister without portfolio. Kamaraj, now the Congress President, had moved to the centre of the power structure, and it seemed that the affairs of the Government for the first time since independence were run by collective leadership.

A variety of reasons might have induced Nehru to remain in office. It is possible that he did not believe (or want to believe) that his illness had permanently incapacitated him and that the end was near at hand. He struggled optimistically to regain his physical powers. In his last press conference, held on 22 May, when he was asked whether it would not be in the interest of the country for him to solve the problem of succession during his lifetime, he replied: 'My life time is not ending so very soon.'[2] It is, however, possible that he feared unconsciously that this was not true. In that case, he would, as he had always hoped, die in harness. Nothing would have discomforted him more than the idea of withering away in retirement.

In this continuous tug-of-war between hope and reality the former seemed, in mid-May, to be winning. He seemed definitely improved when attending the All-India Congress Committee session in Bombay on 16–17 May. Mrs Pandit, then Governor of Maharashtra, noticed that her brother's appetite had returned and that he was overflowing with a renewed zest for life. Nehru returned to Delhi on 17 May but on the following day he suddenly felt unwell. Doctors prescribed rest, and on 23 May he was taken to Dehra Dun for a three-day holiday. There he showed signs of recovery. He played with children and enjoyed chatting with his old friend Sri Prakash. On 26 May he returned to Delhi looking forward to attending the Commonwealth Prime Ministers' Conference in June. He asked Shastri, who met him at the airport, to accompany him to London for the Conference.

On that evening of 26 May nobody had any grounds to suspect that the Prime Minister had only hours to live. Nehru went to his residence, had his dinner, retired to his study where he dictated correspondence and notes on official papers, and then went to sleep around 11 p.m. with only a male attendant nearby – Indira's rooms were at the opposite end of the house. During the night he woke twice complaining of pain, and each time he took a sedative. At about six in the morning he awoke with severe pains in the lower back and abdomen. Doctors arrived within half an hour to discover that Nehru's aorta artery had burst, and death was inevitable. He had by then relapsed into a coma. A blood transfusion, using Indira's blood, was tried, but it was of no avail. By half-past eight any small hope had faded. He breathed his last at 1.44 p.m. on 27 May. He was seventy-four years and six months old.

The news travelled fast to all corners of India and the world. Millions of Indians felt orphaned by his death; outside India many felt that the world was somehow darker without the man who had done so much honour to humanity, the man who was at once the great nationalist and the devout citizen of the world.

Within hours of Nehru's death the question of succession was on its way to being resolved. G. L. Nanda, as the most senior member of the Cabinet, was sworn in by President Radhakrishnan to act as prime minister until the Congress Parliamentary Party could choose its new leader. Indeed the succession game began on the very afternoon of Nehru's death. Morarji Desai was the first to enter the arena, but the choice of the Congress Party was to fall on Lal Bahadur Shastri. In choosing the successor to Nehru by means of a consensus the Congress Party displayed great political maturity.

The funeral took place the following day, on 28 May. Nearly three million people lined the six-mile route of the funeral procession. Many foreign dignitaries (including Sir Alec Douglas-Home, Prime Minister of Britain, and A. N. Kosygin, the First Deputy Premier of the Soviet Union) attended the funeral. At 4 p.m. the cortège reached the cremation ground on the bank of the River Yamuna, only 300 yards from the place where Gandhi's body had been cremated in January 1948. At about half-past four his grandson Sanjay lit the pyre amidst the chantings of Hindu and Buddhist priests; a volley of small arms was fired three times and twenty-four buglers sounded the Last Post; while his body was being consumed by fire the Muslim leader Sheikh Abdullah leapt on the platform, wept and threw flowers on to the flames. A synthesis of the ancient and modern, of eastern and western, of Hindu and Muslim, such as he had tried to achieve in his life, now attended the last farewell the nation gave him on that evening.

India observed twelve days of state mourning and, what was more remarkable, the United Arab Republic observed seven days and Nepal, Kuwait and Cambodia three days of state mourning. The ashes of his body were dispersed in the manner which he had laid down in the will which he had written in 1954. A portion of his ashes was dispersed, on 9 June, in the sacred River Ganges at Allahabad, his home town. It was not for any religious reason that he had wished this, but because the Ganges had been to him 'a symbol and a memory of the past of India, running into the present, and flowing on to the great ocean of the future'. A major portion of his ashes, however was disposed of in a different manner. As he had wished, this portion was carried high up in the air in an aeroplane and scattered from that height 'over the fields where the peasants of India toil, so that they might mingle with the dust and soil of India and become an indistinguishable part of India'.

Nehru had never been concerned about life after death. He did not know whether it existed or not; hence, as was his style, he neither denied nor asserted it. But he had always been conscious of history and consequently a little curious about the place historians would assign to him when he was gone. However, a historian himself, he must have known that in the abbey of history demolition and restoration are carried on continuously and that the leaders of men and of thought have no fixed positions and postures. Interpretations of the past are as fickle, uncertain and diverse as speculations about the future. It is the present which sets the norms and standards by which the past is judged and the future fathomed.

A dozen years have now passed since he died. Has Nehru's position changed over these years? Many statements were made about his statesmanship on the day he died. The Soviet leaders acclaimed him as 'the outstanding statesman of our time'.[3] Charles de Gaulle called him the great democrat. U Thant, the Secretary-General of the United Nations, remarked that 'few men of this age have left their mark on the history of their country as he has' and that he had also affected the course of world events. Hayato Ikeda, the Prime Minister of Japan, thought that Nehru was 'the world's greatest peacemaker'. For Tito of Yugoslavia, Nehru was 'deeply human for the people of the world'. And so on.

Comparing these statements, which were then made, with

a number of studies of Nehru which have appeared over the last decade, one retains the impression that he is one of the very few who continue to occupy the same high position today that they held when they died. At the same time one feels that, in assessing Nehru's place in history, statesmen and historians have been influenced more by the personality of Nehru – his ideas, vision and humanity – than by the impact he made on the course of history. In fact many have found difficulty in assessing his practical achievements. Of course, some have succeeded in preparing a long list of his achievements as a nationalist, a democrat, a prime minister and an internationalist, but they have left the impression that this has been done principally with a view to finding rational justification for their intuitive liking for Nehru. He has been the most liked leader of the twentieth century, and at the same time an enigma to those who have wondered – why? Nehru's uniqueness also lies in the fact that people have been apologetic for his failures rather than critical of them. Indeed, to many Nehru became more endearing, more human, for his innocent faults and human failings. His case has also been uniquely gratifying to those who wish to see an essentially good man succeed in his life and command the affairs of men.

Nehru is the only one of his kind in the galaxy of twentieth-century statesmen. Though he is placed in that select group which includes Lenin and Mao, Churchill and Roosevelt, he has hardly anything in common with them, not even the power which they all seem to have wielded, for Nehru was more the custodian than the user of power. In fact Nehru seems to be a complete outsider in the company of notable politicians and statesmen.

What distinguished Nehru from others was the fact that throughout his life he lived and worked in the realm of ideas. Filled as he was with the qualities of imagination, perception and intuition, he used them to identify new norms and trends which were taking shape in every field of human progress. Through this exercise he acquired an idea of the world as it was going to be, a vision which coincided with his concept of the world as it ought to be. He made his abode in this desired, expected world, and therefore lived in a future which history had yet to bring into existence. Perhaps he was the kind of man who would always be ahead of his time no matter when and where he lived. The present, for him, was always in the melting-pot, hence it was less real than the future. Not all of the present distressed him – only those aspects of it which he thought contravened the values on which the future was to be based. Communalism (or for that matter any grouping based on religion, caste or race), capitalism, colonialism and racialism were those aspects of the present which he thought were dying, and had no purpose and meaning for the future. Likewise, the Cold War, for him, was a temporary phase. Those who were perpetuating it were, in his opinion, standing against the inevitable trends of history. At a time when Soviet–American tension was at its highest, Nehru was perhaps the only man who believed that in the not too distant future these super-powers were bound to become friends.

Living in this future world Nehru often ignored, and sometimes derided, the ugly facets of the present world; but he never fought these realities ruthlessly. This was not because he lacked courage but because he was reluctant to destroy. Evolution, not revolution, was his style. He believed that change should come about through people's own volition, as a result of their experience, and that it should not be foisted upon them through any kind of force or pressure. This made him less effective in creating changes, both on the domestic and on the international front, and he was well aware of it:

> In the pursuit of change, we should seek to carry the mass of the people with us and win their support. This way of dealing with our problems may not result in as swift or spectacular a transformation as we might wish, but at least the progress achieved will have a solid basis in the nation's consent and avoid a degree of dislocation and disorganization that we can ill afford.[4]

His achievements, therefore, lay more in preventing distractions from the course of human progress than in urging it forward. He was sustained by that sense of the inevitability of progress which he had imbibed in his youth. It was sufficient for a statesman to hold the ring while the natural goodness of man, his reason progressively unchained from the shackles of ignorance and prejudice, steadily ameliorated his own condition. Among the distinguished statesmen of the twentieth century he alone could prophesy the future with any certainty, for he almost lived in it. He deliberately under-estimated the strength of what he considered the reactionary and dying forces of the present world, and as a result he was often tormented, and sometimes defeated and disillusioned by them; but until the end of his life he refused to acknowledge them as real. Communalism defeated his secular nationalism and Pakistan was created; the Chinese aggression challenged his concept of peaceful co-existence. But he took these reverses as merely the temporary victories of vice and falsehood over virtue and truth. In believing that the truth would always win and in abstaining, almost religiously, from returning evil for evil he excelled even Gandhi. But he did not match his master in ascertaining accurately the strength of the adversary forces and opposing them relentless. More commonly, Nehru provoked his opponents by pretending that they did not exist.

His spiritual loneliness was, however, real, although he sought to submerge it in his romantic love for the people of India. No man in the twentieth century was loved by so many millions of people. Gandhi was revered and worshipped; Nehru was adored, loved and cherished. In acknowledging this in his will he wrote: 'I have received so much love and affection from the Indian people that nothing that I can do can repay even a small fraction of it, and indeed there can be no repayment of so precious a thing as affection.'[5] But he did try to repay. He gave the people of India unity, regarded them as God, and framed them in democracy. It was not just that he himself was more ardently devoted to democracy than was any other Indian; he also believed that the democratic system was that best suited to the genius of India. Through democracy he wanted to adore and preserve the dignity and freedom of the Indian people, and protect them against the humiliation and coercion from which they had suffered enough in the past.

In the last year of his life, while lying in the shadow of illness and loneliness, conflicts and frustrations, he could reflect that the world was moving steadily towards peaceful co-existence, and India was firmly rooted in the democratic way of life.

If it were so, it was no mean achievement.

Notes

ABBREVIATIONS

AICCP	All-India Congress Committee Papers
GP	Gokhale Papers
JN	Jawaharlal Nehru (in Chapters 1–7 only)
JP	Jayakar Papers
MN	Motilal Nehru
MP	Mahmud Papers
MPP	Mrs Pandit Papers
Nehru	Jawaharlal Nehru (in Chapters 8–13 only)
NP	Nehru Papers
PP	Prasad Papers
TP	Thakurdas Papers

CHAPTER 1 Sowing of the Seed

1. MN to JN, 19 Sept 1920, NP.
2. Ibid.
3. MN to JN, 23 Nov 1905, NP.
4. MN to JN, 8 Nov 1905, NP.
5. MN to JN, 20 Oct 1905, NP.
6. MN to JN, 31 Dec 1908, NP.
7. MN to JN, 23 Dec 1910, NP.
8. MN to JN, 30 June 1927, NP.
9. Lansdowne on legislative councils, 16 March 1893, in *The Evolution of India and Pakistan. Select Documents 1858–1947*, ed. C. H. Philips and others, p. 69.
10. Ibid. p. 68.
11. Gokhale's resolution of 5 Feb 1898, GP, File 203.
12. The inner circle of Congress included, from Bengal – S. N. Banerjea, B. N. Basu, W. C. Bonnerjee, R. C. Dutt; from Madras – G. Subramania Iyer, S. Subramania Iyer; from Bombay – Pherozeshah Mehta, Dadabhai Naoroji, G. K. Gokhale, D. E. Wacha.
13. Dufferin on Congress, Nov 1888, in *Select Documents*, ed. Philips, p. 145.
14. Curzon to Hamilton, 18 Nov 1900, in ibid. p. 151.
15. See GP, File 382, 1897.
16. The leaders of militant nationalism were B. G. Tilak (a teacher and journalist), Aurobindo Ghose (an educationist who later turned into a philosopher and mystic) and B. C. Pal (an author and journalist). Lajpat Rai (a lawyer and social reformer from the Punjab) was a sympathiser but not a committed member of the militant group.
17. MN to JN, 4 Dec 1905, 22 March 1906, 20 Dec 1906, NP.
18. See *India List*, 1905.
19. *Islington Commission Report*, vol. 1, pp. 24–5.
20. *Report of the Royal Commission on Superior Civil Service in India*, p. 129.

CHAPTER 2 The Growth of an Intellectual, 1905–12

1. JN to Mrs V. L. Pandit, 7 Sept 1943, MPP
2. JN, *Autobiography*, p. 8.
3. Ibid. p. 7.
4. JN to S. R. Nehru, 28 Nov 1907, NP. (All letters of JN to his mother S. R. Nehru are written in Hindi and are translated by the author.)
5. MN to JN, 4 Dec 1905, NP.
6. JN to S. R. Nehru, 28 March 1907, NP.
7. JN to S. R. Nehru, 31 May 1907, NP.
8. JN to S. R. Nehru, 17 Feb 1910, NP.
9. JN to S. R. Nehru, 24 June 1910, NP.
10. JN to S. R. Nehru, 5 July 1912, NP.
11. JN to S. R. Nehru, 4 Dec 1908, NP.
12. JN, *Autobiography*, p. 15.
13. Ibid. p. 16.
14. Ibid. p. 14.
15. Ibid. p. 6.
16. Ibid. p. 6.
17. Ibid. p. 16.
18. Ibid. p. 16.
19. Ibid. p. 12.
20. Ibid. p. 17.
21. C. M. Fox to JN, 18 Jan 1913, NP.
22. MN to JN, 19 Jan 1911, NP.
23. Ibid.
24. Gandhi to Spiegal, 10 Feb 1933, Spiegal Papers.
25. N. D. Parikh, *Sardar Vallabhbhai Patel*, p. 19.
26. JN to S. R. Nehru, 20 Dec 1907 and 14 Feb 1908, NP.
27. JN to MN, 24 Oct 1907, NP.
28. JN to MN, 1 Nov 1906, NP.
29. JN to MN, 24 Jan 1907, NP.
30. JN to MN, 17 May 1906, NP.
31. JN to MN, 22 March 1907, NP.
32. JN to MN, 8 Nov 1906, NP.
33. Ibid.
34. JN to MN, 25 July 1907, NP.
35. JN to MN, 3 Dec 1908, NP.
36. JN, *Autobiography*, p. 19.
37. JN to MN, 29 Oct 1908, NP.
38. JN to MN, 15 July 1910, NP.
39. MN to JN, 24 June 1910, NP.
40. JN to S. R. Nehru, 4 Oct 1907, NP.
41. MN to JN, 24 June 1910, NP.
42. Ibid.
43. Ibid.
44. MN to Bansidhar Nehru, 30 Jan 1910, NP.
45. JN to MN, 19 Aug 1910, NP.
46. JN to MN, 8 Sept 1910, NP.
47. JN to MN, 1 Sept 1910, NP.
48. MN to JN, 22 Sept 1910, NP.
49. JN to MN, 22 Sept 1911, NP.
50. JN to MN, 5 Dec 1911, NP.
51. MN to Bansidhar Nehru, 9 Oct 1912, NP.
52. JN to MN, 18 Jan 1907, NP.
53. JN to MN, 18 March 1909, NP.
54. JN to MN, 10 June 1911, NP.
55. JN to MN, 8 Feb 1907, NP.
56. MN to JN, 16 Nov 1905, NP.
57. JN to MN, 3 Dec 1905, NP.
58. MN to JN, 29 March 1906, NP.
59. H. A. Vachell, *The Hill.*
60. JN to MN, 4 March 1906, NP.
61. MN to JN, 4 Jan 1906, NP.
62. MN to JN, 27 Dec 1906, NP.
63. MN to JN, 24 Jan 1907, NP.
64. JN to MN, 8 Feb 1907, NP.
65. K. D. Malaviya, *Pandit Motilal Nehru: his life and speeches*, p. 109; cited in B. R. Nanda, *The Nehrus*, p. 60.
66. JN to MN, 19 April 1907, NP.
67. MN to JN, 17 May 1907, NP.
68. MN to JN, 18 Oct 1907, NP.
69. Brooks visited Ireland in the autumn of 1906 and wrote for the *Daily Mail* a series of articles on the new Irish nationalism. The book emerged from these articles and ran into two editions in the first year of its publication.

70. Brooks, *The New Ireland*, pp. 1–2.
71. JN to MN, 7 Nov 1907, NP.
72. JN to MN, 2 Jan 1908, NP.
73. JN to MN, 16 Jan 1908, NP.
74. JN to MN, 4 June 1908, NP.
75. JN to MN, 3 Dec 1908, NP.
76. JN to MN, 14 May 1909, NP.
77. MN to JN, 1 March 1906, NP.
78. MN to JN, 1 Sept 1910, NP.
79. JN to MN, 30 Sept 1910, NP.
80. MN to JN, 28 Oct 1910, NP.
81. See his presidential speech to the United Provinces Social Conference, April 1909, cited in Nanda's *Nehrus*, p. 107.
82. Rameshwari Nehru to JN, 29 Oct 1906, NP.
83. JN to S. R. Nehru, 7 May 1909, NP.
84. JN to MN, 17 Nov 1909, NP.
85. MN to JN, 8 Sept 1910, NP.
86. Krishanlal Nehru to JN, 8 March 1912, NP.
87. JN to MN, 30 Jan 1907, NP.
88. MN to JN, 9 Dec 1910, NP.
89. JN to MN, 22 Sept 1911, NP.
90. An unidentified Miss Roy who appears in the letter of Krishanlal Nehru to JN, 8 March 1912, NP.
91. JN to S. R. Nehru, 14 March 1912, NP.
92. MN to JN, 5 April 1912, NP.
93. JN to MN, 26 April 1912, NP.
94. MN to JN, 5 April 1912, NP.
95. JN to MN, 26 April 1912, NP.
96. JN to MN, 29 Dec 1911, NP.

CHAPTER 3 Waiting for a Leader, 1913–19

1. JN, *Autobiography*, p. 27.
2. Eva Willis to B. G. Khaparde, 4 Aug 1911, Khaparde Papers.
3. T. T. Krishnamachari to the author.
4. W. S. Blunt to Syed Mahmud, 17 Jan 1910, 30 Oct 1910, 24 July 1913, MP.
5. Some representatives of this section of the Muslim political community (consisting of both the English-educated members of the middle-class and the school-educated ulama) were: Shaukat Ali, Muhammad Ali, Muhammad Iqbal, Abdul Kalam Azad, Shibli Nomani and Hasrat Mohani.
6. Muhammad Iqbal's lecture delivered at Aligarh in 1910, cited in P. Hardy's *The Muslims of British India*, p. 179.
7. JN, *Autobiography*, p. 48.
8. *The Leader*, 23 June 1916; also in the *Selected Works of JN*, ed. S. Gopal, vol. 1, p. 104.
9. MN to JN, 27 June 1916, NP.
10. JN, *Autobiography*, p. 28.
11. MN to JN, 26 April 1914, NP.
12. MN to JN, 10 Aug 1915, NP.
13. Mrs Pandit to the author.
14. MN to JN, 14 June 1916, NP.
15. Ibid.
16. Diaries of JN, NP. The October 1916 entries record the arrival of some Hindu and Muslim leaders.
17. JN, *Autobiography*, p. 34.
18. Ibid.
19. The leaders among the young nationalists who supported Mrs Besant's Home Rule League were Umar Sobhani, P. K. Telang, Jamandas Dwarkadas, Shankerlal Banker, Indulal Yagnik, K. M. Munshi, R. D. Morarji and K. T. Shah.
20. D. G. Tendulkar, *Mahatma: life of Mohandas Karamchand Gandhi*, vol. 1, p. 224.
21. Mrs Besant to Gokhale, 15 Nov 1914, GP.
22. Gokhale to B. N. Basu, 14 Dec 1914, GP.
23. J. Dwarkadas, *Political Memoirs*, pp. 92–6.
24. Letter to the editor, *The Leader*,

21 June 1917; *Selected Works*, vol. 1, pp. 106–7.

25. Ibid.
26. JN to A. M. Khwaja, 12 Dec 1917, *Selected Works*, vol. 1, pp. 109–10.
27. *Report on Indian Constitutional Reforms*, p. 119.
28. MN to JN, 13 Dec 1918, NP.
29. JN, *Autobiography*, pp. 129–30.
30. Ibid.
31. Gandhi in *Young India* of 10 Dec 1919, quoted in Tendulkar *Mahatma*, Vol. 1, p. 334.
32. For Tilak's estimate of Gandhi, see Dwarkadas's *Political Memoirs*, pp. 245–51.
33. Dharna was the ancient Indian custom of recovering a debt through the creditor sitting doggedly, and fasting, for days at the debtor's door.
34. M. K. Gandhi, *An Autobiography*, p. x.
35. Tendulkar, *Mahatma*, vol. 1, pp. 281–5.
36. Chelmsford to King-Emperor, 21 May 1919, Chelmsford Papers. MSS.EUR.E.264.1.
37. Two Bills, based on the Rowlatt Committee Report of April 1918, were introduced in the central legislature in March 1919, and one of them was enacted for three years on 18 March; the other was dropped.
38. Gandhi to Sastri, 9 Feb 1919, *Collected Works of Mahatma Gandhi*, vol. 15, pp. 87–8.
39. Tendulkar, *Mahatma*, vol. 1, p. 317.
40. Gandhi, *Autobiography*, pp. 363–6.
41. MN to JN, 16 Feb 1919, NP.
42. Ibid.
43. MN to JN, 4 Oct 1919, NP.
44. MN to P. S. Sivaswamy Aiyar, 12 Dec 1919, NP.
45. The Congress sub-committee (consisting of Gandhi, Motilal Nehru, C. R. Das, Malaviya and a few other co-opted members) was appointed on 8 June 1919 to enquire into the Punjab tragedy independently of the Government-appointed Hunter Committee.
46. MN to P. S. Sivaswamy Aiyar, 12 Dec 1919, NP.
47. *Report of the 34th Session of Congress*, p. 123.
48. JN's political thinking at this stage is reflected in a review article he wrote in 1919 for Bertrand Russell's book, *Roads to Freedom*; *Selected Works*, vol. 1, pp. 140–4.
49. Ibid.
50. Ibid.
51. Ibid.
52. JN to R. Dar, 29 Jan 1920, NP.

CHAPTER 4 The Plunge into the Politics of Suffering, 1920–1

1. JN, *Autobiography*, 104.
2. JN to Mrs Pandit, 29 Jan 1944, MPP.
3. Ibid.
4. JN's Prison Notebooks, NP.
5. In *Young India*, 4 Aug 1920, quoted in Judith M. Brown's *Gandhi's Rise to Power: Indian Politics 1915–1922*, p. 251.
6. JN, *Autobiography*, p. 75.
7. See JN to M. Desai, Sept 1923, *Selected Works*, vol. 1, p. 382.
8. MN to JN, 27 Feb 1920, NP.
9. MN to JN, 29 Feb 1920, NP.
10. AICCP, File 8, 1920.
11. Ibid.
12. In July 1920 the House of Lords supported Dyer by 129 votes against 86. The British public collected £26,317 within a month to mark their support for Dyer.
13. MN to JN, 21 March 1920, NP.
14. Ibid.
15. JN to MN, 14 May 1920, NP.
16. Ibid.
17. MN to JN, 3 June 1920, NP.

18. JN, *Autobiography*, p. 51.
19. Ibid. p. 52.
20. Ibid. p. 78.
21. *Selected Works*, vol. 1, pp. 165–7.
22. MN to JN, 27 June 1921, NP.
23. Ibid.
24. Mrs Pandit to the author.
25. In support of the boycott of foreign cloths the Nehrus parted with their garments made of foreign cloth and four cartloads of them were taken to the park in Allahabad and burnt. K. N. Katju. Oral History.
26. MN to Gandhi, 10 July 1924, File No. 403, JP.
27. Gandhi to MN, 3 July 1924, File No. 403, JP.
28. JN, *Autobiography*, 73.
29. Prison Papers, 1920–1, NP.
30. JN's speech at Bundhelkhand conference, 13 June 1921, *Selected Works*, vol. 1, p. 179.
31. Ibid. p. 182.
32. JN, *Autobiography*, p. 61.
33. Gandhi to S. R. Nehru, 28 Nov 1934, NP.
34. F. Gunther to JN, 6 July 1938, NP.
35. *The Independent*, 22 Jan 1921.
36. JN to Gandhi, Nov 1921, *Collected Works of Mahatma Gandhi*, vol. 21, pp. 535–7.
37. Prison Papers, 1920–1, NP.
38. *The Independent*, 8 Dec 1921.
39. Quoted in Nanda's *Nehrus*, p. 196.
40. Gandhi to S. R. Nehru, 7 Dec 1921, NP.

CHAPTER 5 Beginnings of Compromise, 1922–5

1. JN, *Autobiography*, pp. 91–3.
2. Dr Moonje to Jayakar, 3 June 1925, JP.
3. Dr Moonje to Jayakar, 23 June 1922, JP.
4. Gandhi to JN, 19 Feb 1922, NP.
5. Ibid.
6. Not many Indians gave up their titles, resigned their government offices or wound up their legal practice. For example, only 24 out of 5186 Indian title-holders resigned by Jan 1921. Only 87 honorary magistrates had resigned by March 1921, and just over 180 lawyers had given up their practice by March 1921. The boycott of schools and colleges, though impressive in the beginning was weakened by the middle of 1921. See Brown's *Gandhi's Rise to Power*, pp. 309–10.
7. Reading to the Prime Minister, 4 May 1922, Reading Papers.
8. Gandhi's statement as quoted in the *Indian Annual Register* (1922), vol. 1, p. 212.
9. Gandhi to MN, 27 Sept 1924, NP.
10. Reading to Prime Minister, 4 May 1922, Reading Papers.
11. For Gandhi's statement and C. N. Broomfield's judgement see, *Select Documents*, ed. Philips pp. 222–4.
12. The mass civil disobedience consisting of non-payment of revenue was to be started in Bardoli (Gujarat) but was suspended owing to the occurrence of the Chauri Chaura tragedy.
13. JN's circular to congress committees, 5 May 1922, *Selected Works*, vol. 1, pp. 249–50.
14. JN's Prison Diary, 1922–3, NP.
15. JN to MN, 17 Oct 1922, NP.
16. JN to MN (in Hindi), 13 July 1922, NP.
17. JN to MN, 1 Sept 1922, NP.
18. Ibid.
19. MN to JN, 25 Aug 1922, NP.
20. JN to MN, 13 July 1922, NP.
21. JN's Prison Diary, 1922–3, NP.
22. See K. M. Munshi, *Pilgrimage to Freedom*, p. 23.
23. MN to S. Satyamurti, 27 Nov

1922, Satyamurti Papers. The election of delegates for the Congress session had been regularised by the Congress constitution of 1920, which Gandhi had drafted. It was no longer possible to flood Congress sessions with delegates of one's own choice.

24. JN's speech, 18 Feb 1923, *Selected Works*, vol. 1, p. 353.
25. V. Patel to JN, 24 June 1923, NP.
26. JN's presidential address to the United Provinces conference, 13 Oct 1923, NP.
27. Ibid.
28. JN's message from Nabha jail, *Selected Works*, vol. 2, pp. 31–2.
29. JN on electoral reform, 7 May 1923, *Selected Works*, vol. 2, pp. 9–11.
30. *Selected Works*, vol. 2, p. 14.
31. JN, *Autobiography*, p. 146.
32. In March 1923 the district authority of Nagpur banned the flying of the national flag on the municipal building. First the local congress body and later the All-India Congress Committee organised the civil disobedience against the ban. Patel took charge of the movement in July and succeeded in securing the release of all prisoners by the beginning of September. For a further account of the episode see Parikh's *Sardar Vallabhbhai Patel*.
33. MN to JN, 28 Sept 1923, NP.
34. Ibid.
35. JN to Sri Prakash, 7 Oct 1923, Sri Prakash Papers.
36. However, JN was too ill to address the conference personally. His speech was read in his absence on 13 Oct 1923.
37. See JN–Dr N. S. Hardikar correspondence, Sept 1924, NP. Hardikar was the General Secretary of the organisation.
38. Gandhi's statement, AICCP, File 15, 1925.
39. Gandhi to S. Mahmud, 6 May 1924, MP.
40. MN to P. Thakurdas, 8 Sept 1924, TP. Gandhi's five-fold boycott was of titles, legislature, schools and colleges, law courts, and foreign clothes.
41. *Collected Works of Mahatma Gandhi*, vol. 24, p. 27.
42. JN, *Autobiography*, p. 126.
43. *Collected Works of Mahatma Gandhi*, vol. 24, p. 341.
44. MN to C. R. Das, 27 July 1924, NP.
45. Gandhi to JN, 15, April 1924, 30 Sept 1925, NP.
46. Gandhi to Rajaji, 6 Sept 1924, *Collected Works of Mahatma Gandhi*, vol. 25, p. 98.
47. *Collected Works of Mahatma Gandhi*, vol. 25, p. 259.
48. Ibid. vol. 25, pp. 360–3.
49. Ibid. vol. 25, pp. 471–89.
50. JN, *Autobiography*, p. 132.
51. For JN'S views on this issue, see his letter to the editor, *The Leader*, 7 Nov 1924, reprinted in *Selected Works*, vol. 2, pp. 197–8.
52. JN, *Autobiography*, p. 137.
53. JN to Gandhi, 12 Sept 1924, *Selected Works*, vol. 2, p. 169.
54. JN, *Autobiography*, p. 140.
55. JN to K. M. Pannikar, 2 April 1924, AICCP, File No. 4 (i), 1924.
56. Jayakar to Malaviya, 15 Nov 1925, JP, File 406, 22–3.
57. JN to Padmaja Naidu, 29 Jan 1926, NP.

CHAPTER 6 Emergence of a Leader, 1926–9

1. MN to JN, 20 May 1926, NP.
2. MN to JN, 30 March 1927, NP.
3. MN to JN, 7 May 1926, NP.
4. Mrs V. L. Pandit to MN, 6 Oct 1926, NP.
5. JN to S. Mahmud, 1 Dec 1926, MP.

6. Kamala Nehru to S. Mahmud, original in Urdu, undated, but written sometime in 1926 from Montana. MP.
7. Kamala Nehru to S. Mahmud, original in Urdu, June 1927, MP.
8. Kamala Nehru to S. Mahmud, undated [1927], original in Urdu, MP.
9. JN, *Autobiography*, p. 156.
10. JN wrote an article on his impressions of the strike for the October 1926 issue of the Hindustan Seva Dal monthly *The Volunteer.* Reprinted in *Selected Works*, vol. 2, pp. 247–9.
11. JN's report to AICC on the Brussels Congress, 19 Feb 1927, AICCP, File G. 29/1927, Part 2.
12. JN to Mrs Pandit, 12 Nov 1927,NP.
13. JN's note on a proposal for a Parliamentary Bill for India, 10 March 1927, NP.
14. MN to JN, 30 March 1927, NP.
15. Ibid.
16. MN to JN, 11 Aug 1927, NP.
17. MN to JN, 2 Sept 1926, NP.
18. Viceroy to Secretary of State, 26 March 1927, Government of India to Secretary of State, 28 April 1927. Home Political File 6/27.
19. MN to JN, 14 April 1927, NP.
20. MN to JN, 4 Jan 1928, NP.
21. For an understanding of JN'S goals and concepts see: (*a*) his letter to the editor, *Journal de Genève,* dated 3 Aug 1926 and published in the issue of 28 Oct 1926 (letters to editors, NP); (*b*) JN'S report to the Working Committee of Congress on the International Congress Against Imperialism held in Brussels from 10 to 15 Feb 1927 (AICCP, File G. 29/1927, Part 2); (*c*) JN's, 'A Foreign Policy for India', written on 13 Sept 1927 (AICCP, File 8, 1927); and (*d*) JN's *Soviet Russia.*
22. JN's report on the Brussels Congress, AICCP, File G.29/1927, Part 2.
23. JN's note on a proposal for a Parliamentary Bill for India, 10 March 1927, NP.
24. JN, 'A Foreign Policy for India', NP.
25. Ibid.
26. Ibid.
27. H. K. Hales to JN, 25 Oct 1933, NP.
28. JN to Hales, 28 Oct 1933, NP.
29. JN, 'A Foreign Policy for India', NP.
30. Ibid.
31. JN, *Soviet Russia*, in *Selected Works*, vol. 2, p. 448.
32. Ibid. vol. 2, p. 451.
33. JN's report on the Brussels Congress, AICCP, File G. 29/1927, Part 2.
34. JN to Hardikar, 26 June 1928, Hardikar Papers.
35. JN's report on the Brussels Congress, AICCP, File G. 29/1927, Part 2.
36. JN to S. Mahmud, 12 Sept 1926, MP.
37. Ibid.
38. JN to Gandhi, 11 Jan 1928, NP.
39. Gandhi to JN, 25 May 1927, NP.
40. JN to Gandhi, 22 April 1927, NP.
41. Report of the Congress proceedings, Madras, 1927.
42. JN to Gandhi, 11 Jan 1928, Gandhi Papers.
43. See Government of India telegram to Government of Bombay, 29 Dec 1928, Home Political File 179/29/Pols.
44. AICCP, File 12, 1928.
45. JN's address at the Indian Youth Conference, Dec 1927, *Selected Works*, vol. 3, p. 179.
46. JN to Gandhi, 13 July 1929, NP.

47. JN's speech, 4 Sept 1928, *Selected Works*, vol. 3, p. 61, and his speech at the All-Parties Conference, 29 Aug 1928, *Report of the All-Parties Conference* (1928).
48. Gandhi to JN, 4 Jan 1928, NP.
49. Gandhi to JN, 1 April 1928, NP.
50. JN to Gandhi, 11 Jan 1928, Gandhi Papers.
51. Gandhi to JN, 11 Jan 1928, NP.
52. JN to Gandhi, 23 Jan 1928, Gandhi Papers.
53. Home Political File 20/5/1929.
54. JN, *Autobiography*, p. 187.
55. JN to Mrs Pandit, 24 and 31 May 1928, NP.
56. Correspondence between MN and P. Thakurdas, 18 and 22 Aug 1928. TP, File 72.
57. Ibid.
58. MN to Gandhi, 24 Nov 1928, NP.
59. MN to Gandhi, 14 Aug 1929, NP.
60. AICCP, File AP.1, 1928.
61. Government of India to Government of Bombay, 29 Dec 1928, Home Political File 179/29.
62. Ibid.
63. AICCP, File G. 68, 1929.
64. Ibid. File 43, 1929.
65. Report of the committee appointed by AICC to revise Congress Constitution, AICCP, File G. 27, 1928.
66. Home Political File 236, 1929.
67. Ibid.
68. MN to JN, 11 Aug 1927, NP.
69. JN to Gandhi, 22 April 1927, Gandhi Papers.
70. Gandhi to Ansari, 10 Aug 1927, NP.
71. JN to S. Mahmud, 30 June 1928, MP.
72. Constitution of the Indian National Congress as amended in 1923. AICCP, File 28(ii), 1929.
73. AICCP, File 43, 1929. Gujarat did not make any recommendation, and Ajmer and Punjab were not entitled to – the former on account of its being a very small constituency and the latter because it was the host province for the 1929 Congress session.
74. Tendulkar, *Mahatma*, vol. 2, p. 490.
75. JN, *Autobiography*, p. 194.
76. V. Chattopadhyaya to JN, 6 Oct 1929, AICCP, File FD.1, Part III, 1929.
77. JN to Congress President, 4 Nov 1929, AICCP, File G. 117, 1929–30.
78. JN to Gandhi, 4 Nov 1929, NP.
79. JN to Bridgeman, 23 Nov 1929, AICCP, File F. D. 23, 1929–30.
80. Presidential address, 29 Dec 1929, *Selected Works*, vol. 4, pp. 189–90.

CHAPTER 7 The Introspective Warrior, 1930–6

1. 'When shall India get Swaraj? Prophecy of Indian situation.' AICCP, File G.40(1), 1930, undated but based on the prophecy made in December 1929.
2. JN's speech, 6 Feb 1930, Home Political, File 90, 1930.
3. JN, 'Inqilab Zindabad', 24 March 1930, NP.
4. Government report on Abdul Gaffar Khan's speeches, Home Political File 33/24/31.
5. See P. Thakurdas to MN, 22 Sept 1930, TP, File 104 (1930).
6. Ibid.
7. JN to N. Chaudhuri, 15 Oct 1933, NP.
8. JN to the Secretaries, League Against Imperialism, 30 Jan 1930 and 9 April 1930, AICCP, File F.D.I., 1929–30.
9. Ibid.
10. MN to JN, 4 Feb 1930, NP.
11. Gandhi to JN, 6 Feb 1930, NP.
12. Tendulkar, *Mahatma*, vol. 3, p. 15.

13. JN's circular to provincial Congress committees, 22 Feb 1930, AICCP, File P-1-1930.
14. JN was in prison from 14 April to 11 Oct 1930, 19 Oct 1930 to 26 Jan 1931, 26 Dec 1931 to 30 Aug 1933, and 12 Feb 1934 to 4 Sept 1935.
15. JN to A. Horace, 17 Sept 1935, NP.
16. JN to A. Horace, 20 Nov 1933, NP.
17. JN, *Glimpses of World History*, p. 947.
18. Mahadev Desai to JN, 25 Sept 1935, NP.
19. Mahadev Desai to JN, 19 Dec 1935, NP.
20. JN to Goswami, 25 May 1936, also JN's letter to the editor, *Servants of India*, 13 June 1936, NP.
21. Jayakar to Polak, 22 May 1936, JP.
22. Dr Urchs to JN, 26 Aug 1936, AICCP, File G5(KW) (ii).
23. Narendra Dev to JN, June 1936, NP.
24. Malkani's review of JN's *Autobiography*, Malkani Papers, Accession No. 100, 1936.
25. JN to Malkani, 9 July 1936, Malkani Papers.
26. JN, *India and the World*, p. 63.
27. JN to S. Mahmud, 24 Sept 1935, MP; also JN's essays in Hindi, July 1935, NP.
28. JN to Mrs Pandit, 7 April 1932, MPP.
29. JN's Prison Diary, 15 March 1932, NP.
30. JN to Superintendent, Dehra Dun district jail, 14 July 1934, NP.
31. JN's Prison Diary, 10 May 1932, NP.
32. JN to Mrs Pandit, 25 June 1930, MPP.
33. Irwin to P. Thakurdas, 29 Sept 1930, TP.
34. JN's report on the rent and revenue situation in United Provinces, 18 April 1931, AICCP, File 4, 1931, Part 1.
35. See Sapru to Jayakar, 10 Nov 1934, JP, File 408.
36. The official note on the history of negotiations, Home Political File 31/97/32.
37. JN to Gandhi, 28 July 1930, Gandhi Papers.
38. MN to Dr Mehta, 30 Oct 1930, NP.
39. JN, *Autobiography*, p. 236.
40. MN to Mrs Pandit, 25 Nov 1930, NP.
41. Ibid.
42. JN, *Autobiography*, p. 246.
43. Tendulkar, *Mahatma*, vol. 3, p. 66.
44. JN to Krishna (Betty), 21 Feb 1931, *Nehru's Letters to his Sister*, ed. Krishna Nehru Hutheesing, p. 20. A similar assurance and support he gave to Mrs Pandit after her husband's death. See JN to Mrs Pandit, 13 March 1944, MPP.
45. Ibid.
46. Sapru to Bikaner, 11 Feb 1931, quoted in D.A. Low's 'Sir Tej Bahadur Sapru', in *Soundings in Modern South Asian History*, p. 319.
47. JN, *Autobiography*, 259.
48. *Gazette of India*, 5 March 1931, Home Political File 5/45/31.
49. JN'S speech at Allahabad, 10 March 1931, *Selected Works*, vol. 4, p. 490.
50. JN's speech in Bombay, 7 June 1931, ibid. vol. 5, p. 1.
51. A fairly accurate account of Gandhi's role in the Karachi Congress session is contained in the government note which was based on information acquired

from some Congressmen who were close to the Congress High Command. (Note on Congress session, 7 April 1931, also Viceroy's telegram to Secretary of State, 2 April 1931, Home Political File 136/31.)

52. *Report of the 45th Session of the Indian National Congress*, pp. 139–41. In April 1931 the Congress Working Committee appointed a Fundamental Rights Committee. This committee enlarged upon the main points of the resolution passed at Karachi, and its recommendations were adopted by the All-India Congress Committee in August 1931 (AICCP, File G. 157, 1931).
53. Viceroy to Secretary of State, 24 June 1932, Haig Papers, File 115/1.
54. P. Khan to JN, 23 Oct 1931, also JN to A. G. Khan, 2 Oct 1931, AICCP, File P.17, 1931.
55. Report of Devadas Gandhi on the North-West Frontier Province, Aug 1931, AICCP, File P. 17, 1931.
56. JN to Mrs Pandit, 8 June 1931, MPP.
57. Ibid.
58. The account of JN's involvement in United Provinces peasant politics during 1931 is based on: (*a*) JN–Patel correspondence with government officials dating from June to Nov 1931 (Home Political File 33/36/31; (*b*) Gandhi–JN correspondence, 20 and 24 June 1931, AICCP, File G(40) (KW) iii, 1931; (*c*) correspondence between Chief Secretary, United Provinces, and Home Secretary, Government of India (Home Political Files 33/24/31, 83/24/31); (*d*) Viceroy to Secretary of State, telegram, 19 Nov 1931 (Home Political File 33/36/31); (*e*) note by Home Secretary (H. W. Emerson) of his discussion with Nehru on 19 and 20 July 1931 (Home Political File 14/13/32); and (*f*) JN to Gandhi, 19 Sept, 1 and 4 Oct 1931, Gandhi Papers.
59. Working Committee's note containing decisions reached at its meetings held on 8, 9 and 10 Sept 1931, enclosure to JN's letter to Gandhi, 12 Sept 1931, Gandhi Papers.
60. JN to Gandhi, 27 Sept 1931, Gandhi Papers.
61. JN to Gandhi, 16 Oct 1931, NP.
62. Devadas Gandhi to JN, 2 Oct 1931, NP.
63. United Provinces Government's express letter to New Delhi, 10 Dec 1931, Home Political File 33/36/31.
64. District Magistrate's order, 21 Dec 1931, AICCP, File P. 21, 1931.
65. Circular to all provincial congress committees (undated), AICCP, File P. 22, 1932.
66. AICCP, File 22, 1932.
67. AICCP, File 35, 1932, Part III.
68. Notes by Miss K. Behn, also report on police excesses, JN's Miscellaneous Papers, 1932, NP.
69. 'How fines are recovered', AICCP, File P. 35, 1932, Part III.
70. Report on circulation of nationalist newspapers, 1932, JN's Miscellaneous Papers, NP.
71. Prime Minister to Viceroy, 31 March 1932, Haig Papers, F. 115/1.
72. A report by a Congress worker on Congress organisation in Allahabad district, Nov 1933, JN's Miscellaneous Papers, NP.
73. JN to Mahadev Desai, 25 May 1933, Gandhi Papers.

74. JN's Prison Diary, 22 Sept 1932, NP.
75. Ibid. 4 June 1933, NP.
76. JN to K. R. Luckmidas, 10 Nov 1933, NP.
77. JN, 'Reality and Myth', 4 Jan 1934, NP.
78. JN to the editor, *Pioneer*, 23 Nov 1933, NP.
79. JN's speech at Albert Hall, Calcutta, 18 Jan 1934, Home Political File 4/1/34.
80. JN to V. R. Kalappa, 17 Dec 1933, NP.
81. JN to Mahadev Desai, 23 May 1933, Gandhi Papers.
82. JN to B. Das, 17 Sept 1933, NP.
83. JN to B. Das, 23 Sept 1933, NP.
84. Gandhi to JN, 21 Jan 1934, NP.
85. JN's Prison Diary, 22 Sept 1932, NP.
86. Gandhi to JN, 9 Oct 1933, NP.
87. K. D. Malaviya to JN, 13 Jan 1934, NP.
88. JN to B. Das, 23 Sept 1933, NP.
89. JN to Gandhi, 27 Sept 1931, Gandhi Papers.
90. JN to S. M. Alam, 29 Sept 1933, NP.
91. JN, *Autobiography*, p. 479.
92. Gandhi to JN, 14 April 1934, NP.
93. Note by JN, undated but most probably written in April or May 1934, NP.
94. JN to Gandhi 14 Aug 1934, intercepted by police hence in Home Political File 3/XI/ 34.
95. Constitution of the All-India Congress Socialist Party, AICCP, File G. 23, 1934.
96. R. A. Kidwai to Rajendra Prasad, 4 Aug 1935, also Rajendra Prasad to Satyamurti, 30 Sept 1935, PP.
97. Congress policy towards the states, 1934, AICCP, File G. 27, 1934.
98. J. P. Narayan's circular, 1935, Sampurnanand's thesis, Feb 1935, AICCP, File G. 23, 1934.
99. R. Prasad to S. Patil, 22 Sept 1935, PP.
100. Gandhi to Rajaji, 3 Sept 1934, PP.
101. Gandhi to R. Prasad, 28 Sept 1934 (in Hindi), PP.
102. Note by JN on Indira, May 1934, NP.
103. JN to Mrs Pandit, 2 June 1934, MPP.
104. Ibid.
105. See Johnson to Hallet, 22 Oct 1934, Home Political File 39/20/ 34.
106. JN's Prison Papers, NP.
107. Government Report, 29 Sept 1935, Home Political File 4/7/35.
108. Gandhi to JN, 25 April 1934, NP.
109. Gandhi to Sardar Patel, Sept 1934, Tendulkar, *Mahatma*, vol. 3, pp. 387–8.
110. Gandhi to JN, 22 Sept 1935, intercepted letter, Home Political File 4/7/35.
111. Sardar Patel to R. Prasad, 22 Nov 1935, PP.
112. R. Prasad to JN, 19 Dec 1935, NP.
113. JN to R. Prasad, 20 Nov 1935, PP.
114. JN to R. Prasad, 29 Dec 1935, PP.
115. See JN to Mrs Pandit, 4 Oct 1932, MPP.
116. AICCP, File 17, 1936.
117. JN to Mrs Pandit, 10 Feb 1936, MPP.
118. JN to R. Prasad, 20 Nov 1935, PP.
119. JN to Mrs Pandit, 20 Dec 1935, MPP.
120. S. C. Bose to JN, 12 Jan 1936, NP.

CHAPTER 8 Farewell to Revolution, 1936–42

1. Nehru to Sri Prakash, 15 Aug 1939, NP.
2. Rajaji to R. Prasad, 24 Feb 1936, PP.
3. Proceedings of the Congress Parliamentary Board, AICCP, File G.9, 1934–6.
4. Kripalani to R. Prasad, 15 Feb 1936, PP.
5. Masani to Nehru, 10 Jan 1936, NP.
6. Jayakar to Polak, 26 June 1936, JP.
7. S. C. Bose to Nehru, 4 March 1936, NP.
8. Nehru, *Unity of India*, p. 98.
9. Ibid. p. 96.
10. Nehru to N. G. Ranga, 31 Oct 1936, AICCP, File G. 5(KW) (i), 1936.
11. For Nehru's reasoning see his presidential speech (*India and the World*, p. 89) and his two subsequent speeches, one delivered in May in Bombay (Home Political File 4/32/36) and the other in Sind in July 1936 (Home Political File 4/23/36); also his circular to Congress election candidates, 7 Dec 1936, AICCP, File E. 1, 1936.
12. See government reports on the Lucknow Congress, by D. Pilditch, Home Political File 4/8/36. This report, based as it is on inside information, is fairly accurate in its analysis.
13. See Haig to Linlithgow, 19 Oct 1936, Haig Papers.
14. Nehru, presidential address, *India and the World*, p. 93.
15. Ibid, p. 82.
16. Nehru's additional speech made in Hindi on 12 April 1936, Home Political File 4/10/36.
17. Gandhi to Miss A.Harrison, 4 May 1936, Home Political File 32/4/36.
18. Ibid.
19. Governor of Madras (Erskine) to Home Member, Government of India, 20 April 1936, also United Provinces Governor to Home Member, 13 April 1936, Home Political File 4/6/36.
20. See Patel to Prasad, 23 May 1936, PP.
21. Patel to Prasad, 29 May 1936, PP.
22. Nehru's speech, 2 June 1936, Indian News Agency telegram, Home Political File 4/14/36.
23. See K. D. Malaviya to Nehru, 6 June 1936, NP.
24. S. L. Polak to Jayakar, 12 June 1936, JP.
25. R. A. Reynolds to Nehru, 23 June 1936, NP.
26. Resignation letter signed by seven members of Working Committee, 29 June 1936, NP.
27. Gandhi to Nehru, 8 July 1936, NP.
28. R. Prasad to Nehru, 1 July 1936, NP.
29. See Tendulkar, *Mahatma*, vol. 4, p. 132.
30. Nehru to Stafford Cripps, 22 Feb 1937, NP.
31. Nehru, *The Discovery of India*, p 60.
32. Nehru to P. V. Gadgil, 11 March 1938, NP.
33. Congress Manifesto, 12 Oct 1936, AICCP, File G. 71, 1936.
34. Linlithgow to all governors, 7 March 1936, Haig Papers.
35. Nehru to Stafford Cripps, 22 Feb 1937, NP.
36. Muslim Mass Contact Committee report on the progress of the movement, AICCP, File G.22, 1938.
37. See Nehru to R. Prasad, 7 July 1939, PP.
38. Moonje to Karandikar, 29 June 1939, TP, File 24, 1939.

39. Patel to Prasad, 21 May 1939, PP.
40. Nehru to Gandhi, 28 April 1938, NP.
41. Haig to Linlithgow, 3 June 1939, Haig Papers, File 116/6.
42. Haig to Linlithgow, 12 June 1939, Haig Papers, File 115/2.
43. Gandhi to Nehru, 30 March 1939, NP.
44. Patel to Prasad, 2 Oct 1937, PP.
45. Prasad to Nehru, 18 Dec 1937, PP.
46. Prasad to Patel, 11 Oct 1938, PP.
47. S. C. Bose to Gandhi, 21 Dec 1938, NP.
48. Patel to Nehru, 12 Dec 1937, NP. Also Nehru to Prasad, 29 Nov 1937; and Prasad to Nehru, 24 Dec 1937; PP.
49. Prasad to Patel, 6 Dec 1937, PP.
50. Nehru to Rajendra Prasad, 21 July 1937, PP.
51. See Haig to Linlithgow, 7 and 24 May 1937, Haig Papers, File 115/17.
52. Nehru to Chaman Lall, 7 Oct 1937, and Nehru to S. C. Bose, 20 Oct 1937, AICCP, Files P. 17 and P.5, 1937.
53. Ibid.
54. See *Speeches and Writings of Mr Jinnah*, ed. Jamil-ud-din Ahmad, vol. 1, p. 30.
55. Some notes on the general approach and propaganda methods of the All-India Muslim League, AICCP, File B. 9, 109–37.
56. See Shams-ul-Kuda to Dr Ashraf, 3 Aug 1937, AICCP, File 49, 1937.
57. See Nehru to S. C. Bose, 20 Oct 1937, AICCP, File P. 5, 1937.
58. National Flag, AICCP, File G. 57, 1931.
59. See Haig to Linlithgow, 23 Oct 1938, Haig Papers, File 115/2.
60. Haig to Linlithgow, 3 June 1939, Haig Papers, File 115/6.
61. See Syed Mahmud to Nehru, 23 March 1939, NP.
62. Jinnah to S. C. Bose, 2 Aug 1938, PP.
63. See Haig to Linlithgow, 21 Nov 1939, Haig Papers, File 115/2.
64. R. Prasad to Patel, 10 Dec 1938, PP.
65. Jinnah to S. C. Bose, 2 Aug 1938, PP.
66. S. C. Bose to Jinnah, 1 Oct 1938, PP.
67. Haig to Linlithgow, 8 Oct 1939, Haig Papers, File 115/2.
68. Nehru to Jinnah, 18 Oct 1939, NP.
69. Ibid.
70. Linlithgow to Haig, 17 April 1939, Haig Papers, File 115/3.
71. Nehru to S. Mahmud, 12 Dec 1939, MP.
72. See Linlithgow to Haig, 1 Dec 1939; Haig to Linlithgow, 4 Dec 1939, Haig Papers, File 115/2.
73. Jinnah to Nehru, 13 Dec 1939, NP.
74. Nehru to R. Prasad, 14 Nov 1939, PP; also Nehru to S. Cripps, 17 Jan 1940, NP.
75. Patel to R. Prasad, 16 Oct 1939, PP.
76. Prasad to Nehru, 12 Nov 1939, NP.
77. Nehru to R. Prasad, 16 Oct 1939, PP.
78. Nehru to S. Cripps, 17 Jan 1940 NP.
79. See Haig to Linlithgow, 19 Sep 1939, Haig Papers, telegrams.
80. See Nehru's long letter from the Mediterranean, 11 June 1938, AICCP, File G.60, 1938.
81. See Nehru to A. K. Azad, 1 Oct 1938; also Nehru to Nahas Pasha, 1 Oct 1938; AICCP, File G. 71, 1938.

82. Nehru to Dr Olsvanger, 25 Sept 1936, AICCP, File G.5 (KW), 1936.
83. Nehru to J. B. Kripalani, 24 Sept 1938, AICCP, File G.71, 1938.
84. Nehru to Agatha Harrison, 18 April 1937, NP.
85. Nehru's confidential letter to Congress Working Committee, 30 July 1938, NP.
86. Nehru's confidential note to the Working Committee, 6 Sept 1938, NP.
87. Nehru's article, 'Day by Day', 7 Oct 1938, Chalpat Rao Papers.
88. Nehru's article, 'The Great Betrayal', 1 Oct 1938, Chalpat Rao Papers.
89. Patel to Prasad, 15 July 1938, PP.
90. Gandhi to Nehru, 21 Dec 1938, NP.
91. See Patel to Prasad, 2 Nov 1938, and Azad to Patel, 28 Oct 1938, PP.
92. Prasad to Patel, 21 Nov 1938, PP.
93. See Patel to Nehru, 8 Feb 1939, NP.
94. AICCP, File G.79, 1939.
95. AICCP, File G. 20, Part III, 1939.
96. Bose to Gandhi, 29 March 1939, PP.
97. Gandhi to Bose, 2 April, 1939, PP.
98. Nehru to Prakash, 15 Aug 1939, NP.
99. See A. K. Chandra to Nehru, 28 Nov 1938, NP.
100. Nehru to S. C. Bose, 3 April 1939, NP.
101. S. C. Bose to Nehru, 28 March 1939, NP.
102. S. Cripps to Nehru, 18 March 1940, NP.
103. Note by R. A. Kaur of conversation between Azad Nehru and Gandhi, 13 Oct 1940, Kaur Papers.
104. Conversation between Nehru and Gandhi, 30 Oct 1940, ibid.
105. Intelligence Bureau Note, 5 Oct 1940, Home Political File 3/3/40.
106. Nehru to J. Gunther, 16 March 1938, NP.
107. ' The Rastrapati', NP.
108. Ibid.
109. See Sri Prakash to Nehru, 29 Jan 1942, NP.
110. Gandhi to Nehru, 5 Dec 1941, NP.
111. Frances Gunther to Nehru, March 1938, NP.
112. Mrs Pandit to author.
113. Nehru to A. K. Azad, 10 May 1940, NP.
114. Nehru to J. H. Smith, 10 Jan 1940, NP.
115. See G. S. Bajpai to Linlithgow, 12 March 1942, *The Transfer of Power* 1942–47, ed. N. Mansergh and others, vol. 1, p. 415.
116. Madame Chiang Kai-shek to Nehru, 2 May 1942, NP.
117. Nehru to K. Rama Rao, 2 April 1942, NP.
118. Nehru to Mahadev Desai, 9 Dec 1939, NP.
119. Note by S. Cripps, 29 March 1942, *Transfer of Power*, vol. 1, p. 530.
120. Nehru to Johnson, 8 April 1942, AICCP, File G.26, Pt 1, 1942.
121. Churchill to Cripps, 10 April 1942, *Transfer of Power*, vol. 1, p. 721.
122. Churchill to Cripps, 11 April 1942, Ibid. vol. 1, p. 739.
123. Roosevelt to Hopkins, 12 April 1942, ibid. vol. 1, p. 759.
124. Nehru's speech on 29 April 1942 in the open session of AICC held in Allahabad, Home Political File 4/1/42.
125. Tendulkar, *Mahatma*, vol. 6, p. 174.
126. Nehru to A. K. Azad, 5 June 1942, NP.
127. Nehru to Sampurnanand, 28 July 1942, Sampurnanand Papers, File 35.
128. Nehru's instructions to Congress workers, 24 July 1942, NP.

CHAPTER 9 The Defeat of a Nationalist, 1942–7

1. K. M. Munshi's statement as recorded on 18 Oct 1966. Oral History.
2. Nehru, *Discovery of India*, p. 21.
3. Ibid. p. 33.
4. Ibid. p. 598.
5. Ibid. p. 598.
6. Ibid. p. 599.
7. Ibid. p. 561.
8. Ibid. p. 58.
9. Ibid. p. 582.
10. Nehru to Mrs Pandit, 6 May 1944 and 14 Feb 1945, MPP.
11. Nehru to Mrs Pandit, 27 Feb 1945, MPP.
12. Nehru to Mrs Pandit, 9 April 1943, MPP.
13. Nehru to Mrs Pandit, 29 Jan 1944, MPP.
14. Nehru to Mrs Pandit, 9 Nov 1943, MPP.
15. Nehru to Mrs Pandit, 29 June 1943, MPP.
16. Halifax to Eden, 20 April 1943, *Transfer of Power*, vol. 3, pp. 903–4.
17. Linlithgow to Amery, 16 April 1943, Ibid. vol. 3, p. 893.
18. See Nehru's own estimate in *Discovery of India*, p. 519; also statistics connected with Congress disturbances for the period ending 31 Dec 1943 as reprinted in F. G. Hutchins's *Spontaneous Revolution: the Quit India Movement*, p. 337.
19. Linlithgow to provincial governors, 30 Aug 1942, *Transfer of Power*, vol. 2, pp. 847–8.
20. Linlithgow's talks to Wavell as recorded by latter in his journal on 19 Oct 1943, *The Viceroy's Journal*, pp. 32–4.
21. *Transfer of Power*, vol. 3, pp. 1052–3.
22. *Viceroy's Journal*, p. 33.
23. *Transfer of Power*, vol. 3, p. 730.
24. Ibid. vol. 3, p. 737.
25. *Viceroy's Journal*, p. 79.
26. Wavell to Prime Minister, 24 Oct 1944, *Viceroy's Journal*, pp. 94–9.
27. See Sir B. Glancy (Governor of Punjab) to Wavell, 2 and 23 Aug 1944, *Transfer of Power*, vol. 4, pp. 1148–9, 1223–4.
28. Lord Mountbatten to author, June 1970.
29. *Viceroy's Journal*, p. 168.
30. Congress's confidential instructions to Congressmen attending Simla Conference, 25 June 1945, AICCP, File G. 58, 1945.
31. *Viceroy's Journal*, p. 154.
32. Nehru to Malkani, 16 July 1945, Malkani Papers.
33. M. Hatta to Nehru, 1, Dec 1945, NP.
34. Nehru to Macmanage, 1 Nov 1945, NP.
35. *Viceroy's Journal*, p. 165.
36. Ibid. pp. 169–70.
37. Ibid. p. 199.
38. Nehru to R. Prasad, 9 Oct 1945, PP.
39. Patel to Nehru, 22 Feb 1946, NP.
40. Gandhi to Nehru, 5 Oct 1945, in Hindi, NP.
41. Nehru to Gandhi, 9 Oct 1945, NP.
42. Patel to R. Prasad, 25 Feb 1946, PP.
43. See Mrs A. Asaf Ali to Nehru, 8 Dec 1945, NP.
44. H. V. Hodson, *The Great Divide: Britain-India-Pakistan*, p. 205. Also report by Nehru on his visit to Malaya, 28 March 1946, PP.
45. Nehru's presidential address to the States Peoples' Conference, 31 Dec 1945, AICCP, File G.20, Pt 1, 1942–6.
46. S. M. Abdullah's thoughts on Pakistan in *Tribune*, 9 Jan 1946.

47. Nehru's press statement on his Malaya visit, March 1946, AICCP, G.11, 1945–6.
48. Azad to Pethick-Lawrence, 20 May 1946, India, Cabinet Mission, Cmd 6861 (1946).
49. Muslim League's resolution, 6 June 1946, India Cabinet Mission, Cmd 6861.
50. *Viceroy's Journal*, p. 295.
51. Pethick-Lawrence to Azad, 22 May 1946, Cmd 6835.
52. *Viceroy's Journal*, p. 271.
53. Ibid. p. 305.
54. Jinnah to Wavell, 28 June 1946, India, Cabinet Mission, Cmd 6861.
55. Nehru's statement, 10 July 1946, *Indian Annual Register* (1946), vol. 2, pp. 145–7.
56. Nehru to Bardoloi, 22 July 1946, AICCP, File 71, 1946–7.
57. Nehru to those members of the provincial assemblies who had been elected members of the Constituent Assembly, 22 July 1946, AICCP, File 25.
58. *Viceroy's Journal*, pp. 330–2, 344–5.
59. *Jawaharlal Nehru's Speeches 1946–1964*, vol. 1, p. 4.
60. See Bardoloi to Patel, 15 Nov 1946, *Sardar Patel's Correspondence*, vol. 3, pp. 297–9.
61. Patel to Cripps, 15 Dec 1946, *Patel's Correspondence*, vol. 3, pp. 313–5.
62. Nehru to Wavell, 5 Feb 1947, PP.
63. *Viceroy's Journal*, pp. 426–7.
64. Nehru's resolution, 13 Dec 1946, *Nehru's Speeches*, vol. 1, pp. 5–16.
65. Nehru to Mrs Pandit, 14 Nov 1946, MPP.
66. *Nehru's Speeches*, vol. 1, p. 298.
67. Kripalani to Nehru, 25 July 1947, PP.
68. Nehru to Kripalani, 15 July 1947, AICCP, File 71, 1946–7.
69. Mountbatten to author.
70. Krishna Menon to author.
71. Nehru to Mountbatten, 1 May 1947, AICCP, File 71, 1946–7.
72. Ibid.
73. Constituent Assembly of India, Report of the Committee appointed to negotiate with the States Negotiating Committee, 24 April 1947, AICCP, File 29, 1946–7.
74. *Speeches and Documents on the Indian Constitution 1921–47*, ed. Sir Maurice Gwyer and A. Appadorai, vol. 2, pp. 681–3.
75. Mountbatten to author. See also V. P. Menon to Patel, 10 May 1947, *Patel's Correspondence*, vol. 4, pp. 111–8.
76. Nehru to Mountbatten, 9 June 1947, PP.
77. Nehru to Ismay, 19 June 1947, PP.
78. V. P. Menon, *The Story of the Integration of the Indian States*, p. 94.
79. Nehru's Speech, *Hindustan Times*, 29 July 1947.
80. Ibid. 10 Aug 1947.
81. JN to R. Prasad, 7 Aug 1947, PP.
82. *Nehru's Speeches*, vol. 1, p. 25.

CHAPTER 10 The Years of Statesmanship, 1947–51

1. Nehru's speech in the Constituent Assembly, 8 March 1949, *Nehru's Speeches*, vol. 1, p. 238.
2. Nehru to Mrs Pandit, 6 Aug 1949, MPP.
3. Nehru's speech in the Constituent Assembly, 8 March 1949, *Nehru's Speeches* vol. 1, pp. 238–9.
4. Sampurnanand to Nehru, 18 Oct 1950, Sampurnanand Papers.
5. Nehru to Sampurnanand, 21 Oct 1950, Sampurnanand Papers.
6. Nehru's speech, 23 Dec 1947, *Hindustan Times*, 25 Dec 1947.
7. R. Prasad to Nehru, 17 Sept 1947, PP.

8. Nehru to Prasad, 17 Sept 1947, PP.
9. Nehru's speech in the Constituent Assembly, 3 April 1948, *Nehru's Speeches* vol. 1, p. 73.
10. Nehru's speech in the Parliament, 9 Aug 1950, ibid. vol. 2, p. 175.
11. Nehru's speech, 30 Sept 1947, *Hindustan Times*, 1 Oct 1947.
12. Nehru's speech, 4 Oct 1947, ibid. 5 Oct 1947.
13. Nehru's speech, 29 Jan 1948, ibid. 30 Jan 1948.
14. Nehru's speech, 2 Oct 1951, ibid. 3 Oct 1951.
15. Nehru to Mrs Pandit, 6 Aug 1950, MPP.
16. R. Prasad to Patel, 22 Sept 1948, PP.
17. *Patel's Correspondence*, vol. 1, p. 122.
18. Nehru to Mrs Pandit, 25 Aug 1950, MPP.
19. As quoted in A. Stein's, *India and the Soviet Union: the Nehru era*, p. 29.
20. K. M. Panikkar, *In Two Chinas: memoirs of a diplomat*, p. 105.
21. Nehru to Mrs Pandit, 27 Nov 1949, MPP.
22. Nehru to Mrs Pandit, 12 April 1950, MPP.
23. *Report of the First General Election in India, 1951–52*.
24. Nehru to G. B. Pant, 10 April 1950, Pant Papers.
25. Nehru's speech, 12 Nov 1948, *Hindustan Times*, 13 Nov 1948.
26. Nehru's speech, 10 Dec 1948, ibid. 11 Dec 1948.
27. Nehru's press conference, ibid. 6 Aug 1949.
28. Nehru to G. B. Pant, 13 April 1951, Pant Papers.
29. Ibid; also Nehru to Sampurnanand, 13 April 1951, Sampurnanand Papers.
30. R. Prasad to S. P. Mookerjee, 29 Jan 1948, PP.
31. Tendulkar, *Mahatma*, vol. 8, p. 345.
32. *Nehru's Speeches*, vol. 1, p. 42.
33. Ibid. vol. 1, p. 44.
34. Nehru's speech, *Hindustan Times*, 2 May 1948.
35. Nehru's speech, 2 Jan 1948, ibid. 3 Jan 1948.
36. Nehru to Mrs Pandit, 28 Oct 1947, MPP.
37. Ibid.
38. Nehru's speech, 24 Sept 1949, *Hindustan Times*, 25 Sept 1949.
39. Quoted by Nehru in his letter to Mrs Pandit, 21 Sept 1948, MPP.
40. See Nehru to the Maharaja, 1 Dec 1947, and Nehru to Patel, 17 April 1949, *Patel's Correspondence*, vol. 1, pp. 101–6, 261–3.
41. Abdullah's address to a press conference, *Hindustan Times*, 7 March 1948.
42. *Patel's Correspondence*, vol. 1, p. 266.
43. Nehru to Mrs Pandit, 17 May 1949, MPP.
44. Patel to Nehru, 3 July 1950, *Patel's Correspondence*, vol. 1, p. 317.
45. Nehru to Mrs Pandit, 18 July 1950, MPP.
46. Nehru's speech, *The Statesman*, 1 Oct 1950, also Nehru to Mrs Pandit, 21 Sept 1948, MPP.
47. Nehru's speech in Parliament, *Hindustan Times*, 13 Feb 1951.
48. Nehru's speech, 4 June 1951, ibid. 5 June 1951.
49. Syed Mahmud to author. Abdullah was arrested on the night of 8 Aug 1953, He was to remain in custody for nearly twenty years, interrupted by a few releases and re-arrests. His political wilderness came to an end in February 1975 when Mrs Gandhi restored him to the chief ministership of Kashmir. Abdullah in return accepted Kashmir's accession to India as irrevocable.

50. Nehru's address to the Indian Chemical Manufacturers' Association, 26 Dec 1950, *Nehru's Speeches*, vol. 2, pp. 44–50.
51. Ibid. vol. 2, pp. 44–50.
52. Nehru's speech delivered in the Legislative Assembly, 17 Feb 1948, ibid. vol. 1, pp. 113–4.
53. Ibid.
54. Nehru to K. T. Shah, 13 May 1939, National Planning Committee Files, NP.
55. Ibid.
56. See File No. 341 (1945–50), TP.
57. Nehru's speech in Parliament, 15 Dec 1952, *Nehru's Speeches*, vol. 2, p. 87.
58. Ibid. vol. 2, p. 89.
59. Nehru's speech to Asian Conference on labour problem, New Delhi, 27 Oct 1947, *Hindustan Times*, 27 Oct 1947.
60. Nehru to Mrs Pandit, 13 Feb 1950, MPP.
61. Ibid.
62. *The Memoirs of Harry S. Truman*, vol. 2, p. 247.
63. Ibid. p. 245.
64. Nehru's speech in Parliament, 6 April 1949, *Hindustan Times*, 7 April 1949.
65. Nehru to R. Prasad, 22 July 1948, PP.
66. Nehru's speech in the Constituent Assembly, 4 Dec 1947, *Nehru's Speeches*, vol. 1, p. 202.
67. Nehru's speech in the Constituent Assembly, 8 March 1948, *Nehru's Speeches*, vol. 1, p. 211.
68. Nehru to S. Patel, 27 Oct 1948, *Patel's Correspondence*, vol. 7, pp. 667–72.
69. Nehru's speech, 7 March 1948, *Hindustan Times*, 9 March 1948.
70. Nehru, *Visit to America*, p. 29.
71. Nehru to S. Patel, 27 Oct 1948, *Patel's Correspondence*, vol. 7, p. 668.
72. Nehru, *Visit to America*, p. 9.
73. Nehru's speech, 8 March 1949, *Hindustan Times*, 9 March 1949.
74. R. Prasad to Nehru, 11 Jan 1948, Nehru to R. Prasad, 11 Jan 1948, PP.
75. Nehru's speech, 4 Dec 1947, *Nehru's Speeches*, vol. 1, p. 204.
76. Nehru to Mrs Pandit, 1 July 1949, MPP.
77. Ibid.
78. Nehru to Mrs Pandit, 8 June 1949, MPP.
79. Ibid.
80. Ibid.
81. Nehru to Mrs Pandit, 24 Aug 1949, MPP.
82. Ibid.
83. See *Hindustan Times*, 25 Oct 1949, for some American interpretations of Nehru's importance.
84. Ibid. 11 Jan 1950.
85. Nehru to Mrs Pandit, 10 May 1950, MPP.
86. Nehru to Mrs Pandit, 12 Sept 1950, MPP.
87. Ibid.
88. See Nehru's speech in Parliament, 6 Dec 1950, *Nehru's Speeches*, vol. 2, pp. 254–5.
89. Nehru to Mrs Pandit, 14 Sept 1950, MPP.
90. Nehru to Mrs Pandit, 1 Nov 1950, MPP.
91. Ibid.
92. Ibid.
93. Patel to Nehru, 7 Nov 1950, as reprinted in D. V. Tahamankar's *Sardar Patel*.
94. Nehru's speech in Parliament, 6 Dec 1950, *Nehru's Speeches*, vol. 2, pp. 256–7.
95. Nehru to Mrs Pandit, 6 Aug 1951, MPP.
96. Ibid.
97. Nehru's note to Gandhi, 6 Jan

1948, *Patel's Correspondence*, vol. 6, pp. 17–21.
98. Patel's note to Gandhi, 12 Jan 1948, ibid. vol. 6, pp. 21–4.
99. Nehru to Mrs Pandit, 24 July 1951, MPP.
100. Nehru to Mrs Pandit, 25 June 1949, MPP.

CHAPTER 11 The Leader of the Third World, 1952–8

1. Nehru to R. Prasad, 15 Feb 1948, PP.
2. Nehru to R. Prasad, 22 Sept 1948, PP.
3. Nehru's speech in Lok Sabha, 21 Dec 1955, *Nehru's Speeches*, vol. 3, pp. 170–83.
4. Ibid.
5. Ibid.
6. Nehru's speech, 6 Oct 1955, *Nehru's Speeches*, vol. 3, pp. 25–35.
7. Ibid.
8. Nehru to R. Prasad, 22 July 1948, PP.
9. R. Prasad to Nehru, 24 July 1948, PP.
10. Nehru's speech in Lok Sabha, 22 May 1954, *Nehru's Speeches*, vol. 3, pp. 440–2.
11. Nehru's speech in Lok Sabha, 16 Sept 1954, ibid. vol. 3, pp. 443–5.
12. Nehru's speech in Lok Sabha, 5 May 1955, ibid. vol. 3, pp. 446–54.
13. Nehru's speech in Lok Sabha, 28 March 1957, ibid. vol. 3, pp. 154–8.
14. Nehru to Mrs Pandit, 2 May 1950, MPP.
15. Nehru to Mrs Pandit, 4 Nov 1953, MPP.
16. Nehru to Mrs Pandit, 13 Feb 1957, MPP.
17. Nehru to M. Desai, 19 Feb 1953, Desai Papers.
18. M. Desai to Nehru, 23 Feb 1953, Desai Papers.
19. Nehru to Mangla Prasad and Muzaffar Hasan, 3 Sept 1958, Sampurnanand Papers.
20. *The Hindu*, 20 and 25 March 1953.
21. Nehru's speech, 26 Dec 1955, *Nehru's Speeches*, vol. 3, pp. 134–7
22. Nehru to Sampurnanand, 6 May 1958, Sampurnanand Papers.
23. Nehru's speech, 26 Dec 1955, *Nehru's Speeches*, vol. 3, pp. 134–7.
24. Ibid.
25. Nehru on communism, *Asian Recorder*, 19–25 Oct 1957.
26. Nehru to Mrs Pandit, 5 March 1955, MPP.
27. Ibid.
28. Ibid.
29. Nehru's speech on communist victory in Kerala, June 1957, *Asian Recorder*, 6–12 July 1957.
30. Nehru's speech, 21 Jan 1957, *Nehru's Speeches*, vol. 3, pp. 152–4.
31. Ibid.
32. Nehru's letter to chief ministers, 11 Oct 1954, Desai Papers.
33. Nehru's statements, 29 April, 3 May 1958, *Asian Recorder*, 3–9 May 1958.
34. Nehru to Sampurnanand, 6 May 1958, Sampurnanand Papers.
35. Nehru's 'odd notes' made at Manali, 30 May 1958, NP.
36. Nehru's speech, 3 Feb 1958, *Nehru's Speeches*, vol. 4, pp. 110–13.
37. Nehru's speech, 4 Jan 1957, ibid. vol. 3, pp. 51–4.
38. Ibid. vol. 3, pp. 51–4.
39. Nehru's speech, 15 Aug 1958, ibid. vol. 4, pp. 114–23.
40. Ibid. vol. 4, pp. 114–23.
41. Nehru's speech on his impressions of China, 8 Nov 1954, *Leader*, 9 Nov 1954.
42. Nehru's speech, 2 Oct 1955, *Nehru's Speeches*, vol. 3, pp. 23–6.

43. Chester Bowles, *Ambassador's Report*, pp. 131–8.
44. Nehru's speech, 6 April 1957, *Nehru's Speeches*, vol. 3, pp. 158–66.
45. Nehru's speech, 10 Sept 1956, ibid. vol. 3, pp. 145–51.
46. Nehru to M. Desai, 25 Dec 1952, Desai Papers.
47. Nehru's speech in the Lok Sabha 18 Feb 1953, *Nehru's Speeches*, vol. 2, pp. 338–55.
48. Nehru's speech in the Lok Sabha, 20 Nov 1956, ibid. vol. 3, pp. 44–6.
49. Nehru's speech in the Council of States, 16 Feb 1953, ibid. vol. 2, pp. 325–6.
50. Nehru to Syed Mahmud, 17 Dec 1953, MP.
51. *Asian Recorder*, 6–12 July 1957.
52. B. N. Mullik, *My Years with Nehru: the Chinese betrayal*, pp. 178–80.
53. See Margaret W. Fisher and Joan V. Bondurant, *Indian Views of Sino-Indian Relations*, pp. 83–4.
54. Nehru's statement in Lok Sabha, 25 Aug 1954, *India's Foreign Policy*, 401–4.
55. Chou En-lai's speech, 28 June 1954, *Leader*, 29 June 1954.
56. Nehru to M. Desai, 1 Feb 1954, Desai Papers.
57. Nehru's memorandum of July 1954, cited in D. R. Mankekar, *The Guilty Men of 1962*, p. 138.
58. See Nehru to Chou En-lai, 14 Dec 1958, *White Paper on China*, vol. 1, pp. 48–51.
59. Ibid.
60. In March 1957 the Chinese first announced the completion of their Sinkiang–Tibet highway. In Oct 1957 the road was formally opened. Mullik, *The Chinese Betrayal*, pp. 197–8.
61. See *Prime Minister on Sino-Indian Relations*, vol. 1, pp. 251–2.
62. Nehru to Mrs Pandit, 12 Oct 1958, MPP.
63. Ibid.
64. Nehru's statement, 8 Nov 1954, *Leader*, 9 Nov 1954.
65. For the text of the agreement see *Documents on China's Relations with South and South-East Asia (1949-1962)* ed. G. V. Ambekar and D. V. Divekar, pp. 334–5.
66. Nehru's speech, 4 Dec 1956, *India's Foreign Policy*, pp. 437–8.
67. Nehru to Mrs Pandit, 31 Dec 1954, MPP.
68. Ibid.
69. Shah's conversation with the Indian ambassador as reported by Tara Chand to Syed Mahmud, 27 Sept 1953, MP.
70. Nehru to Mrs Pandit, 14 April 1955, MPP. Also see Nehru's speech in Lok Sabha on Baghdad Pact, 29 March 1956, *Nehru's Speeches*, vol. 3, pp. 319–20.
71. Ibid.
72. Nehru to Mrs Pandit, 3 April 1955, MPP.
73. Ibid.
74. Nehru's notes for his speech at the Bandung Conference, April 1955, NP.
75. Nehru's speech at the Bandung Conference, 24 April 1955, *India's Foreign Policy*, pp. 269–72.
76. Chou En-lai's speech, 19 and 23 April 1955; *Documents on China's Relations*, pp. 13–21.
77. Nehru's statement in the Lok Sabha, 30 Sept 1954, reported in the *Leader*, 1 Oct 1954.
78. Wilson, *A Quarter of Mankind*, p. 266, as cited in Neville Maxwell's *India's China War*, p. 261.
79. John Kotelawala, *An Asian Prime Minister's Story*, p. 187.
80. Tara Chand to Syed Mahmud, 12 May 1955, MP.

81. Nehru on Bandung Conference in the Lok Sabha, 30 April 1955, *Nehru's Speeches*, vol. 3, pp. 292–301.
82. Nehru to M. Desai, 28 April 1955, Desai Papers.
83. Ibid.
84. *Khrushchev Remembers*, p. 466.
85. K. P. S. Menon, *The Flying Troika*, pp. 110–20.
86. *Khrushchev Remembers*, p. 507.
87. Nehru to Mrs Pandit, 2 Dec 1955, MPP.
88. Nehru to Mrs Pandit 15 Dec 1955, MPP.
89. Ibid.
90. Nehru to Mrs Pandit, 5 Dec 1955, MPP.
91. Nehru to Mrs Pandit, 22 Aug 1955, MPP.
92. Nehru's speech in Lok Sabha, 17 Sept 1955, *India's Foreign Policy*, pp. 122–4.
93. Nehru to Mrs Pandit, 15 Dec 1955, MPP.
94. Nehru's statement in Lok Sabha, 20 March 1956, *India's Foreign Policy*, p. 578.
95. See Anthony Eden, *Full Circle*, pp. 354–66.
96. Nehru to Mrs Pandit, 4 Aug 1956, MPP.
97. Ibid.
98. Nehru's speech in Lok Sabha, 19 Nov 1956, *Nehru's Speeches*, vol. 3, pp. 321–34.
99. Ibid.
100. Nehru's speech in the U.S.A., Dec 1956, *Asian Recorder*, 22–31 Dec 1956.
101. Menon, *Flying Troika*, pp. 171–3.
102. Nehru's speech in Lok Sabha, 19 Nov 1956, *India's Foreign Policy*, p. 557.
103. Nehru's speech in Lok Sabha, 16 Nov 1956, ibid. pp. 555–6.
104. Nehru 'The Basic Approach', in *Nehru's Speeches*, vol. 4, pp. 114–23.
105. Nehru's speech in Lok Sabha, 19 Nov 1956, ibid. vol. 3, p. 328.
106. Nehru's speech in Lok Sabha, 12 June 1952, ibid. vol. 2, p. 314.
107. *Asian Recorder*, 22–31 Dec 1956.
108. Nehru's press statement, 7 Aug 1958, *India's Foreign Policy*, pp. 414–5.
109. Nehru's speech in Lok Sabha, 25 March 1957, *Nehru's Speeches*, vol. 3, pp. 342–4.
110. Ibid. vol. 3, pp. 342–4.
111. Nehru's speech in Lok Sabha, 14 Aug 1958, ibid. vol. 4, pp. 310–12.
112. Nehru's appeal to the U.S.A. and the U.S.S.R., ibid. vol. 4, pp. 308–9.
113. Nehru to Mrs Pandit, 12 Jan 1958, MPP.
114. Nehru's statement in the Lok Sabha, 3 July 1958, *India's Foreign Policy*, pp. 563–4.
115. Statement made on 12 Jan 1956 and quoted in UNESCO's *History of Mankind*, vol. 6(II), p. 994.

CHAPTER 12 Defeat into Victory, 1959–63

1. Morarji Desai to the author in a recorded interview.
2. Nehru to Mrs Pandit, 9 Feb 1958, MPP.
3. Ibid.
4. Morarji Desai to the author.
5. Nehru to Mrs Pandit, 27 Nov 1956, MPP.
6. T. T. Krishnamachari to the author in a recorded interview.
7. Ibid.
8. Nehru to Mrs Pandit, 19 March 1955, MPP.
9. Nehru to Mrs Pandit, 7 Nov 1959, MPP.
10. Zareer Masani, *Indira Gandhi: a biography*, p. 112.
11. Nehru's speech in Lok Sabha on

Kerala, 19 Aug 1959, *Nehru's Speeches*, vol. 4, pp. 82–92.
12. Ibid.
13. *Asian Recorder*, 5–11 Sept 1959.
14. Nehru's statement at a press conference, 15 Dec 1960, *Nehru's Speeches*, vol. 4, p. 100.
15. Nehru's speech, 28 Sept 1961, ibid. vol. 4, pp. 19–20.
16. Nehru's speech, 11 Dec 1961, ibid. vol. 4, pp. 31–5.
17. Ibid. vol. 4, pp. 31–5.
18. Nehru's statement at press conference, 28 Dec 1961, ibid. vol. 4, pp. 35–43.
19. Ibid.
20. B. M. Kaul, *The Untold Story*, pp. 300–1.
21. J. K. Galbraith, *Ambassador's Journal*, pp. 284–5.
22. *Asian Recorder*, 30 April–6 May 1962.
23. Morarji Desai came to believe that the entire purpose of the plan had been to push him out of the Cabinet. Desai to the author.
24. Nehru's speech in Lok Sabha, 17 Aug 1959, *India's Foieign Policy*, p. 244.
25. Nehru to Mrs Pandit, 7 Dec 1960, MPP.
26. Nehru's statement on Congo, 31 Aug 1960, *India's Foreign Policy*, p. 512.
27. Nehru's statement on Algeria, 4 July 1962, *Nehru's Speeches*, vol. 4, p. 396.
28. Nehru's speech, 9 April 1958, *India's Foreign Policy*, p. 543.
29. Galbraith, *Ambassador's Journal*, p. 353.
30. Nehru's speech at the UN. General Assembly, 5 Oct 1960, *India's Foreign Policy*, pp. 227–34.
31. *Asian Recorder*, 22–8 Oct 1961.
32. Nehru's speech in New York, 11 Nov 1961, *Nehru's Speeches*, vol. 4, pp. 375–8.
33. Ibid. vol. 4, pp. 375–8.
34. Nehru's statement on a television interview in Washington, 12 Nov 1961, ibid. vol. 4, p. 379.
35. His interpretation of the situation was right as evinced by *Khrushchev Remembers*, pp. 493–504.
36. Nehru's statement to a press Conference, 31 Dec 1962, *Nehru's Speeches*, vol. 4, p. 402.
37. Nehru's speech at the Commonwealth Prime Ministers' Conference, London, 11 Sept 1962, ibid. vol. 4, p. 397.
38. *Asian Recorder*, 29 Oct–4 Nov 1963.
39. Ibid.
40. *White Paper on China*, vol. 1, pp. 52–4.
41. Nehru to Sampurnanand, 25 April 1959, Sampurnanand Papers.
42. Nehru to Mrs Pandit, 15 April 1959, MPP.
43. Nehru's statement in Rajya Sabha, 10 Sept 1959, *India's Foreign Policy*, p. 347.
44. Ibid. p. 349.
45. *Khrushchev Remembers*, pp. 472–3.
46. *Prime Minister on Sino-Indian Relations*, vol. 1, p. 156.
47. Nehru's statement in Rajya Sabha, 23 June 1962, *Nehru's Speeches*, vol. 4, pp. 447–50.
48. Klaus Mehnert, *Peking and Moscow*, p. 410.
49. Ibid. p. 428.
50. Nehru's statement, 20 March 1963, *Asian Recorder*, 7–13 May 1963.
51. Nehru's statement in Lok Sabha, 12 Sept 1959, *India's Foreign Policy*, p. 354.
52. Ibid. p. 355.
53. M. Brecher, *India and World Politics: Krishna Menon's view of the world*, p. 149.
54. Nehru's speech in Rajya Sabha, 20 Dec 1960, *India's Foreign Policy*, pp. 441–3.

55. Nehru's speech on 15 Jan 1960, ibid. pp. 97–8.
56. Nehru's speech in Lok Sabha, 22 Dec 1959, ibid. pp. 381–3.
57. Mullik, *Chinese Betrayal*, pp. 438–9.
58. N. Maxwell, in *India's China War* follows this line of enquiry most resolutely.
59. *Premier Chou En-lai's Letter to the Leaders of Asian and African Countries on the Sino-Indian Boundary Question, 15 November 1962*, pp. 21–2.
60. Brecher, *Krishna Menon's View of the World*, p. 169.
61. Galbraith, *Ambassador's Journal*, p. 477.
62. *Prime Minister on Chinese Aggression*, p. 46.
63. Ibid. p. 20.
64. Ibid. p. 1.
65. *Prime Minister on Sino-Indian Relations*, vol. 2, p. 11.
66. Ibid. p. 15.
67. Nehru 'Changing India', April 1963, *Nehru's Speeches*, vol. 4, pp. 403–17.
68. Ibid.
69. *Prime Minister on Chinese Aggression*, p. 54.
70. Ibid. p. 72.
71. Ibid. p. 87.
72. Nehru's speech, 17 Jan 1960, *India's Foreign Policy*, p. 83.
73. Ibid.
74. Nehru, 'Changing India', April 1963, *Nehru's Speeches*, vol. 4, p. 415.

CHAPTER 13 The Last Struggle, January–May 1964

1. B. N. Mullik, *Kashmir*, p. 123.
2. Nehru's statement at a press conference, 22 May 1964, *Nehru's Speeches*, vol. 5, p. 228.
3. *Asian Recorder*, 17–23 May 1964.
4. Nehru, 'Changing India', April 1963, *Nehru's Speeches*, vol. 4, p. 412.
5. *Asian Recorder*, 17–23 June 1964.

Bibliography

Private Papers

Nehru Memorial Museum and Library, New Delhi (NMML)

The Library has collected a vast number of private papers, most of which have been examined. But only those which have been useful for this work are listed below.

B. N. Basu Papers
S. S. Caveeshar Papers
G. M. Chitnavis Papers
Bhulabhai Desai Papers
N. S. Hardikar Papers
John H. Holmes Papers
Alexander Horace Papers
Rajkumari Amrit Kaur Papers
Syed Mahmud Papers
N. R. Malkani Papers
B. S. Moonje Papers
G. A. Natesan Papers
Nehru Papers. Papers of Motilal and Jawaharlal Nehru, including the latter's journals, diaries, notebooks and typescripts of articles.
Rameshwari Nehru Papers
Mrs V. L. Pandit Papers
Vitalbhbhai Patel Papers
R. P. Paranjpye Papers
Sri Prakash Papers
Chalpat Rao Papers. This collection consists mostly of typed articles by Jawaharlal Nehru written from 1938 to 1945 and published in the nationalist daily, the *National Herald*, of which C. Rao was the editor.
E. Raghavendra Rao Papers
Mohanlal Saksena Papers
S. Satyamurti Papers
Phiroze Sethna Papers
M. Spiegal Papers
Purshotamdas Thakurdas Papers

National Archives of India, New Delhi (NAI)

G. K. Gokhale Papers
M. R. Jayakar Papers
G. S. Khaparde Papers
Sampurnanand Papers

Gandhi Memorial Museum and Library, New Delhi

M. K. Gandhi Papers

India Office Library, London (IOL)

Harcourt Butler Papers
Chelmsford Papers
Curzon Papers
Harry Graham Haig Papers
Irwin (Halifax) Papers
Montagu Papers
Reading Papers

In Private Possession

Morarji Desai Papers. With the special permission of Sri Desai these papers were consulted while they were in the private custody of Sri H. M. Shah, Baroda, Gujarat.

Mrs V. L. Pandit Papers. With the special permission of Mrs Pandit this part of her collection was consulted at her house in Dehra Dun, Uttar Pradesh.

G. B. Pant Papers. Consulted by courtesy of Sri K. C. Pant at the Pant Memorial Society, New Delhi.

Rajendra Prasad Papers. Consulted while in the private custody of the late Sri Vishwanath Varma, New Delhi.

Papers of Political Organisations

All-India Congress Committee Papers (at NMML)
Indian States Peoples' Conference (at NMML)

Government Papers

Records of the Home Department of the Government of India (to 1947), filed as Home Political (*at* NAI).

Oral History (at NMML)

Since its foundation the NMML has been conducting interviews with individuals in India and abroad who have closely witnessed or participated in the political growth of India in the twentieth century. Of a vast number of recorded interviews, those which have been useful for this work are listed below.

Mrs S. Ambujammal
Frank Anthony
Dr N. P. Asthana
Dr D. M. Bose
Miss Vera Brittain
Lord Brockway
Lord Butler
James Cameron
Prof. George Catlin
Prof. S. Chandrasekhar
Justice S. R. Das
M. C. Davar
C. D. Deshmukh
Mrs Durgabai Deshmukh

C. C. Ganguli
Dr P. S. Gill
Alexander Horace
Begum Iftikharuddin
Dr K. N. Katju
S. S. Khera
Mrs Hansa Mehta
Tibor Mende
Dr K. M. Munshi
S. Narayanswami
P. A. Narialwala
G. Ramachandra
Mrs Nayantara Sahgal
K. G. Saiyidain
B. Saklatwala
Dr Vatsala Samant
K. Santhanam
Brig. Gyan Singh
S. Iqbal Singh
Lord Sorensen
N. S. Sreeraman
Indulal Yajnik

Interviews

A number of Nehru's colleagues, friends and relations were interviewed by the author, but only those whose statements have been particularly useful for this work are listed below.

M. C. Chagla. A High Court judge and a diplomat, who in 1964 became Minister of Education in Nehru's Cabinet.

Morarji Desai. Chief Minister of Bombay 1951–7; Finance Minister in Nehru's Cabinet 1958–63; Deputy Prime Minister 1967–9.

H. V. R. Iyengar. Principal Private Secretary to Nehru 1947–8.

S. P. Khanna. Private Secretary (personal) to Nehru.

T. T. Krishnamachari. Finance Minister in Nehru's Cabinet 1956–8 and 1964.

Harold Macmillan. Prime Minister of Britain 1957–63.

Syed Mahmud. Minister of External Affairs 1955–6.

V. K. Krishna Menon. Defence Minister in Nehru's Cabinet 1957–62.

Lord Mountbatten. Governor-General of India 1947–8.

K. Kamaraj Nadar. Chief Minister of Madras 1953–63; President of Congress 1964.

S. Nijalingappa. Chief Minister of Mysore 1957–8, 1962–4.

Mrs V. L. Pandit. Sister of Jawaharlal Nehru; Minister in the United Provinces Government 1937–9; Indian ambassador to the Soviet Union 1947–9, to the United States 1949–52; President of the United Nations General Assembly 1953–4; High Commissioner in the United Kingdom 1954–62; Governor of Maharashtra 1962–4.

Jagjivan Ram. Minister in Nehru's Cabinet 1948–63.

B. Gopala Reddi. Minister of Information and Broadcasting in Nehru's Cabinet 1962–3.

Swaran Singh. Minister in Nehru's Cabinet 1957–64.

Published Sources

Letters, Writings and Speeches of Jawaharlal Nehru

An Autobiography, Indian edition (1962).

A Bunch of Old Letters (Bombay, 1958). This contains letters to rather than letters from Nehru.

The Discovery of India, Indian reprint (Bombay, 1967).

Eighteen Months in India, 1936–37 (Allahabad, 1938).

Glimpses of World History (London, 1949).

Independence and After (Delhi, 1949).

India and the World (London, 1936).

India's Foreign Policy (Government of India Publication, 1961). Selected speeches of Nehru, September 1946–April 1961.

Jawaharlal Nehru's speeches 1946–1964, 5 vols (Government of India Publication, 1949–69).

Letters from a Father to His Daughter, 2nd ed. (Calcutta, 1955).

Nehru's Letters to His Sister, ed. Krishna Nehru Hutheesing (London, 1963).

Prime Minister on Chinese Aggression (Government of India Publication, n.d.).

Prime Minister on Sino-Indian Relations, vol. 1, *In Parliament*, vol. 2, *Press* (Government of India Publication, 1961–3).

Selected Works of Jawaharlal Nehru, ed. S. Gopal (Delhi, 1972–). This publication is intended to contain select writings and speeches of Nehru from 1903 to 1964. Six volumes have been published to date.

Soviet Russia (Allahabad, 1928). This work is now contained in vol. 2 of the *Selected Works.*

The Unity of India (London, 1942). Collected writings 1937–40.

Visit to America (New York, 1950).

Documents: Official and Non-official

Chou En-lai, *Premier Chou En-lai's Letters to the Leaders of Asian and African Countries on the Sino-Indian Boundary Question, 15 November 1962* (Peking, 1973).

Congress Reports. Reports of the annual sessions of Congress.

Documents on China's Relations with South and South-East Asia (*1949–1962*), ed. G. V. Ambekar and V. D. Divekar (Bombay, 1964).

Election Commission (India) *Report on the First General Elections in India, 1951–52*, 2 vols (Government of India Publication, 1955).

—, *Report on the Second General Elections in India, 1957*, 2 vols (Government of India Publication, 1958).

—, *Report on the Third General Elections in India, 1962*, 2 vols (Government of India Publication, 1963).

The Evolution of India and Pakistan. Select Documents 1858–1947, ed. C. H. Philips and others (London, 1962).

Indian Constitutional Documents, ed. K. M. Munshi, vols 1 and 2 (Bombay, 1967).

Islington Commission Report (1917).
Planning Commission, Government of India, *The First Five Year Plan* (1953).
—, *Second Five Year Plan* (1956).
—, *Third Five Year Plan* (1961).
Report of the Officials of the Government of India and the People's Republic of China on the Boundary Question (Government of India Publication, 1961).
Report of the Royal Commission on Superior Civil Service in India (1924).
Report of the States Reorganization Commission (1955).
Report on the Indian Constitutional Reforms (1918). The Montagu–Chelmsford Report, Cd. 9109.
Speeches and Documents on the Indian Constitution 1921–47, ed. Sir Maurice Gwyer and A. Appadorai, 2 vols (London, 1957).
The Transfer of Power 1942–47, ed. N. Mansergh and others (Her Majesty's Stationery Office, London, 1970–). Five volumes have so far been published.
White Paper: Notes, Memoranda and Letters Exchanged and Agreements Signed between the Government of India and China (Government of India Publication, 1959–63).

Memoirs, Correspondence and Journals

Bowles, Chester, *Ambassador's Report* (London, 1954).
Butler, Lord, *The Art of the Possible* (London, 1971).
Dwarkadas, J., *Political Memoirs* (Bombay, 1969).
Eden, Anthony (Lord Avon), *Full Circle* (London, 1960).
Eisenhower, Dwight D., *The White House Years, Mandate for Change* (New York, 1963).
Galbraith, J. K., *Ambassador's Journal* (London, 1969).
Gandhi, M. K., *An Autobiography*, reprint (Ahmedabad, 1969).
—, *Collected Works of Mahatma Gandhi*, vols 14–56 (Government of India Publication, in progress).
Jinnah, M. A., *Speeches and Writings of Mr Jinnah*, ed. Jamil-ud-din Ahmad, 2 vols (Lahore, 1960, 1964).
Katju, K. N., *The Days I Remember* (Calcutta, 1961).
Khan, Badshah, *My Life and Struggle* (Delhi, 1969).
Khrushchev, Nikita, *Khrushchev Remembers*, trans. Strobe Talbott (London, 1971).
Kotelawala, John, *An Asian Prime Minister's Story* (London, 1956).
Macmillan, Harold, *Tides of Fortune, 1945-55* (London, 1969).
—, *Riding the Storm, 1956–1959* (London, 1971).
—, *Pointing the Way, 1959–61* (London, 1972).
Narayan, Sriman, *Letters from Gandhi, Nehru, Vinoba* (Bombay, 1968).
Patel, Vallabhbhai, *Sardar Patel's Correspondence*, vols 1-10 (Ahmedabad, 1971–4).
Sampurnanand, *Memoirs and Reflections* (Bombay, 1962).
Truman, Harry S., *The Memoirs of Harry S. Truman*, 2 vols (New York, 1968).
Wavell, Lord, *The Viceroy's Journal*, ed. Penderel Moon (London, 1973).

Newspapers and Periodicals

Asian Roecrder (library of the School of Oriental and African Studies, London).
The Bombay Chronicle (NMML).
The Hindu (IOL).
The Hindustan Times (NMML).

The Independent (NMML).
Indian Annual Register (IOL).
The Leader (NMML).
The Statesman (NMML).
The Tribune (NMML).

Secondary Works

Auty, Phyllis, *Tito: a biography* (London, 1970).
Baxter, C., *The Jan Sangh: a biography of an Indian political party* (Philadelphia, 1969).
Bhatia, K., *Indira* (London, 1974).
Brecher, M., *India and World Politics: Krishna Menon's view of the world* (London, 1968).
—, *Nehru: a political biography* (London, 1959).
—, *Succession in India* (London, 1966).
Brooks, Sydney, *The New Ireland* (London, 1907).
Brown, Judith M., *Gandhi's Rise to Power: Indian Politics 1915–1922* (London, 1972).
Cousins, N., *Talks with Nehru* (London, 1951).
Crocker, W., *Nehru: a contemporary estimate* (London, 1966).
Dalvi, J. P., *Himalayan Blunder* (Delhi, n.d.).
Das, Durga, *India from Curzon to Nehru and After* (London, 1969).
Erdman, H. L., *The Swatantra Party and Indian Conservatism* (London, 1967).
Fisher, Margaret W., and Bondurant, Joan V., *Indian Views of Sino-Indian Relations* (Berkeley, Calif., 1956).
Floyd, David, *Mao against Khrushchev* (London, 1964).
George, T. J. S., *Krishna Menon: a biography* (London, 1964).
Hardy, P., *The Muslims of British India* (London, 1972).
Hodson, H. V., *The Great Divide: Britain-India-Pakistan* (London, 1969).
Hutchins, F. G., *Spontaneous Revolution: the Quit India Movement* (Delhi, 1971).
Kaul, B. M., *The Untold Story* (Bombay, 1967).
Kavic, Lorne J., *India's Quest for Security: defence policies 1957–1965* (Berkeley, Calif., 1967).
Lacouture, Jean, *Ho Chi Minh* (Harmondsworth, 1969).
Lamb, Alastair, *The China-India Border: the origins of the disputed boundaries* (London, 1964).
Legge, J. D., *Sukarno: a political biography* (Harmondsworth, 1973).
Malaviya, K. D., *Pandit Motilal Nehru: his life and speeches* (Allahabad, 1919).
Mankekar, D. R., *The Guilty Men of 1962* (Bombay, 1968).
Masani, M. R., *The Communist Party of India* (London, 1954).
Masani, Zareer, *Indira Gandhi: a biography* (London, 1975).
Maxwell, Neville, *India's China War* (Bombay, 1970).
Mehnert, Klaus, *Peking and Moscow* (London, 1963).
Menon, K. P. S., *The Flying Troika* (London, 1963).
Menon, V. P., *The Story of the Integration of the Indian States* (Madras, 1961).
Moraes, Frank, *Jawaharlal Nehru: a biography* (New York, 1956).
Morris-Jones, W. H., *Parliament in India* (Philadelphia, 1957).
Mullik, B. N., *My Years with Nehru: the Chinese betrayal* (Bombay, 1971).

Mullik, B. N., *Kashmir* (Bombay, 1971).
Nanda, B. R., *The Nehrus* (London, 1965).
Nutting, Anthony, *Nasser* (London, 1972).
Overstreet, G. D., and Windmiller, M., *Communism in India* (Berkeley, Calif., 1959).
Panikkar, K. M., *In Two Chinas: memoirs of a diplomat* (London, 1955).
Parikh, N. D., *Sardar Vallabhbhai Patel* (Ahmedabad, 1953).
Patterson, G. N., *Peking versus Delhi* (London, 1963).
Poplai, S. L., and Talbot, Philips, *India and America* (Indian Council of World Affairs, n.d.).
Sar Desai, B. R., *Indian Foreign Policy in Cambodia, Laos and Vietnam 1947-1964* (Berkeley, Calif., 1968).
Seton, Marie, *Panditji: a portrait of Jawaharlal Nehru* (London, 1967).
Singh, Baljit, and Vajpeyi, D. K., *Political Stability and Continuity in the Indian States during the Nehru Era, 1947-1964: a statistical analysis* (Michigan, 1973).
Smith, D. E., *India as a Secular State* (Princeton, N. J., 1967).
Soundings in Modern South Asian History, ed. D. A. Low (London, 1968).
State Politics in India, ed. M. Weiner (Princeton, N. J., 1968).
Stein, Arthur, *India and the Soviet Union: the Nehru era* (Chicago, 1969).
Stephens, R., *Nasser: a political biography* (Harmondsworth, 1973).
A Study of Nehru, ed. Rafiq Zakaria (Bombay, 1959).
Tahamankar, D. V., *Sardar Patel* (London, 1970).
Taylor, A. J. P., *English History* 1914–1945, Pelican ed. (Harmondsworth, 1970).
Tendulkar, D. G., *Mahatma: life of Mohandas Karamchand Gandhi*, 8 vols (Bombay, 1951–4).
Tyson, G., *Nehru: the years of power* (London, 1966).
Vachell, H. A., *The Hill* (London, 1905).
Weiner, M., *Party Politics in India: the development of a multi-party system* (Princeton, N.J., 1957).

Index